continued

For volumes in the NCRLL Collection (edited by JoBeth Allen and Donna E. Alvermann), the Practitioners Bookshelf Series (edited by Celia Genishi and Donna E. Alvermann), and other titles in this series, please visit www.tcpress.com

Educating Emergent Bilinguals

Policies, Programs, and Practices for Multilingual Learners

THIRD EDITION

Ofelia García, Jo Anne Kleifgen,
and Claudia Cervantes-Soon

Foreword by Jim Cummins
Afterword by Ramón Antonio Martínez

Teachers College Press
Teachers College, Columbia University

For all those emergent bilingual students around the world who have come through our classroom doors and enriched our lives as educators.

And to the memory of two women who taught us so much about language, bilingualism, and education—Muriel Saville-Troike and Tove Skutnabb-Kangas.

Published by Teachers College Press,® 1234 Amsterdam Avenue, New York, NY 10027

Copyright © 2025 by Teachers College, Columbia University

Cover art: Emiliano C. Carrillo.

Library of Congress Cataloging-in-Publication Data is available at loc.gov

ISBN 978-0-8077-8738-0 (paper)
ISBN 978-0-8077-8739-7 (hardcover)
ISBN 978-0-8077-8324-5 (ebook)

Printed on acid-free paper
Manufactured in the United States of America

Contents

Foreword

Perhaps once or twice a decade you read a book that is so lucid, convincing, and inspirational that you want to order copies for every teacher, administrator, and policymaker across the nation. Ofelia García, Jo Anne Kleifgen, and Claudia Cervantes-Soon have written such a book. Their message is very simple: If you want students to emerge from schooling after 12 years as intelligent, imaginative, and linguistically talented, then treat them as intelligent, imaginative, and linguistically talented from the first day they arrive in school.

Woven throughout the pages of *Educating Emergent Bilinguals* is the reminder to educators and policymakers that effective schooling has much more to do with the quality of human relationships orchestrated between teachers and students than with the simple transmission of content. These relationships are obviously influenced by the conditions within which educators work—the curricula they are mandated to teach, the standardized tests that often operate as a proxy curriculum, the language(s) and varieties thereof that are considered legitimate within the ideological space of schooling. Yet, despite the myriad constraints within which educators (including administrators) operate, there are always degrees of freedom that permit and require them to make choices on a continuing basis.

Thus, individual educators are never powerless; they always exercise agency, understood as the power to act. Although they rarely have complete freedom, educators do have choices in the way they structure the interactions in their classrooms. They determine for themselves the social and educational goals they want to achieve with their students. There are always options with respect to educators' orientation to students' language and culture in the forms of parent and community participation they encourage and in the ways they implement pedagogy and assessment.

The choices we make in the classroom are infused with images: images of our students as we perceive them now and in the future, and images of our own identities as educators. To what extent are we communicating to the students in our classrooms an image of themselves as capable of becoming bilingual and biliterate? Capable of higher-order thinking and intellectual accomplishments? Capable of creative and imaginative thinking? Capable of creating literature and art? Capable of generating new knowledge? Capable of thinking about and finding solutions to social issues?

As García, Kleifgen, and Cervantes-Soon point out, when students see themselves (and know that their teachers see them) as emergent bilinguals rather than as English language learners (or some other label that defines students by what they lack), they are much more likely to take pride in their linguistic abilities and talents than if they are defined in deficit terms. Similarly, when students are given opportunities to engage in critical inquiry with their peers aimed at generating knowledge, they are likely to adopt what Patrick Manyak (2004) has called identities of competence. These identities of competence propel students into active engagement with literacy and learning.

Unfortunately, far too few low-income students in North American classrooms are given opportunities to engage in cognitively powerful and identity-affirming learning experiences in comparison to their higher-income peers. The No Child Left Behind legislation implemented by the federal government in the early 2000s institutionalized high-stakes standardized testing as the simultaneous gauge of student learning and teacher effectiveness, thereby reinforcing the pedagogical divide between schools serving economically privileged communities and those serving the impoverished and dispossessed. Frequently, dispossession continues within the school as emergent bilingual students are further stripped of their home language and culture. Defined by their limited English skills and their low standardized test scores, emergent bilingual students struggle, often unsuccessfully, to escape from the externally imposed identity cocoon within which they find themselves.

One of the most powerful messages woven into this book is that, as educators, we do have the power to push back against myopic and irresponsible policies that ignore the research evidence in relation to bilingual students' academic development. When we articulate our choices, individually and collectively, we will find ways of connecting academic content with our students' prior knowledge; we will identify ways of enabling students to engage in higher-order thinking through the translanguaging instructional strategies outlined in this book; we will explore how technological tools can be used creatively by students to generate knowledge; and we will infuse a sense of pride and affirmation of identity into the projects that our students undertake. In this process of articulating and acting on our choices, our own identities as educators will expand. The classroom interactions we orchestrate with our students will shape, rather than simply reflect, our society.

—Jim Cummins

Acknowledgments

The third edition of this book builds on the work of the first two editions. We have been fortunate to have been joined by Claudia Cervantes-Soon in this third edition. Claudia brings conceptual freshness and diversity of experience to the work. This edition is not just an update; it is an expansion that reflects our changing world and the ways in which we perceive the presence of many in it.

We are especially grateful to Emily Spangler from Teachers College Press for convincing us to work on this third edition. Emily has been receptive, helpful, and generous with her time, and we are grateful. Several former doctoral students, who read and commented on different parts of past editions as well as this one, deserve our heartfelt thanks—Gladys Aponte, Laura Ascenzi-Moreno, Heidi Batchelder, Ivana Espinet, Nelson Flores, Kristin Gorski, Laura Kaplan, Tatyana Kleyn, Khánh Lê, Kate Menken, Briana Ronan, Karen Velasquez, and Heather Woodley. We also thank Meg Lemke from Teachers College Press for her encouragement and support in the preparation of the first edition.

This book is an extension of a report that Ofelia and Jo Anne originally wrote for the Campaign for Educational Equity at Teachers College, Columbia University (García, Kleifgen, & Falchi, 2008). We thank the campaign, executive director Michael Rebell, research director Amy Stuart Wells, and policy director Jessica Wolff for giving us the opportunity to write the report and for offering excellent suggestions. In particular, we owe a special debt of gratitude to our coauthor in the report, Lori Falchi, who supported our original thinking and writing as the report took shape.

A number of people contributed significantly in the preparation of the review we conducted for the Campaign for Educational Equity. We are most grateful to Jim Crawford for his willingness to share his expertise from the very beginning and to continue to support us as we updated the information for the first edition. Besides Crawford, a number of people read and commented on parts of the first edition—Jamal Abedi, Bruce Baker, Luis Moll, and Terry Wiley. And others provided us with essential pieces of information—Lyle Bachman, Tim Boals, Ellen Forte, Margot Gottlieb, Luis Reyes, Roger Rice, Pedro Ruiz, and Mariano Viñas. Chris Bacon and his students from Boston University also provided us with feedback on the first edition, for which we are grateful. For the second edition, we want to express our gratitude to Michel DeGraff, who provided us with feedback about his project on Haitian Creole and technology in Haiti; we also thank David Wible for suggestions regarding the digital writing platform developed in Taiwan. Our gratitude also goes to Robert Linquanti, who was most helpful in clarifying for us the recent policy changes. Many scholars read parts of the update to this third edition, and we want to particularly thank Tim Boals, Michel DeGraff, Juan Freire, and Alexis López. For his invaluable help with writing software, we are indebted to Khánh Lê. We also thank Emiliano Carrillo, the 12-year-old bilingual artist who created the beautiful art for the cover of this book. Finally, we want to express our gratitude to our partners—John Borghese, Juan F. Carrillo, and Ricardo Otheguy. Claudia also thanks her two young children, Emiliano and Natalia. They all have exercised much patience while we engaged again with the preparation of this third edition.

Gracias to all for contributing to the efforts to improve the education and lives of language-minoritized students in the United States.

Preface

In the almost two decades since the publication of the first edition of *Educating Emergent Bilinguals*, much has changed in educational policies and in the world. However, little has changed in the inequitable practices that continue to be used to educate emergent bilinguals. Meanwhile, new research continues to confirm and extend the importance of the role of students' home language practices in education.

At the time we write, we are experiencing unprecedented uncertainty in the ways that federal and state policies are being interpreted and implemented. The federal Every Student Succeeds Act (ESSA) supplanted the No Child Left Behind (NCLB) act in 2015, but this has had little impact on state education policy and on the education of emergent bilinguals. The Common Core State Standards (CCSS) initiative, a set of rigorous standards for K–12 mathematics and English language arts that was introduced with much fanfare in 2009, started to be questioned a decade later. Many states that had previously adopted the Common Core have repealed their participation. Years later, states are still scrambling to figure out how emergent bilinguals are to meet what standards. On March 20, 2025 President Trump signed an Executive Order calling for the closing of the Department of Education. We are now unsure of the future role of the federal government in education.

With regard to the students who are the subject of this book—emergent bilinguals—the socioeducational climate has never been less auspicious. For newcomers and immigrants, negative discourse on immigrants is affecting how they are viewed in schools and society, with talk of them being murderers, criminals, or animals. Many immigrants are afraid of walking home from school, fearful that they will be deported. Children of immigrants, and even grandchildren of immigrants, are also afraid that their loved ones might be deported.

Furthermore, today's educators, families, and students are navigating a complex education system that is increasingly shaped by capitalist principles, emphasizing consumer choice, competition, innovation, efficient resource allocation, and accountability through specific performance indicators that may not accurately reflect emergent bilinguals' capabilities. Concerns have been raised that the growing demand for school choice policies may exacerbate existing inequities due to unequal access to high-quality options for minoritized students. This can lead to increased segregation and reduced resources for traditional public schools, which often serve the majority of emergent bilingual students.

Despite changes in policies that affect the education of emergent bilinguals, research findings in the past 50 years have only continued to assert the importance of leveraging *all* the linguistic and cultural practices of emergent bilinguals to educate them. In the past decade, considerable literature on translanguaging and the dynamic languaging practices of bilinguals has emerged, and this edition pays attention to its potential in education. New technologies have also been developed, altering the ways in which we educate. This third edition pays attention to the affordances provided by other modal resources when combined with the linguistic modes to educate emergent bilinguals. Discussion is also included about the promises and pitfalls of artificial intelligence in their education. There is also today greater critical consciousness among educators about the role that colonialism has played in education, and how schools have helped carry out discriminatory practices. This third edition uncovers the ensuing coloniality that has resulted from the colonial logic surrounding language, and it reveals the deleterious effects not only of colonialism but also of capitalism, patriarchy, and racism. It particularly highlights the role that raciolinguistic ideologies have played in the education of emergent bilinguals.

We have emerged from a worldwide pandemic in 2020 that significantly changed education. Instruction went remote as teachers, students, and parents scrambled to educate online. During this period, we observed changes in teacher, student, and parent attitudes and engagement. Some teachers saw, maybe for the first time, the conditions in which students learned at home. They observed parents who did not speak English engage with the education of their children, using their own language and literacy practices to explain to their children texts in English. In addition, the relationship of students with schools was forever changed, with some starting to understand that official buildings called schools are not the only source of education. This has resulted in the lower school-attendance rates that we are still experiencing today. In addition, the Black Lives Matter movement, as well as the #MeToo movement, engaged many communities and students as the pain of death and illness, and the fear, turned to societal rage over inequalities. We write this third edition conscious of the social cataclysm that has occurred during this period and how it has affected minoritized communities as well as the teachers and students who are the focus of this book. We write to ensure that we do not forget the inequities and racism that have plagued the education of these students, and the policies that in early 2025 seem more cruel than ever.

Despite the greater number of bilingual students in classrooms, the availability of alternative language and literacy practices and technology today, and despite greater consciousness of inequity based on racial, gender, and social class, educational policies and practices continue to center white,[1] monolingual students, silencing the voices of racialized emergent bilingual students.

There has been one noticeable change concerning bilingualism in schools in the past two decades. We have witnessed a growing acceptance in some school districts of programs that educate students bilingually. However, the term *bilingualism* has been silenced by naming these programs "dual-language" programs, which also open the door to English speakers. This semantic change implies that bilingualism receives its legitimacy from the presence of English-monolingual, middle-class students.

When we wrote the first edition of this book, we chose to call the students who are the object of our attention "emergent bilinguals," mainly to emphasize their bilingualism rather than their lack of English, as signaled by other terms (*English language learner, limited English proficient*). But the growing popularity of two-way dual-language programs (what we call here dual-language bilingual education, or DLBE, to emphasize its bilingual nature) has complicated the term, as language-majority students learning languages other than English can also be considered emergent bilinguals. In this book, however, we reserve the term *emergent bilingual* for *racialized* and *minoritized* students—usually Brown, Black, and other students not considered white, whose emergent bilingualism educational policymakers often prefer to neglect rather than nurture. This third edition also emphasizes that bilingualism is performed in interaction with our interlocutors and the communicative tasks in which we are engaged. We therefore recognize that all bilingual students, whether speakers of English or not, can be placed along a bilingual continuum depending on the task that they are performing; thus, all students' bilingualism is always emergent. Educational policy and practice for bilingual students focuses mostly on those who are developing English (those called English learners), and these students are the focus of this book. However, whenever possible, we also pay attention here to the emergent bilingualism of students whose bilingualism has been shuttered in homes and communities and ignored in education.

Little has changed in the education of minoritized emergent bilingual students in the past two decades, as we make obvious in the text. In fact, the reality of educational practice for them is that there is less bilingual education and more English-only education. Despite our growing knowledge of the value of dynamic bilingual practices in the world today, emergent bilingual students are minoritized precisely by ignoring their dynamic bilingualism.

The central idea in this third edition continues to be what we stated clearly at the end of the first chapter of the first edition—that there is a growing dissonance between research on the education of emergent bilinguals, policy enacted to educate them, and the practices we observe in schools. What the past two decades have taught us is that this dissonance only exists when the students are those who are racialized, minoritized, and excluded from social and educational opportunities. We are not ignorant about the assets that bilingualism can bring in a globalized world. But this privilege seems to be granted only to those whom political and educational institutions really want to educate well—white, middle-class, English-speaking monolinguals. Minoritized emergent bilinguals continue to experience the educational inequities that we identify in this book. We write this third edition hoping that our work will raise awareness of the inequities in which emergent bilinguals are educated. And we write hoping that educators develop *the will* to change, transform, and imagine the possibilities.

—Ofelia García,
The Graduate Center, CUNY

—Jo Anne Kleifgen,
Teachers College, Columbia University

—Claudia Cervantes-Soon,
Mary Lou Fulton College of Teaching and Learning Innovation,
Arizona State University

Educating Emergent Bilinguals

CHAPTER 1

Introduction

There is no equality of treatment merely by providing students with the same facilities, textbooks, teachers, and curriculum; for students who do not understand English are effectively foreclosed from any meaningful education.

—Lau v. Nichols, 1974

This introductory chapter:

- Discusses the labels used for students who are not yet proficient in English and advocates for using the term *emergent bilingual,*
- Gives reasons why thinking of students as emergent bilinguals can result in a more equitable education for these students, and
- Provides an overview of the book.

EMERGENT BILINGUALS

One of the most misunderstood issues in prekindergarten to 12th-grade education today is how to educate students who are not deemed proficient in English. These students are often called English language learners (ELLs) or, as in the 2015 Every Student Succeeds Act (ESSA), simply English learners (ELs). Before 2015, the federal government referred to these students as limited English proficient (LEP). The designation refers to students who speak a language other than English and are acquiring English in school. Although local and state education agencies may use different definitions (see Chapter 2), the official definition in ESSA is of students "ages 3–21, enrolled in elementary or secondary education, born outside of the United States or speaking a language other than English in their homes, and not having sufficient mastery of English to *meet state standards and excel in an English-language classroom"* (Title III, Elementary and Secondary Education Act [ESEA], as cited in National Research Council, 2011, p. 5; emphasis added). NCLB, which is the previous U.S. federal law enacted in January 2002 that reauthorized the ESEA of 1965, had described these students as those "whose difficulties in speaking, reading, writing, or understanding the English language may be sufficient to deny the individual the ability to meet the *State's proficient level of achievement on State assessments"* (No Child Left Behind Act, 2001, Sec. 9101[37]; emphasis added).

Although the change is subtle and holds the same meaning, it is indicative of the greater emphasis in ESSA on meeting academic standards in English rather than simply doing well on state standardized tests.

Students classified as ELLs were 10.4% of the total school population of the United States during school year 2019–2020, accounting for 5,115,887 students (Office of English Language Acquisition [OELA], 2022). Despite their staggering presence, these students lag in reading and math, according to the National Assessment of Educational Progress, and their median graduation rate in four years of 69% pales in comparison with the 87% national average (OELA, 2023; U.S. DoE, 2022d). And yet, as we will see, these students also have great linguistic, cultural, and intellectual/academic strengths that are being ignored in schools. Part of how we perceive these students has to do with how we name them, which we discuss in the next section.

WHAT'S IN A NAME?

Referring to these students as ELLs or ELs—as many school district officials and educators presently do—signals the omission of a critical idea in the discussion of equitable education for these students.

English learners are, in fact, *emergent bilinguals*.[1] That is, through school and through acquiring English, these students become *bilingual*, able to continue to function with their home language practices[2] as well as in English—the new language practices that they acquire in school. The home language practices are a significant educational resource for these students as they develop their English for academic purposes. Moreover, their home language practices are an essential resource for their sense of connection, understanding of the world, and overall well-being. When officials and educators ignore the bilingualism that these students can and must develop through schooling in the United States, they perpetuate inequities in the education of these students. That is, they discount the linguistic and cultural practices and understandings of these students and assume that their educational needs are the same as those of a monolingual child. Or they assume that these students are inferior and need a remedial English language, skills-based education, thus robbing them of meaningful academic content and of ways to use their entire language repertoire to make meaning. Therefore, in our definition of emergent bilinguals, we include those who may be perceived as proficient in their home language but not in English, as well as students who have been developing English alongside another language from an early age and whose linguistic repertoire involves features of both languages, which they may use at home and in school depending on their audience.

There is little agreement about what name best describes these students. In addition to the terms LEP, ELL, and EL, students who are acquiring English in the nation's schools are also variously referred to in the literature as *culturally and linguistically diverse* (CLD), students with *English language communication barriers* (ELCB), *English as a second language* (ESL) students, *English as a new language* (ENL) students, *language minority* (LM), *language minoritized, dual-language learner* (DLL), *bilingual/multilingual learner*, or *racialized bilinguals*. Each label has different connotations, and all have limitations.

Critics of the LEP label used formerly by the federal government argued convincingly that it focuses on the students' limitations rather than their potential. State and local educational authorities most often prefer the term ELL or EL because these are protected legal labels. That is, once students are given this label, their English learning needs are recognized, and funds are allotted to their education. But the ELL/EL label has serious limitations: It devalues other languages and puts the English language in a sole position of legitimacy. It also focuses solely on the development of what is often referred to as "academic English," ignoring other parts of students' language and education.

The terms *CLD* and *LM students* can include culturally and linguistically different minority students who are already bilingual, although the LM label may better offer a legal basis for rights and accommodations (May, 2011). The recent use of the term *language minoritized* (used without abbreviation in critical scholarship of bilingualism) points to the power of language-majority groups over those they deem inferior, and it resists a categorization of "minority." Critical scholars who work on language and race often refer to these children as *racialized bilinguals*.

ESL or *ENL* refers to a subject and not to people; also, this label of *ESL/ENL student* does not recognize students for whom English is not a "second" language but one spoken fluently at home or those for whom English is a third, fourth, or even fifth language and beyond. Furthermore, to tell students that they are learners or speakers of English as a second language robs them of the opportunity to appropriate "English" features as part of their very own linguistic repertoire.

Since 2010, the term *DLL* has gained much currency. This has to do first and foremost with the silencing of the term *bilingual* in the United States since the late 1990s (for more on this history, see especially Crawford, 2007; see also Chapter 3, this volume). It also has to do with the rise of what in the United States are increasingly called dual-language programs, bilingual programs that typically teach language-majority and language-minoritized students together. But referring to these students as dual-language learners constructs them as having two discrete language systems that have to be developed separately, when in fact, as we will see later, bilinguals develop one complex linguistic system that they use regularly to learn.

Recently, the term *dual-language learner* has been increasingly used to refer to young learners, under 8 years of age, who are learning English in school while continuing to develop basic proficiency in their home language (Williams, 2015). The Dual Language Learners National Work Group, a group dedicated to raising awareness about very young bilingual learners, reserves the term *English language learner* for those who are older than 8 and who are said to have basic proficiency in their home language (Williams, 2015). But many children entering early childhood educational settings and preschools today are simultaneous bilinguals (see Escamilla et al., 2014), being raised in bilingual and multilingual homes and in communities where more than one language is spoken and heard. Although we applaud the efforts of early childhood educators to bring attention to the capacities of very young emergent bilinguals, we take exception with the unequivocal adoption of the term *DLL* for very young children. The way in which the DLL label has been constructed around very young children leaves out the recognition of the complex bilingualism of those who grow up bilingual from birth and who also need development and expansion of their entire language repertoire, and not just "dual" languages as if they were two autonomous entities.

The terms *bilingual/multilingual learner* or *multilingual learner* have many advantages over the *English learner* label. Identifying students as bilingual/multilingual learners does not focus on the needs of these students to learn English. Instead, it celebrates these students for their bilingual/multilingual capacities.

We prefer, and use here, the term *emergent bilingual* because it has become obvious to us that much educational inequity is derived from obfuscating the fact that a meaningful education will not only turn these English learners into English proficient students, but more significantly, into bilingual and multilingual students and adults. *Emergent bilingual* most accurately indexes the type of student who is the object of our attention—those whose bilingualism is emerging and who have been minoritized and racialized in schools. By choosing to refer to these students as emergent bilinguals, we want to stress and amplify the term *bilingualism*, as well as emphasize the concept of *emergence*. In affirming the term *bilingual*, we recognize the early political struggles over bilingual education that were tied to antiracism, better housing and jobs, and more voting rights. For us, *bilingual* refers not simply to the addition of a second language. This term points to political struggles over inclusion and equality for minoritized students with different language practices. It also includes the many minoritized students who speak what are considered more than two languages, that is, those who some people refer to as multilingual. The concept of *emergence* for us is related to that of the Chilean biologist Francisco Varela (1995), who argues:

> Forget the idea of a black box with inputs and outputs. Think in terms of loops. . . . The inputs and outputs are completely dependent on interactions within the system, and their richness comes from their internal connectedness. Give up the boxes, and work with the entire loopiness of the thing. (n.p.)

As we will see, this concept of emergence fits our own vision of how bilingualism emerges, not by focusing on "bits and pieces" of languages, as Guadalupe Valdés would say (2001, p. 13), but on the "loopiness" of language development, on the dynamic practices.

Thinking of these students as emergent bilinguals has important consequences not only for them but also for teachers, policymakers, parents, the language education profession, and U.S. society at large (García, 2009b). The use of the term *emergent bilinguals* allows us to imagine a different scenario. Instead of being regarded as limited in some way or as mere learners of English, as the terms *limited English proficient* or *English language learner/English learner* suggest, students are seen instead for their potential to become bilingual or multilingual. Their emergent bilingualism begins to be recognized as a cognitive, social, and educational resource to be leveraged, which is consistent with research on this topic (see Chapter 4).

For teachers, working with these students as emergent bilinguals means holding higher expectations of them rather than simply remediating their limitations and focusing on their English learning. In recognizing the emergent bilingualism of students, educators are building on their strengths—their linguistic and cultural practices. They are thereby making positive use of the students' home language and bilingual practices rather than suppressing or ignoring them.

In recognizing these students as emergent bilinguals, policymakers can begin to require a more rigorous curriculum and more challenging instructional material for them and recognize that language development takes time and happens through meaningful interactions. Educational policymakers become more patient, understanding that—as research has clearly shown—living and learning as bilingual takes time (Hakuta, Butler, & Witt, 2000). And it becomes easier to demand that assessment be valid for *all* bilinguals. A more flexible norm can then be adopted that includes all students along a bilingual continuum instead of insisting on a rigid monolingual standard.

As we said before, the term *emergent bilingual* recognizes the fact that our linguistic performances are always emerging, depending on the languaging task that we are asked to perform. By focusing on emergence, we heed Varela's call to work with the entire loopiness of language, a complex network of significance. Our linguistic performances are never done, completed, finished, or isolated from our other parts of being. Teachers of emergent bilingual students are thus challenged to provide rich affordances (cultural, historical, social) that will encourage students to want to use language to perform academic tasks for a particular audience.

Giving emergent bilinguals a name that does not focus on their limitations means that their family and community's lived language practices are seen as an educational resource. Instead of assigning blame to parents and community for language practices that may not include English, the school can begin to see the parents and community as the experts in the students' linguistic and cultural practices, which are the basis of all learning. As a result, family and community members will be able to participate in the education of their children from a position of strength, not a position of limitations.

The language education profession is presently compartmentalized in ways that do not support the holistic education of students. Focusing on students' emergent bilingualism/multilingualism can facilitate the integration of four approaches to language education that presently exist separately in the United States—the teaching of English to speakers of other languages (TESOL), bilingual education (BE), the teaching of the heritage language (HL), and the teaching of a foreign language (FL). As a result of a more unifying focus, teaching begins to be centered on *the students* rather than on a profession or on a curriculum.

Finally, we know that bilingual practices in the 21st century are more important than ever, and thus important for U.S. society. It is clear that having flexible language practices, being able to do language in ways described by many scholars as *translanguaging* (García, 2009a; see also García & Li Wei, 2014; Otheguy, García, & Reid, 2015; see also Chapter 4, this volume), can become an important resource for all in the future. The linguistic resources of the United States have never been greater. Despite the insistence on being identified as a monolingual nation-state, the United States has perhaps the world's most complex language practices, given its long history of immigration. The benefits of harnessing the lived multilingualism of Americans are more evident than ever.

THIS BOOK

The central idea that we present in this book is that there is a growing dissonance between *research* on the education of minoritized emergent bilinguals, *policy* enacted to educate them, and the *practices* we observe in communities and schools. Whereas research has consistently shown the importance of building on students' complex home language practices as they develop ways of using English, whether in ESL instruction or bilingual education,[3] U.S. educational policy has often ignored these research findings. In fact, in recent years in the United States—as we explain subsequently—educational policy toward minoritized emergent bilinguals has become more rigid, embodying a view of these students solely from a deficit perspective and demanding that English alone be used in their education. It is interesting to note, however, that language-majority families, as well as second- and third-generation bilingual families, have had a growing interest in developing their children's bilingual abilities, accounting for the growth of immersion programs in languages other than English (often called dual-language immersion), the increase of two-way dual-language bilingual education programs where language-majority students participate, and the development of dual-language bilingual programs where bilingual children who are positioned differently along a bilingual and social continuum are educated together. These last programs are often called one-way dual-language or developmental bilingual programs because most students are considered to be of one ethnolinguistic group. But because of the students' different national identities and various historical and generational immigration experiences, students perceived as being of one language group engage in linguistic and cultural practices that are quite heterogeneous. This book focuses on emergent bilingual students who because of race, poverty, immigration status, and English language proficiency are subjected to an impoverished education that contradicts research on language acquisition, bilingualism, and learning in general.

Educators, who are closer to the ground than many policymakers and researchers, are often caught in the middle of the dissonance between research, policy, and the immediacy of having to educate emergent bilinguals. As a result, educators' teaching practices sometimes suffer as they strive to find alternative ways of acting on top-down national and local educational policies that are plainly misguided for the education of these students. This frequent incompatibility between research, policy, and teaching practice is responsible for much of the miseducation of emergent bilinguals in the United States and their failure in school.

Chapter 2 in this book characterizes the students who are the subject of our attention: emergent bilinguals. We raise questions regarding the ways in which demographic data on these students are collected at state and national levels and used to identify them for educational purposes. Chapter 3 briefly historicizes the educational policies targeted toward this group of students and reviews the programs and practices that have been developed over the past 50 years. We then turn to Chapter 4, where we consider theoretical constructs, empirical evidence, and practices related to what we think are the five most important aspects of the education of emergent bilinguals—language and literacy considerations (Chapter 5), curriculum and pedagogy (Chapter 6), family and community engagement (Chapter 7), assessment (Chapter 8), and digital technologies and learning (Chapter 9). The objective of these chapters is to expose the educational inequities that directly affect the education of emergent bilinguals and to provide descriptions of alternative practices that alleviate these injustices. Most of the inequities stem from policymakers' and often educators' lack of understanding of bilingualism/multilingualism itself. Thus, we will discuss how misunderstandings about the nature of bilingualism have educational equity consequences for some of the most disadvantaged students. Finally, Chapter 10 offers recommendations for advocates, policymakers, educators, and researchers.

STUDY QUESTIONS

1. Discuss some of the issues that emerge from the different labels that have been assigned to students who are developing English proficiency in schools.
2. What are the reasons why García, Kleifgen, and Cervantes-Soon name these students emergent bilinguals? Discuss how using this term affects students, teachers, policymakers, parents, the language education profession, and U.S. society.
3. What is the central idea in this book?

CHAPTER 2

Who Are the Emergent Bilinguals?

This chapter provides background information on emergent bilinguals. Specifically, the chapter asks the following key questions:

- How do we know who they are?
- How many are there?
- How are they designated as English language learners?
- How are they reclassified as fluent English speakers?
- Where do they live and go to school?
- What languages do they speak?
- What are their demographic characteristics with respect to:
  » Ethnicity/race, socioeconomic status, and other characteristics,
  » Age distribution and access to pre-K and other programs, and
  » Nativity?
- How do they use language?
- Who are the Latine students?
- What do all emergent bilinguals have in common?

In this chapter, we address the issue of how students are identified, counted, and designated as English learners, as we elucidate their sociolinguistic characteristics. The chapter also brings to the forefront the mismatch between the policy that dictates how data on their characteristics are collected and considered, the reality of the students themselves, and what research tells us about how best to educate emergent bilingual students. In other words, the dissonance between the research and the policies and practices enacted, which is the central theme of this book, begins with descriptive data that have shaped the way these students are defined. As we consider the data, we will point out these contradictions.

HOW DO WE KNOW WHO THEY ARE?

Part of the difficulty in understanding the characteristics of emergent bilinguals results from the great inconsistency in the data that purport to describe them. Primary data on students needing services are collected using a variety of measures across different states. As we will see, states use different assessments for the identification of emergent bilinguals, sometimes measuring different abilities. The federal government, in its most recent legislation (ESSA, 2015), has not resolved the inconsistencies in the data.

HOW MANY EMERGENT BILINGUALS ARE THERE?

However inaccurately these students are counted, we do know that the numbers of emergent bilinguals are increasing and growing much more rapidly than is the English-speaking student population. There are many different methods used to identify emergent bilingual students, including the U.S. Census, as well as data gathered by the National Clearinghouse for English Language Acquisition in an effort to hold states accountable for the education of these students. Because in this book we attempt to include the educational issues pertaining not just to students who are classified as English learners but also to those who are bilingual and who are usually not addressed in educational policy, we use a combination of data sources. At times, we rely on the data gathered by the Office of English Language Acquisition, which relies exclusively on the data from states on their English learners and how they are being serviced. But sometimes, we describe student demographics by including data from the American Community Survey of the U.S. Census, which is more inclusive of bilingual students who are not exclusively those identified by states as English learners and whose bilingualism is most often ignored in education.

Between 1995 and 2005, the enrollment of emergent bilinguals in public schools nationwide grew by 56%, whereas the entire student population grew by only 2.6% (Batalova, Fix, & Murray, 2007). According to data reported by the U.S. Department of Education, National Center for Education Statistics (2020), although the total enrollment of students has remained flat, the number of emergent bilinguals increased from 4.6 million students in 2010 to 5.1 million students in the fall of 2019, with a small dip in population to 4.9 million in the fall of 2020 as a result of the pandemic (U.S. DoE, NCES, 2020; see Table 2.1).

Table 2.1. shows that emergent bilingual students accounted for 10.1% of the total preschool through 12th grade enrollment in U.S. public schools in the fall of 2020 (U.S. DoE, Office for Civil Rights, 2024). That is, one out of 10 students in the United States in 2020 spoke a language other than English at home. This proportion has not significantly increased since the fall of 2009, when they accounted for 9.7% of the school population.

According to the American Community Survey (ACS, 2022a) of the U.S. Census Bureau, there were 2.5 million 5- to 17-year-old emergent bilinguals in 2022; in contrast, the states reported a total of 4,929,989 million ELLs for the same year. This discrepancy has to do with the fact that the Census Bureau relies on self-reports and asks only whether or not students speak English, but not whether they can read and write English. In addition, the census undercounts the undocumented population, which the states are more likely to count because they collect their data through the schools themselves. However, even school data may depict an inaccurate picture because ELL identification in schools is based on home language surveys, which we will discuss further subsequently, and which often mask

Table 2.1. Emergent Bilingual (EBL) Students Enrolled in Public and Elementary U.S. Schools

Year	# of EBL students	% of EBL students as % of total enrollment
2009–2010	4,647,016	9.7%
2011–2012	4,635,185	9.6%
2012–2013	4,850,293	10.0%
2013–2014	4,929,989	10.1%
Fall 2014	4,813,693	9.8%
Fall 2015	4,854,285	9.9%
Fall 2016	4,949,423	10.1%
Fall 2017	5,010,505	10.2%
Fall 2018	5,024,177	10.2%
Fall 2019	5,115,887	10.4%
Fall 2020	4,963,888	10.1%

Source: U.S. Department of Education, NCES (2020b, Table 204.27).

important nuances. Finally, the federal government also gives states the flexibility to count students who were formerly classified as English learners for up to four years to ensure that schools remain accountable for their outcomes. While this provision provides a more accurate picture, it further adds to the discrepancies in number.

The U.S. Census provides information about the number of students between the ages of 5 and 17 who speak a language other than English (LOTE) at home. The census also asks families who report that they speak a LOTE at home to indicate their ability to speak English as either "very well," "well," "not well," or "not at all." Students who live in households where English is spoken less than "very well" are considered eligible for English language support. Table 2.2 indicates the number of 5- to 17-year-olds who speak languages other than English at home, as well as the number who live in families that speak English less than "very well." Table 2.2 tells an interesting story. It is important to note that, although the percentage of youths who speak languages other than English at home, according to the U.S. Census, has significantly increased (21.4% in 2022 compared to 8.5% in 1979), the percentage of LOTE speakers who speak English less than "well" has decreased (21.5% in 2022 compared to 34.2% in 1979). That is, there is a rise in the number of *bilingual* students who are both speakers of other languages and also fluent speakers of English.

In fact, the increase in the number of bilingual students who are proficient in both English and another language in the U.S. school population has been considerable. From 1979 to 2022, while the number of students who spoke English less than very well increased (from 1.3M to 2.5M), the number of students who spoke

Table 2.2. Speakers of LOTEs and Emergent Bilinguals (EBLs), 5 to 17 Years Old

Year	Total 5–17 years*	Number of speakers of LOTEs*	% total speakers of LOTEs	Number of EBLs**	% speakers of LOTEs who are identified as EBLs
1979	44.7	3.8	8.5%	1.3	34.2%
1989	42.3	5.2	12.3%	1.8	34.6%
1995	47.5	6.7	14.1%	2.4	35.8%
2000	52.5	9.5	18.1%	2.9	30.5%
2004	52.9	9.9	18.8%	2.8	27.9%
2008	53.0	10.9	20.5%	2.7	24.7%
2014	53.8	11.8	21.9%	2.4	17.7%
2022	53.9	11.6	21.4%	2.5	21.5%

* Numbers are given in the millions.
** Emergent bilinguals here are those designated by the federal government as English learners. They are those who speak languages other than English at home and who speak English less than very well.
Sources: U.S. Census Bureau, 1979, 1989, 1995, 2005; U.S. Department of Education, National Center for Education Statistics, 2006; U.S. Census Bureau (2008, 2014, 2022b) ACS 1-year estimates, Table C16004 (2022a).

LOTEs and at home who were proficient in English, and thus considered fluent bilinguals, grew even more. That is, in 1979 there were 3.8 million students speaking LOTEs at home, of whom 1.3 million spoke English less than very well; thus 2.5 million students could be considered fluent bilinguals. In 2022 there were 11.6 million students speaking LOTEs at home of whom 2.5 million spoke English less than very well; thus 9.1 million could be considered fluent bilinguals. In short, from 1979 to 2022 the increase in the number of students who spoke a LOTE at home but who were fluent bilinguals was a staggering 264%.

Certainly, the growth in the number of bilingual English-proficient students is greater than that of emergent bilinguals considered English learners, making bilingualism a central educational topic for teachers of *all* U.S. students, not just those who are learning English, since about one out of every four 5- to 17-year-olds in the U.S. speaks a language other than English at home, and of those only one out of four reports that they speak English less than very well. It is also important to remember that any ranking less than "very well" does not simply imply that these students cannot speak English at all, for the other choices are "well" and "less than well," besides "not at all."

Although the growing bilingual student population is an important resource in a globalized world, our focus in this book is on minoritized emergent bilinguals because their bilingualism is a consequential resource for them and their families, which is too often devalued by others. Thus, these are also the students who need the most support from the educational system. We warn, however, that as García

(2006) noted, English learners are "only the tail of the elephant"—2.5 million of the 11.6 million bilingual and multilingual U.S. students in 2022. When educators and policymakers use the term *bilingual students* to refer only to the elephant's tail, or those students who are not yet proficient in English, they lose sight of the incredible potential of the millions of multilingual students in this country. Focusing narrowly on the beginning points of the bilingual continuum blinds them to the strength and potential of bilingualism. This makes all bilingualism suspect for policy and practice, when, instead, being bilingual/multilingual is becoming the norm for students in an increasingly multilingual United States.

HOW ARE THEY DESIGNATED AS ENGLISH LEARNERS?

The question of how many emergent bilinguals there are has to do with the ways in which they are designated and then reclassified as a specific category of student. Unlike other categories of identification such as ethnicity, race, and gender, the EL classification is fluid—that is, students move in and out of being classified according to their progress. And we emphasize that being classified as an English learner or reclassified as a "fluent English speaker" is based on a cutoff score that sometimes has little relationship to the actual performances of these students in school tasks.

Since the 1970s, based on federal civil rights legislation and federal case law, states have had to identify emergent bilinguals and ensure that their schools serve them (Linquanti, 2001). Guidance from the U.S. Departments of Education and Justice in January 2015 reminded schools of their obligation to "identify English learner students in a timely, valid and reliable manner" (U.S. Department of Education, 2015). ESSA requires that emergent bilinguals be identified 30 days after the beginning of a school year, or two weeks after enrollment if students enter during the school year. But the criteria used to identify emergent bilinguals continue to vary by state and sometimes even by districts within a state (Linquanti & Cook, 2013; Rafa et al., 2020).

Because so many studies have pointed to the variations across states in ways of identifying those classified as English learners, the U.S. Department of Justice Civil Rights Division and the U.S. Department of Education Office for Civil Rights (2015b) published a set of guidelines to ensure the adequacy of identification and classification. In addition, also in 2015, the U.S. Department of Education's National Center for English Language Acquisition (NCELA) published an "English Learner Toolkit," providing guidance on how to identify English learners (U.S. Department of Education, 2015).

An initial step in identifying students as ELs usually takes place when students first register for a new school: They are given a *home language survey*, which contains questions for students' parents or guardians about the language used at home by students and others. But as Bailey and Kelly (2013) have demonstrated, states vary in what is asked in the home language survey. Almost half the states have a single form and mandate its use in schools statewide; other states, however, allow school districts to create their own surveys.

Home language surveys tend to view bilingualism through a monolingual lens and ignore the complexity of linguistic practices of multilingual populations. For example, many states' and schools' home language surveys ask which was the first language the student learned, ignoring the fact that many students are simultaneous bilinguals, growing up in homes with complex language practices where members of families use their multilingual repertoire flexibly. The surveys also often ask which language is spoken to the child in the home, overlooking the bilingual/multilingual practices of parents and caregivers when interacting with one another and their children. Because there is no label and/or identification process in the home language survey that accurately reflects bilingual students' language practices, sometimes bilingual students, even those fluent in English, may still be classified as English learners if their families indicate that a LOTE is spoken at home.

Home language surveys may result in highly inaccurate data as parents' responses reflect decisions that are influenced by their context. For example, in states with English-only policies that restrict designated English learners' access to bilingual programs, like Arizona and formerly California and Massachusetts (up until 2016), parents may mark English as the home language in order to secure opportunities for bilingual education (Darriet & Santibañez, 2024). In contrast, in other places where dual-language programs may be gentrifying (meaning that English speakers begin to outnumber speakers of the other language) and therefore have to prioritize the enrollment of English learners, English speakers or bilingual families may indicate that a LOTE is used at home in order to get a place in the program.

Moreover, because of the monolingual bias in many states' home language surveys and the stigmatization that often follows a student's designation as an English learner, many bilingual parents hide their bilingualism, refusing to acknowledge their home bilingual practices. The construction of inferiority that accompanies being categorized as an emergent bilingual in many schools means that some parents prefer to say that the child only speaks English.

While we are not saying that these strategies are the most common responses to home language surveys, being aware of them helps us recognize that the current practices to identify ELs mask important nuances and even families' strategic moves in attempts to counter restrictive language policies or stigma.

Students identified by the home language survey as potentially needing services are then referred for an English language proficiency assessment (Rafa et al., 2020). More than half the states use a screener or placement test for identification as English learner. Of these, the majority use a screener test for designation developed by WIDA (no longer an acronym), which is a consortium of state departments of education that designs standards and assessments for English learners.

Some states, however, use their own screening assessment. At the time of this writing, California, for example, uses the California English Language Development Test (CELDT). New York has developed the New York State Identification Test for English Language Learners (NYSITELL). Still other states provide their school districts with a list of tests from which the districts can select. The National Research Council's (2011) report concludes the section on the identification of English learners by saying:

> Because of the differing state policies, practices, and criteria for initially identifying students as linguistic minority and for classifying them as an English language learner (ELL), individuals who are classified as ELL students in one state may not be classified as ELL students in another. In states that permit local control, students classified as ELL in one district may not be classified as ELL in another district in that state. (p. 86)

In conclusion, school districts classify students as English learners through a combination of information on the home language survey and formal assessment or screening. The home language survey, although designed to ensure language support for students who need it, has unfortunately become a highly outdated tool. It forces bilingual children into monolingual categories, requiring them to identify as either English speakers or speakers of another language, but not both. This approach fails to acknowledge the fluid language practices of bilingual students. To offer beneficial instruction that leverages students' bilingual abilities, schools must change the negative perceptions of speakers of languages other than English and dispel the mistaken belief that bilingualism is rare among students or that EL classification equates to perpetual underperformance (Flores & Lewis, 2022). García, Johnson, and Seltzer (2017) include a Bilingual Student Identification and Profile instrument that teachers can adapt to ensure that families identify their home language practices with pride.

HOW ARE THEY RECLASSIFIED AS FLUENT ENGLISH SPEAKERS?

Equally important to the question of how many students are designated as emergent bilinguals in U.S. public schools is the question of how these students get reclassified as English proficient. Even though *language proficiency* is the focus for designation as English learner, *academic achievement in English* is key to students' reclassification as English proficient (Linquanti, 2001). This means that the assessment used for the reclassification process should be much more complex because multiple dimensions of communicative competence have to be considered (Bachman, 2001; Canale & Swain, 1980). In other words, to be reclassified, students must not only be able to comprehend and communicate effectively but also do cognitively demanding work in the content areas at the appropriate grade level in English (Bachman, 2002; Linquanti, 2001).

One of the advances toward the educational equity of emergent bilinguals made since No Child Left Behind (more in Chapter 3) has been the requirement that states develop English language proficiency standards for emergent bilinguals, as well as an assessment instrument aligned to these standards that measure listening, speaking, reading, writing, and comprehension. In addition, grants have been made available to develop, validate, and implement such assessments. As a result, the states' English language proficiency tests used in reclassification of students have improved dramatically, although there still is much room for improvement.

Furthermore, the Common Core State Standards (CCSS) in English language arts and mathematics released in 2010 (more on this in Chapter 3) led to efforts to develop standards for English learners, as well as for assessment systems.

The WIDA consortium of states, which at the time of this writing includes 42 states, territories, and federal agencies, has built a standards-based, criterion-referenced English language proficiency test for reclassification (ACCESS for ELs). WIDA continues to refine its comprehensive and balanced technology-based assessment system for English learners and provides standards-based resources and professional learning to member states. The other smaller consortium is ELPA21 (English Language Proficiency Assessment for the 21st Century), which includes nine states at the time of this writing. ELPA21's assessment system consists of a screener to assess baseline English language proficiency, as well as a summative assessment. Both consortia have alternate assessments for ELs with disabilities.

Some states, which together account for the largest populations of English learners in the country, have not joined consortia; they use other English proficiency tests. In 2022, some of the "big states" with large numbers of emergent bilinguals used their own assessments for English language proficiency: California—California English Language Development Test (CELDT); Texas—Texas English Language Proficiency Assessment (TELPAS); New York—New York State English as a Second Language Achievement Test (NYSESLAT); and Arizona—Arizona English Language Learner Assessment (AZELLA).

Not all tests focus on the same skill domains or weigh each skill domain equally. For example, California's CELDT assigns equal weights to listening, speaking, reading, and writing. However, ACCESS for ELLs weighs its overall composite in favor of literacy. As a result, students reclassified in one state would not be considered reclassified in another state.

On average, emergent bilinguals are reclassified three years after school entry, in second grade (Slama, 2014). Reclassification rates are lowest in kindergarten through second grade as well as in grade 9, the grade levels when many emergent bilinguals enter the U.S. school system for the first time. A longitudinal study of reclassification rates in the Los Angeles Unified School District confirmed that reclassification occurred between four to seven years of enrollment. However, one-fourth of students had not been reclassified after nine years in the district (Thompson, 2015).

An important finding is that Spanish-speaking emergent bilinguals are reclassified at half the rate of those who speak other languages, even after controlling for income (Slama, 2014). That is, emergent bilinguals who speak Spanish are twice as likely as those who speak other languages to remain categorized as English learners. There may be many reasons why this is so, but it might be important to consider causes that have to do with what some scholars call *raciolinguistic ideologies* (see Flores & Rosa, 2015). Language and race have been mutually constitutive, with language used to construct race, and ideas about race being shaped by language (Alim, Rickford, & Ball, 2016). In the United States, Spanish-speaking students have traditionally been considered non-white. The Spanish language has been used often as a proxy for race, a way to segregate and exclude the minoritized Spanish-speaking students from rich educational opportunities. For instance, Flores and Lewis (2022) highlight the raciolinguistic ideology embedded within California's EL reclassification policy, impacting the state's largest population of English learners, who are primarily Spanish speakers. In their 2023 study, the authors noted that a California state education leader critiqued the expectation that English learners not only demonstrate proficiency on the state English Language Proficiency assessment but also on the state English Language Arts (ELA) assessment and other content areas depending on the district. This dual requirement sets a higher bar for achieving full English proficiency. Flores and Lewis argue that by linking academic performance measures to English proficiency assessments, the state perpetuates a raciolinguistic ideology. This ideology casts doubt on racialized bilingual individuals' linguistic capabilities, fearing misclassification if such criteria are not met. Under this framework, academically struggling students classified as "never-ELs," that is, those who have never been classified as ELs and have not received language services, may be seen as proficient language users, while those labeled as ELs may not receive the same benefit of the doubt. Moreover, California's reclassification criteria also involve teachers' evaluations, which may be influenced by raciolinguistic perspectives of their students.

The failure to provide an equitable, rigorous, and consistent education to emergent bilinguals results in much academic failure. Despite excellent English proficiency, many students are unable to pass English proficiency exams for reclassification because these exams rely heavily on reading and writing skills. The number of students who are designated as English learners for more than six years has increased over time, leading to the creation of another subgroup of emergent bilinguals known as long-term English learners (LTEL) (Chang-Bacon, 2021; Menken, Kleyn, & Chae, 2012; Olsen, 2014). They represent one-fourth of all emergent bilinguals. This points to the failure of the U.S. education system to provide a meaningful and equitable education to these students, as well as problematic reclassification policies, often stemming from the system's refusal to see their bilingualism as a resource for learning. With EL assessments increasingly emphasizing academic language mastery, the rising number of students identified as long-term English learners (LTELs) comes as little surprise.

Reclassification of English learners is as problematic as identification. On the whole, reclassification criteria are left up to states and school districts, although they must be based on test scores. But as we have seen, assessment systems and reclassification criteria differ widely.

WHERE DO THEY LIVE AND GO TO SCHOOL?

Nine states accounted for more than two-thirds of the emergent bilingual population in the United States in 2022. They are, ranging from highest to lowest emergent bilingual population: California, Texas, Florida, New York, Illinois, Washington, Georgia, Virginia, and North Carolina. These states all had over 100,000 students classified as English learners. Table 2.3 gives the number of public school emergent bilinguals in 2020 in these nine states, as well as the percentage of students they represent (U.S. DoE, IES, NCES, 2020). When the second edition of this book was published, neither Georgia nor Virginia were among the top states.

Table 2.3. Number of Public-School Emergent Bilinguals (EBLs), Fall 2020 (States With More Than 100K EBLs)

State	Number	% of EBLs among students
California	1,062,264	17.7%
Texas	1,034,543	20.1%
Florida	264,546	9.7%
New York	239,954	9.4%
Illinois	218,480	12.0%
Washington	129,564	11.8%
Georgia	125,963	7.5%
Virginia	117,553	9.6%
North Carolina	114,901	7.7%

Source: U.S. Department of Education, Institute of Education Science, National Center for Education Statistics, 2020a. Table 204.20, fall 2000 through fall 2020. EL students enrolled in public elementary and secondary schools, by state.

Emergent bilingual students make up a large proportion of the total pre-K to 12 population in several other states, even if their actual numbers there are not as large as in these nine states. In 2020, Texas had the greatest proportion of students designated as English learners in the country (20.1%), followed by California (17.7%). In fact, the Texas EL population jumped by almost 80% between 2012 and 2020, whereas California's enrollment of ELs decreased from 39% to 22% in the same period (OELA, August 2022). These two states are followed by states whose numbers do not exceed 100,000 (and thus do not appear in Table 2.3) but whose proportions are sizable: New Mexico (16.0%), Nevada (13.3%), Rhode Island (12.2%), District of Colombia (12.0%), Alaska (11.0%), Delaware (10.7%), Colorado (10.5%), Maryland (10.3%), and Massachusetts (10.2%). This is also a change from the numbers reported in the second edition of this book, for students classified as English learners are now present in more states. The greatest *growth* in the number of students who are developing English proficiency in the past decade has occurred clearly outside the nine top states in population.

In previous years, the majority of designated English learners tended to be enrolled in public schools in urban areas, but there was a shift in 2021 (NCES, 2024). While cities still enrolled about 1.5 million emergent bilinguals, most emergent bilinguals were found in suburban areas (1.6 million). In contrast, about 742,000 emergent bilinguals were enrolled in towns and rural areas.

In 2022–2023, the Los Angeles Unified School District had the largest number of students classified as English learners (145,983), constituting 22.6% of the Los Angeles school population. But if we consider the proportion of EL designated students in school districts, Santa Ana Unified School District in California leads in the proportion of English learners in their student body (45.3%). Santa Ana is followed by four Texas school districts—Dallas Independent School District (38.7%), Houston Independent School District (36%), Aldine Independent School District (29.9%), and Fort Worth Independent School District (28.6%). These four Texas districts were then followed by Denver County School District in Colorado (27.7%), Houston (26.6%), Austin (24.6%), San Diego (24.1%), Los Angeles (22.6%), and Fairfax, Virginia (20.2%) (U.S. Department of Education, IES, NCES, 2020). The state of Texas's five school districts constitute the greatest proportion of English learners.

Despite the spread of emergent bilinguals across the United States, they seem to be concentrated in fewer than half the school districts in the country. In 2015, 46% of English learners were enrolled in school districts where ELs comprised over 20% of the school population; that is, they tend to go to school with a large number of peers who are also English learners (U.S. DoE, 2020a). This points to the high degree of racial and linguistic segregation in the United States (Orfield & Frankenberg, 2014). Furthermore, the level of linguistic segregation in the United States has risen steadily (Frankenberg et al., 2019).

Notably, the school choice movement that has led to the expansion of charter schools has also influenced EL student enrollment. For example, in Texas, the percentage of ELs in charter schools nearly doubled from 16 percent in 2016 to just under 30 percent in 2021. During this time, the overall enrollment in charter schools in Texas also more than doubled. As a result, the number of English learners in Texas charter schools has increased fivefold over the past decade, rising from under 25,000 in 2010 to almost 120,000 in 2021 (Carlson, 2023). Nationally, there has also been an upward but less drastic trend of EL enrollment in charter schools, rising from 9% in 2011–2012 to 11% in 2017–2018 (U.S. Department of Education, 2021).

WHAT LANGUAGES DO THEY SPEAK?

Emergent bilinguals in the United States are speakers of many different languages, although Spanish remains by far the language spoken by the highest number of them. The National Center for Education Statistics of the Institute of Education (2024) reports that in fall 2021, 76.4% of those students designated as English learners spoke Spanish at home. One of the limitations of the ways in which the census gathers language data is that the heterogeneity of language groups is erased. Many Native American languages are not accounted for. Immigrants from Latin America are speakers of the many Indigenous languages of the Americas. And yet, they have no way to name these languages in the census except by claiming to be Spanish speakers, when Spanish is often a language that they have learned in school but that does not reflect their linguistic practices at home (Martínez, 2017).

According to the Office of English Language Acquisition (OELA), Arabic is the second language most spoken by emergent bilingual students (2.5% of the population in 2020). In 2018, Arabic was the second most spoken language by emergent bilinguals in 16 states and was among the five most common languages in 39 states

(Bialik, Scheller, & Waler, 2018). In Michigan, over a quarter of all emergent bilinguals (26.3%) speak Arabic (OELA, 2023).

Arabic is followed surprisingly by English (2.2%). The fact that so many students designated as English learners speak English at home is important to note. The National Center for Education Statistics (2023) gives the following example as a reason for this claim: "[S]tudents who live in multilingual households and students adopted from other countries who were raised speaking another language but currently live in households where English is spoken" (Table 1, footnote 2). However, the fact that so many students designated as ELs speak English at home is another indication of the complexity of language practices in the homes of emergent bilinguals. It also accounts for the change in immigration that has brought many bilingual English-speaking students from Africa and Asia to the United States.

English as a home language of emergent bilinguals is then followed by Chinese, representing fourth place and 1.8% of students who are classified as English learners. It is important, however, to understand that this group is also linguistically heterogenous, with most speaking Mandarin, but many also speaking Cantonese and other Chinese languages, such as Fuzhounese, Wu, Hokkien, and Hakka. In 2018, Chinese was among the five most common languages in 32 states. West Virginia has the greatest percentage of English learners who speak Chinese (9.9%), followed by New York (9.2%).

Vietnamese then follows, representing 1.4% of all emergent bilinguals in the United States. Other languages spoken at home by more than 25,000 students who are English learners include Portuguese (1%), Russian (0.7%), Haitian/Haitian Creole (0.6%), Hmong (.06%), and Urdu (0.5%).

Table 2.4 provides the distribution of the languages other than English spoken by students in the United States, including those who are emergent bilinguals, according to calculations from the U.S. Census[1] (U.S. Census Bureau, ACS, 2022). It shows the number of youth (ages 5 to 17) who speak a language other than English at home, as well as those who speak English less than very well and are considered emergent bilinguals. The table also shows the percentage of emergent bilinguals speaking a given language group compared to others. In addition, the last column of the table shows the percentages within each language group who are emergent bilinguals.

Despite the fact that the greatest proportion of emergent bilinguals as shown in Table 2.4 is Spanish speaking (69.0%), it is important to point out that, proportionately, Spanish-speaking youth are *not* less proficient in English than other groups. In fact, the proportion of speakers of Asian/Pacific languages who speak English less than very well (23.6%) is greater than that of the Spanish-speaking group (22.5%).

Spanish is the leading language of emergent bilinguals in all but five states, where other languages dominate: Alaska (Yup'ik), Hawai'i (Iloko), Maine (Somali), Montana (German), and Vermont (Nepali) (U.S. DoE, 2018). Maine and Vermont have large settlements of Somali and Nepali refugees. Yup'ik is a major indigenous language in Alaska. Iloko is the language spoken among most Filipino immigrants to Hawai'i. Most surprisingly, the variety of German spoken by the Hutterites, a religious group in Montana, is the leading home language of emergent bilinguals in that state.

Table 2.4. Numbers and Percentages of Languages Spoken by Emergent Bilinguals (EBLs),
5 to 17 Years Old

Language group	Number of LOTE speakers	Number of EBLs	% of all EBLs	% of EBLs within language group
Spanish	7,972,525	1,789,893	69.0%	22.5%
Indo-European[2]	1,680,851	384,057	15.09%	22.9%
Asian/Pacific[3]	1,255,736	296,250	11.0%	23.6%
Other	662,489	125,101	5.0%	18.9%
Total	11,571,601	2,595,301	100.00%	

Source: U.S. Census Bureau, American Community Survey, 2022, one-year estimate, Table C16004.

WHAT ARE THEIR DEMOGRAPHIC CHARACTERISTICS?

Ethnicity/Race and Socioeconomic Status

When we look at racial or ethnic classifications according to the categories of the U.S. Census,[4] emergent bilinguals are overwhelmingly Hispanic or Latino (78.1%). Asians account for 10.6% of the emergent bilingual population, whereas whites account for 5.8% and Blacks for 3.5%. There are also many emergent bilinguals who are categorized in the census as American Indians and Pacific Islanders, although their numbers pale in comparison to those of the other racial or ethnic categories. Although the U.S. Census allows self-identification of two or more races, this also makes little sense, for example, to people of Latin American ancestry who have learned to think of themselves as mestizo or mulato or simply mezclao (mixed) and whose complex racial background has been erased for generations. And yet, among the foreign-born English learners who consider themselves Black, 57% are from Latin America, pointing to a greater consciousness of the racial categories in the United States (OELA, March 2020).

There is much more racial and linguistic heterogeneity among emergent bilinguals than ever. For example, among emergent bilinguals who are counted as French speakers, we now find students from all over West Africa who are multilingual. The Africans arriving in the United States have brought their many languages (and their various multilingual practices), the most numerous being Ibo, Yoruba, Kru, Amharic, Cushite, Swahili, Bantu languages, Fulani, and Mande. And among emergent bilinguals from the Indian subcontinent, we find not only students who speak Hindi and Urdu but also substantial numbers of speakers of Gujarati, Bengali, Punjabi, Telugu, Malayalam, and Tamil, who are also multilingual. In addition, emergent bilingual students in large numbers are found among Native Americans, especially Navajo (Diné) but also Yup'ik, Keres Pueblo people, Yaqui, Apache, Cherokee, Choctaw, Dakota, Ojibwa, and others.

Turning now to the socioeconomic characteristics of emergent bilinguals, *Statista* (2019) reported that 31.9% of students who lived below the poverty threshold did not speak English at home. However, 20.9% of those who lived above the poverty threshold also did not speak English at home. This great variance in socioeconomic status among emergent bilinguals was also noted by Quintero and Hansen (2021), who found that only 37% of students classified as ELs come from households with low socioeconomic status. The profile of the emergent bilingual student has changed drastically from 2003, when Zehler and colleagues (2003) estimated that 75% of English learners lived in poverty. This is an important finding, for bilingualism in the United States and the development of English language and literacy is not limited to children of poor parents but also includes children of middle-class parents.

It is also important to note other social categories where English learners are overrepresented. Although emergent bilinguals make up only 10% of the total student population, they are overrepresented among students experiencing homelessness (16%), and they are more likely to experience homelessness in urban settings (OELA, February 2022). English learners are also overrepresented in the migratory population and among emergent bilinguals labeled as disabled (Cioè-Peña, 2021). In 2017–2018, 11.2% of students identified with disabilities were English learners (OELA, August 2021). Notably, English learners were overrepresented in the categories of specific learning disability (12.3% percentage points higher than other students), speech or language impairment (2.0% higher), and intellectual disability (0.5% higher) (OELA, August 2021).

Gender and Age Distribution

According to Office for Civil Rights data (U.S. Department of Education and Office for Civil Rights, 2024), slightly more than half of emergent bilinguals in the nation's schools identify as male (54%), with just less than half as female (46%).

Emergent bilingual students in the United States are younger than the average pre-K–12 student and thus clustered more in elementary schools. In the fall of 2020, for instance, 57% of all emergent bilingual students were in K through grade 3, and only 27% were enrolled at the grade 9–12 high school level. Moving higher up in the grades, we find that the number of emergent bilinguals decreases.

The drop in the number of emergent bilinguals as we move up the grades reflects two important trends. On the one hand, at the elementary level, the change points to the success of educators in moving emergent bilinguals along the bilingual continuum, so that they can test out of the English learner classification. But the reasons for the decline in the numbers of emergent bilinguals in high school should be interrogated. The decline might reveal the high dropout rate in this age group, as well as the secondary schools' policies of pushing out students who might not succeed in the standardized tests and graduation exit exams that are required so that schools can claim success. We return to this issue in later chapters.

Nativity

Despite popular perceptions, emergent bilinguals are by no means all immigrants or foreign born. Zong and Batalova (2015a) report that 77% of emergent bilinguals are *U.S. born*. In prekindergarten to 5th grade this proportion is even greater at 85% (Zong & Batalova, 2015b). The high number of American-born children who enter U.S. schools and are designated as English learners points to the increased multilingualism in the United States. American children are increasingly growing up in homes where English is not the only language spoken. Bilingualism is not a *foreign* phenomenon. It is an American sociolinguistic reality, chosen by many who see it as important to family and community life. The fact that U.S. schools do not understand the value of bilingualism to families points to how out of touch they are with their communities.

At the middle and high school levels, U.S.-born students still account for 57% of all students designated as ELs (Grantmakers for Education, 2013). This has to do with three factors—the complex nature of immigration and family settlement, the presence of individual disability, and the failure of our school system to meaningfully educate emergent bilinguals.

The complex nature of immigration and families today refers to the fact that, although in the past children born in the United States have also grown up in the United States, travel across national borders is currently more frequent. And this is not only happening with migrant rural families. Urban families are increasingly moving back and forth across borders, and their U.S.-born children often end up also being schooled in languages other than English. Additionally, many families send their U.S.-born children to live with grandparents in other countries while they work long hours in the United States. Only when the children are older and able to care for themselves do they return to live with their parents.

Many of the U.S.-born children who remain emergent bilinguals after middle school have language disabilities. Some students who are designated as emergent bilinguals when they enter school are afterward referred for evaluation to receive special education services. Because they have been designated as English learners, they then have to pass the state's exam—which assesses performance in listening, speaking, reading, and writing—for reclassification as English fluent. Despite being quite fluent in English, many students with disabilities cannot be reclassified because of poor scores on exams that have been normed on students without disabilities. Therefore, their designation as English learners and later as long-term English learners travels with them throughout their education.

The majority of emergent bilinguals who are born in the United States (77%) are the children of immigrants or have at least one immigrant parent (Zong & Batalova, 2015a, 2015b). Although some may continue to speak languages other than English at home, this fact does not explain why so many others continue to be designated English learners when, in fact, they may not speak anything but English.

On the other end of the spectrum are *foreign-born emergent bilinguals*. They vary in the number of years they have been in the United States, but most have been in the United States for less than five years (Zehler et al., 2003). It is difficult to determine the number of foreign-born emergent bilinguals who are refugees, temporary sojourners,[5] or migrant workers.[6]

The U.S. foreign-born population was approximately 14.1% of the U.S. population in 2021 (Passel & Krogstad, 2023). In 2023, the top six countries of immigrant origin to the United States were Mexico (24%), India (6%), China (5%), the Philippines (5%), El Salvador, (3%) and Vietnam (3%) (Schumacker et al., 2023). Of the 46.2 million immigrants in the United States in 2022, approximately one-fourth (10.5 million) were undocumented. The number of undocumented immigrants has remained mostly stable since 2017 (Passel & Krogstad, 2023).

Of those immigrants who were documented, approximately half are naturalized citizens or permanent residents. A total of 2.3 million are refugees or asylum seekers, and in 2023, 43% of refugees were from Africa, 28% from the Middle East and South Asia, 13% from East Asia, 11% from Latin America and the Caribbean, and 4% from Europe and Central Asia. The top origin countries for refugees in 2023 were the Democratic Republic of Congo, Myanmar, and Syria (Ward & Batalova, 2023). Finally, 1.5 million immigrants had legal temporary status (mostly foreign students and temporary workers). But we know little of how these figures relate to students enrolled in schools.

Some foreign-born students, mostly from the middle class, come to the United States from well-resourced schools and often have had some instruction in English. But other foreign-born students come from societies torn by war and poverty, where the educational system has declined or collapsed. Some come from poor rural communities where it has been difficult to go to school consistently. These students have minimal literacy in their home language. For them, achieving proficiency in the ways of using English for academic tasks is a struggle because they have little familiarity with these tasks.

In particular, migrant students, those whose families work seasonally in agriculture or fisheries across the United States, face significant marginalization in the educational system. While about half of migratory agricultural workers are U.S. citizens or have visas, 47% of them are considered "unauthorized" (NCFH, 2018). This undocumented status, coupled with their transient living conditions, exacerbates their precarious circumstances. For these children and their families, the demands of English language proficiency, intensive academic engagement, and active parental involvement in school clash with their daily realities, creating severe challenges and exclusion (Free & Križ, 2022).

We know that approximately 1.1 million to 1.6 million students under the age of 18 are undocumented immigrants (Suárez-Orozco, Suárez-Orozco, & Todorova et al., 2008; Zong & Batalova, 2015a). As of 2018, approximately 6.1 million U.S.-citizen children lived with an undocumented family member, and between 2011 and 2013, up to half a million U.S.-citizen children experienced the deportation of at least one parent (American Immigration Council, 2021). While we do not know how many of these students are emergent bilinguals, we do know that a child's risk of mental health issues like depression, anxiety, suicidal thoughts, PTSD, and more increases after a parent's detention or deportation (Lovato, 2019; Rojas-Flores et al., 2017). This toxic stress impacts students' daily life, including their academic, social, and linguistic performance in school. While mixed status and deportation are often viewed as taboo in schools, attending to the socioemotional ramifications is essential. The education of undocumented students in K–12 classrooms was guaranteed by the Supreme Court in 1982, when it ruled in *Plyler v. Doe* that a K–12 education is a fundamental and protected right that needs to be provided to all students, regardless of citizenship or residency status.

Unaccompanied minors are immigrants under 18 years of age who have no lawful immigration status and no parent or legal guardian in the United States. The number of unaccompanied minors who have come into the United States has increased significantly since 2012, when there was a total of 13,625 unaccompanied minors. In 2023, there were 118,938 (U.S. Department of Health and Human Services, 2024a). In 2023, the unaccompanied minors received were from Guatemala (42%), Honduras (28%), El Salvador (9%), Mexico, (8%), and other countries (13%). The states into which they were released to sponsors tells the story of the changing demographics of the United States. From October 2023 to February 2024, as expected, Texas received the most unaccompanied minors (6,916), followed by Florida (5,349) and California (5,276). These states were followed by New York (3,440), and then surprisingly by Georgia (2,343), New Jersey (2,079), and Tennessee (2,042) (U.S. Department of Health and Human Services, 2024b).

It is imperative to understand that, although important, the education of emergent bilinguals is not just about immigrant or refugee education alone. As we have said, according to the Migration Policy Institute, 82% of English learners in prekindergarten through fifth grade were born in the United States (Corey, 2016) and are native-born U.S. citizens.

HOW DO THEY USE LANGUAGE?

The U.S. Census Bureau only asks families about spoken English, but what is at issue for educational attainment is the ability to complete academic work, which requires written, along with spoken, proficiency. Therefore, relying on census figures may be misleading and may underestimate the population of students who are emergent bilinguals.

Estimates of the percentage of emergent bilinguals who can use their home language in complex academic tasks vary, but school coordinators report that between one-fourth to one-third of these students nationwide have lower levels of literacy in their home language compared to what might be expected of students going to school in a country where it is the language of schooling. This fact should be of vital importance to those who coordinate and plan for the education of these students because it turns out that the benefits of what is known as linguistic transfer of literacy skills from one language to another will not be enjoyed completely by emergent bilinguals who are not familiar with literacy practices for academic purposes in what is considered their home language.

Many emergent bilinguals struggle with literacy in their home language, particularly secondary school students categorized as students with interrupted formal education (SIFE) or students with limited or interrupted formal education (SLIFE). It has been estimated that between 11% and 20% of emergent bilinguals in middle schools and high schools have missed more than two years of schooling since the age of six (Custodio & O'Loughlin, 2020). This group also has very high dropout rates, with estimates as high as 75% at the secondary level (Montero, Newmaster, & Ledger et al., 2014). Furthermore, even students who have consistently attended school in their countries of origin have often learned to use language for literacy purposes that are very different from those literacies required by U.S. schools (Yip, 2016; more on this in Chapter 4).

WHO ARE THE LATINE EMERGENT BILINGUALS?

Because Spanish-speaking students make up the majority of emergent bilinguals in the United States, we pay special attention to them in this book. We start by contextualizing our use of the term *Latine* in this book to refer to them, when up to now we have used the terms preferred by government agencies and much scholarship—*Latino/a* or *Hispanic*. In 1970, the U.S. Census used the term *Hispanic* for the first time, although much of the population of Latin American origin in the United States preferred the term *Latino/a*. In 1997, the census expanded the category to "Hispanic or Latino origin," legitimizing the use of the word *Latino*. At the same time, a battle was brewing over who was included as Latino and whether the masculine ending "o" was gender normative. The alternatives—*Latino/a* or *Latin@*, introduced by many scholars—were not satisfactory for many because the terms reified the gender binary. In the past decade, the term *Latinx*, a gender-neutral alternative to *Latino*, *Latina*, or *Latin@*, has been increasingly used by scholars and the community to include those who are trans or gender nonconfirming. In the second edition of this book, we adopted *Latinx* as our preferred term. Lately, the term *Latine* is being increasingly used by the community itself. In addition to being gender neutral, it has the advantage that it is easier to say in Spanish than *Latinx*. Also, it allows the easier use of plural forms, *Latines*. Because, for us, the act of naming oneself is important, we have adopted the term *Latine* in this edition, except when referring to the work of the government and others who name them differently.

In 2022, and according to the U.S. Census Bureau, there were approximately 63.7 million Latines in the United States, accounting for 19% of the population of the country. It is projected that by 2060 that figure will be 111 million (Statista, 2024). In 2021, there were 14 million Latine students in U.S. schools. Latine students made up 26% of the country's prekindergarten and kindergarten pupils, 26% of elementary school students, and 26% of high school students (U.S. Census Bureau, 2021). Between 2011 and 2021, the school-age Latine population increased in every state, and it is expected to reach 30% by 2030 (Jimenez, K., 2022). The U.S. Census Bureau has forecasted that Latine students will make up a third of the nation's 3- to 17-year-old learners by 2036.

Two of the five largest school districts in the country are Los Angeles County and Miami–Dade County, with 74% and 73% of students respectively being of Latine background.

The Latine population is complex. In 2020, over two-thirds were born in the United States (67%), and the number of U.S.-born Latine people is growing. In 2019, 72% of all Latines ages five and older indicated they spoke English very well. This rise in English proficiency has been accompanied by a decline in the number of Latines who claim to speak Spanish at home. However, there is no doubt that the use of Spanish has more holding power than the traditional three-generation language shift that occurred during the 20th century (Fishman, 1965). In 2022, 94% of Latine immigrants spoke Spanish at home, the same rate as in 1980 (Funk & López, 2022).

The Latine group also represents many national origin groups, although in 2020 almost two-thirds are considered Mexicans (62%), either because they were born in Mexico or they trace their ancestors' roots to Mexico. Puerto Ricans constituted the second largest group (9.7% of the Latine population in 2020), and Cubans, Salvadorans, Dominicans, Guatemalans, Colombians, and Hondurans each had a population of around a million. Nevertheless, the fastest growing origin group is now Venezuelan. From 2010 to 2019, the Venezuelan population grew by 126%, whereas the Mexican population only grew 13% over the same period (Funk & López, 2022).

Regardless of where Latine people have settled and the sociohistorical circumstances of their settlement, U.S. schools have rarely built upon their funds of knowledge (Moll et al., 1992; see also Chapter 8) or used pedagogy that leverages and sustains their cultural practices (Ladson-Billings, 1995; Paris & Alim, 2014; Villegas & Lucas, 2002). Speaking specifically about the importance of leveraging Latine cultural and linguistic practices in their education, Pedraza and Rivera (2005) use the image of *sankofa*, a Swahili word that refers to going back to the source, and suggest that it is important for Latine students to explore their "historical, sociocultural and familial traditions and legacies" (p. 234). The education system's lack of attention to Latine students' sociohistorical context has resulted in these students not faring well in U.S. schools (Gándara & Contreras, 2009).

In 2021, there was a total of more than 13 million Latine students in U.S. elementary and secondary schools (Fabina et al., 2023). The sheer number of Mexican-origin students makes them the group with the most Spanish-speaking students, as well as the group with the most emergent bilinguals. Mexicans are, however, neither the group that speaks Spanish the most at home nor the group that has the most emergent bilinguals, comparatively speaking. The Latine national groups with the highest percentages of students who are emergent bilinguals are the following: Honduran (17.3%), Salvadoran (17.1%), Guatemalan (16.7%), Paraguayan (16.7%), Dominican (16.6%), Venezuelan (15.6%), Mexican (13.2%), and Ecuadorean (12.6%) (Office of English Language Acquisition, 2015).

Latine immigrant students account for more than half (58%) of all immigrant youth in the United States, and more of these students are in the upper grades than in the lower grades. Despite the lack of data on undocumented immigrant students, we know that many Latine immigrant students are undocumented or are the children of undocumented immigrants, since about three-quarters (76%) of undocumented immigrants are of Latine origin (Passel & Cohn, 2009).

One of the most alarming facts about Latine emergent bilinguals is their high dropout rate of 7.8% compared to 4.1% for white English learners. This dropout rate is only superseded by that of Native Americans who are English learners (National Center for Education Statistics, 2023). Clearly, practitioners, researchers, and policymakers must redouble their energies toward better serving Latine students, who constitute the overwhelming proportion of the emergent bilingual population.

EDUCATING EMERGENT BILINGUALS: KNOWING WHO THEY ARE

Despite the differences among emergent bilinguals that we have identified in this chapter, a few generalizations can be gleaned from our prior discussion:

- Their numbers are increasing overall, but so is the number of fluent bilingual students.
- There are discrepancies regarding how they are identified and reclassified among state and local educational authorities.
- Most are racialized as non-white, and of those approximately one-third are poor.
- Most live in urban areas and attend under-resourced schools that are segregated, although the suburban population has grown in recent years.
- Three out of every four were born in the United States.
- Although approximately half are in elementary schools, the greatest increase in the number of emergent bilinguals is in high school–age students, although many of them do not graduate.
- Most emergent bilinguals are of Latine origin, although there is great linguistic, cultural, and social diversity among the Latine population.

STUDY QUESTIONS

1. Identify some of the contradictions in counting, classifying, and reclassifying emergent bilinguals. What are some of the inconsistencies in the data?
2. Describe the population of emergent bilinguals in the United States. What do all students have in common?
3. Find out who the emergent bilinguals are in your school district. How many are there? What are their characteristics, and what languages do they speak? How have they been counted? What method is used to identify, classify, and reclassify them?
4. Why is bilingualism a vital topic in the education of *all* children in the United States?

CHAPTER 3

Programs and Policies for Educating Emergent Bilinguals

This chapter:[1]

- Considers programs and policies for educating emergent bilinguals;
- Describes types of educational programs for emergent bilinguals;
- Reviews educational policies for these students in a historical context, including:
  - » The antecedents,
  - » Title VII: The Bilingual Education Act,
  - » Legal precedents,
  - » The 1990s,
  - » No Child Left Behind (NCLB),
  - » Common Core State Standards (CCSS), and
  - » Every Student Succeeds Act (ESSA); and
- Presents a critical review of the present.

Since the 1960s, language-minoritized students have been the focus of many U.S. educational policy decisions at the national, state, and local levels and in all three branches of government. As a result of top-down educational policies and negotiations with teachers and communities, different types of educational programs for these students exist in the United States. In what follows, we first review the educational programs that are available for emergent bilinguals. We then turn to a brief historical section in which we discuss the roots of bilingual education, as well as the evolution of federal and state policies to educate these students. It will become evident that federal bilingual education policy has moved away from the initial sociopolitical, as well as linguistic, demands of the language minoritized communities in the 1960s. Federal bilingual education policy has also changed over the past five decades from taking into account the students' home language practices and being flexible about educational approaches to being far more rigid in emphasizing English-only instruction or strict separation of languages in dual-language instruction. As we also illustrate, the high-stakes standardized testing movement, spurred by NCLB (2001) and continued under ESSA (2015) despite the greater flexibility afforded to states, has had much to do with this new rigidity. At the same time, there has been a discourse shift in terminology—from *bilingual education* programs to *dual-language* programs. The latter term often carries a narrower focus on language and academics, frequently overlooking the sociopolitical issues of social and racial justice that were central to the bilingual education movement championed by Chicanx, Puerto Rican, and Native American communities in the 1960s. As we will see, dual-language programs often focus not on leveraging and developing the bilingualism of emergent bilinguals who are progressing toward spoken and written skills in English along with their home language, but on programs that often also include language-majority students, speakers of English who are learning an additional language for "enrichment." (We discuss the consequences of this discourse shift in more detail later in this chapter.) These developments mean that there is even greater dissonance today between policy and research on the education of emergent bilinguals than there has been in the past.

EDUCATIONAL PROGRAMS FOR EMERGENT BILINGUALS

Within the U.S. public educational system, there are different educational programs used in schools for working with emergent bilinguals. These programs range from those that expect students to learn English after simply exposing them to it and treating them like all other students, to those specifically designed to support students' academic, emotional, and linguistic development through the deployment of their home language practices. The educational policies we discuss in this chapter are critical to the form of instruction that emergent bilinguals receive.

The tendency over the past two decades has been for policymakers, and the public more generally, to provide more English-only programs for emergent bilinguals and move away from programs that use students' home languages. Before we discuss this shift and its (dis)connection with the research literature, we briefly describe these different programs or approaches and display them in Table 3.1.

In the first category, *nonrecognition*, often referred to as *submersion* or *sink-or-swim* programs, schools and educators provide emergent bilinguals with exactly the same educational services that are provided to monolingual English speakers. That is, they neither provide alternative educational services nor use the students' home language practices to teach them. These submersion programs were prevalent before 1970 and still are used in different ways in many parts of the country, especially in light of recent English-only initiatives in certain states.

A second category of educational programs falls under the umbrella of *English as a second language (ESL) programs*, also called *English as a new language (ENL)* in some states. There are *pull-out ESL/ENL programs*, which provide some support for students in special sessions outside of the regular classroom. Although these programs are meant to offer instruction exclusively in English, some home language support is allowed. There are also *push-in ESL/ENL programs*, in which an ESL teacher works collaboratively with the content-area teacher to support emergent bilingual students in the class. Some home-language support is also possible in these programs. Still another type of program, called *structured English immersion*, also known as *sheltered English* or *content-based ESL*, provides emergent bilinguals with pedagogical support and scaffolding tailored specifically for these students. Usually, instruction is only in English in these programs, although some teachers do provide home-language support.

The federal government makes a distinction between English as a second language programs and *high-intensity language programs* (see U.S. Department of Education, NCES, 2015d). This latter term is being used in some localities for programs that focus on intensive instruction in the features of English (lexicon, phonology, morphology, syntax). Usually, this is combined with sheltered English content courses or with mainstream classes in English only. This type of instruction is used especially in middle schools and high schools. These programs are also used in states that deny bilingual education to emergent bilinguals. For example, in Arizona, emergent bilingual students at present spend two hours a day in these high-intensity language classes (Kaveh et al., 2022). Previously, students in Arizona had spent four hours in these classes (Gándara & Orfield, 2010; Johnson & Johnson, 2015). Because of their focus on the structure of English, and not its use, these programs fail to provide students with adequate opportunities to use English meaningfully and develop proficiency (Ríos-Aguilar, Gonzalez-Canché, & Sabetghadam, 2012). High-intensity language programs are also often implemented in *newcomer programs*. Newcomer programs are short-term, specialized educational initiatives designed to support newly arrived immigrant students, particularly at the secondary level. These programs serve as a bridge aiming to help students transition into the regular school system by providing intensive English language instruction, acculturation support, and academic skills development. Because these programs bring together immigrant students from multiple countries of origin and language backgrounds, providing bilingual education is not feasible, but individual teachers may still provide bilingual supports when possible. Not all newcomer programs rely on intensive English language instruction, as will become evident in our discussion of high schools that are part of the Internationals Network for Public Schools.

Moving toward the other end of the pedagogical spectrum, there is a third category of programs that takes a more *bilingual* approach, in that students' home languages are used to teach subject matter for a variety of reasons—sometimes to support their transition to English and other times to develop their bilingualism and biliteracy. The first such type is known as *transitional bilingual education*, also known as *early-exit bilingual education*. These transitional programs group students by home language and use it to some degree, but the focus is on students' acquiring English as quickly as possible and exiting them into mainstream English-only classrooms. Another type of bilingual program is known as *developmental bilingual education*, or simply as *maintenance bilingual education*[2] (also known as *late-exit bilingual education* or in some places as *one-way dual-language education*). This type of program also groups language-minoritized students by home language and supports the development of their bilingualism. In some localities, these developmental bilingual education programs are now called one-way dual-language bilingual programs and serve students of a language group other than English whose bilingualism falls along all points of the bilingual continuum. That is, these programs may serve emergent bilinguals, as well as more experienced bilinguals. In some cases, the emergent bilinguals are developing English, and in others, more experienced bilingual students are developing what is considered their heritage language. Developing students' bilingualism and biliteracy is the goal of these programs.

It is important to understand, however, that in some places, particularly in regions without a longstanding presence of bilingual education, so-called one-way dual-language programs may actually refer to programs serving exclusively English speakers who want to develop a new language from an early age through an *immersion approach*. In these contexts, developmental bilingual education and programs called one-way dual language differ in their goals and in the populations they serve. In some states these programs for language majority children who want to develop an additional language are called *dual-language immersion*. Because they concern mostly language majority children, they are not the focus of this book.

Significant attention has recently been focused on *two-way dual-language bilingual education* (DLBE), also known as two-way bilingual, dual-language, or two-way immersion (see, for example, Freire, Alfaro & de Jong, 2024). This increased interest warrants a more in-depth examination of this program type. DLBE programs support the development of two languages within classrooms that enroll, in theory, students of two distinct language backgrounds: speakers of the same language other than English (LOTE) (e.g., Spanish or Chinese) developing English, and English monolingual speakers developing a LOTE. These students learn academic content together through both languages. The goal is for both the language-minoritized students and the language-majority students to become bilingual and biliterate, achieve highly academically, and develop cross-cultural competence. The sociolinguistic reality of these programs, however, is much more complex, for it reflects the dynamics of bilingualism and bilingual use, as well as the politics of the locale. For example, in many places, the English-fluent children are members of minoritized groups, and their dynamic language practices also include what is perceived as the language other than English. That is, although originally conceived as a way to socially and racially integrate two different ethnolinguistic groups, in reality, as we will see, many language minoritized communities have used DLBE programs to provide an education for their bilingual students who are positioned along different points of the bilingual continuum.

In the current landscape of school choice, with the proliferation of charter schools and schools' competition for student enrollment, as well as increased public interest in the cognitive, economic, and sociocultural benefits of multilingualism, DLBE programs are often utilized to attract majority families (Bernstein et al., 2020; Cervantes-Soon et al., 2021; Duarte, 2022). DLBE programs have thus rapidly expanded across 41 states and the District of Columbia (Dual Language Schools, 2024). As we have said, these programs aim to integrate students linguistically and promote equity, but they are also seen as a means to integrate students racially and economically (Dorner et al., 2023; Gándara & Aldana, 2014; Uzzell & Ayscue, 2021), either implicitly or explicitly, such as to comply with desegregation orders (López, 2016). However, these programs are not inherently designed to ensure racial or economic integration, and therefore this assumed benefit has been contested (Chávez-Moreno, 2023; Flores, Tseng, & Subtirelu, 2020; Palmer Cervantes-Soon, & Freire, 2024).

Students in these programs usually start in kindergarten or first grade and can continue, in principle, through secondary school (although there are few programs for older students). English speakers benefit from learning a new language from an early age and from practicing it with authentic speakers. Because English speakers participate in DLBE, these programs are supposed to escape the stigma of bilingual education as remediation. Therefore, they are seen as not only offering emergent bilinguals the possibility of developing their home language and accelerated English language acquisition, but also providing a context in which they can develop positive cultural and academic identities. The academic and linguistic gains of DLBE for emergent bilinguals compared to mainstream and other programs have been documented in the literature (Lindholm-Leary & Block, 2010; Steele et al., 2017), and thus at first sight, this appears to be a win-win solution to the education of emergent bilinguals.

However, research also suggests DLBE programs might disproportionately benefit privileged English-speaking students, marginalizing English learners and low-income students through a variety of ways, such as strict language separation and language allocation policies that exclude emergent bilinguals' authentic language practices or increased attention to the demands of parents from the dominant group (Cervantes-Soon et al., 2017). These findings question the equity vision of DLBE programs and highlight concerns about the gentrification of bilingual education, where wealthier, predominantly English-speaking families displace racialized emergent bilinguals, shifting the focus of teachers, resources, policies, curriculum, and instruction in ways that perpetuate inequities (Chaparro, 2021; Delavan, Freire, & Menken, 2021, 2024; García-Mateus, 2023; Heiman & Murakami, 2019; Valdez, Freire, & Delavan, 2016, 2021). These issues have often been documented especially in regions without a politicized history of bilingual education, such as Delaware, Georgia, North Carolina, and Utah, among many others (Cervantes-Soon et al., 2021; Freire & Delavan, 2021), or in rapidly gentrifying cities (Cervantes-Soon, Degollado, & Nuñez, 2020; Chaparro, 2021; García-Mateus, 2023; Heiman & Murakami, 2019).

Although the white-streaming of these dual-language programs is likely widespread, demographic gentrification of DLBE programs is not universal. For instance, most DLBE programs in Los Angeles serve mostly Latine students in segregated low-income communities (Asson et al., 2023). In this and other Latine majority settings, DLBE programs may serve Spanish-speaking English learners and Latine English speakers who have not had the privilege of bilingual education in the past. Furthermore, some students may be bilingual or have Indigenous home languages and cultures unrecognized by the program. Thus, while DLBE programs imagine two distinct language groups, there is significant diversity within them. Nonetheless, inequities persist, with African American students and students with disabilities often underrepresented, underserved, or implicitly excluded (Cervantes-Soon, Degollado, & Nuñez, 2020; Cioè-Peña, 2020; Palmer, 2010; Valdés, 2002).

Given the persistence of inequities, some advocate for the explicit inclusion of *critical consciousness* as both the foundation and goal of these DLBE programs (Cervantes-Soon et al., 2017; Dorner et al, 2022; Heiman, Cervantes-Soon, & Hurie, 2021). Drawing on Paulo Freire's (1970) notion of conscientization, critical consciousness refers to the ability of individuals to critically analyze and understand the social, political, and economic conditions that shape their lives. It involves questioning and challenging oppressive structures and ideologies. It requires individuals to engage in dialogue, reflection, and collective action or praxis in pursuit of social justice and human liberation. Heiman and colleagues (2023) describe actions integral to developing critical consciousness in DLBE, which include continuously challenging power structures to address injustice; examining and incorporating global, local, and personal histories in program planning, implementation, and curriculum; fostering meaningful connections through critical listening to historically marginalized voices; and confronting discomfort to understand and counteract personal privileges that perpetuate social injustices. These interconnected actions align with Freire's praxis cycle of reflection, dialogue, and action, aiming to humanize educational relationships. In DLBE, they involve teachers, students, parents, and policymakers fostering justice and nurturing critical consciousness.

We have presented the general characteristics of a variety of language education programs available for emergent bilinguals in U.S. schools. All of these programs vary in implementation and terminology depending on the context where they are established, the student populations that they serve, and the way practitioners understand the goals, components, and approaches of their program. In general, they develop from institutional structures that characterize themselves as being either monolingual or bilingual. Notice that throughout this book, we explicitly name the *bilingual* condition of all types of dual-language programs (whether one-way or two-way). For example, we refer to two-way dual-language as "dual-language bilingual education," or DLBE (see Sánchez , García & Solorza, 2017).

In contrast, some educational programs for emergent bilinguals function as a *blend* of ESL and bilingual education programs. To acknowledge their existence, we are calling this type here *dynamic bi/multilingual education*. The secondary schools that make up what is called the Internationals Network for Public Schools fall under this category.[3] In these schools, newcomer students of different language backgrounds are educated with teachers who teach in English but focus on leveraging the students' home language practices. They follow distinct pedagogical principles that include project-based experiential learning, language and content integration, and student/teacher collaboration (for more on these principles, see García & Sylvan, 2011).

To help differentiate programs in terms of their pedagogy, philosophy, and focus, we display all programs in Table 3.1, which is adapted and expanded from Crawford (2004). Readers are encouraged to study this table carefully, as it expands our descriptions of the programs (for other categorizations of programs, see Baker & Wright, 2021). Although we present different program categories, in practice, the most innovative and committed educators start with designing a program for their actual community of students. For this reason, we have found many times

Table 3.1. Types of Educational Programs for Emergent Bilinguals

Program	Language used in instruction	Components	Duration	Goals
I. Nonrecognition				
Submersion (sink-or-swim)	100% English	Mainstream education; no special help with English; no teachers qualified to teach emergent bilinguals	Throughout K–12 schooling	Linguistic assimilation (shift to English only)
II. ESL/ENL				
English as a second/new language (ESL/ENL) Pull-out (submersion plus ESL)	90–100% in English; may include some home language support or not	Mainstream education; students pulled out approximately for 30–45 minutes of ESL daily; teachers certified in TESOL	As needed	Linguistic assimilation; remedial English
English as a second/new language (ESL/ENL) Push-in	90–100% in English; may include some home language support or not	Mainstream education; ESL teacher works alongside the subject teacher as needed; teachers certified in TESOL	As needed	Linguistic assimilation; remedial education within mainstream classroom
Structured English immersion (sheltered English, content-based ESL, stand-alone ESL)	90–100% English; may include some home language support or not	Subject-matter instruction at students' level of English; students usually grouped for instruction; teachers certified in TESOL; should have some training in immersion	Usually 1–3 years	Linguistic assimilation; exit to mainstream education

High-intensity English language training	100% English; focus on English features; usually combined with mainstream or sheltered English for content	Focus on features and structures of the English language, usually combined with mainstream or sheltered English for content; teachers certified in TESOL/ELA for language instruction	Usually 1–3 years, especially used in high school and middle school, newcomer programs, and antibilingual education school districts	Linguistic assimilation; remedial English focus; exit to mainstream education

III. Bilingual

Transitional bilingual education (early-exit bilingual education)	Initially 50–90% home language and 10–50% English; home language gradually reduced to 10% and English increased to 90%	Initial literacy usually in home language; some subject instruction in home language; ESL and subject-matter instruction at students' level of English; sheltered English subject instruction; teachers certified in bilingual education	Usually 1–3 years; students exit as they become proficient in English	Linguistic assimilation; English acquisition without falling behind academically
Developmental bilingual education (late-exit bilingual education, one-way dual-language bilingual education-for language minoritized students)	90% home language initially; gradually decreasing to 50% or thereabouts; or 50/50 from beginning; home language subject instruction always available	Initial literacy focus in home language, although English usually simultaneously introduced; always some subject instruction in home language; ESL initially and English subject-matter instruction at students' level of English; teachers certified in bilingual education	At least 5–6 years	Bilingualism and biliteracy; academic achievement in English

(continued)

Table 3.1. (continued)

Program	Language used in instruction	Components	Duration	Goals
Two-way dual-language bilingual education (DLBE) (two-way dual-language, dual-language bilingual, two-way immersion bilingual)	50/50 model or 90/10 model: 90% home language, 10% additional language in early grades; parity of instruction in both languages from the beginning	English speakers *and* speakers of a LOTE taught literacy and subjects in both languages; teachers certified in bilingual education	At least 5–6 years; more prevalent at the elementary level	Bilingualism and biliteracy; academic achievement in English
IV. Blend				
Dynamic bi/multilingual education	English and students' home languages in dynamic relationship; students are the locus of control for language used; peer teaching	Teacher-led whole classroom in English, coupled with collaborative project-based student learning using home language practices	Used especially at the secondary level, when students have already developed literacy in their home languages	Bilingualism, academic achievement in English

that educators blend features of different types of programs to fit their students' needs. And although we provide the percentage of time in which each language is typically used in instruction, in reality this *varies widely, and must be adjusted to the needs of the local community and students.*

As Table 3.1 illustrates, students' home language practices can be used in a wide variety of ways within educational programs. For instance, they can either be used *fully*, as in the case of bilingual education programs in which the students' home language is a medium of instruction and the goal is biliteracy, or *partially*, as when teachers teach only in English but use the students' home language practices for support. Sometimes students' home language practices are used to ensure comprehension or scaffold instruction in English; other times, they are used to support emergent bilinguals' work on collaborative projects. For example, the Sheltered Instruction, Observation Protocol model, a widely used program of sheltered English instruction for English learners, supports the use of the students' home language to clarify concepts and assignments. The developers of this approach state:

> [W]e believe that clarification of key concepts in students' L1 [first language] by a bilingual instructional aide, peer, or through the use of materials written in the students' L1 provides an important support for the academic learning of those students who are not yet fully proficient in English. (Echevarría, Vogt, & Short, 2004, p. 107)

Whether to use students' home language as a medium of instruction as in bilingual education or simply as a scaffolding mechanism in many ESL classrooms often depends on the number of students of the same language group in the same school and classroom, as well as the ability to find teachers who speak that language. Clearly, in classrooms where emergent bilinguals are from different language backgrounds, traditionally structured bilingual education is not feasible. However, some form of bilingualism in education *is always* attainable, as demonstrated, for example, by the work of the schools of the aforementioned Internationals Network for Public Schools (see García & Leiva, 2014; García & Nuosy, 2024; Sylvan & Romero, 2002) and other schools that are purported to provide only some form of ESL instruction (García, Flores, & Woodley, 2015; García & Kleyn, 2016; Manyak, 2004). Nevertheless, as we noted in Chapter 2, approximately three-fourths of all emergent bilinguals in the United States speak Spanish as their home language. Therefore, the recent shift toward increased efforts to teach Spanish-speaking emergent bilinguals exclusively in English, thereby omitting the use of their home language practices to transform their learning, can be attributed to a lack of public knowledge about the nature of bilingualism and its benefits (detailed in Chapter 4), as well as cultural politics that have little to do with what is educationally sound for the students.

Further, as Table 3.1 shows, the duration of different programs for emergent bilinguals varies considerably. These variations need to be considered in light of the research evidence that we introduce in Chapter 4, which suggests that to be able to use an additional language successfully in academic contexts takes considerably longer than to attain interpersonal communication skills in that language.

But first, we demonstrate how American language-in-education policy changes have placed limits on program options that aim to develop bilingualism and biliteracy.

A BRIEF HISTORY OF EDUCATIONAL POLICIES FOR EMERGENT BILINGUALS

The Antecedents

Before examining contemporary policies for emergent bilinguals, it is important to situate them within the colonial vestiges that led to the emergence of the nation state and that remain in various forms. Since precolonial times, the linguistic landscape of what is now the United States has been incredibly diverse and rich. Before European colonizers settled in what became U.S. land, Indigenous peoples spoke an estimated 300 languages across several major language families (Campbell & Bright, 2016). These languages represented diverse and intricate linguistic groups, each possessing distinct characteristics and cultural importance. Before colonization, the linguistic environment was vibrant, marked by robust trade networks, alliances, and interactions among various Indigenous nations, fostering multilingualism and the interchange of linguistic practices. Beyond mere means of communication, these language practices held profound significance for Indigenous peoples, shaping their identities, spirituality, and worldviews. Language played a pivotal role in their social structure, rituals, and profound connection to their ancestral lands. The arrival of European colonizers, however, brought significant disruption to this linguistic diversity. Although the colonial project encouraged the influx of Europeans from diverse language backgrounds, Native Americans were victims of disease, warfare, displacement, and forced assimilation policies, leading to a dramatic decline in the number of Indigenous language speakers (Iyengar, 2014).

Beginning in the 16th century, Spanish and French missionaries imposed their languages and cultures on Native American communities in regions that became Arizona, California, New Mexico, Texas, Canada, and along the St. Lawrence and Mississippi Rivers. These missionaries taught Spanish and French alongside Roman Catholicism and other worldviews. Despite later English efforts at Indian education and conversion to Christianity in the 17th century, which involved teaching English and Christian doctrine, earlier Spanish and French colonizers established their languages as primary among European languages in North America until the rise of English (Dussias, 1999). However, Indigenous resistance to colonization continued to be a problem for European settlers. In 1867, Congress established the Indian Peace Commission, shifting policy toward peaceful resolutions over military solutions for issues associated with Native American presence, as advocated by white settlers and others, and prompting the use of education to eradicate Indigenous languages. In the 19th century, boarding schools for Native American children were established to assimilate them through traumatic schooling and cultural genocide (Adams, 1995; Wolfe, 2006). Lieutenant Richard Henry Pratt, founder of the

Carlisle Indian Industrial School, described their purpose to "kill the Indian and save the man" (Pratt, 1892). The fabricated superiority of European languages and the construction and classification of Indigenous and African languages as primitive reinforced racial hierarchies that justified genocide and slavery (Iyengar, 2014). Newly developed social and biological sciences facilitated this hierarchy by providing methods to measure and classify human quality.

Furthermore, 19th-century U.S. imperialism was exemplified by events such as the acquisition of more than half of Mexico's land that significantly expanded U.S. territory westward to the Pacific Ocean, as well as the acquisition of Puerto Rico and other territories. This expansion triggered demographic shifts with important implications; for example, Mexicans living in newly acquired U.S. land were forced to navigate challenges concerning their cultural identity, language, and rights as they became U.S. citizens. In this context, Mexican Americans and Puerto Ricans (and later other Latines) emerged as a racialized group largely produced on the basis of language (García, 2015).

At the turn of the 20th century, education and psychological sciences began to view, classify, and study children in new ways, focusing on their brains and language practices. Children and their homes became subjects of research and policy interventions for social and cultural "improvement" with a particular focus on the poor, immigrants, and racialized groups who were perceived as a societal problem (Hernando-Lloréns & Cervantes-Soon, 2023). Within this context, minoritized languages emerged as a problem (Ruiz, 1984), and as in colonial times, educational initiatives aimed to make English the primary home language. This gave way to a normalizing view that labeled emergent bilingual children's behaviors as deviant. Intelligence tests, presented as scientific evidence, reinforced myths that bilingualism in non-white communities hindered learning (Flores, 2005). It was also believed that those who became bilingual later in life were "more real bilinguals" than those who grew up bilingual. These ideas had a significant impact on students from Spanish-speaking backgrounds. For example, during the 1920s and 1930s, Mexican segregation policies in the United States were instituted to separate Mexican American children in schools or classrooms from white children based on ideologies of white supremacy and English superiority (Menchaca & Valencia, 1990). These schools were often underfunded, lacked adequate resources, and provided inferior education compared to schools attended by white children.

However, the social protests and antiracist movements of the 1960s, which viewed language reclamation as a crucial form of resistance against colonization and assimilation, catalyzed significant federal policy shifts supporting bilingual education in the United States (García & Sung, 2018). The battle over racial equality and rights that dominated the civil rights era culminated in the 1965 Watts race riots. Drawing inspiration from the struggles for Black Power, the Mexican American, Puerto Rican, and Native American communities recognized their shared histories as a conquered and colonized people. For example, the Chicano Movimiento demanded "bilingual education, better school conditions, Chicano studies and more Chicano teachers," as well as "a return of our land, release of prisoners, jobs, education, housing, an end to the destruction of the environment" (Thirteen Point Program, 1970, n.p.). García and Sung (2018) concluded:

> To the extent that El Movimiento espoused bilingual education, it was always with connection to the broader *race radical political economic project of self-determination* as tied to alleviating inequality, exclusion, segregation, racism, and poverty. Bilingual education was never meant to be isolated from the structural racism and material oppression that needed to be alleviated in the larger U.S. society, as well as in schools. (our italics, p. 322)

In 1954, the U.S. Supreme Court had ruled in *Brown v. Board of Education* that segregated schools were unconstitutional. Congress passed the Civil Rights Act in 1964, prohibiting discrimination on the basis of race, color, or national origin. According to Title VI of this act: "No person in the United States shall, on the ground of race, color, or national origin, be excluded from participation in, be denied the benefits of, or be subjected to discrimination under any program or activity receiving Federal financial assistance" (Civil Rights Act, sec. 601, 1964). Thus, Title VI of the 1964 Civil Rights Act has played an important role in protecting the educational rights of language-minority students in the United States (see Crawford, 2004; E. García, 2005; O. García, 2009a; and especially the National Clearinghouse for English Language Acquisition [NCELA], 2006). In addition to Title VI of the Civil Rights Act, the Equal Educational Opportunities Act of 1974 requires states to ensure that education agencies take "appropriate action to overcome language barriers that impede equal participation by its students in its instructional programs" (20 USC Sec.1703(f)).

Title VII: The Bilingual Education Act

In 1968, the U.S. Congress reauthorized the landmark Elementary and Secondary Education Act (ESEA), the largest and most influential federal education policy to date. Title VII of that Act, known as the Bilingual Education Act, established a federal goal of assisting "limited-English-speaking" students in the acquisition of English. The Bilingual Education Act became a way to shift focus away from racial and political self-determination and more toward cultural pride and linguistic support of these language minoritized communities (García & Sung, 2018). This genealogy of bilingual education is described fully in Flores (2024).

At first, only poor students were eligible to participate. Title VII of the Elementary and Secondary Education Act did *not* require bilingual education. Rather, Congress put aside money for school districts enrolling large numbers of language-minoritized students that chose to start bilingual education programs or create bilingual instructional materials. The Bilingual Education Act (1968) stated:

> In recognition of the special educational needs of the large numbers of children of limited English-speaking ability in the United States, Congress hereby declares it to be the policy of the United States to provide financial assistance to local educational

agencies to develop and carry out new and imaginative elementary and secondary school programs designed to meet these special educational needs. (Sec. 702)

When the Bilingual Education Act was first reauthorized in 1974, eligibility for educational services was expanded to include students of any socioeconomic status who had limited English-speaking ability (LESA). The 1974 reauthorization also defined bilingual education for the first time as "instruction given in, and study of, English and *(to the extent necessary to allow a child to progress effectively through the education system)* the native language of the children of limited English speaking ability" (quoted in García, 2009a, p. 169; emphasis added). The subsequent 1978 reauthorization of the Bilingual Education Act expanded eligibility for services even further, from students with limited English speaking ability to those with limited English proficiency while reinforcing the transitional nature of bilingual education. The central focus during this time of expanding access was to ensure that students who needed bilingual education services were receiving them; the pedagogy was left to the educators who were tasked with carrying out imaginative programs.

By the mid-1980s, the tone and focus of the federal Bilingual Education Act had begun to shift to support English-only programs. For the first time, the 1984 reauthorization of the Bilingual Education Act also provided funding for programs that used only English in educating English language learners, although only 4% of the funding was reserved for these types of programs. The 1988 reauthorization of the Bilingual Education Act further expanded the funding for programs in which only English was used to 25% of programs funded. Additionally, it imposed a three-year limit on participation in transitional bilingual education programs, meaning that schools had three years to move English language learners to fluency in English.

In 1994, Congress reauthorized the provisions of the Elementary and Secondary Education Act, including the Bilingual Education Act, this time under the new Improving America's Schools Act. Although this reauthorization gave increased attention to two-way bilingual education programs, the cap for English-only programs that was previously legislated was lifted.

These legislative efforts, beginning with the Elementary and Secondary Education Act in 1968, were the first to focus on the need to provide language-minoritized students with an equal opportunity for an education. Not long after the 1968 legislation, a series of legal battles began for an equitable education for emergent bilinguals.

Legal Precedents

In the early 1970s, a group of Chinese American parents brought a judicial case against the San Francisco school board on the grounds that their children were not receiving an equitable education. The case was brought under the equal protection clause of the Fourteenth Amendment of the Constitution and Title VI of the Civil Rights Act. The case, known as *Lau v. Nichols*, was eventually appealed up to the U.S. Supreme Court and was decided on the basis of Title VI. Justice William O. Douglas wrote the majority opinion of the Court, stating:

[T]here is no equality of treatment merely by providing students with the same facilities, textbooks, teachers and curriculum; for students who do not understand English are effectively foreclosed from any meaningful education. . . . Basic skills are at the very core of what these public schools teach. Imposition of a requirement that, before a child can effectively participate in the educational program, he must already have acquired those basic skills is to make a mockery of public education. We know that those who do not understand English are certain to find their classroom experiences wholly incomprehensible and in no way meaningful. . . . No specific remedy is urged upon us. Teaching English to the students of Chinese ancestry who do not speak the language is one choice. Giving instructions to this group in Chinese is another. There may be others. (*Lau v. Nichols*, 1974)

The Court offered no specific method of instruction as a remedy. It merely instructed school districts to take "affirmative steps" to address the educational inequities for these students and called upon the federal Office for Civil Rights, as part of the executive branch, to guide school districts (For a 50th year retrospective of Lau and its effects see Jiménez-Castellanos et al., 2024). The Office for Civil Rights set up a task force that eventually promulgated guidelines for schools and districts. These guidelines eventually became known as the Lau Remedies (1975). In addition to instructing school districts on how to identify and serve emergent bilinguals, these guidelines specifically required bilingual education at the elementary level. Emphasizing that English as a second language was a necessary component of bilingual education, the guidelines continued, "since an ESL program does not consider the affective nor cognitive development of the students . . . an ESL program [by itself] is not appropriate" (as cited in Crawford, 2004, p. 113). At the secondary level, however, ESL programs were permitted. In 1979, the Lau Remedies were rewritten for release as regulations. However, they were never published as official regulations, and in 1981, they were withdrawn by Terrel Bell, the incoming secretary of education under Ronald Reagan, who called them "harsh, inflexible, burdensome, unworkable, and incredibly costly" (cited in Crawford, 2004, p. 120).

Yet, even as the executive branch of the federal government was signaling retrenchment from meaningful bilingual education, emergent bilinguals continued to have the courts on their side. In another important federal court case (*Castañeda v. Pickard*, 1981), the U.S. Court of Appeals for the Fifth Circuit upheld the *Lau* precedent that schools must take "appropriate action" to educate language-minoritized students and that such action must be based on sound educational theory; produce results; and provide adequate resources, including qualified teachers and appropriate materials, equipment, and facilities. The case, however, did not mandate a specific program such as bilingual education or ESL.

English-Only Education at the Polls: The 1990s and the Aftermath

In the 1990s, the use of the child's home language to support learning came under political siege (see Gándara & Hopkins, 2010). The most effective attack against bilingual education was spearheaded by Silicon Valley software millionaire Ron Unz.

Proposition 227 (California Proposition 227, 1998, sec. 300–311), also known as the English for the Children Initiative, was presented to California voters in June 1998. The proposition prohibited the use of home-language instruction in teaching emergent bilinguals. It mandated English-only instruction for a period not to exceed a year, after which students were put into mainstream classrooms. Parents were able to request a waiver from the one-year English immersion program if the child was over 10 years of age, had special needs, or was fluent in English. Sixty-one percent of Californians voted in favor of this proposition, making it state law. The vote of the Latine population was two to one against the initiative. However, some Latine citizens also supported this proposition. In part, this was due to misinformation perpetuated by the political language used in the media, which cast a very negative light on bilingual education (Baltodano, 2004). Urrieta (2010) suggests that Mexican American parents who supported the English-only proposition did so because they were victims of cultural whitestreaming—the imposition of white norms, including language, as the societal standard, leading to the perception of English as superior to Spanish. This perception is reinforced in schools through whitestream curricula, which associate bilingual education with remedial programs and view students in bilingual programs as deficient. This stigma was exploited in the political spectacle surrounding Proposition 227. As a result, some Latine parents may have supported the English-only policy out of fear of the negative connotations associated with bilingual education.

Proposition 227 passed despite the fact that only a minority of emergent bilinguals were in bilingual programs in California in the first place. Prior to its passage, only 30% of emergent bilinguals were in bilingual programs, with the rest in either ESL programs or regular classrooms (Crawford, 2003). Of the 30% of California English learners in bilingual programs, less than 20% were being taught by a credentialed bilingual teacher (Cummins, 2003). A year after the passage of Proposition 227, California students in bilingual programs declined from 29.1% to 11.7% (Crawford, 2007). Four years after Proposition 227 was passed, only 590,289 emergent bilinguals (just 42% of the total in 1998) had become proficient in English, and annual redesignation rates—that is, the rates of English acquisition—remained unchanged. According to the California Department of Education (2006a, 2006b), in 2006, only 7.6% of English learners in California were in transitional bilingual education classrooms because their parents had signed waivers requesting these programs (California Department of Education, 2006a, 2006b). Baca and Gándara (2008) attest to the inadequate English-only instruction that emergent bilinguals in California were receiving, as well as their poor assessment results (also Wenworth et al., 2010). In fact, the number of students who were not able to become proficient in English for six or more years increased dramatically as a result. A space for bilingual education was found during this time in the gradual implementation of dual-language programs, a label that, as we have said, does not name its bilingualism, and in programs where English learners are said to be taught with fluent English speakers.

A year after California's Proposition 227 was passed, Unz took his English-only efforts to Arizona. In 2000, 63% of Arizona voters approved Proposition 203, which banned bilingual education for emergent bilinguals in that state. Arizona's statute was even more restrictive than California's. It limited school services for emergent bilinguals to a one-year English-only structured immersion program that included ESL and content-based instruction exclusively in English. Waivers were almost impossible to obtain, and schools were continuously surveilled to enforce the policy and ensure that parents were not encouraged to request the waiver. This not only created an environment of fear among teachers and principals but also resulted in real emotional distress and psychological trauma for emergent bilingual children (Parra et al., 2014). In 2006, the Arizona Legislature passed HS2064, which reshaped the structured immersion programs into a very prescriptive four-hour-a-day block of instruction specifically on English language development (Johnson & Johnson, 2015). This four-hour requirement, which was in addition to the content areas core curriculum, left little room for anything else, such as elective courses or opportunities for extracurricular activities. It also resulted in the segregation of emergent bilinguals for most of the day, restricting their opportunities to interact with proficient English speakers despite being forced to an English-only education (Gándara & Orfield, 2012).

In 2002, a similar proposition to outlaw bilingual education in Massachusetts (Massachusetts Question 2, G.L. c. 71A) passed by 68%. Emergent bilinguals continued to be the lowest-performing subgroup in the state by every measure—English language arts and math, and graduation rates.

In 2002, Amendment 31 to Colorado's state constitution, which would have made bilingual education illegal, was defeated, with 56% of voters opposing it. Ironically, the campaign to defeat the amendment focused on the threat to parental choice and local control of schools, as well as the possibility that non-English-speaking children would be in the same classrooms as other children. A TV commercial warned that the Unz-backed English-only amendment would "force children who can barely speak English into regular classrooms, creating chaos and disrupting learning" (Crawford, 2004, p. 330).

No Child Left Behind

An important stage of the policy movement away from bilingual education and toward an English-only approach was the reauthorization of the Elementary and Secondary Education Act under the more ambitious No Child Left Behind Act (NCLB), which was signed into law by President George W. Bush in January 2002.

As we said in Chapter 1, NCLB's definition of *limited English proficient* as referring to those who could not meet *proficiency levels in English on state assessments* signaled a significant shift in political culture and ideology. From an earlier era that provided language-minoritized students and their families with greater access to educational resources and more equal educational opportunities to become truly bilingual, NCLB heralded a period focused solely on closing the achievement gap through testing in English and English immersion instruction.

NCLB mandated that, by the 2013–2014 school year, all students would achieve the level of "proficient" in state assessment systems. To accomplish this lofty goal, NCLB required schools and districts to ensure that all their students meet specific state-developed annual targets of adequate yearly progress (AYP) for reading, math, and science. In addition, it was not enough for schools or districts to meet their goals in terms of their aggregate data; they also were required to show that all subgroups of students—meaning students of different races, ethnicities, income groups, gender, and so on—were meeting AYP goals.[4] One of the subgroups that NCLB required schools and districts to keep track of was "limited English proficient students." As a result, local school officials had to pay attention to their emergent bilinguals' yearly progress in English proficiency (Capps et al., 2005).

NCLB required assessments for emergent bilinguals under Title I (funding for poor students)[5] and Title III (funding for limited English proficient students) of the act. Under Title I, which is the federal compensatory education program for poor students, if English learners or other subgroups did not meet their test score targets, their schools could be subject to interventions. Parents whose children attended schools in need of improvement were permitted to send their children to an alternative school in the same school district, provided that the school had room and the services each student required. Parents of students in schools designated as in need of improvement were also offered supplemental services such as after-school tutoring programs. If the schools continued to fail to meet the performance targets, they were to be eventually restructured or closed (NCLB, 2001).

Under NCLB, Title VII of the Elementary and Secondary Education Act, known as the Bilingual Education Act, was replaced by Title III. The purpose of Title III, now called "Language Instruction for Limited English Proficient and Immigrant Students," was "to help ensure that children who are limited English proficient, including immigrant children and youth, attain English proficiency" (2001, sec. 3102). Schools were required to evaluate the English proficiency of all students enrolling for the first time in school, establish criteria to determine eligibility for programs and services for emergent bilinguals, and implement appropriate educational services. States were to hold schools receiving Title III funding accountable for meeting annual measurable achievement objectives for their emergent bilinguals, which placed unprecedented demands on the states for improvements in both the academic proficiency and the English proficiency of emergent bilinguals. From the beginning, NCLB regulations proved problematic for emergent bilinguals. Unlike other subgroups, emergent bilinguals eventually become bilingual, and thus, they move out of the English learner category. Therefore, emergent bilinguals' progress toward proficiency was difficult to demonstrate, because only those who failed to progress remained in the category. By 2010, the difficulties inherent in NCLB were obvious: States lowered their standards so that more students would appear proficient, schools that missed a single target were considered failing, interventions were one-size-fits-all, and the focus was on tests, forcing teachers to teach to the test and eliminating subjects such as history and the arts (Duncan, 2013). Arne Duncan, Obama's then secretary of education, started granting states waivers from some NCLB provisions and giving them greater flexibility in exchange for commitments to adopt higher standards, target the lowest-performing schools, and choose teacher and principal evaluation and support systems that took into account student growth.

The state waivers were coupled with the 2009 announcement of Race to the Top, the $4.35 billion U.S. Department of Education competitive grant that created incentives for states to adopt common standards (see the next section), performance-based evaluations for teachers and principals, and data systems, as well as to give increased attention to the lowest-performing schools. Race to the Top also gave extra points to states that expanded high-quality charter schools; this competitive grant officially ended in July 2015.

Common Core State Standards (CCSS)

In 2009, the Common Core State Standards (CCSS) in English language arts and mathematics were released. This was an initiative of the National Governors Association and the Council of Chief State School Officers, which outlined what students were expected to know at the end of each grade. But the CCSS document devoted only two and a half pages to English learners and acknowledged that "these students may require additional time, appropriate instructional support, and aligned assessments as they acquire both English language proficiency and content area knowledge" (www.corestandards.org, n.p.). By 2016, all but four states had adopted the CCSS; however, by October 2017, 10 states had either rewritten or replaced the CCSS. The withdrawal of states from the CCSS signaled increasing opposition to the role of the federal government in supporting the adoption of the CCSS and its attendant emphasis on testing. The passage of the Every Student Succeeds Act (ESSA) in 2015 (see the next section) explicitly forbids the federal government from requiring adoption of the CCSS by states. Texas, the state with the second highest number of emergent bilinguals in the country, has never adopted the CCSS.

With respect to emergent bilinguals, the problem with the CCSS was that the standards do not seem to have a coherent theory of language. At first glance, the English language arts standards seem to support a view of language as human action in the standards related to listening, speaking, reading, and writing. García (2016) summarizes this by saying:

> Students are asked to use a greater variety of complex texts—oral, visual, quantitative, print and non-print—that technology has enabled. The purposes for which language is used have also changed—from recreation or factual declaration giving way to analysis, interpretation, argument, and persuasion. Even language itself has gone from being acknowledged as simply grammar and vocabulary of printed texts to include its many levels of meaning—figurative language, word relations, genres, and media. Finally, students are now being asked to perform language socially through cooperative tasks. It is not enough to organize information on one's own and write as an individual; it is important to build upon others' ideas, whether those of peers, teachers, or authors of texts, to find evidence to articulate one's own ideas, adjusting the presentation according to the different purposes or audiences. (p. 48)

All of these are lofty goals, ones that emergent bilinguals can meet with the appropriate support, especially by leveraging their home language practices (for an analysis of the CCSS from a multilingual perspective, see García & Flores, 2014). However, on closer inspection, the strand of the CCSS known as the Language Standards requires something completely different. These standards reinforce the learning of grammar and vocabulary in English only—that is, of English as a system of structures that are to be taught in progressive and linear order. As we will see later on, emergent bilinguals need experience using English in legitimate academic tasks. They do not benefit by merely analyzing the structure of the English language in isolation; linguistic features are acquired in authentic use.

When the CCSS were adopted, educators immediately had to scramble to put together resources to help prepare emergent bilinguals for the new ways in which language was being assessed (see, for example, Heritage, Walqui, & Linquanti, 2015). As we said in Chapter 2, WIDA and ELPA21 emerged as two consortia of state departments of education, which focused on developing English language proficiency standards to indicate progression of language development. Both California and New York developed their own progression standards toward English language proficiency for emergent bilinguals. California adopted the California English Language Development Standards. All of the standards for language progression of emergent bilinguals support the use of home language practices to help emergent bilinguals meet academic standards. This is especially so for students situated along the beginning points of the English language progression.

Every Student Succeeds Act (ESSA)

On December 10, 2015, President Barack Obama signed the new reauthorization of the Elementary and Secondary Education Act (ESEA) of 1968, which was ESSA. This law continues the goal of preparing all students for success in college and career, while providing flexibility for some of NCLB's more prescriptive requirements.

As with NCLB, the needs of English learners are addressed in ESSA under Title III, now called "Language Instruction for English Learners and Immigrant Students." According to Section 3003, "English Language Acquisition, Language Enhancement, and Academic Achievement," the purposes of Title III of ESSA are:

1. to help ensure that English learners, including immigrant children and youth, attain English proficiency, and develop high levels of academic achievement in English;
2. to assist all English learners, including immigrant children and youth, to achieve at high levels in academic subjects so that all English learners can meet the same challenging State academic standards that all children are expected to meet;
3. to assist teachers (including preschool teachers), principals, and other school leaders, State educational agencies, local educational agencies, and schools in establishing, implementing, and sustaining effective language

instruction educational programs designed to assist in teaching English learners, including immigrant children and youth;

4. to assist teachers (including preschool teachers), principals and other school leaders, State educational agencies, and local educational agencies to develop and enhance their capacity to provide effective instructional programs designed to prepare English learners, including immigrant children and youth, to enter all-English instructional settings;
5. to promote parental, family, and community participation in language instruction educational programs for the parents, families, and communities of English learners. (Section 3102, 129 STAT. 1954)

ESSA reauthorized Title III of NCLB and in 2023 has continued to increase funding of awards to states. As with NCLB, ESSA requires that states establish and implement standardized statewide entry and exit procedures for emergent bilinguals.

As we said in Chapter 1, whereas NCLB focused on emergent bilinguals' achievement on assessments, ESSA looks at their achievement on academic standards, taking the onus off standardized tests, although not quite. It continues the requirement that states administer assessments in English language arts and mathematics aligned with their standards annually in grades three to eight and once in high school. It also requires testing of science content once in grades 3 to 5, once in grades 6 to 9, and once in grades 10 to 12.

One major change between NCLB and ESSA is that the accountability provisions for English learners were moved to Title I, incorporating the English language proficiency of these students not as an add-on but as part of the general life of the school. Schools are now required to have an English language proficiency indicator as part of adequate yearly progress (AYP), and to have goals and interim targets for emergent bilinguals. But as in NCLB, ESSA requires states to have standardized statewide entrance and exit procedures for identifying emergent bilinguals. It also continues the requirement that states annually assess emergent bilinguals' English language proficiency and specifies that it be "aligned with their academic standards in a valid and reliable manner" and provide "appropriate accommodations (including, to the extent practicable, assessments in the language and form most likely to yield accurate information on what those students know and can do in the content area assessed)" (ESSA, 2015, n.p). A noteworthy new requirement is that states identify languages that are present to a "significant extent" as well as those languages for which there are no assessments (CCSO, 2016; ESSA, 2015).

As with NCLB, the English language arts and math scores of emergent bilinguals who have been enrolled in U.S. schools for less than 12 months are excluded for accountability purposes. ESSA, however, does not require states to count the scores of emergent bilinguals until their third year of enrollment. Furthermore, ESSA expands NCLB in allowing states to include for accountability purposes students designated as English learners for four years after reclassification. ESSA also adds that states report not only the data for emergent bilinguals but also the data for two subgroups of emergent bilinguals: those with disabilities and those who have not achieved English proficiency after five years (now labeled long-term ELs) (U.S. DoE, 2016).

The future enforcement of the ESSA 2015 regulations is not clear, given the support for less federal oversight over education. States and school districts are encouraged to implement the law with flexibility (U.S. DoE, 2016).

A Critical Review of the Present

ESSA is only the most recent iteration of a broader change in policy orientation toward the education of language-minoritized students in the United States. In fact, as many have remarked, the word *bilingual*—what Crawford (2004) has called "the B-word"—is disappearing; public discourse about bilingualism in education has been increasingly silenced (Cervantes-Soon, 2014; Hornberger, 2006; Kaveh et al, 2022; Wiley & Wright, 2004). García (2009a) portrays this silencing of the word *bilingual* within the context of federal educational policy by illustrating some of the key name and title changes that occurred in legislation and offices in Washington, D.C., since the passage of No Child Left Behind. These changes are shown in Table 3.2.

As shown in the first row of Table 3.2, the replacement of Title VII of the Elementary and Secondary Education Act (the Bilingual Education Act) by Title III (Language Instruction for Limited English Proficient [English Learner for ESSA] and Immigrant Students) is indicative of the shift away from the support of instruction in students' home languages through bilingual education.

The greatest efforts to silence the complex multilingualism of the United States and its citizens have been made by proponents of making English the official language of the land. In the 1980s Senator Samuel Hayakawa and Dr. John Tanton founded U.S. English and proposed a constitutional amendment to make English the official language. But by the 1990s this movement was in disarray because it was said to have links to the "threats" of Latines and their "low educability" (cited in García, 2009). Although many states passed English only laws, the

Table 3.2. Silencing of Bilingualism

Title VII of Elementary and Secondary Education Act: The Bilingual Education Act		Title III of No Child Left Behind, Public Law 107–110: Language Instruction for Limited English Proficient and Immigrant Students
Office of Bilingual Education and Minority Languages Affairs (OBEMLA)	→	Office of English Language Acquisition, Language Enhancement and Academic Achievement for LEP Students (OELA)
National Clearinghouse for Bilingual Education (NCBE)		National Clearinghouse for English Language Acquisition and Language Instruction Educational Programs (NCELA)

federal government paid little attention to the officialization of English. However, on March 1, 2025, President Trump issued an Executive Order designating English as the official language of the United States. This official English order restricted language access services for immigrants, and was based on the greater animosity toward immigrants and Latines in the country at the time.

It has not been only the government—whether federal, state, or local—that has carried out this discursive shift silencing multilingualism. Educators and scholars of bilingualism have also been complicit by not directly naming bilingualism, perhaps fearful of more backlash against it. One example of this discursive shift among educators and scholars has been the increased use of the term *dual-language* instead of *bilingual*. One speaks about *dual-language programs* instead of *bilingual programs*, about *dual-language learners* instead of *bilingual learners*, of *dual-language books* instead of *bilingual books*.

The change, however, is not just discursive; it is real. Crawford (2007) estimates that approximately half of emergent bilinguals in California and Arizona who would have been in bilingual classrooms in 2001–2002 were reassigned to all-English programs. In 2019–2020, only 8% of students served by Title III were in dual-language bilingual programs. In New York City, 79% of students designated as English learners were in English as a new language programs in 2022, with 10% in transitional bilingual education programs and 9% in dual-language bilingual programs (NYC DoE, 2022–2023). Clearly, most emergent bilinguals are overwhelmingly receiving instruction in English as a second language programs, with little use of students' home language practices. In 1997 Guadalupe Valdés issued a cautionary note about dual language programs. Cervantes-Soon (2014) noted that dual-language programs are often established and led by world-language education state departments and initiatives, which intentionally distance them from the field and history of bilingual education in the United States in order to sanitize them from any political baggage. This distancing may contribute to a greater focus on English speakers in dual-language bilingual programs.

Despite educational policy that has silenced the growing bilingualism of U.S. language-minoritized students, there are apparent new efforts to revive bilingualism in the United States under different names and for different purposes. Among the most promising measures is the implementation of the Seals of Biliteracy (also deliberately sidestepping the term *bilingualism* with its political implications) in many states. These seals are generally awarded at the time of graduation from secondary schools to recognize students who have studied and attained proficiency in more than one language. Significantly, California was the first state to award the Seal of Biliteracy in 2012. By 2024, all 50 states and Washington, D.C., offered the state's Seal of Biliteracy (www.sealofbiliteracy.org).

In a way, the Seal of Biliteracy can extend the ways in which policymakers and educators view the languages with which emergent bilinguals enter classrooms. If they consider these languages as a resource not only to acquire English but also for emergent bilinguals themselves, their high school graduation, and their future careers, perhaps emergent bilinguals would not be subjected to punitive English-only programs that rob them of the opportunity to be and become truly bilingual and biliterate. The danger, however, is that these awards would only become affirmations of foreign-language ability for language-majority students. The Seals of Biliteracy are but a step into a multilingual future that has the potential of changing the unequal education that emergent bilinguals are receiving today. It remains to be seen to what extent this first step will overcome the largely monolingual approaches to their learning and achievement.

The global economy is being used by proponents of these Seals of Biliteracy as a reason to bring back bilingualism and bilingual ways of educating. Faced with this movement, the questions for all educators who are working to provide an equitable education to language-minoritized students needs to be: Who are these policies for? And how do we ensure that they benefit the most vulnerable—those who are classified as English learners? Many have argued that this push to become multilingual in order to compete globally is related to a neoliberal economy (Cervantes-Soon, 2014). That is, the commodification of multilingualism is tied to the push for privatization and the free flow of capitalism in ways that benefit transnational corporations and economic elites (Flores, 2013). As Valdez, Delavan, and Freire (2014) argue, the economic logic of a neoliberal economy ultimately privileges those with the most access to wealth.

The neoliberal stance toward bilingualism in the United States in the second decade of the 21st century is evident even in states like California and Massachusetts, which had banned bilingual education at the turn of the century. Proposition 58, the California Multilingual Education Act, was passed in November 2016, effectively lifting restrictions on bilingual education. Proposition 58 passed by a 73% to 27% margin. The Massachusetts state senate passed a bill in July 2017 permitting school districts to reinstate a bilingual education option; in June, the Massachusetts house had passed a similar bill. This interest in reversing language education policy in Massachusetts is supported by a 2009 report compiled by the state showing that only about 20% of students receiving structured English immersion achieved proficiency in English, even after five years or more; that proficiency rates in science and mathematics academic content were also very low; and that high school dropout rates for these students were twice that of the state's language-majority students (English Language Learners Sub-Committee of the Massachusetts Board of Elementary and Secondary Education's Committee on the Proficiency Gap, 2009; Karp & Uriarte, 2010). Although Arizona has upheld Proposition 203, Senate Bill 104 passed in 2018 scaled back the restrictions of the Structured English Immersion (SEI) Program, reducing the English language development requirement to two hours daily from the original mandated four hours and providing flexibility about the programs that can be used to meet such requirement. This seemingly small change opened the back door in 2019 for students classified as English learners to access dual-language bilingual programs for the first time in 20 years. However, because Proposition 203 has not been overturned, this opening remains susceptible to proponents of English-only education, including the superintendent elected in 2022, who persists in opposing it (Kaveh et al., 2022).

The changes in California and Massachusetts point to the greater interest in the United States in teaching languages other than English for economic purposes. As López (2005) has said: "Educational opportunities for minority students exist only when the students' interests and the nation's interests converge" (p. 2016). Even in Arizona, where the policy change was enacted largely by invoking the harms inflicted by the restrictive four-hour structured English immersion (SEI) block, it succeeded because those harms converged with the overall national orientation toward choice and Arizona's core value of local control (Kaveh et al., 2022).

Callahan and Gándara (2014) have shown that bilinguals coming of age today are entering a different job and career market, one that has been transformed not only by globalization and the online era, but also by the growth of a multilingual consumer base. Yet, in a country where so many people speak languages other than English, especially Spanish, bilingualism and biliteracy cannot be valued only as an instrument of a neoliberal economy (Flores, 2013; Petrovic, 2005; Ricento, 2005). Bilingualism and biliteracy can only be sustained and developed if they also empower minoritized speakers and their communities—that is, if bilingualism connects with its social justice and equal education opportunity origins. The success of Seals of Biliteracy, as well as dual-language bilingual programs, can only be measured if indeed these policies encompass and benefit the most vulnerable students—those who have been minoritized and racialized as bilinguals and who have seldom been able to use their full linguistic repertoire in schools without fear, shame, or stigma.

PROGRAMS AND POLICIES FOR EMERGENT BILINGUALS: UNDERSTANDING THE SHIFTS

In this chapter, we have laid out the range of educational programs for emergent bilinguals and shown how U.S. language-in-education policies have shifted the program options away from focus on the home language and cultural practices and toward English-only instruction and assessment. We ended by arguing that present policies that seem to embrace bilingualism and biliteracy can only be measured as successful if they also work against the present minoritization of bilinguals in the United States.

In the next six chapters, we uncover the fallacies of present educational policy and practices with regard to emergent bilinguals. We explore what has been learned through research in sociolinguistics and psycholinguistics, education and curriculum, sociology, economics, and psychometrics, about educating emergent bilinguals to achieve high standards. We focus on the questions: *What does the research tell us about how best to educate and assess emergent bilingual students? Are we using accepted theories and evidence in the education of these students?* We provide evidence that the gap between policy and practices and the research is indeed wide. In addition, we offer descriptions of alternative practices that do benefit emergent bilinguals.

STUDY QUESTIONS

1. What are the different types of educational programs for emergent bilinguals in public schools? Discuss how they differ in their practices and goals.
2. How are emergent bilinguals being educated in your district? Give specific examples.
3. Discuss how it is possible to encourage students' home language practices in all classrooms regardless of whether there are a few or many who speak a language other than English, whether the group is diverse, or whether the teacher speaks their home language.
4. Discuss the development of educational policies targeting emergent bilinguals in our recent past. Make sure to address the changes in the Bilingual Education Act, as well as *Lau v. Nichols* and *Castañeda v. Pickard.*
5. How have federal and state policies, as well as judicial decisions, on the education of emergent bilinguals differed in purpose from those policies and decisions for Chicano, Puerto Rican, and Native American communities in the 1960s?
6. What have been the recent changes in educational policies with regard to emergent bilinguals? What is the difference between No Child Left Behind (NCLB) and the Every Student Succeeds Act (ESSA)?
7. Discuss the recent shifts in policies toward the education of emergent bilinguals. What have been some promising policies?
8. How do you view the commodification of bilingualism? Do you think it will benefit poor and racialized emergent bilinguals?

CHAPTER 4

Bilingualism and Achievement
Theoretical Constructs and Empirical Evidence

In this chapter, we:

- Review the following theories related to bilingualism:
  » Cognitive benefits,
  » Linguistic interdependence and common underlying proficiency,
  » Developing language for academic purposes,
  » Literacy and biliteracy,
  » Dynamic bilingualism,
  » Translanguaging,
  » Decolonial and borderland theories, and
  » Raciolinguistic ideologies.
- Consider the empirical evidence on the relationship between bilingualism and academic achievement.

So far, we have seen that a growing number of language education programs and policies have failed to recognize language-minoritized students' bilingualism and the role of their home language practices in supporting their learning. In this chapter, we consider the theoretical constructs and empirical findings that support the use of students' home language practices in the classroom. Within this context, we also examine the theories and research on bilingualism and bilingual acquisition that speak to the developmental process of acquiring English as well as additional languages, not just for spoken communication but also for academic work.

THEORETICAL CONSTRUCTS

Over the past five decades, researchers have developed frameworks for understanding the relationship between bilingualism and academic achievement. We describe here some of the theoretical frameworks that are useful in considering the equitable education of emergent bilinguals. We also outline here associated empirical studies from the fields of anthropology, education, linguistics, philosophy, psychology, and sociology that are useful for addressing equity goals in the education of emergent bilinguals.

Cognitive Benefits

Ever since the seminal article by Peal and Lambert (1962), which found that bilingualism is an important factor in cognitive development, the literature on this topic has been extensive. In their Montreal study, Peal and Lambert (1962) found bilingual 10-year-olds to be "more facile at concept formation, and [to] have greater mental flexibility" than monolingual students (p. 22). Many empirical studies have followed, detailing various aspects of cognitive advantages for bilingual learners (for a review of these, see Baker, 2011; Baker & Wright, 2021; Blanc & Hamers, 1985; Díaz & Klinger, 1991; García, 2009a; Hakuta, 1986). Bilingual speakers constantly select some features from their linguistic repertoire and inhibit others, relying on what psycholinguists call the executive function of the brain. Bialystok and her colleagues, who study how bilingualism affects the mind and brain, have used behavioral and neuroimaging methods to show that bilinguals, because of their constant use of two languages,[1] perform better on executive control tasks than do monolinguals (Barac & Bialystok, 2012; Bialystok, 2011, 2015, 2016; Kroll & Bialystok, 2013). In an article reviewing studies showing the cognitive benefits of bilingualism, Bialystok (2011) concludes that

> research with bilinguals . . . provides clear evidence for the plasticity of cognitive systems in response to experience. One possible explanation in the case of bilinguals is that the executive control circuits needed to manage attention to the two languages become integrated with the linguistic circuits used for language processing, creating a more diffuse, more bilateral, and more efficient network that supports high levels of performance. (p. 233)

It has been found that bilinguals' constant use of their different language practices strengthens the control mechanisms of the brain (the inhibitory control) and changes the associated brain regions (see also Abutalebi et al., 2012; Bialystok et al., 2012; Green, 2011). In addition, because blood flow (a marker of neuronal activity) is greater in the brain stem of bilinguals in response to sound, this also creates advantages in auditory attention (Krizman et al., 2012).

Researchers have found other positive cognitive consequences of being bilingual. Bialystok (2004, 2007, 2016) has pointed out that children's bilingualism results in a more analytic orientation to language itself, a facility that is known as greater *metalinguistic awareness*. Bilingual children also have more than one way to describe the world and thus possess more flexible perceptions and interpretations—that is, more *divergent* or *creative thinking* (Ricciardelli, 1992; Torrance et al., 1970). Also, bilingual children have more practice in gauging communicative situations, giving them more *communicative sensitivity* (Ben-Zeev, 1977).

Young children's potential for metalinguistic awareness, creative thinking, and communicative sensibility is forcefully documented in Perry Gilmore's (2016) close analysis of two 5-year-old boys who shared no common language but soon fashioned their own language during daily play together on a hillside in Kenya. Gilmore's English-speaking son interacted with his newfound Kenyan friend, a speaker of Samburu and some degree of Swahili. With these linguistic tools, they generated novel forms "never before heard or uttered" (p. 55). They invented what Gilmore called Kisisi, their private language.

The development of bilingual practices has been associated with enhancements in cognitive function. August and Hakuta (1997) conclude: "Bilingualism, far from impeding the child's overall cognitive linguistic development, leads to positive growth in these areas. Programs whose goals are to promote bilingualism should do so without fear of negative consequences" (p. 19).

Bilingualism has also been associated with creativity (Kharkhurin, 2015; Li Wei, 2011). Bilingual practices have been shown to strengthen certain cognitive mechanisms, which in turn may increase one's creative potential. Hugo Baetens Beardsmore (2018) points to five characteristics of bilinguals that result in greater creativity: a flexible mind, a problem-solving mind, a metalinguistic mind, a learning mind, and an interpersonal mind. In their study of creativity in Montreal, researchers Stolarick and Florida (2006) quote a respondent from a consulting firm who tells them that whenever he is faced with difficult problems to solve, he forms strategy groups with multilingual staff. The respondent observed:

> being multilingual means you understand the world from different perspectives and are more likely to devise creative and innovative solutions: it's "good for the brain to have to learn how to work and think in [multiple languages]." (p. 1812)

All programs to teach emergent bilinguals should capitalize on the cognitive and creative advantages of bilingualism. Because bilingualism develops cognitive capacities and enhances sensory processes, educational programs for emergent bilinguals can be effective if they leverage the home language practices along with English in the learning process.

Linguistic Interdependence and Common Underlying Proficiency

Jim Cummins has been a pioneer in developing theoretical frameworks that help us understand the relationship between a student's home language and the development of an additional language. It might seem counterintuitive to imagine that using the home language at school can support higher levels of English proficiency. However, the benefits of such practices are explained by the concept of *linguistic interdependence*, which means that both languages bolster each other in the student's acquisition of language and knowledge (Cummins 1979, 1981). Cummins (2000) explains linguistic interdependence by stating: "To the extent that instruction in Lx [one language] is effective in promoting proficiency in Lx [that language], transfer of this proficiency to Ly [the additional language] will occur provided there is adequate exposure to Ly" (p. 38). Cummins is not positing here that the child's home language needs to be fully developed before the additional language is introduced, but he argues that "the first language must not be abandoned before it is fully developed, whether the second language is introduced simultaneously or successively, early or late, in that process" (p. 25).

Linguistic interdependence is stronger in the case of languages that share linguistic features (such as, for example, Spanish and English) where students can derive interdependence from similar linguistic factors, as well as familiarity with language and literacy practices and ways of using language. Yet, even in cases where the two languages are not linguistically congruent, such as Chinese and English, Chinese-speaking students learning English will benefit academically if they have developed literacy in Chinese because they will understand, for example, that reading is really about making meaning from text and that writing requires the ability to communicate to a distant and sometimes unknown audience. In addition, they will have had practice in decoding, a sense of directionality of print and the mechanics of writing in their own language—all useful metalinguistic understandings that help orient learners to text in another language (Fu, 2003, 2009; Fu et al., 2019).

A related theoretical construct called *common underlying proficiency* (Cummins, 1979, 1981) posits that knowledge and abilities acquired in one language are potentially available for the development of another. Researchers have consistently found that there is a cross-linguistic relationship between the student's home and additional language, and proficiency in the home language is related to academic achievement in an additional language (Riches & Genesee, 2006). This is particularly the case for literacy. Lanauze and Snow (1989), for example, found that emergent bilinguals, even those students who were not yet orally proficient in their additional language, exhibited similar complexity and semantic content in their writing in both their home and additional languages.

Language for Academic Purposes

Skutnabb-Kangas and Toukomaa (1976), working with Finnish immigrants in Sweden, proposed that there is a difference between the way in which language is used for academic tasks as opposed to its use in informal spoken and written communication.[2] The *surface fluency* so evident in conversational language or in writing to someone we know intimately is most often supported by cues that elaborate and accompany language—gestures, repetition, intonation, emoticons, and so on. Cummins (1981) has called this use of language, which is supported by meaningful interpersonal and situational cues outside of language itself, *contextualized language*. Contextualized language is used for what Cummins (1981) has called *basic interpersonal communication* (BICS). Contextual support, Cummins (2000) explains, can be *external*, having to do with aspects of the language input itself. Contextual support can also be *internal*, having to do with the shared experiences, interests, and motivations that people communicating may have.

To complete school tasks, and especially assessment tasks, a different set of language practices is needed. Students in school often must be able to use language with little or no extralinguistic support. Cummins (1981) has claimed that what he calls *decontextualized language*[3] is needed in order to participate in some classroom discourse, read texts that are sometimes devoid of pictures and other semiotic cues, or interpret texts requiring background knowledge that students do not always have. Students also need to use this abstract language in order to write academic essays that require an unknown audience with whom communication is important and to participate in the specialized discourse of test-taking such as multiple-choice tests that force students to choose only one answer. Cummins (1979, 1981, 2000) refers to the mastery of this type of language abilities as cognitive academic language proficiency (CALP) and has proposed that it takes five to seven years to develop these skills in an additional language. Cummins also estimates that students can usually acquire the language of everyday communication in an additional language in just one to three years. As shown in Table 3.1 in Chapter 3, many educational programs for emergent bilinguals do not afford sufficient time to develop complex ways of using language.

The finding that the development of ways of using language for academic tasks in an additional language takes time is supported by other empirical research. Hakuta, Butler, and Witt (2000) also have found that it takes five years or longer to fully develop academic skills in English. They add: "In districts that are considered the most successful in teaching English to EL students, oral proficiency takes 3 to 5 years to develop and proficiency in English for academic purposes can take to 7 years" (p. 13). High school students are said to need a vocabulary of approximately 50,000 words, and the average student learns 3,000 new words each year (Graves, 2006; Nagy & Anderson, 1984). Thus, in four years of high school, emergent bilinguals might have acquired 12,000 to 15,000 words in English, falling short of what they would need in order to engage in English with the complex coursework of high school (Short & Fitzsimmons, 2007). In their review of longitudinal research over 32 years on the efficacy of bilingual instruction, Collier and Thomas (2017) confirm that it takes students at least six years with good-quality instruction that includes their home language, and at least ten years without it, to achieve "on-grade" levels of performance in reading in English.

Although oral language development is most important to make sense of literacy activities, emergent bilinguals develop receptive skills in an additional language, especially those of listening, long before they can use the additional language well to read and, especially, to write. Gándara (1999) reports that by grade 3, listening skills in English may be at 80%, but reading and writing lag behind this number. Oral language development and reading/writing development are intertwined, but it is important to understand the special demands of reading and writing for academic contexts, especially those that are targeted in state-developed standards.

While acquiring the necessary linguistic proficiency to perform decontextualized academic tasks is clearly a complex and challenging process, there has been a tendency to dichotomize language practices as either "social" or "academic," assuming that "academic language" is more difficult to develop and distinct from everyday language. However, both types of language proficiency are important, and rigidly separating them can be misleading (Bigelow, 2014; García & Otheguy, 2020). For example, highly educated emergent bilinguals who learn an additional language later in life through traditional approaches may often find that social language or the language required in nonacademic social settings—with its nuances like humor, sarcasm, figurative language, cultural references, and other knowledge necessary to engage in socially appropriate discourse—can be more challenging than the language needed for academic tasks, which can be more readily learned from books and grammar instruction.

Flores (2020) further critiques the emphasis on teaching academic language as a separate, superior form of communication, which suggests that the language practices of racialized emergent bilinguals are deficient, rather than recognizing them as legitimate and valuable forms of expression. Flores and Rosa (2015) argue that academic language is not merely a set of empirical linguistic practices but rather an ideology that perceives the language practices of racialized communities as inherently deficient. By framing academic language as a gatekeeping tool, Flores and others highlight how it can serve to exclude nondominant students from rich academic opportunities by relegating them to perpetual remedial education. This is clearly illustrated in a study by Adair and colleagues (2017) involving over 200 educators, parents, and children. Their study found that well-meaning educators often perceived Latine immigrant students as lacking the necessary vocabulary for dynamic learning, thus depriving them of sophisticated educational experiences. Instead, children in these classrooms were taught to equate learning with stillness, silence, and obedience. Given these issues, it is important that educators redefine what constitutes academic language or create new constructs to include diverse, fluid, and dynamic linguistic practices in the learning process.

Literacy and Biliteracy

Brian Street, a key figure in new literacy studies, challenges scholars and educators to examine the uses of language for academic purposes as a series of social practices. Rather than thinking of literacy as a monolithic construct made up of a discrete set of skills, he recommends that we consider first, that literacies are multiple, and second, that they are embedded in a web of social relations that maintain asymmetries of power (Street, 1985, 1996, 2003, 2005). He notes that literacy practices can also entail privileging some forms of literacy over others, and he reminds us to interrogate "whose literacies are dominant and whose are marginalized or resistant" (2003, p. 77). In other words, learning to "do language" in schools is not a neutral activity, easily divided into two modes of communication—spoken and written. Rather, developing literacy for academic purposes entails much more: It requires using language in ways that are increasingly complex and contingent upon wider societal factors beyond the school. Paulo Freire and Donaldo Macedo remind us that literacy is about "reading the word and the world" (Freire & Macedo, 1987).

Nancy Hornberger (1990) has defined biliteracy as "any and all instances in which communication occurs in two or more languages in and around writing" (p. 213). Hornberger's (2003) framework of the *Continua of Biliteracy* identifies the major social, linguistic, political, and psychological issues that surround the development of biliteracy as they relate to one another. The interrelated nature of Hornberger's continua supports the potential for positive networks of relationships across literacies. Hornberger (2005) says that "bi/multilinguals' learning is maximized when students are allowed and enabled to draw from across all their existing language skills (in two or more languages), rather than being constrained and inhibited from doing so by monolingual instructional assumptions and practices" (p. 607). The nested nature of Hornberger's (2003) continua also shows how literacy can be promoted or hindered by different contextual factors (Hornberger & Skilton-Sylvester, 2003).

Initially, much of the discussion around biliteracy focused on whether to first master literacy in what was considered the student's home or first language or develop simultaneous biliteracy. However, at the turn of the 21st century, scholars began to consider the meaning-making process in biliteracy, focusing on the *interaction or bidirectionality* between the two languages, which inform each other as bilingual readers interpret texts (Dworin, 2003; Gutiérrez, Baquedano-López, & Alvarez, 2001). Later, De la Luz Reyes (2012) challenged the linear development of biliteracy. Since then, the work of Kathy Escamilla and her colleagues (2014) has further changed the conversation around biliteracy, arguing that it needs to be developed simultaneously, from the start. Focusing on the many Latine students who are entering U.S. schools with different levels of proficiency in English *and* the language other than English, Escamilla and colleagues propose that literacy can be squared. This means that by introducing students to reading and writing in two or more languages simultaneously, literacy multiplies itself and its effects. As a result of this vision of biliteracy, alternative conceptualizations about instruction and assessment are being developed.

The New London Group (1996) coined the term *multiliteracies* to refer to the increased modes of meaning-making that characterize the production and use of texts today especially given the influx of new media (including not only the linguistic but also the visual, the audio, and the spatial/gestural); the term also accounts for the increased local linguistic diversity around the world. In advocating for a different type of pedagogy, they argue for one that develops "an epistemology of pluralism that provides access without people having to erase or leave behind different subjectivities" (p. 72). (For more on this, see Chapter 9.) Moreover, Martin-Jones and Jones (2000) coined the term *multilingual literacies* to refer to the "multiple ways in which people draw on and combine the codes in their communicative repertoire when they speak and write" (p. 7). Building on these new frameworks and the ones developed by Street and Hornberger, authors García, Bartlett, and Kleifgen (2007) proposed the concept of *pluriliteracy practices*, which are grounded in an understanding that equity for emergent bilinguals must take into account the power and value relations that exist around the various language practices in the school setting and in society. Importantly, while Hornberger's (1990) definition of biliteracy focused on writing as the primary source of meaning, pluriliteracies expanded this concept to include multiple semiotic forms together with written text for decoding, production, and interpretation. In this way, the notion of pluriliteracies recognizes the more dynamic and fluid uses of literacies in and out of schools in a context of new technologies and increased movements of people, services, and goods in a globalized world. Schools that value the use of pluriliteracy practices—including diverse language practices, scripts, and modes—can provide a more equitable education for emergent bilinguals; they are enabling students to develop a powerful repertoire of multiliteracies that includes practices associated with English and/or other additional language and cultural practices.

Scholarship on biliteracy is slowly moving toward understanding the dynamic nature of students' bilingual practices. For instance, recent research has revealed that bilingual individuals possess a profound grasp of language usage, adapting specific linguistic features (e.g., in English or Spanish) based on their audience (Durán, 2017; Nuñez, 2018). This adaptation involves interpreting and utilizing both linguistic and nonlinguistic culturally embedded codes, often resulting in the creation of multimodal texts. Furthermore, scholars have developed a more heightened awareness of power asymmetries in literacy instruction. Palmer and Martínez (2016) have urged language arts and biliteracy educators, researchers, and policymakers to resist policies and instructional practices that uphold conventional language views and stigmatize the dynamic bilingualism of emergent bilinguals.

Dynamic Bilingualism

Wallace Lambert (1974), working in the context of Canadian immersion bilingual education for Anglophone majorities in the 1970s,[4] proposed that bilingualism could be either *subtractive* or *additive*. According to Lambert, language-minoritized students usually experience subtractive bilingualism as a result of schooling in another language. Their home language is subtracted as the school language is learned. (Such is the case in the United States with ESL/English-only programs, as well as programs in transitional bilingual education.) On the other hand, claims Lambert, language-majority students usually experience additive bilingualism as the school language is added to their home language (for a review of additive bilingualism, see Cummins, 2017). These models of bilingualism are represented in Figure 4.1.

Responding to the intensified movements of peoples across national borders and attendant language interaction and change brought about by globalization and new technologies, it has been proposed that bilingualism is not *linear* but *dynamic* (García, 2009a). This conceptualization of bilingualism goes beyond the notion of two autonomous languages and of additive or subtractive bilingualism, and it instead suggests that the language practices of *all* bilinguals are complex and interrelated; they do not emerge in a linear way. Bilingualism does not result in either the balanced wheels of two bicycles (as the additive bilingual model purports) or in a monocycle (as the subtractive bilingual model suggests). Instead, bilingualism is like an all-terrain vehicle with individuals using their different language practices and features to adapt to both the ridges and craters of communication in uneven terrains (see Figure 4.2). Like a banyan tree, bilingualism is complex as it adapts to the soil in which it grows (see García, 2009a).

Figure 4.1. Subtractive Versus Additive Bilingualism*

Subtractive Bilingualism	Additive Bilingualism
$L1 + L2 — L1 = L2$	$L1 + L2 = L1 + L2$

*L1 refers to first language, L2 to second language.

Figure 4.2. Types of Bilingualism

Subtractive Bilingualism	Additive Bilingualism	Dynamic Bilingualism

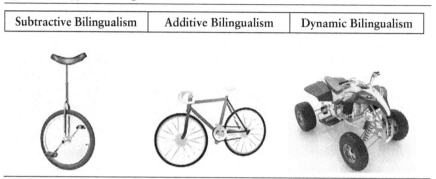

Dynamic bilingualism refers to the development of different language practices to varying degrees in order to interact with increasingly multilingual communities and bilinguals along all points of the bilingual continuum. In some ways, dynamic bilingualism is related to the concept of *plurilingualism* as defined by the Council of Europe (2000): the ability to use several languages to varying degrees and for distinct purposes and an educational value that is the basis of linguistic tolerance. Jim Cummins (2017) has proposed the term *active bilingualism* to support the dynamic nature of multilingual practices, while maintaining the idea that bilinguals indeed have two separate languages that can support cross-linguistic transfer. There is a subtle difference between the concept of dynamic bilingualism on the one hand, and on the other hand the concepts of plurilingualism and of active bilingualism. Within a dynamic bilingual perspective, languages are not simply perceived as autonomous and separate systems that people "have," but rather as linguistic and other multimodal features of a unitary semiotic meaning-making repertoire from which people subjectively select and "do." We will expand on this when we discuss *translanguaging* subsequently.

Educating for dynamic bilingualism for *all* students builds on the complex and multiple language practices of students and teachers, not simply on standardized conventions of named languages. Unlike additive and subtractive models of bilingualism, a dynamic bilingualism model proposes that we start by leveraging the complex practices of bilingual speakers—that is, that we *put their practices front and center.*

In most bilingual encounters today, the language practices of bilingual users function as those portrayed in the graphic on the left in Figure 4.3. The dynamism refers to the interrelatedness of language features and practices taking place in a moment-by-moment interaction with different interlocutors in the present, but also to the intermingling of features and practices as speakers blend together remnants of past experiences and histories with those of the present. This is consonant with Bakhtin's (1981) concept of *heteroglossia*, and his idea that "one's own language is never a single language: in it there are always survivals of the past and a potential for other-languagedness" (p. 66).

Speakers in language-minoritized communities, who have experienced extreme language loss and who attend bilingual schools for purposes of language revitalization,

Figure 4.3. Kinds of Dynamic Bilingualism

Dynamic Bilingualism	Recursive Dynamic Bilingualism

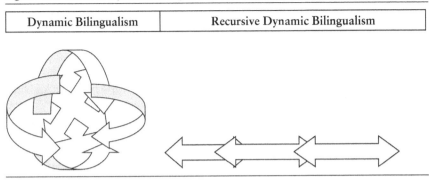

undergo a process of what García (2009a) has called *recursive dynamic bilingualism*. They do not start as simple monolinguals (as is assumed in the subtractive and additive models). Instead, they recover features of their existing ancestral language practices as they develop a bilingualism that continuously reaches back to former language practices in order to move forward and revitalize their language use. Their bilingualism cannot be called balanced, as in the two wheels of a bicycle, because their language practices need to adapt to the bilingually complex terrain in which they interact. This is the case, for example, of many Native American communities in the United States whose ancestral language practices have been persecuted and forbidden, resulting in language loss (see, for example, Leonard, 2017: Wyman, McCarty, & Nicholas, 2013). This is also the case of groups who have lived in the United States for generations and who are revitalizing the language their ancestors brought to the United States as immigrants.[5] And this is also evident in the language practices of African Americans who use alternate ancestral linguistic features than those deemed to be standard white English depending on their audience and context. This recursive dynamic bilingualism is portrayed in the graphic on the right in Figure 4.3. Although we portray it as a series of arrows that go back and forth, the recursive bilingualism of these minoritized groups is also dynamic, experiencing the same dynamism that the multidirectional circular arrows on the left depict. That is, the language practices of language-minoritized groups may start out by reaching backward, but in order to go forward they experience the same heteroglossic practices of all bilingual speakers.

Educators meaningfully educate when they draw upon the full linguistic repertoire of all students, including language practices that are multiple and fluid, as we will see subsequently. Any language-in-education approach—be it monolingual or bilingual—that does not acknowledge and build upon the fluid language practices in bilingual communities is *more concerned with controlling language behavior than with educating* (Blackledge & Creese, 2010; Creese & Blackledge, 2010; García, 2009a; García & Li Wei, 2014; García et al., 2021; Li Wei, 2011, 2018). Effectively educating emergent bilinguals, even in programs that teach through the medium of English, must include and support the dynamic bilingual practices by which bilinguals construct knowledge and understandings.

This conceptualization of dynamic bilingualism builds on and challenges traditional second language acquisition work. In the 20th century, researchers in the field of second language acquisition (SLA) were concerned with the degree to which a language learner's "interlanguage" (Selinker, 1972) conformed to what they called the *target language*. They often cataloged what is called *fossilization* behavior—that is, "errors" associated with interlanguage. Selinker and Han (2001) list some of these fossilizations: low proficiency, non-target-like performance, backsliding or the reemergence of "deviant" forms, and errors that are impervious to negative evidence. The emphasis on fossilization and "ultimate attainment" in second language acquisition studies have impacted the ways in which some language educators view their learners—as somehow incomplete. In such a view, learning an additional language is linear, as if a static and complete set of grammar rules were available for acquisition. However, recent scholarship has increasingly questioned what Ortega (2014) has called "the monolingual bias in SLA." Socioculturally oriented SLA researchers now focus on the meaning-making semiotic resources of speakers rather than narrowly focusing on what is considered "the linguistic" itself (Block, 2014). Additionally, scholarship on language education has increasingly focused on what Conteh and Meier (2014) and May (2015) have called the *multilingual turn*, a recognition that those involved in language education are, or are in the process of becoming, multilingual.

Scholars have also increasingly questioned the idea of a "native speaker" and of "native-like proficiency" (Bonfiglio, 2010; Canagarajah, 1999; Cook, 2008; Doerr, 2009; García, 2009a; Pennycook, 2006; Valdés, 2005). Kramsch (1997) has argued that the concept of native speaker, which had been considered a privilege of birth, is closely linked to social class and education, since the ways of speaking of many poor and working-class native-born citizens are considered suspect. Bonfiglio (2010) has focused on how it is the concept of race that determines who is considered a native speaker. He documents how advertisements for "native English-speaking teachers" in Singapore actually means white teachers are wanted for hire and not those who are ethnically Chinese and have spoken English "natively" since birth.

In addition, scholars in the field of bilingualism have long argued that bilinguals are not two monolinguals in one (Grosjean, 1985, 1989). By proposing the concept of *multicompetence,* Cook (2002) contends that second language users are different from monolingual speakers because their lives and minds are also different; that is, they hold knowledge of two named languages in the same mind. Likewise, Herdina and Jessner (2002) have also proposed that speakers of more than one language have dynamically interdependent language systems whose interactions create new structures that are not found in monolingual systems. This view of bilingualism has implications for teaching English to emergent bilinguals. As Larsen-Freeman and Cameron (2008) explain:

> Learning is not the taking in of linguistic forms by learners, but the constant adaptation of their linguistic resources in the service of meaning-making in response to the affordances that emerge in the communicative situation, which is, in turn, affected by learners' adaptability. (p.135)

& Martin, 2006; Jacobson & Faltis, 1990; Lin, 2013). But the idea that code-switching could be used constructively in education seldom has had acceptance, since it is considered too much a violation of what is accepted as two separate, autonomous languages.

Translanguaging theory shifts our epistemological understandings, positing that there is no such "switch," because bilingual speakers are selecting and/or inhibiting different features in their unitary linguistic/semiotic repertoire based on the moment-to-moment communicative situation (Otheguy, García, & Reid, 2015). In other words, when called upon to perform using what society calls "English," bilinguals may inhibit those features from their repertoire that are socially associated with Arabic, Chinese, Spanish, Vietnamese, and so on. But when bilinguals are among other bilinguals and in bilingual communities where their language use is not monitored by school authorities or others, they do not always have to exercise such social restraint. Translanguaging then is the norm, with bilingual speakers having free access to their entire language repertoire in a social context where this language behavior is accepted, where they perceive themselves as belonging and powerful, without having to leave behind any part of themselves or their experiences. Translanguaging thus focuses on the complex language practices of bilinguals in actual communicative settings (Li Wei, 2018) and not on the use of language codes whose distinctness is monitored by the standardizing agencies of nation-states such as language academies, grammar books, and, of course, schools.

The *trans-* in translanguaging is *not* about going from one language to another. Instead, the *trans-* refers to the act of *transcending* the concept of named language that erases and stigmatizes the language practices of speakers; translanguaging transcends or goes beyond the borders established by dominant society and nation-states.

Li Wei (2011) describes translanguaging spaces as "interactionally created" and emphasizes the performative nature of those spaces. He adds:

> For me, translanguaging is both going between different linguistic structures and systems, including different modalities (speaking, writing, signing, listening, reading, remembering) and going beyond them. It includes the full range of linguistic performances of multilingual language users for purposes that transcend the combination of structures, the alternation between systems, the transmission of information and the representation of values, identities and relationships. The act of translanguaging then is transformative in nature; it creates a social space for the multilingual language user by bringing together different dimensions of their personal history, experience and environment, their attitude, belief and ideology, their cognitive and physical capacity into one coordinated and meaningful performance, and making it into a lived experience. I call this space "translanguaging space," a space for the act of translanguaging as well as a space created through translanguaging. (p. 1223)

This *creative* use of language by bilinguals not only transforms our traditional notions of "named languages" and the ways in which we view the language practices of bilingual students but also makes room for bilinguals to be themselves rather than "two monolinguals in one" (for more, see García, 2009a and García & Li Wei, 2014). In other words, translanguaging is also *critical*, transforming ideologies and subjectivities.

The social construction of named languages is most important and real, and bilinguals have to learn to gauge when to use what features for what situation and with whom, but in the view of García and Li Wei (2014) and Otheguy, García, and Reid (2015, 2019), this is a social selection based on *external social norms*, not one based on a dual linguistic reality of two languages. This is the perspective of translanguaging that we adopt in this book, because as we will see in Chapters 5 and 6, a translanguaging lens makes a difference as to how we view and teach emergent bilinguals.

In contrast to the *unitary repertoire* view of translanguaging that we support, MacSwan (2017) has advocated for what he calls "multilingual translanguaging." But in MacSwan's view, the concept of a named language, as a product of colonization and nation-building, is left intact, thus protecting the privilege of those monolingual—usually white—speakers with dominant ways of using language. However, in the unitary theory of translanguaging adopted by García and Li Wei (2014) and Otheguy, García, and Reid (2015), among many others, the colonial logic that produced standard named languages is disrupted, giving bilingual and other language minoritized speakers the privilege to be agentive language users, and acknowledging the bodily-emotional aspects of their lived languaging. In fact, as García and Wong (in press) have said: "Translanguaging can be considered a *fugitive practice* (Givens, 2023), by which speakers, similarly to Black enslaved people in the Americas, escape from the language and literacy constraints imposed by dominant white societies and their institutions." García et al. (in press) name three principles of translanguaging—a decolonial logic of language, support of fluid languaging practices, and multimodalities beyond what is considered "the linguistic."

There is an important additional reason for advancing the unitary repertoire view of translanguaging that we are espousing in this book. Without understanding the bilingual's unitary repertoire and the decolonizing goal of translanguaging, bilingual students will continue to be taught as two monolinguals in one instead of leveraging translanguaging pedagogical practices. Understanding translanguaging gives us a different starting point for teaching them, as we will see in Chapters 5 and 6, for it is important not just to add linguistic features but to engage with the feelings, perceptions, and experiences of students as they do language, and integrate them holistically (Otheguy, García, & Reid, 2015; see also García & Kleyn, 2016; García, Johnson, & Seltzer, 2017). And as we will see, translanguaging is also important for valid assessments since disregarding the bilingual's unitary repertoire will always put them in a position inferior to that of dominant monolinguals. Translanguaging in assessment will be considered in Chapter 8.

Only by disrupting the idea of the named language that is upheld with a colonial logic of language (Mignolo, 2000) will translanguaging enable bilingual speakers to name and be themselves. In other words, it is the unitary repertoire theory of translanguaging that has the potential of becoming a political act in the transformation of these racialized/minoritized speakers. Our view of translanguaging has emerged from decolonial or borderland visions of the world as well as raciolinguistic perspectives. We consider these subsequently because without these alternative theories, translanguaging cannot fulfill its transformative potential.

Decolonial and Borderland Theories

As we have seen, theories regarding bilingualism have evolved as scholarship has questioned many of the ways in which bilingualism was first studied and the subjugated or inferior positions in which minoritized bilinguals were placed. An important theoretical lens for this shift has been *decolonial theories*. Decolonial scholarship emerging from Latin America demands that scholars situate our epistemological perspective on what Boaventura de Sousa Santos (2007) has called "the other side of the line." Santos explains how the knowledges and lifeways of Indigenous populations were positioned by colonial powers on a side of the line that rendered them invisible, relegating them to an existential *abyss*, erasing their existence. According to Santos (2007), *post-abyssal thinking* requires bringing to light the vast system of knowledge and practices of Indigenous people and those from the Global South, which had been previously relegated to that existential abyss. Post-abyssal thinking challenges the existence of the colonial line itself. To do so requires that we take up a *locus of enunciation* (Mignolo, 2000), which is different from that of the nation-state and dominant populations. By locus of enunciation, Mignolo refers to the specific positionality or standpoint from which a person speaks, interprets, or makes meaning. The term highlights the fact that knowledge, beliefs, and ideas are not neutral or universally applicable but are instead rooted in particular experiences, places, and identities. Part of the colonial project was to situate the dominant locus of enunciation not only as the normative one but also as the only reasonable one by erasing, extinguishing, and delegitimizing as much as possible the knowledges and worldviews that already existed and that continue to exist even if in suppressed ways. A decolonial lens enables scholars to observe and describe the *actual language practices* of diverse communities, while rectifying histories of exclusions and guaranteeing minoritized bilingual students the greatest level of participation (see García et al., 2021). Translanguaging and decoloniality are always linked (García & Alvis, 2019).

Bilingual students often are not situated on one side of the line or another but on *borderlands*, on the cracks between worlds, on an *entre mundos* (Anzaldúa, 1987). Gloria Anzaldúa (1987) identified, with the Nahuatl word *nepantla*, the place in the middle where duality of nationhood, identity, language, gender, race, and social positions is transcended. By navigating the cracks between different sides of the line, borderland theory (often referred to as nepantlera theory) advances that life can be reconstructed, identities can be rewritten, and alternatives constructed (Anzaldúa & Keating, 2002).

Decolonial and borderland/nepantlera theories have been responsible for providing a different angle from which to view traditional theories of bilingualism and find them lacking. In fact, focusing on decolonial and borderland/nepantlera theories is transforming the traditional ways in which we had thought about dual-language bilingual education (García, Alfaro, & Freire, 2024). Without the alternative epistemological perspective that adopts the locus of enunciation of communities that have been subjugated (Mignolo, 2000), alternative theories of bilingualism like dynamic bilingualism and translanguaging would not have emerged.

Raciolinguistic Ideologies

As we saw in the previous chapter, language minoritized communities in the 1960s called for antiracist bilingual education. But race was soon divorced from language, as government policy toward the education of emergent bilinguals was directed exclusively to language aspects (see Chávez-Moreno, 2020; García & Sung, 2018; García, Cioè-Peña, & Frieson, 2024). And yet, both race and language have been produced precisely by processes of colonization that made it possible to categorize "the other" as inferior. As the Brazilian decolonial theorist Lynn Mario de Souza has said (2007), dominance came first, and it was later that this superiority came to be biologized as race and naturalized as language.

The close link between language and race and the discriminatory effects it has produced has been theorized in the work on raciolinguistic ideologies by Flores and Rosa (2015) and the many scholars who now center raciolinguistic perspectives in thinking about the education of emergent bilinguals. It is not language itself, but racialization processes that produce the perception that the language of racialized subjects is deficient. As Flores and Rosa have said: "No language variety is objectively distinctive or nondistinctive, but rather comes to be enregistered as such in particular historical, political and economic circumstances" (2015, p. 632).

The work on raciolinguistic ideologies has brought us full circle to confront the racism that has surrounded the education of emergent bilinguals. While governmental policies and traditional theories of bilingualism have historically focused on language, raciolinguistic ideologies remind us of how race and the antiracist/ sociopolitical demands of the language-minoritized communities in the 1960s were silenced. As García, Cioè-Peña, and Frieson (2024) have said: "The government's response to Latinx activists' broader political, racial, and economic struggle was to promote the ideologies of the War on Poverty, focusing on the cultural deficit discourse of handicaps that Mexican Americans and Puerto Ricans had to overcome" (p. 104). Melamed (2011) has referred to this response as *liberal multiculturalism*, that is, rather than engage critically with race and oppression, the government focused on differences in culture, thus distancing itself from the antiracism demands of communities in the 1960s.

The complete separation of language from race in theoretical discussions of bilingualism has resulted in the silencing of the racialized experience of most emergent bilinguals. For example, in discussions of the education of Latine emergent bilinguals, the presence of Afro-Latine, Asian-Latine, and Indigenous-Latine groups has been rarely addressed. Also silenced is the profound absence of African, Asian, and Native Americans in bilingual education programs (Cervantes-Soon et al., 2021; Chávez-Moreno, 2020, 2024).

Translanguaging has to be understood in the light of work on decolonial theories and raciolinguistic ideologies (Flores, 2019). The manifesto jointly written by García, Flores, Seltzer, Li Wei, Otheguy, and Rosas (2021) delineates how rejecting the type of thinking that erases the epistemologies of the Global South is the core of a just education for racialized bilingual students. In translanguaging work, language is not simply defined as a category that belongs to a specific group and identifies them, but as practices that can be dynamically used to interact with interlocutors moment-to-moment. Because of the dynamism of the interactional encounters, both speakers and listeners are always positioned differently, with listeners having a most important role in the construction of linguistic and social messages. White listening subjects often act on their raciolinguistic ideologies when evaluating the language practices of racialized speakers as inferior without grounding this assessment on the language practice itself.

EMPIRICAL EVIDENCE ON THE RELATIONSHIP BETWEEN BILINGUALISM AND ACHIEVEMENT

Around the world there is near consensus among researchers that greater support for emergent bilinguals' home language practices, and academic development using those practices, is "positively related to higher long-term academic attainment" (Ferguson, 2006, p. 48). Because in the United States the notion of bilingual education itself is so politically loaded, research about the question of whether bilingual education or monolingual (English-only) education works best for emergent bilinguals is often contradictory. Nevertheless, and on balance, there is much research support for the positive effects of the use of students' home language practices over English-only education (for a comprehensive review, see Baker & Wright, 2021).

Several large-scale evaluations (e.g., Ramírez, 1992; Thomas & Collier, 2002) have demonstrated that using the home language in instruction benefits language-minoritized students. For instance, Ramírez (1992) carried out a longitudinal study of 554 kindergarten-to-sixth-grade Latine students in five states (New York, New Jersey, Florida, Texas, and California) who were in English-only structured immersion programs, transitional early-exit programs, and late-exit developmental bilingual programs. The results of the study favored late-exit developmental bilingual programs that use students' home languages for five to six years. Although there were no differences between programs among students in the third grade, by sixth grade, students in late-exit developmental programs were performing better in mathematics, English language arts, and English reading than students in the other programs.

In 2002, Thomas and Collier published a study of the effectiveness of different types of educational programs for language-minoritized student achievement. They compared the achievement on nationally standardized tests of students in different kinds of programs, who entered school in kindergarten or first grade with little or no proficiency in English, and followed them to the highest grade level reached. They determined that bilingually schooled students outperformed comparable monolingually schooled students in all subjects. Furthermore, they found that the strongest predictor of the students' English language achievement was the amount of formal schooling they had received in the home language. Developmental bilingual education programs (one-way dual language) and two-way bilingual education programs (two-way dual language) were the only kinds of programs that enabled emergent bilinguals to reach the 50th percentile in both languages in all subjects. These bilingual education programs also produced the fewest dropouts. Two types of two-way and developmental bilingual education programs were included in the study: (1) the 50:50 model, meaning that 50% of the instruction is in the child's home language and 50% in the additional language; and (2) the 90:10 model, meaning that *initially* 90% of the instruction is in the child's home language and 10% in the other language, but gradually moves to a 50:50 arrangement. Thomas and Collier (2002) found that the 90:10 type of instruction was more efficient than the 50:50 instructional model in helping students reach grade-level achievement in their additional language.

In 2017, Collier and Thomas summarized the findings of 32 years of research on the effects of bilingual instruction on achievement. Their summary concludes that only high-quality long-term bilingual programs are effective in making bilingual students achieve academically, whereas bilingual students in English-only and transitional bilingual programs of the early-exit type are not successful.

Lindholm-Leary (2001) conducted a comprehensive evaluation of programs serving emergent bilinguals in California. These included English-only programs, transitional bilingual education, and two types of two-way bilingual education (what she called simply dual-language education or DLE—90:10 and 50:50). Like Thomas and Collier (2002), Lindhom-Leary found that students who were in instructional programs in which initially English was used for only 10% to 20% of the time (whether transitional or 90:10 dual language) did as well on English proficiency tests as those in English-only programs or 50:50 two-way dual-language bilingual programs. By grade 6, however, Latine students in what Lindholm-Leary called "dual-language education" (which for her is two-way bilingual education) outperformed transitional bilingual education students. In mathematics, all students in dual-language education outperformed by 10 points those educated only in English.

In their synthesis of the research evidence in the education of emergent bilinguals, Genesee, Lindholm-Leary, Saunders, and Christian (2006) confirmed that students who are in educational programs that provide extended instruction in their home language through late-exit bilingual education programs (developmental/one-way dual-language and two-way bilingual education/dual language) outperform students who receive only short-term instruction through their home language (early-exit transitional bilingual education). They also found that bilingual proficiency and biliteracy were positively related to academic achievement in both languages. Finally, Genesee and colleagues (2006) found that emergent bilinguals in primary school programs providing home language support had acquired the same or superior levels of reading and writing skills as students in English-only programs by the end of elementary school.

Five independent meta-analyses of experimental studies (August & Shanahan, 2006; Greene, 1997; Rolstad, Mahoney, & Glass, 2005; Slavin & Cheung, 2005; Willig, 1985) concluded that learning to read in the child's home language promotes reading achievement in an additional language (Goldenberg, 2008). Likewise, the National Literacy Panel on Language Minority Children and Youth, appointed by the George W. Bush administration, concluded that bilingual education approaches, in which the student's home language is used, are more effective in teaching students to read than are English-only approaches (see August & Shanahan, 2006). Thus, there is firm evidence that learning to read in the student's home language promotes reading achievement in English. In a guide to the research on how to promote academic achievement among English learners, Goldenberg and Coleman (2010) say:

> Primary-language reading instruction is clearly no panacea, just as phonics instruction is no panacea. But relatively speaking, it makes a meaningful contribution to ELLs' reading achievement in *English*. (p. 27, emphasis added)

In 2014, Umansky and Reardon conducted an analysis of reclassification patterns among Latine emergent bilinguals in schools in California in three different types of programs—sheltered English immersion, transitional bilingual education, and two-way dual-language bilingual (dual-immersion) programs. They found that Latine emergent bilingual students in two-way dual-language bilingual education (DLBE) programs were reclassified (as fluent bilinguals) more slowly than were students in other programs. However, they also found that, over time, students in DLBE programs had higher overall reclassification rates and higher English proficiency and academic performance.

Lindholm-Leary and Genesee (2014) synthesize all these studies by concluding:

> Over three decades of research in the U.S. indicates that minority language students in two-way and DBE [developmental bilingual education] programs acquire English speaking, listening, reading and writing skills as well and as quickly as their minority language peers in mainstream programs. (p. 172)

Despite the support for two-way immersion or two-way dual-language bilingual education, we cannot conclude that they are the *only* way to educate language-minoritized students successfully and bilingually. The promise of two-way DLBE notwithstanding, not all localities can implement these programs in all languages because many language-majority communities are not eager to have their children schooled with language-minority children. For example, even though two-way DLBE programs are growing in English/Chinese and English/Spanish, other language groups—Haitians, for example—are not benefiting from such programs. Why? Language-majority parents are many times reluctant to have their children learn Haitian Creole, which they consider to be a low-prestige language. Haitian Creole is, however, essential for the meaningful education of Haitian children and youth (Ballenger, 1997; Cerat, 2017; DeGraff, 2009; DeGraff & Stump, 2018;

Hudicourt-Barnes, 2003; Kleifgen, 1991, 2009), and thus, it would be important to develop bilingual education programs for the Haitian community. The same can be said of Native American communities where the ancestral languages are important in the education of the community itself, but where two-way DLBE would have little relevance.

It is also important to point out that, depending on demand and availability, in some cases students are selected for participation in two-way DLBE programs on the basis of good scores on screening instruments and parental interviews (see, for example, the case of some schools in New York City in García, Menken, Velasco, & Vogel, 2018). Emergent bilinguals who are considered less "gifted" linguistically when they enter kindergarten are assigned to ESL programs or transitional bilingual education programs because room has to be made for English-speaking monolingual students in the DLBE program. Thus, emergent bilingual students in two-way DLBE programs where half of the students are white English-speaking students may not always be the same type of students as those in transitional bilingual education or ESL programs.

As August and Hakuta (1998) state in their National Research Council report, any type of program to educate emergent bilinguals can be implemented well or poorly. However, what is evident from the research is that the classroom use of students' home language practices over a longer period of time is crucial for their long-term cognitive growth and academic achievement in English and in the home language. De Jong and Bearse (2011) report a positive correlation between level of bilingualism and academic achievement, as well as between level of bilingualism and level of proficiency in English and the home language. All teachers, both those who are required to deliver instruction in English only and those who do so bilingually, can take a more effective pedagogical path by constructing bilingual instructional spaces, as we will describe in the next chapter.

EDUCATING EMERGENT BILINGUALS:
BUILDING ON BILINGUALISM FOR ACADEMIC SUCCESS

Although *additive schooling practices* are important (see, for example, Bartlett & García, 2011), additive conceptions of bilingualism fail to capture the complexity of bilingual acquisition and development. A linear conception of additive bilingualism does not adequately describe the ever-changing multilingual practices of the 21st century; thus, we have chosen instead to use the term *dynamic bilingualism*. We make evident that some language-minoritized students who speak languages that are not prevalent in the school community cannot be schooled bilingually, given the ways in which many bilingual education programs have been constructed. It is, of course, easier to build bilingual education programs for large language groups—especially Spanish speakers, the largest and most rapidly growing linguistic minority in the United States. Yet every teacher, even those teaching in spaces that are formally denominated as ESL or English only, can draw on students' linguistic practices (see García, Johnson, & Seltzer, 2017).

By way of summary, Table 4.1 shows the types of educational programs described in Chapter 3, alongside linguistic goals, and the kind of bilingualism that they promote according to the understandings that we have proposed in this chapter.

Table 4.1. Types of Educational Programs and Bilingualism

Program	Goal	Bilingualism
Submersion	Monolingualism	Subtractive
ESL pull-out	Monolingualism	Subtractive
ESL push-in	Monolingualism	Subtractive
Structured English immersion (sheltered English)	Monolingualism	Subtractive
High-intensity English language training	Monolingualism	Subtractive
Transitional bilingual education (early exit)	Monolingualism	Subtractive
Developmental bilingual education (one-way DLBE/late exit)	Bilingualism	Dynamic and recursive dynamic
Two-way bilingual education (two-way DLBE or two-way immersion)	Bilingualism	Dynamic
Dynamic bi-/multilingual education	Bilingualism	Dynamic

STUDY QUESTIONS

1. What, according to a number of studies, are the cognitive benefits of bilingualism?
2. Discuss Cummins's theories of "linguistic interdependence" and "common underlying proficiency." Describe the distinction, according to Cummins, between basic interpersonal communication skills and cognitive academic learning proficiency.
3. Identify types of bilingualism. Discuss why dynamic bilingualism fits closely with the concept of multicompetence and the complexity of bilingualism.
4. What is translanguaging? How does the concept differ from the notion of "named languages"? Can you imagine how building on the concept of translanguaging might change instruction in ESL and bilingual education?
5. What is the epistemological difference between translanguaging and code-switching?
6. How do decolonial and borderland/nepantlera theories transform our understandings of bilingualism?
7. What is the relationship of raciolinguistic ideologies and the perception of language and bilingualism?
8. Discuss the research evidence that exists for drawing on home language practices in the schooling of emergent bilinguals.

CHAPTER 5

Language and Bilingualism

Practices

In this chapter, we will:

- Identify three inequitable practices with regard to language use in education:
  - » Insufficient support and development of home language practices,
  - » Isolation of English, and
  - » Compartmentalization of English and languages other than English in instruction.
- Consider four alternative practices:
  - » Heteroglossic bilingual instructional practices,
  - » Translanguaging pedagogy,
  - » Critical multilingual raciolinguistic awareness, and
  - » Complex dynamic language/literacy use.

Our task in this chapter is twofold: We first identify some of the inequitable language education practices that educators should avoid. We focus on these because they are the most commonly found in schools, and also because some of them are advocated in professional guides for policymakers and educators of emergent bilingual students. We then describe in detail four alternative language education practices that we advocate.

INEQUITABLE LANGUAGE/LITERACY PRACTICES

Having established that educational policy and practice does not reflect current research on emergent bilinguals and their education, we examine here three inequitable school practices—insufficient support and inadequate development of home language practices in instruction, the isolation of English and other languages of instruction into a monolingual learning space, and the compartmentalization of languages in ways that devalue students' own fluid bilingual community practices, that is, their translanguaging. In the second part of this chapter, we propose alternatives that we believe could address some of the problems in the present practices.

Insufficient Support and Inadequate Development of
Home Language Practices

The NCLB and ESSA laws, described in Chapter 3, as well as the greater multilingualism in the U.S. population, have generated some attention by scholars and the public to the education of emergent bilinguals. Yet, as we will see in this section, there has been a decrease in the number of students receiving an adequate education, and support is insufficient. We will also see that the participation of emergent bilingual students in educational programs that meet their needs remains inadequate both because of the types of programs offered and the length and level of service rendered.

Decrease in numbers receiving adequate services. As reported in Chapter 3, emergent bilingual students are increasingly educated in English-only programs despite the growth of the emergent bilingual student population. According to the Office for Civil Rights, in 2011, approximately 9% of students who had been identified as English learners (420,826) were not enrolled in any targeted language instructional programs.

New York City, as we said in Chapter 3, exemplifies the decline in the use of students' home language practices in education. In 1974, the Aspira Consent Decree mandated transitional bilingual education programs for the city's Latine students (Reyes, 2006); today, however, fewer than ever emergent bilingual students are in New York City bilingual classrooms. In the school year 2002–2003, 53% of emergent bilinguals in New York City were in ESL programs (now called ENL); by the school year 2007–2008, 69% were instructed in ESL programs, and this number increased to 79.2% by 2013–2014, and made up 78.94% of students in 2022–2023. Likewise, whereas 37% of emergent bilinguals were in transitional bilingual education in 2002, only 21% participated in such programs in 2007–2008 and 15.4% in 2013–2014. By 2022–2023 only 10% of emergent bilinguals were in transitional bilingual education programs. In 2002, 2% of emergent bilinguals were in two-way dual-language bilingual programs, 3.6% were in such programs in 2007–2008, 4.5% in 2013–2014, and 8.73% in 2022–2023. Although the number of emergent bilinguals is increasing in dual-language bilingual programs, in 2022–2023, less than 20% of the emergent bilingual student population in New York City participated in any type of bilingual program (NYC Public Schools, 2022–2023).

Inadequate educational programs: Program types. English as a second language/new language programs have been reshaped in the past 20 years, with more attention paid to students' funds of knowledge, including home language practices (García, 2023; Paulsrud, Tian, & Toth, 2021; Tian et al., 2020). But pull-out ESL/ENL, where the focus is on English as an isolated subject of study, continues to be the most commonly used type, although research has shown that the use of English in content-area instruction, as in push-in programs or in structured English immersion programs, is associated with higher long-term educational attainment (Collier & Thomas, 2017; Thomas & Collier, 1997).

Even with the growth of dual-language bilingual programs, most bilingual programs in the United States are still early-exit transitional bilingual programs, which often have the secondary consequence of tracking emergent bilinguals into remedial programs. The effect of such policies is that bilingualism and biliteracy for academic purposes does not emerge; instead, the result for these students is academic failure.

All types of bilingual education programs in the United States, even dual-language bilingual education programs, focus primarily on the development of English and its use for literacy purposes. As we have seen, ESSA (2015) requires schools to help their students achieve the rapid development of English literacy as measured by standardized tests. As a result, many schools do not take the development of academic literacy in the home language seriously, because literacy in the language other than English is rarely assessed. In transitional bilingual education programs, the home language is often used and viewed only as a "bridge" to facilitate the learning of English. In dual-language bilingual programs, where the intent is to use the language other than English at least 50% of the time and facilitate the development of bilingualism and biliteracy, students and teachers also tend to value the development of English literacy much more than that in the other language, given the importance of scores in standardized tests in English. Thus, more time and resources are spent ensuring that students do well in the language that "counts."

Although dual-language bilingual programs might be a step in the right direction for the future possibility of a less monolingual society, only 50% of students in these programs are language-minoritized emergent bilinguals. Thus, dual-language bilingual programs tend to serve fewer English learners. As we said in Chapter 3, the appeal of these programs is their focus on the commodification of bilingualism for the global economy and the gentrification of neighborhoods rather than the provision of the bilingual education that language-minoritized students deserve (see, for example, Cervantes-Soon, 2014; Cervantes-Soon et al., 2017; Chávez-Moreno, 2024; Fitts, 2006; Flores, 2016; Flores, Tseng, & Subtirelu, 2020; Freire, Alfaro, & de Jong, 2024; Palmer, 2010; Valdez et al., 2014; Varghese & Park, 2010). Some scholars have cautioned that emergent bilingual students are being used as "commodities that can be consumed by white, English-speaking students" (Pimentel, 2011, p. 351). Petrovic (2005) provocatively has said:

> Dual immersion programs have the potential of becoming the Epcot Center of foreign language curriculum, providing language majority students an opportunity to view live specimens of the second language. (p. 406)

Utah leads the nation in the state-wide development of a dual-language immersion (DLI) initiative for English-speaking students, a model that is being replicated in some states like Delaware and Georgia.[1]

Inadequate educational programs: Length and levels. Beyond the inadequate types of educational programs in which emergent bilinguals are being educated today, these support services are offered for an inadequate length of time. The failure of the services offered also stems from the fact that they are mostly found at the elementary level.

As we pointed out in Chapter 3, substantial research evidence reports that bilingualism develops over time. And yet, emergent bilinguals are reclassified on average after three years (Slama, 2014). Thus, according to the research, emergent bilinguals are receiving educational support for about half the time that they will most likely need it. Many states permit emergent bilinguals to remain in special programs for only one year (for example, Arizona) or a maximum of three to four years. In fact, ESSA requires states to include in their reports any student who does not attain English proficiency in five years or more; ESSA designates those students as long-term English learners.

Although emergent bilinguals at the secondary level arguably have a more difficult task than students at the elementary level, given the complexity of the subject matter they must master to graduate, elementary-level students are far more likely to have instruction in which their home language practices are used in any significant way. Because all types of bilingual education programs exist primarily at the elementary school level, there is insufficient development of students' literacies in the home language in middle and high schools. In effect, most students who attend bilingual elementary programs then go to secondary schools where instruction is exclusively in English.

Middle and high school bilingual programs most often serve recent immigrants, except in the case of students coming from elementary school classrooms who have been unable to pass the English proficiency assessments. These long-term English learners have experienced considerable home language loss, and some have even become monolingual English speakers. Although these students are labeled as English learners, they do not share the characteristics of those for whom instruction is usually planned: They may be fluent speakers of English, although their use of English for school literacy purposes might be inadequate. As we have said, this is often the result of an inconsistent or poor-quality primary educational experience.

Isolation of English

Most education programs for emergent bilinguals in the United States are based on the belief that English is best taught monolingually (García, 2009a). Harmer (1998) summarized this uninformed yet commonplace advice to ESL teachers by saying that "the need to have them [students] practicing English (rather than their own language) remains paramount" (p. 129).

The emphasis on getting emergent bilinguals to perform as English proficient in assessments means that many teachers forbid the use of students' home languages in their classrooms. They do so with the mistaken belief that, if they allow home language use, they will fail as educators to adapt instruction to the English language needs of the students (Cloud et al., 2000).

Schools in the United States have played a vital role in controlling the language practices of minoritized and racialized students and making them "governable subjects" (Flores, 2013; Foucault, 1979). Named language constructions, such as standard English, have been used as gatekeepers to exclude minoritized students from entry into meaningful and authentic opportunities to use English. When English is isolated and demands are made that only English be used to learn and to participate in educational opportunities, emergent bilinguals are also excluded from dominant social circles and important roles (for more on the construction of "English," see Pennycook, 2007, 2024). When students express sophisticated understandings of math, science, and history using language features considered nonstandard, their knowledge is invalidated because only standard English is accepted. This further restricts emergent bilinguals' opportunities to become the mathematicians, scientists, and historians that we so desperately need.

Compartmentalization of English and Languages Other Than English in Instruction

Bilingual education programs have also fallen prey to a monoglossic ideology that treats bilinguals' languages as one autonomous language added to another instead of understanding these students' dynamic, fluid linguistic practices (García, 2009a). Thus, bilingual schools usually strictly separate the languages. It was Wallace Lambert (1984) who perhaps best expressed this ideology of language separation in his discussion about French immersion programs in Canada in the 1980s:

> No bilingual skills are required of the teacher, who plays the role of a monolingual in the target language . . . and who never switches languages, reviews materials in the other language, or otherwise uses the child's native language in teacher-pupil interactions. In immersion programs, therefore, bilingualism is developed through two separate monolingual instructional routes. (p. 13)

This practice of strict language separation and sheltering of languages has prevailed in many bilingual education programs. Jacobson and Faltis (1990) explain the reasons for this practice: "By strictly separating the languages, the teacher avoids, it is argued, cross contamination, thus making it easier for the child to acquire a new linguistic system as he/she internalizes a given lesson" (p. 4).

There are four language allocation strategies traditionally used to separate languages in bilingual education:

- Time-determined, with one language exclusively used half the day, on alternate days, or even alternate weeks;
- Teacher-determined, with two teachers who speak one language exclusively;
- Place-determined, with one room or an entire building used for one language exclusively; and
- Subject-determined, with one language being used exclusively to teach one subject (García, 2009a).

In bilingual education, language-allocation policies are important. But those policies that adhere to complete language separation—what Cummins (2008) called "the two solitudes"—should be reexamined. Rigid adherence to one language or another without regard to students' own practices and how they make meaning contradicts research findings. Unless these strict language allocation policies become more flexible, they will keep language-minoritized students within a closed circle from which they cannot access opportunities and knowledge.

Bilingual education programs understandably must maintain instructional spaces for one language or another so that students receive adequate input and have opportunities to use the language of instruction. This is especially important for the development of a minoritized or threatened language. But language development (whether in English or in the additional language) cannot occur in isolation from the world and the complex language practices of its speakers. *Minoritized languages need to be protected, but they cannot be isolated as if they were pieces in a museum because bilinguals use these languages in interaction with speakers who use other languages.* Students develop new linguistic practices when they learn to use language for meaningful purposes, particularly when they learn something of interest and want to use language to show that understanding.

Sánchez, García, and Solorza (2017) point out that even though instructional spaces where one language is used are important, it is equally important for teachers to understand how to open *translanguaging spaces* (Li Wei, 2011) where students are free to use their different language practices. They point to three reasons for doing so: (1) *scaffolding* for students who need additional assistance to understand; (2) *assessment/evaluation* to differentiate between what students understand and know how to do, and being able to perform these actions with specific standardized language features; and (3) *transformation* so as to ensure that bilingual students' subjectivities of deficiency are transformed into potentialities.

Heller (1999) has made us aware of the dangers of valuing only what she calls "parallel monolingualisms," practices in which "every variety must conform to certain prescriptive norms" (p. 271). Because languages other than English are not validated publicly in powerful spheres (even when they are spoken in local communities), they are often valued only when they are used according to standardized monolingual conventions and norms, what Guadalupe Valdés (2018) has called "the curricularization of language." And thus, unless language allocation policies are adhered to judiciously and flexibly, there is the potential that bilingual education would further alienate language-minoritized bilingual students from what is assigned to them by schools as their "first language," "L1," "mother tongue," or even "home language." Language-minoritized students' own bilingual practices often have little relationship to what is taught in school as "their" language.

ALTERNATIVE LANGUAGE/LITERACY PRACTICES

Whether teaching exclusively in English or teaching bilingually, effective educators make room in the classroom for emergent bilinguals' leveraging the existing features of their repertoire in order to acquire new ones. How do teachers manage this, given policies that many times run counter to these practices? They can do so, as we will demonstrate here, by negotiating educational policies for the benefit of their students, thus becoming policymakers themselves (Menken & García, 2010). In what follows, we describe educational practices that work for emergent bilinguals given the dynamic nature of bilingualism that we have laid out previously. We describe the following four language-focused educational practices that build on theoretical constructs and research evidence that we have been considering:

- Heteroglossic bilingual instructional practices
- Translanguaging pedagogy
- Critical multilingual raciolinguistic awareness
- Complex dynamic language/literacy use

Heteroglossic Bilingual Instructional Practices

Language teaching has traditionally excluded the students' home language practices from ESL and bilingual classrooms, whether the approach used has been communicative, immersion, or focused on linguistic structures. In ESL classrooms, many teachers continue to believe that it is best to use what is considered appropriate English exclusively. In bilingual classrooms, the separation of languages has been the most accepted practice, with only "appropriate English," but also only "appropriate language other than English" accepted during the times allotted to each of the languages.

A meaningful and rigorous education for emergent bilinguals will *always* leverage the home language practices as much as possible. Some ESL/ENL educators may be constrained by program structures that require English-only instruction. Others might be inhibited because the emergent bilinguals in their classrooms speak many languages. Bilingual educators may be confined by strict language allocation policies. But *all* educators—bilingual, ESL, and mainstream—can draw upon the language practices of their bilingual students for a meaningful education. We call them *heteroglossic bilingual instructional practices* here because they disrupt the monoglossic nature of programs that purport to be in English only or solely in two standard languages with separate articulations. These heteroglossic bilingual instructional practices are grounded on the ways in which emergent bilinguals use language, and not simply on the restrictive ways of using language that schools impose.

There are many classrooms in the United States where educators are finding ways of leveraging the students' home language practices regardless of program structure or model used. As Cummins (2009) says, "bilingual instructional strategies can be incorporated into English-medium classrooms, thereby opening up the pedagogical space in ways that legitimate the intelligence, imagination, and linguistic talents of ELL students" (p. xi). Describing how all teachers can include the students' home language practices in instruction, Cummins (2007) suggests that "[W]hen students' L1 is invoked as a cognitive and linguistic resource through bilingual instructional strategies, it can function as a stepping stone to scaffold more accomplished performance in the L2" (p. 14).

In their discussion about modifications needed to advance literacy instruction for emergent bilinguals, Goldenberg and Coleman (2010) recommend what they call "strategic" uses of the language other than English. In teaching vocabulary, they recommend presenting words in the LOTE before teaching them in English, previewing lessons using texts in the LOTE, providing teachers with translation equivalents of the target words, using cognates, and selecting texts and topics that would be culturally appropriate for their students. In developing emergent bilinguals' reading comprehension, they recommend previewing English reading texts in the LOTE, teaching metacognitive reading strategies in the students' home language, and pointing out similarities and differences between English and the students' home language.

Wright (2010) refers to what he calls "primary language support," a form of scaffolding. Wright identifies several such strategies that use the home language: (1) preview–review, in which teachers preview lessons in the home language, present in English, and review in the home language; (2) giving quick explanations; (3) labeling and displaying words and works; (4) providing resources (dictionaries, books, technology); and (5) accepting all students' contributions to the lesson. Furthermore, given the increased use of the internet as a resource, teachers can find information on their students' home languages; they can also direct students to online opportunities to strengthen the home language. For example, teachers working with Haitian Creole–speaking students can access useful curricular materials at the Haitian-Creole Institute of New York (https://haitiancreoleinstitute.com/). To continue developing their home language, students can go to blogs and other sites such as Kreyòl Pou Timoun/Haitian Creole for Kids (https://jadentimoun.com/) and Duolingo (https://blog.duolingo.com/haitian-creole-duolingo).

García, Flores, and Chu (2011) have described how two high schools include bilingual instructional practices despite the fact that neither has an official bilingual education program. In one high school where all the students are emergent bilinguals of different language backgrounds, students decide which language they want to use when researching topics and reading and writing about them. Students develop their own strategies for making sense of the academic lesson in English, often using Google Translate and other websites as a resource. As they develop their projects, students teach one another phrases in both English and additional languages. Whenever possible, the teacher interacts with small groups and individual students in the languages they are using. When students are using a language that the teacher does not understand, one of the more advanced emergent bilinguals provides translation.

In an ESL elementary school classroom, Christina Celic (2009) "stretches" her self-contained ESL class by getting students to read and write in languages other than English. Most of her emergent bilinguals are Spanish speaking, but there are also Mandarin speakers and students from Nepal, India, and Bangladesh. Students are paired strategically so that fluent bilingual students work with emergent bilingual students. Celic uses a workshop model of teaching literacy (Calkins, 1994). Calkins' workshop model recommends mini-lessons: short teacher-centered lessons in which teachers model explicit metacognitive strategies used in reading and writing texts (see also Swinney & Velasco, 2011). During the mini-lessons, students "turn and talk," which means they practice what the teacher has been modeling with a peer, using all the linguistic and other semiotic resources at their disposal—Spanish, English, language prompts, drawings, gestures. For independent reading, Celic provides leveled reading material for her emergent bilinguals in English and the other language. During the writing workshop, students have the option to write in any language or to write fully bilingual texts, similar to the bilingual children's books that Celic uses as read-alouds (C. Celic, personal communication, October 31, 2009). Celic also helps emergent bilinguals develop their understanding of new vocabulary in English by making explicit connections between languages. To do that, she asks her students if they know what the word means in their language and, whenever possible, has them add the translation to the "word wall" in their classroom.

In middle schools studied by Danling Fu (2003, 2009), the students use Chinese writing as a stepping-stone to English writing. Teachers allow beginning ESL students to write in Chinese while incorporating the few words they know in English. Gradually, more English writing emerges. Fu (2009) says:

> Learning to write in English for ELLs who are literate in their native language is actually a process of becoming bilingual writers, rather than merely replacing one language or writing ability with another or mastering two separate language systems. . . . If writing reflects who and what the writers are, then ELLs' native language (voice and expressions) will either visibly appear or be blended with English. (p. 120)

The work of Cummins and other researchers in Canadian classrooms also clearly demonstrates how teachers can use bilingual instructional strategies in English-only classrooms. Cummins (2006) calls for the use of *identity texts*, as students use both languages to write about their own immigration and education experiences. Elsewhere, he quotes Madiha, one of the girls involved in a project of producing bilingual identity texts:

> I think it helps my learning to be able to write in both languages because if I'm writing English and Ms. Leoni says you can write Urdu too it helps me think of what the word means because I always think in Urdu. That helps me write better in English. (Cummins, 2009, p. x)

In some classrooms, teachers encourage students to write *double-entry journals* (see García & Traugh, 2002). In this assignment, students copy fragments of academic texts they are reading in one column, then react to the texts from their own personal perspectives in the second column, contributing both their experiences and their cultural and linguistic understandings to make sense of the texts. The reactions or reflections are written using the students' own complex language practices. These double-entry journals are then shared with fellow classmates as a way to build multicultural and multilingual understandings of the same text and to generate different understandings from multiple perspectives.

Lucas and Katz (1994) document more bilingual instructional practices that do not require teachers to be bilingual, such as:

- Teachers devising a writing assignment in which students use their home languages;
- Students reading or telling stories to one another using their home languages and then translating them into English to tell other students;

- Students from same language backgrounds being paired together so that students who are more fluent in English can help those less fluent;
- Students being encouraged to use bilingual dictionaries;
- Students being encouraged to get help at home in their home languages;
- Books being provided in students' home languages; and
- Awards being given for excellence in languages not commonly studied.

A useful resource with examples is the video series called "Teaching Bilinguals Even If You're Not One." This can be found on the website of a project conducted by scholars from City University of New York and funded by the New York State Department of Education (CUNY-NYSIEB), www.cuny-nysieb.org (see subsequent discussion). Two other important websites with resources for teachers of emergent bilinguals are ¡Colorín, Colorado! (http://www.colorincolorado.org/new-teaching-ells) and Edutopia (https://www.edutopia.org/article/resources-for-teaching-english-language-learners-ashley-cronin).

Strengthening the relationship between languages is also the approach taken in Beeman and Urrow (2013) in what they identify as "the Bridge," an important strategy in bilingual instruction. Beeman and Urrow explain: "The Bridge is the instructional moment when teachers purposefully bring the two languages together, guiding students to transfer the academic content they have learned in one language to the other language, engage in contrastive analysis of the two languages, and strengthen their knowledge of both languages" (p. v).

The practices described previously are ways in which bilingualism is used in all types of educational programs for emergent bilinguals. These heteroglossic bilingual practices are consonant with theoretical and empirical evidence for how home language practices support students' development of language for academic purposes. These bilingual instructional practices serve as important instructional scaffolds.

Translanguaging Pedagogy

A pedagogical approach based on translanguaging theoretical perspectives that we considered in Chapter 4 supports and *extends* the heteroglossic bilingual instructional practices described previously. Traditionally, the teaching of English to emergent bilinguals in the United States has been perceived as simply adding an autonomous box of a separate language that could be completely ignored and left behind. To discuss bilingual development, García has often provided teachers with the alternative image of a thread of pearls instead of a separate box. Teachers who base their understandings of language development on translanguaging theory perceive their task as adding new language features and practices, new pearls, to the students' existing rich linguistic repertoire, and not simply a separate autonomous language. By adding new features to the bilingual students' thread of pearls, these teachers understand that emergent bilinguals will always have access to their own pearls and use them agentively in different interactions. Instruction would then focus on providing interactional affordances to emergent bilinguals so that they could use and select features and practices from their repertoire depending on different social contexts and diverse messages. Sometimes bilingual teachers may offer opportunities for students to select and use features of what is seen as one named language or the other in order to develop the students' biliteracy, an important goal of bilingual instruction. Other times, the teachers may offer bilingual students opportunities to engage with their full unitary language repertoire, freeing them from the monolingual social norms of named languages. Always, however, the students' rich unitary language repertoire is leveraged. A translanguaging pedagogy is not simply the use of what is considered the student's first language (Li Wei & García, 2022).

A translanguaging pedagogy is always critical (Selzter, 2019 and 2022), and rests on the idea of teaching as a decolonial process. That is, a translanguaging pedagogy adopts a decolonial logic of language, enabling students to use their full semiotic repertoire rather than restricting them to the use of what schools consider language—a standard that rarely takes into account the ways in which minoritized speakers do language (García et al., in press).

A translanguaging pedagogy is especially useful to educate the many Native Americans whose language practices have been decimated through massacres, forced displacement, exclusion, and schooling. It can assist these minoritized speakers to engage in a recursive dynamic bilingual process to reclaim their own ancestral language practices for their own good, and not simply to be able to use the named language as reconstructed by linguists with good intentions. Translanguaging pedagogy *is more than a simple scaffold*; it leverages the unitary language repertoire of bilingual speakers and can shape their social transformation (Sánchez & García, 2020). It is not simply about using the students' first language, as in the instructional practices described previously as heteroglossic bilingual instructional practices (see also Li Wei & García, 2022). Instead, a translanguaging pedagogy acknowledges that the students' *home language practices* are not simply a first language, a mother tongue, or a home language but are much more complex and dynamic. Because language is done in situ, in moment-to-moment interactions, bilingual students, living in the United States, are doing language in homes and communities where language use is not restricted to the standard definitions of what is considered English, Spanish, Chinese, and so on. Translanguaging pedagogies recognize, as we said before, the bilingual students' complex language use and leverage the students' full semiotic repertoire (i.e., linguistic along with other modes), while at the same time recognizing named languages as important social constructions with colonial baggage.

Li Wei and García (2022) give examples of how translanguaging pedagogies *as a decolonizing project* do not rely on students' first language but on the concept of *repertoire*. As we said before, students must engage with their semiotic repertoires that have been assembled through their lived experiences, including their sense of themselves, of belonging, and of power, in relationship to themselves and to others. Adopting a translanguaging pedagogy as a decolonizing project disrupts the concept of standardized named languages that nation-states and their institutions have constructed (García et al., 2021). In so doing, a translanguaging pedagogy *transforms* practices in schools, as well as societal views of such practices, and develops in students a critical stance toward normed standardized languages (for more on the transformative potential of translanguaging pedagogy, see chapters in Sánchez and García, 2022).

A translanguaging pedagogy is not simply a series of strategies but a philosophy of language and education that is centered on bilingual minoritized communities (García & Li Wei, 2014). It leverages *all* the language practices that bilingual students bring to school. Our understanding of translanguaging pedagogy does not differentiate between spontaneous translanguaging and pedagogical translanguaging, as does, for example, Cenoz and Gorter (2022). For us, *the spontaneous translanguaging of bilingual students in classrooms is in itself pedagogical.*

Because emergent bilinguals are always embodying their translanguaging, educating them cannot be a matter of isolating or compartmentalizing one language from the other, using one language in support of another, or simply promoting "transfer" from one language to another. A translanguaging pedagogy values and supports the translanguaging practices that are the norm in bilingual communities, thus having the potential to transform the contempt with which bilingual fluid language practices are often held by schools and majority society (Canagarajah, 2011).

García and Kleyn (2016) summarize the transformative impact on educators who take up translanguaging theory:

> A theory of translanguaging can be transformative for educators. Once educators start looking at language from the point of view of the bilingual learner, and not simply at the named language with its prescribed features, everything changes. Educators then teach in order to discover what, in the child's arsenal of language features, can be enhanced through interactions with others and texts that have different language features. They do not tell students to stop using their own language features or to stop drawing on them for learning. Educators become co-learners (Li Wei, 2014), instead of simply identifying as teachers who transmit a canon of linguistic knowledge. Equipped with translanguaging theory, educators leverage the students' full language repertoires to teach and assess, enabling a more socially just and equitable education for bilingual students. (p. 17)

García, Johnson, and Seltzer (2017) identify four instructional purposes of translanguaging pedagogy:

1. Supporting students as they engage with and comprehend complex content and texts;
2. Providing opportunities for students to develop linguistic practices for academic contexts;
3. Making space for students' bilingualism and bilingual ways of knowing; and
4. Supporting students' social–emotional development and bilingual identities.

These four purposes work together to advance social justice and to ensure that bilingual learners are educated for success and not just to conform to monolingual norms. With the help of translanguaging pedagogy, the language practices of minoritized speakers cease to be an excuse to deny access to rich educational experiences and instead are leveraged to educate deeply and justly (García, Seltzer, & Witt 2018).

García, Johnson, and Seltzer (2017) identify three interrelated strands that define a translanguaging pedagogy:

1. The translanguaging stance,
2. The translanguaging design, and
3. The translanguaging shift.

Teachers of minoritized bilingual students must have a *translanguaging stance*—the philosophical, ideological, or belief system that students' various and wide-ranging language practices work together and are a resource for learning. Educators with this stance believe that the classroom space must promote collaboration across language and complex multimodal practices, content understandings, students, peoples, home, and school. A translanguaging stance also includes the belief that to truly assess what bilingual students know and can do, both in language and content, students must be allowed to access all the features of their language repertoire, as is the privilege of monolingual students, instead of having to work with less than half of their repertoire (for work on translanguaging assessment, see Azcenzi-Moreno & Seltzer, 2021; Schissel, 2020. See also Chapter 8, this volume).

The *translanguaging design* involves the careful planning of (1) the multilingual resources needed in the classroom and their use, (2) the grouping of students, (3) the unit/lesson planning that includes not only content and language objectives but also translanguaging objectives, (4) pedagogical strategies that open up translanguaging spaces where students can engage with their full repertoire of resources, and (5) translanguaging assessments.

Finally, the term *translanguaging shifts* refers to the many moment-by-moment decisions that teachers make all the time. It indicates a teacher's flexibility and willingness to change the course of the lesson and assessment, as well as the language use, in response to the students' *translanguaging corriente*, the dynamic flow of emotions, thoughts, understandings, and language practices with which students always engage in classrooms.

U.S. scholars increasingly have been providing evidence of how translanguaging enhances understanding of content considered academic and extends the emergent bilinguals' linguistic and semiotic repertoire to incorporate features also considered standard in U.S. schools, as it gives them space to be and express themselves fully. This is evident in ESL/ENL classrooms (see Ebe, 2016; Woodley, 2016), in transitional bilingual education classrooms (Collins & Cioè-Peña, 2016; Kleyn, 2016; Sayer, 2013; Seltzer & Collins, 2016), or in dual-language bilingual education classrooms (Espinosa & Herrera, 2016; Gort & Sembiante, 2015; Palmer et al., 2014).

Developing translanguaging pedagogical strategies that support the education of emergent bilinguals has been the focus of the aforementioned project, CUNY-NYSIEB (2021), which has worked with all types of schools and teachers with large numbers of emergent bilinguals to improve their education. Its vision rests on the development of bilingual students' understandings of their practices as translanguaging, and of teachers able to leverage them in instruction.[2]

Educators who understand the power of translanguaging encourage emergent bilinguals to use their home language practices actively to think, reflect, feel, and extend their meaning-making repertoire. They also encourage students to explore other meaning-making cues that accompany speech: embodied modes such as intonation and other vocal phenomena, gesture, facial expressions, bodily-emotional reactions, and so on. And educators work with emergent bilinguals to ensure that the new language features become appropriated into a repertoire that students perceive and feel as *their own*. English cannot be their "second" language. Instead, the new linguistic features of what schools call "English" must become part of bilingual students' own complex language system. Students cannot simply perceive and use these new features as if they were part of a new, alien, "second language" system. A translanguaging pedagogical approach ensures that students become *agentive* users of the linguistic and other communicative sign systems that they have available to make meaning and learn. By immersing students in opportunities to practice language for authentic and complex operations, students become agentive in *using language for their own purposes, and not always that of others.*

In understanding translanguaging as part of the unitary system of bilingual speakers, educators *transform* ESL/ENL and bilingual education. Adopting translanguaging in ESL/ENL classrooms means that the language practices of *all* students can be used as a resource for learning at all times, even if the teacher's language practices do not overlap with those of students. In bilingual education, it means that *all* the students' language practices, beyond those that reflect the two standardized versions used as a medium of instruction, can be leveraged. It also means that educators judiciously open up translanguaging spaces even when following strict language allocation policies in their bilingual programs (see Sánchez et al., 2017).

García and Li Wei (2014) acknowledge that in today's dynamic world of interaction, "students need practice and engagement in translanguaging, as much as they need practice of standard features used for academic purposes" (pp. 71–72). Emergent bilingual students must be given agency to be creative and critical, "able to co-construct their language expertise, recognize each other as resources, and act on their knowing and doing" (p. 75).

Discussing language practices in a digital age, Cope, Kalantzis, and Tzirides (2024) have proposed the idea of *transposition* to build on the concept of translanguaging. As used by Cope and colleagues, transposition highlights the fluid nature of multimodal meaning-making and underscores the need to rethink theoretical discussions and pedagogical practices in the digital age. We revisit this expanded view in Chapter 9.

Critical Multilingual Raciolinguistic Awareness

Emergent bilingual students foreground language practices that differ significantly from the ways in which language is used in school. These different language practices are often manifestations of social, racial, political, and economic struggles and of histories of subjugation. Instruction that builds on critical multilingual raciolinguistic awareness builds students' understandings of the social, political, racial, and economic struggles surrounding the use of languages (see Fairclough, 1992, 1999; García, 2017; Kleifgen, 2009; Kleifgen & Bond, 2009; Makoni & Pennycook, 2007; van Dijk, 2008). In so doing, they aim to develop students' critical consciousness (Cervantes-Soon et al., 2021; Palmer et al., 2019). Many sociolinguists today are focusing on the politics (not policy) of language through the study of what has become known with the Spanish term *glotopolítica*. This work, stemming from Latin America (Arnoux, 2014; del Valle, 2017), reminds us that one cannot study language unless one centers geopolitical politics having to do with domination (García & Alvis, 2019).

Shohamy (2006) reminds us that it is important for all students to reflect on ways in which languages are used to exclude and discriminate. In calling for ways to work against raciolinguistic ideologies of language inappropriateness, Flores and Rosa (2015) argue that students need to become more aware of the way that language-majority speakers listen to and perceive the linguistic practices of minoritized speakers as deficient, regardless of how closely they follow supposed rules of appropriateness (on this point, see also DeGraff, 2005, 2009).

Instruction that leverages students' critical multilingual raciolinguistic awareness generates greater understandings of the intersectionality between language, geopolitics, race, socioeconomic status, and gender. This awareness also helps students understand how language use in society has been naturalized, falsely claiming that only what are constituted as standard features and uses of language are considered legitimate. Foucault (1979) has argued that this process of establishing an idealized norm of conduct and then punishing individuals who deviate from it is a tactic of social control. This naturalization of language constitutes what Foucault (1979) calls "disciplinary power."

When teachers make students aware that named languages are socially constructed, and thus socially changeable to give voice to others, young people are given agency to redress the historical oppression of certain linguistic groups. As García (2017) has said, this can generate "not only a new order of discourse, but also a new praxis, capable of changing the social order of what it means to 'language' in school" (p. 269).

One useful critical multilingual awareness activity is to have students of different language backgrounds read the same news item published in various languages. The students can analyze how the discourse (and the content) varies across languages and reflect on the reasons for the variation. They also can make recordings and transcriptions of their own rendering of the news in their home languages and reflect on the differences between their language practices and those of the media.

In classrooms with older students, teachers can engage them in becoming critical ethnographers of communities by looking at the ways in which different languages are represented in public spaces—what many call *linguistic landscapes*—and interpreting why they appear as such (Gorter et al., 2012; Landry & Bourhis, 1997; Shohamy & Gorter, 2009). Students can take photographs of signs in the community for analysis of similarities or differences across languages and reflect on the variations of use and the different messages that are communicated. Students can also analyze bilingual signs with their varied designs of text. Other students can analyze the hierarchy of power with regard to languages by studying the order in which languages appear in print, the nature of signage, and what all these different social positionings mean.

Ethnographies of language communities that are part of critical multilingual raciolinguistic awareness practices must also include spoken language. Teachers can ask students, for example, to observe and compare language use in different neighborhoods and places and explore questions such as: Which languages are selected for use in different neighborhood locales—businesses, government offices, places of worship, parks? Students can be asked to explore language use in an upscale store and in a *bodega* in a Latine neighborhood, and answer questions such as: Which clients are attended to in service encounters—English speakers or speakers of other languages—and what are the social and racial indices of the speakers? What are the language practices of the employees and the clients? How do they differ? Why?

Educators also can engage students in studying the languages represented in newspapers and magazines found in their neighborhood stands and in the media—television, radio, and the internet. How do language choice and use differ, and who are the target readers or listeners? Students can critically analyze how different language groups are represented in film, television, and other media outlets.

Then, to ensure that students reflect on translanguaging in society, students can generate banks of examples in media and print, as well as spoken language. These examples should identify sources and keep in mind different audiences and interlocutors. The problem sets then can be subjected to further analysis and become the focus of explicit language and literacy instruction.

The best critical multilingual raciolinguistic awareness instruction encourages students to study their own school: What are the different language practices they hear and see in their school? How do these differ by interlocutor, or task? What is the meaning of this language use? In describing language and literacy practices within the classroom, students can draw from the data they have gathered outside the classroom and in the community for comparative analysis. This comparison can serve well to help students anchor language use in particular domains and for specific purposes, and then reflect on its social meaning.

As part of instruction in critical multilingual raciolinguistic awareness, educators may also present students with an explicit curriculum on multilingualism in the United States. Educators might engage students in researching the following questions: What are the language practices in different regions of the United States, and what are the historical, social, and economic reasons for those differences? Where do bilingual communities live, and what are the differences in their schooling? Why do they live there? How did this come about?

Students looking beyond the United States can be engaged in questions such as: What is the sociolinguistic profile of different nation-states? Whose language practices are represented as official or national? Why? How did this come about? Students can make links between socioeconomic characteristics, race and other sociodemographic attributes, and the status of named languages within different countries. They also can search the internet as they become aware of the variation in scripts used to write different languages and explore the relationship, in some cases, between scripts and cultural history.

Complex Dynamic Language/Literacy Use

Educators who understand theories and empirical evidence about bilingualism in education are aware that language and literacy growth is linked to authentic and rich use of language. For this to happen, educators must trust that emergent bilinguals already have a "language architecture" (Flores, 2020), that is, a rich and complex foundation for a solid education. Often, educators worry that there is not sufficient time in the school day to engage in the kind of analyses previously described while covering the state-required academic standards. This concern stems, again, from the dichotomous framing of school language and literacy tasks as academic and students' authentic language practices as nonacademic. To challenge this, and to make evident the transformative possibilities of shifting perspectives about emergent bilinguals' language practices, Flores (2020) notes that, like architects, language users adhere to broad parameters but also make unique decisions that reflect their voice to effectively communicate messages. Standards should encourage students to be "language architects" by doing close readings of texts and discourses, critically analyzing an author's and speaker's language choices, and applying this knowledge as they use language for specific purposes. Viewing academic language through this lens, educators can recognize that students, especially those from racialized backgrounds, already engage in critical analyses of language and understand language choice and meaning through their cultural practices. Flores points to Latine students discussing language variations and pragmatics, such as the differences between "habichuelas" and "frijoles," debating the appropriateness of "farted" versus "passed gas," or questioning the gendered nature of Spanish. These experiences highlight that bilingual students already possess and practice valuable language architecture skills relevant to academic tasks required by state standards that teachers can build upon (Martínez & Morales, 2014).

Kibler, Valdés, and Walqui (2021) point to the importance of critical dialogue in the classroom to promote equity. Teachers present complex ideas that develop the students' existing metacognitive skills—that is, curricular plans that enable learners to successfully approach academic tasks and help them monitor their thinking, thereby creating greater metalinguistic awareness (Walqui, 2006). Effective teachers do not oversimplify the English language or offer remedial instruction. Instead, they offer intensive support while providing challenging instruction (see Walqui & van Lier, 2010). This is consonant with Cummins's (2000) view that "language and content will be acquired most successfully when students are challenged cognitively but provided with the contextual and linguistic supports or scaffolds required for successful task completion" (p. 71).

These supports or scaffolds can also include:

- Contextualization through translanguaging support that includes the full linguistic repertoire consisting not only of what is understood as "the linguistic," but also through body language, gestures, manipulatives, realia, technology, word walls, and graphic organizers;
- Modeling thorough think-alouds and verbalization of actions and processes of lessons;
- Bridging and schema building by weaving new information into preexisting structures of meaning;
- Thematic planning by which vocabulary and concepts are repeated naturally;
- Multiple entry points, by which some children might use their home language practices, whereas others might be able to conform to the English language of the lesson. Still others might use gestures or drawings; and
- Routines in which language is used consistently and predictably. (García, 2009a, p. 331)

Emergent bilinguals also may need some overt instruction in which the use of certain meaning-making strategies is made explicit. Genesee and his colleagues (2006) summarize their findings from a major meta-analysis by saying: "The best recommendation to emerge from our review favors instruction that combines interactive and direct approaches" (p. 140). Swinney and Velasco (2011) provide guidance to teachers of emergent bilinguals on how to implement what they call "a curriculum of talk" in order to build language use. They also include structures of balanced literacy that support emergent bilinguals. Espinosa and Ascenzi-Moreno (2021) propose that, to root literacy work in the strength of children, the educators' gaze must be turned toward the student and not simply outward toward external standards.

Vocabulary is a central area in teaching emergent bilinguals (Pollard-Durodola, 2020). The consensus among scholars is that vocabulary instruction is important, but that despite the importance of helping students break down words to build meaning (Kieffer & Lesaux, 2007), word study cannot be isolated from its use in narratives, discussions, explanations, and other forms of extended discourse. Words identified in the extended discourse of texts can be identified, studied, posted on word walls, and reused in oral discussion and writing (Carlo et al., 2004). Snow (2017) summarizes:

Everything we know about vocabulary acquisition suggests strongly that children acquire large vocabularies in the context of responsive interactions about topics of interest to them . . . most reliably when those topics are shared with adults, in discussions and negotiations about content. (n.p.)

All disciplines have different linguistic registers, and students must be made aware of such differences (Gibbons, 2002) through actual interactions with the complex texts in which they appear (Wong-Fillmore & Fillmore, n.d.). Emergent bilinguals need support in understanding *juicy sentences* (Wong-Fillmore & Fillmore, n.d.), a process whereby each day, a teacher selects a sentence or two from the texts students are reading to discuss in conversation. The students and teacher then engage in instructional conversation about the linguistic and discourse features of the sentence, thus setting the context for unpacking the content of a text. But instruction for emergent bilinguals about the explicit features of language needs always to be embedded within extended, rich instructional discourses.

The approach to teaching literacy to emergent bilinguals has been deeply monolingual. When emergent bilinguals are taught to read a text written in English (or in a language other than English), they are told to think only in the language of the text. But this advice goes against the common knowledge that to comprehend a written text one needs to build on *background knowledge*. Indeed, bilingual students' thinking cannot be delimited by the language of the text, but by their own language practices and experiences. Bilingual students' engagement with text, whether oral or written, can only happen if they bring themselves into the experience holistically (Cervantes-Soon & García, 2023; García & Cervantes-Soon, 2023).

García and Cervantes-Soon (2023) outline five interrelated principles of literacy education for bilingual learners. These principles are based on findings of different literacy scholars working with emergent bilinguals who have taken up a critical translanguaging perspective. While we indicate in parenthesis some relevant works, there is much more research supporting these principles.

1. Centering bilingual learners' language, experiences, and complex knowledge system as strength (Cervantes-Soon & Carrillo, 2016; de los Ríos & Seltzer, 2017; Degollado, Núñez, & Romero, 2021; Espinosa & Ascenzi-Moreno, 2021; García & Kleifgen, 2019; Harvey-Torres & Degollado, 2021; Lau, Juby-Smith, & Desbiens, 2017; Nuñez, 2022, 2023; Nuñez & Urrieta, 2021)
2. Working en comunidad and collaboratively with students, teachers, families, and communities (España & Herrera, 2020)
3. Identifying temas, textos, and translanguaging (España & Herrera, 2020) by starting with a topic that is meaningful to the students, finding suitable texts that reflect those topics, and employing translanguaging in ways described previously
4. Ensuring that educators are co-learners and teach to raise critical consciousness (Chang-Bacon et al., 2022; España & Herrera, 2020; Heiman, Cervantes-Soon, & Hurie, 2021; Jin & Liu, 2023)
5. Adopting fair literacy assessment (Ascenzi-Moreno, 2018; Ascenzi-Moreno et al., 2024; Bauer et al., 2020; Noguerón-Liu, 2020; Noguerón-Liu et al., 2020; Steele, Dovchin, & Oliver, 2022)

All scholars and educators working with emergent bilinguals agree that students must engage with complex texts and multifaceted dialogic conversations. Pedagogical strategies must acknowledge and leverage the students' translanguaging and knowledge system, as they not only scaffold instruction but transform lives.

EDUCATING EMERGENT BILINGUALS: INCORPORATING MULTILINGUAL PEDAGOGIES

This chapter has presented ways of transforming pedagogies to leverage the dynamic language practices of emergent bilinguals. It has reviewed how to use heteroglossic bilingual instructional practices, how to develop translanguaging pedagogical practices, how to raise students' critical raciolinguistic consciousness, and how to ensure that the complexity of language and literacy use is reflected in instruction. The semiotic meaning-making potential of human beings is not limited just to what we call "language." Also important are bodily-emotional experiences and modes that accompany speech. We will elaborate on these additional semiotic resources in Chapter 9. In the next chapter, we look at the role of the curriculum in either restricting or expanding opportunities for emergent bilinguals. We also consider the role of educators in implementing the curriculum.

STUDY QUESTIONS

1. What is the situation today regarding the use of languages other than English in U.S. education? How is it done in your school district?
2. What does language compartmentalization mean? What are some of the ways in which this is done? What are its potentials and drawbacks?
3. How could bilingualism include all students? Describe some ways in which you might be able to do this in your classroom.
4. How might teachers use the home language practices of their students for more effective academic instruction? Describe one way in which this might be done regardless of program structure.
5. What are translanguaging pedagogies, and how might they be used in classrooms? What is the epistemological difference between bilingual instructional strategies and translanguaging strategies?
6. Describe a critical multilingual raciolinguistic awareness activity that you might conduct. Explain why it would be important in your own teaching context.
7. What are some ways in which teachers of emergent bilinguals could help them engage with complex texts?
8. Why is instruction in the decontextualized isolated features of language not appropriate for emergent bilinguals?

CHAPTER 6

Curriculum and Other Pedagogical Practices

When we narrow the program so that there is only a limited array of areas in which assessment occurs and performance is honored, youngsters whose aptitudes and interests lie elsewhere are going to be marginalized in our schools. The more we diversify those opportunities, the more equity we are going to have because we're going to provide wider opportunities for youngsters to find what it is they are good at.

—Elliot Eisner, 2001

In this chapter, we will:

- Review theoretical constructs that support curricular opportunities and practices for emergent bilinguals:
  - » Orientation of social justice and linguistic human rights,
  - » A curriculum that is challenging and creative,
  - » Pedagogy that is transformative and culturally sustaining, and
  - » Learning that is collaborative and agentic.
- Identify inequalities in curricular opportunities and resources:
  - » Inequitable curricular opportunities: lack of early childhood programs, remedial education and tracking high-stakes accountability pressures, special education placements, exclusion from gifted and AP classes;
  - » Inequitable resources: inadequate instructional materials, school facilities, and funding; and
  - » Inequitable access to high-quality educators.
- Consider some alternative practices:
  - » A challenging inclusive curriculum that starts early, and
  - » Preparing caring, creative, and qualified teachers.

In this chapter, we focus on curricular opportunities and practices affecting the education of emergent bilinguals. Gándara and Contreras (2009) say: "The problem of English learners' underachievement . . . is more likely related to the quality of education that these students receive, regardless of the language of instruction" (p. 145). We consider here the *quality* of the education that emergent bilingual students are receiving, beyond the issue of language or other meaning-making modes of instruction; in doing so, we continue to give attention to the central question in this book: *What does research tell us about how best to educate and assess emergent bilingual students? Are we using accepted theories and evidence in the education of these students?* Just as we observed a gap in Chapters 4 and 5 between language education theory and practice, we note in this chapter a gap between accepted theoretical foundations for curricula and practices and the classroom realities for many emergent bilinguals. We conclude the chapter by laying out alternative practices that can do much to accelerate the academic achievement of these students.

THEORETICAL CURRICULAR AND PEDAGOGICAL CONSTRUCTS

In this section, we identify three theoretical constructs that promote equity in both curriculum and practice for emergent bilinguals—an orientation of social justice and linguistic human rights, a curriculum that is challenging and creative, and a pedagogy that is transformative and collaborative.

Social Justice and Linguistic Human Rights

The idea of teaching for social justice has roots in U.S. social history of democracy and oppression. Consistent with defending the basic human rights and freedoms guaranteed under the Bill of Rights of the U.S. Constitution, educating for social justice also requires that teachers and students act in the construction of a socially just world. This was the case, for example, in the Freedom School movement of the 1960s, when Black students in the segregated South participated in programs that not only engaged them in a rigorous academic curriculum but also in a citizenship curriculum, enabling them to understand their rights and their role in bringing about change (Hale, 2011; Morrell, 2008). Movements to teach for social justice have been inspired by the work of the Brazilian scholar Paolo Freire, who urges educators to engage students in a dialectal praxis so that they can act upon the world in order to transform it.

Rights to education are at the core of these social justice efforts. In this regard, UNESCO (1960) has been most influential. In the UNESCO Convention against Discrimination in Education (adopted December 14, 1960 and entered into force May 22, 1962), Article 1 reads:

> For the purposes of this Convention, the term "discrimination" includes any distinction, exclusion, limitation or preference which, being based on race, colour, sex, language, religion, political or other opinion, national or social origin, economic condition or birth, has the purpose or effect of nullifying or impairing equality or treatment in education. . . .

The focus on social justice and human rights, coupled with the rise of critical theory on the role that language has played in asymmetrical power relations (see

García et al., 2017; García et al., 2021), has led to increasing calls for linguistic human rights (Skutnabb-Kangas, 2000, 2006; Skutnabb-Kangas & Phillipson, 1994, 2017). Skutnabb-Kangas and Phillipson (1994) identify two categories of linguistic human rights that are important to consider in educating emergent bilinguals:

- Individual rights, including the right to identify with one's own language and to use it both in and out of school, and the right to learn the official language of the state; and
- Community rights, including the right of minoritized groups to establish and maintain schools and other educational institutions and to control their curricula.

Taking these categories into account, we can argue that in the United States, linguistic human rights are not fully observed. For example, although many languages other than English are spoken, the use of these languages in everyday situations is sometimes considered suspect (Lippi-Green, 1997). Most of these languages are excluded from schools; in high schools, classes to learn and develop languages other than English may be offered, but these usually only include Spanish and French and to a much lesser degree German, Latin, Mandarin Chinese, and Japanese (American Councils for International Education, 2017). And most dual-language bilingual education programs are in Spanish, followed by Chinese, leaving numerous U.S. peoples such as speakers of Arabic, Diné, Haitian Creole, and Vietnamese with little opportunity to develop their bilingualism and biliteracy. As for minoritized groups' linguistic rights, although these groups have the right to establish their own complementary schools where their languages and cultures are taught after school and on weekends, they do not receive state funding (García, Zakharia, & Otcu, 2013; Peyton, Ranard, & McGinnis, 2001). One of the questions for educators, then, is how to extend these language rights to all students in the curriculum. Social justice and linguistic human rights are the philosophical values that motivate a challenging and creative curriculum for emergent bilinguals.

A Curriculum That Is Challenging and Creative

Research on teaching and learning indicates that all students need to be given opportunities to participate in challenging yet supportive academic work that promotes deep disciplinary knowledge and encourages higher-order thinking skills. Goldenberg (2008) summarizes:

> As a general rule, all students tend to benefit from clear goals and learning objectives; meaningful, challenging, and motivating contexts; a curriculum rich with content; well-designed, clearly structured, and appropriately paced instruction; active engagement and participation; opportunities to practice, apply, and transfer new learning; feedback on correct and incorrect responses; periodic review and practice; frequent assessments to gauge progress, with re-teaching as needed; and opportunities to interact with other students in motivating and appropriately structured contexts. (p. 17)

And yet, as Gibbons (2009) points out, "the development of curriculum distinguished by intellectual quality and the development of higher-order thinking has in reality rarely been a major focus of program planning for EL learners" (p. 2).

Many have called attention to the importance of maintaining high expectations for emergent bilinguals and of providing them with challenging academic work (Carrasquillo & Rodríguez, 2002; Walqui, 2006), while simultaneously providing the necessary supports for them to be successful (Walqui & Bunch, 2019). As with all students, emergent bilinguals require practice in complex thinking; they deserve teachers who engage them in combining ideas to synthesize, generalize, explain, hypothesize, or arrive at some conclusion or interpretation (Walqui et al., 2004). Speaking about the importance of an action-based perspective of language for emergent bilinguals, van Lier and Walqui (2012) explain:

> Language is an inseparable part of all human action, intimately connected to all other forms of action, physical, social and symbolic. Language is thus an expression of agency, embodied and embedded in the environment. . . . In a classroom context, an action-based perspective means that ELs engage in meaningful activities (projects, presentations, investigations) that engage their interest and that encourage language growth through perception, interaction, planning, research, discussion, and co-construction of academic products of various kinds. During such action-based work, language development occurs when it is carefully scaffolded by the teacher, as well as by the students working together. (n.p.)

Gibbons (2009) advances seven intellectual practices in the education of emergent bilinguals:

1. Students engage with the key ideas and concepts of the discipline in ways that reflect how "experts" in the field think and reason.
2. Students transform what they have learned into a different form for use in a new context or for a different audience.
3. Students make links between concrete knowledge and abstract theoretical knowledge.
4. Students engage in substantive conversation.
5. Students make connections between the spoken and written language of the subject and other discipline-related ways of making meaning.
6. Students take a critical stance toward knowledge and information.
7. Students use metalanguage in the context of learning about other things.

Alongside challenge and richness, it is important to provide students, especially emergent bilinguals, with a creative curriculum that provides space for them to experiment and innovate (Greene, 1995). Learning how to make and communicate meaning in another language is in itself a highly creative and innovative activity (Ward et al., 1997). But when additional meaning-making resources— other modes—such as those made available through the arts and technology—are combined with the spoken and written modes and incorporated into the learning process, students can experience a much more empowering and engaging curriculum. Over the past two decades, an increasing body of research has highlighted the advantages of multimodality for emergent bilingual students, such as broadening linguistic skills (Kim, 2018; Smith et al., 2021), and empowering identity expression and criticality (Ajayi, 2015; Cimasko & Shin, 2017). From reading, writing, and performing Mexican *corridos* (de los Ríos, 2018), creating digital aboriginal Dreamtime stories (Mills et al., 2016), or incorporating play and traditional dances (Ascenzi-Moreno, Espinosa, & Lehner-Quam, 2022; Machimana & Genis, 2024) to using spoken word poetry (Burton, 2023) and graphic novels in the critical analysis of social issues (Barter-Storm & Wik, 2020; Chun, 2009), multimodal practices can also transform English-centric classrooms by challenging conventional views on language and literacy and centering students' voices and funds of knowledge, which are typically disregarded or subjugated (Smith et al., 2021).

In sum, responsive schools will not only provide emergent bilinguals with a challenging and rich curriculum but also with a creative one. By having teams of multicultural and multilingual students, who work collaboratively as equals using all their linguistic and cultural resources to address educational challenges presented to them, schools can foster the creative conceptual expansion of all students. To do so, schools must have teachers who can deliver a transformative and culturally sustaining pedagogy, the subject of our next section.

Pedagogies That Are Transformative and Culturally Sustaining

Many scholars, working to redress the educational inequities affecting minoritized students, have advocated several practices, all with the potential to transform society. We have already referred to the potential of translanguaging as part of that transformation.

Focusing on teaching by building on the ethnolinguistic identities of language-minority students, other scholars have advocated a *culturally relevant pedagogy* (CRP) for minority students (Gay, 2002; Ladson-Billings, 1994, 1995; Valdés, 1996; Villegas & Lucas, 2002). Paris and Alim (2014) have gone beyond the "relevant" aspects to propose what they call a *culturally sustaining pedagogy (CSP)*. They explain the difference:

> CSP seeks to perpetuate and foster—to sustain—linguistic, literate and cultural pluralism as part of the democratic project of schooling and as a needed response to demographic and social change. CSP, then, links a focus on sustaining pluralism through education to challenges of social justice and change. (p. 88)

Culturally sustaining pedagogies' foundational tenets can help shape the curriculum in transformative ways. First, they seek community agency in the development of activities, units of study, and other classroom/school practices and decision-making processes. Second, they integrate the authentic language practices of students and their communities and challenge the monolingual standardized English-centric ideology of schools, which, as revealed in our extensive discussion in previous chapters, is inherent in translanguaging pedagogy. Third, they incorporate cultural and historicized content that centers nondominant voices, narratives, practices, and perspectives in the literature, multimodal texts, and classroom discourse and practices.

Thus, culturally sustaining pedagogy seeks not only to promote equity across communities but also to ensure access and opportunity by demanding that outcomes not be centered only on "[w]hite, middle-class, monolingual and monocultural norms of educational achievement" (Paris & Alim, 2014, p. 95). This brings attention to the fundamental role that schooling plays in assuming and ascribing students' identities, the significance of language in shaping identity, and the students' own agency in negotiating them (Crump, 2014; Chávez-Moreno, 2020). As previously mentioned, research on emergent bilinguals has emphasized the importance of affirming students' identities through the curriculum and language practices of the classroom (Cummins, 2000; Nuñez, Villarreal, & DeJulio, 2021). Nevertheless, there is a risk of conceptualizing identity as a process devoid of political significance, an uncomplicated validation of student experience (Giroux, 1988). Therefore, besides aligning classroom experiences with the students' cultural and linguistic practices, culturally sustaining pedagogies attempt to counteract inequitable power relations in society and empower minority students to use their own repertoire of practices (Giroux, 1988). Along these lines, scholars in the field of bilingual education have emphasized the need to foster critical consciousness for education to be truly transformative (Cervantes-Soon et al., 2017; Heiman et al., 2023), noting that it can be traced back as the propelling force in the race-radical roots of bilingual education (Darder, 2012; Flores, 2016; Pacheco & Chávez-Moreno, 2022). The emphasis on critical consciousness can help shape what knowledge systems, language practices, materials, texts, objects or topics of study, histories, narratives, assessments, and activities are prioritized and/or interrogated and the kinds of interactions that are cultivated.

Race, language, gender, social class, ability, immigration/citizenship status, and other social categories place us at various levels of social hierarchies depending on the unique sociopolitical relations and histories of our local contexts. In U.S. contexts, even within bilingual programs, not all students or teachers embody the same degrees of privilege or critical consciousness. Thus, instead of regarding minoritized emergent bilingual children as passively accepting school knowledge, treatment, and discourses without question, Pacheco and Chávez-Moreno (2022) posit that these youth are already actively involved in critically evaluating how power dynamics, language, identities, and school environments impact their daily experiences. They emphasize the importance of acknowledging and building upon the critical evaluations made by minoritized youth, advocating for what they term *bilingual education for self-determination against oppression (BESO)* (p. 253). Additionally, they argue that students express their critical assessments within the classroom, and it is the responsibility of educators, researchers, and others to recognize and respond to them. Therefore, if critical listening is to be practiced in the classroom, some voices, experiences, and perspectives, typically those characterized by privileged normative whiteness, should step down from the center, while the voices and knowledges that are typically disregarded or silenced should be granted thoughtful attention. This also means that critical listening involves paying thoughtful attention to how minoritized emergent bilingual students manifest their critical appraisals, even if silently, and to provide the tools and space for their interrogation of power to be heard. These are only a few examples of how the curriculum can be infused with actions toward critical consciousness and for the self-determination of minoritized emergent bilinguals.

Collaborative and Agentic Learning

Research on teaching and learning has also validated the importance of pedagogy that builds on meaningful collaborative social practices in which students try out ideas and actions and, thus, socially construct their learning (Vygotsky, 1978). According to Vygotsky's sociocultural theory, language is not only a means of communication but also a tool for thought. In this context, language serves as a vehicle for agency; that is, for the individual's ability to act intentionally, make choices, and exert influence over the environment by interacting with others and participating in cultural practices. In language learning, agency is evident in the active engagement of learners as they use language to communicate, solve problems, and negotiate meaning within social contexts. Learners exercise agency when they initiate conversations, ask questions, express opinions and feelings, and negotiate interpretations of texts or experiences. Agentic learning thus entails the capacity of learners to make choices and impact the manner and content of their learning experiences, thereby enabling them to enhance their skills across various domains including social and academic interactions, emotional development, cognitive abilities, cultural understanding, and physical activities (Adair & Colegrove, 2021).

Lave and Wenger (1991) describe learning within a given social group as a process of participation that moves gradually from being "legitimately peripheral" to being fully engaged in what they call a *community of practice*: "a set of relations among persons, activity and world, over time and in relation with other tangential and overlapping communities of practice" (p. 98). This social view of learning and pedagogy takes the position that emergent bilinguals do not come to "possess" or "have" English or any other language; rather, they learn by "doing" and "using" practices and features associated with English repeatedly over the course of a lifetime in communities of practice. As van Lier (2000) explains:

> The ecologist will say that knowledge of language for a human is like knowledge of the jungle for an animal. The animal does not have the jungle; it knows how to use the jungle and how to live in it. Perhaps we can say by analogy that we do not have or possess language, but that we learn to use it and to live in it. (p. 253)

A collaborative agentic pedagogy relies, then, on a great deal of practice of talk, or what Tharp et al. (2000) call *instructional conversation* or what Padrón and Waxman (1999) call *teaching through conversation*. We know, for example, that high-quality instruction for emergent bilinguals must include "efforts to increase the scope and sophistication of these students' oral language proficiency"

(August & Shanahan, 2006, p. 448). That is, a focus on reading and writing alone is insufficient to develop emergent bilinguals' abilities to use and live in English or to understand the world in which they live.

To build this community of practice, groups of students need to be engaged in *cooperative learning* (Kagan, 1986; Kagan & McGroarty, 1993). The National Literacy Panel review found that having students work cooperatively on group tasks increases the literacy comprehension of emergent bilinguals (August & Shanahan, 2006). However, in order for this collaborative learning to be agentic, it should be fostered by consistent opportunities that empower students to pursue their interests and utilize their own sense of urgency, curiosity, and enthusiasm to engage with content and with each other (Adair & Colvegrove, 2021).

Despite research that shows the importance of having curricular programs that emphasize social justice and that are academically challenging and creative, and pedagogy that is culturally sustaining, collaborative, and agentic, emergent bilinguals are often excluded from meaningful educational programs and rigorous instruction. We discuss these inequitable curricular and pedagogical practices before proposing what can be done about it.

INEQUITABLE CURRICULAR OPPORTUNITIES AND RESOURCES

Curricular, pedagogical, and educator-quality issues result in inequities in the education of emergent bilinguals. And because high-quality instruction does not happen without adequate resources, funding is needed to provide high-quality education for emergent bilinguals.

Inequitable Curricular Opportunities

It all starts early. The transition to kindergarten tends to be a time of great vulnerability for many emergent bilinguals, as their families are faced with the challenge of navigating a school system and language that are new to them. Because emergent bilingual kindergartners cannot understand English well enough to be assessed in English, from the very beginning they are often placed in remedial education. Therefore, this transition to kindergarten acts as the foundation for persistent gaps in educational achievement, as even minor variations in early learning tend to magnify over the course of K–12 education, particularly for students from low socioeconomic status and minoritized groups (Ansari & Crosnoe, 2018).

It has been shown that early childhood education programs can help narrow gaps in preparation for elementary school, especially among poor children (Haskins & Rouse, 2005; Takanishi, 2004, in Capps et al., 2005). Additionally, researchers have demonstrated the benefits of early childhood education programs that contribute positively to children's health, emotional adjustment, and cognitive functioning (E. García & Gonzalez, 2006; Karoly & Bigelow, 2005). For example, in a study of the effects of a preschool program on poor children in Ypsilanti, Michigan, a control group received no preschool services. At the age of 40, those who had attended preschool had not only increased earnings but also decreased reliance on public assistance and had lower rates of criminal activity and substance abuse (Nores et al., 2005). A study in North Carolina obtained similar results—the group that had attended preschool had higher IQs, increased levels of high school graduation and college attendance, as well as decreased rates of grade retention and rates of special education classification than a control group that did not attend preschool (Barnett & Masse, 2007).

The benefit of preschool education for Latine emergent bilinguals has also been demonstrated (Ackerman & Tazi, 2015). Gormley Jr. (2008), for example, showed that Latine emergent bilinguals in a prekindergarten program did better in all aspects of the Woodcock-Johnson Test and the Woodcock-Muñoz Battery—assessing letter-word identification, spelling, and answers to applied problem items. Tazi (2014) has likewise shown the value of bilingual education programs for these young students. Very young Latine children who participated in bilingual instruction were evaluated by their teachers as more socially competent, more interested and prepared for early academic skills such as literacy and numeracy, and more ready for school. When allowed to use their entire language repertoire, Latine kindergartners schooled bilingually also showed greater use of language and facility in expressing their ideas.

And yet, emergent bilinguals are less likely than their monolingual counterparts to be enrolled in early childhood programs (Espinosa, 2013b). Some research suggests that attending preschool can boost emergent bilinguals' language development and skills in kindergarten (Cooper & Lanza, 2014). If bilingual instruction is provided, not only can the home language be developed by building expressive vocabulary skills, but also other academic and cognitive skills would be advanced, such as the quantitative reasoning competence that is necessary for building foundational mathematical skills (Partika et al., 2021). Therefore, we know that the best form of early childhood education for emergent bilinguals would be one that builds on the linguistic and cultural strengths that students bring from home (Restrepo-Widney & Sembiante, 2023), and such programs are extremely rare (Figueras-Daniel & Li, 2021; García & Gonzalez, 2006). Due to early childhood teacher demographics, fluent speakers of the students' home language usually work as assistants, not lead teachers (Whitebook et al., 2018), and when these languages are used, it tends to be mainly for purposes other than instructional ones (Jacoby & Lesaux, 2014).

Overall, states have done little to support emergent bilinguals in preschool. Illinois in 2010 and Texas in 2012 became the first states to mandate the use of home language practices to educate emergent bilinguals in prekindergarten. The passage of the ESSA (2015) marks the first time in the reauthorization of the Elementary and Secondary Education Act that some attention has been paid to early childhood education. It includes provisions to strengthen early childhood funding, especially for children of low- and moderate-income families. It remains to be seen whether these programs will support the bilingual practices of very young children.

Deficit thinking, remedial education, and tracking. The concept of *deficit thinking* refers to an ideology that attributes students' academic challenges to their internal factors such as intelligence or other aspects of their identity, and to external factors like family dysfunction (Valencia, 2010, 2012). Deficit thinking places the burden of challenges and inequalities faced by students from historically marginalized groups squarely on their shoulders (McKay & Devlin, 2016; Solórzano & Yosso, 2001; Valencia, 2010, 2012). This belief system ultimately upholds dominant systems and neglects to hold oppressive structures, policies, and practices within educational environments accountable. Deficit thinking is also one major reason why emergent bilinguals and other historically marginalized groups are perceived as lacking the necessary skills, intellectual capacity, language proficiency, discipline, and other attributes necessary to receive a challenging, agentic, creative, and innovative education.

For example, because emergent bilinguals are seen only as English learners from whom little is expected, their schooling often consists of *remedial programs* that emphasize drill and remediation (De Cohen et al., 2005). In their 2017 study of early childhood classrooms across Texas with predominantly Latine immigrant student populations, Adair and colleagues found that educators tended to justify discriminatory and limiting practices by invoking the "word gap" discourse—that is, by arguing that their students lacked the language competence and vocabulary to engage in agentic learning practices. The concept of the *word gap* originated from research in the field of early childhood education and developmental psychology conducted in the early 1990s, which found that children from higher-income families were exposed to significantly more words and language-rich environments compared to children from lower-income families, leading to variations in vocabulary size, language development, and ultimately, academic achievement (Hart & Risley, 1995). While this research and the notion of the word/language gap has been extensively debunked (e.g. García & Otheguy, 2020; Johnson, 2015; Johnson & Zentella, 2017), the harmful effects of denying children agentic learning experiences on the basis of deficit-oriented ideas persists. This is especially true when assessments continue to take place predominantly in English, denying emergent bilinguals the opportunity to demonstrate their learning, and reinforcing deficit thinking among educators (Ascenzi-Moreno & Seltzer, 2021).

As a result, the learning of emergent bilinguals is frequently about compensating for their assumed limited English language skills (Harklau, 1994; Kim, 2017; Olsen, 1997). These students' placement in remedial literacy and mathematics courses and lower-level core academic courses is well documented (Gándara et al., 2003; Parrish et al., 2002).

Emergent bilinguals are often given multiple periods of classes in ESL instead of meaningful content, a product of the emphasis on developing English. This is exacerbated in the high-intensity English language training provided in states such as Arizona, where students spend many hours studying decontextualized language structures. Other times, in order to focus on English acquisition at the expense of other content-related learning, emergent bilinguals are often taken from their regular classes for "pull-out ESL," creating further inequities (Anstrom, 1997; Fleischman & Hopstock, 1993). Furthermore, although it is widely accepted that a balanced approach to literacy that incorporates more time to discuss, create, read and write is central to literacy development (Birch, 2002; Calkins, 1994; Honig, 1996), many emergent bilinguals are taught to read through heavily phonics-based approaches instead of more balanced ones. This trend toward phonics-based approaches has gained ground under the influence of what is called the science of reading, which does not take into account reading research in different languages and scripts or by bilingual students. Advocates of the science of reading reduce meaning-making to the mastery of grapho-phonemic relationships without any meaningful consideration of the sociocultural or sociopolitical dimensions of the reading process. This is the considered critique of Tierney and Pearson (2024), who also affirm "the moral imperative to ensure curricular and pedagogical equity and relevance . . ." (p. 111).

For academic courses other than English, emergent bilinguals are also regularly tracked into courses that do not provide them with challenging content (Callahan, 2003, 2005; Oakes, 1990; Palmer & Henderson, 2016). In fact, many times, their learning of content-area academics is delayed until they have acquired English proficiency (Minicucci & Olsen, 1992). Alternatively, when newcomers are taught subject matter exclusively through English, instruction often takes on a slower pace and less content is covered (Minicucci & Olsen, 1992).

This results in an inferior education, because by the time the emergent bilinguals develop their full proficiency in English, they have not taken the appropriate high-level courses compared with their grade-level English-speaking counterparts, and thus they score lower on college admission tests (Mehan et al., 1992; Pennock-Román, 1994; Umansky, 2016). For example, a report from the U.S. Department of Education National Center for Education Statistics and Office of Civil Rights (2020–2021) notes that Algebra I is considered a "gateway course" due to its pivotal role in readying students for advanced studies in mathematics, science, and computer science. Early exposure to Algebra I, typically by eighth grade, grants students additional time to enroll in the advanced mathematics coursework frequently mandated for college majors in science, technology, engineering, and mathematics (STEM). Given that even at the high school level, only 7% of designated English learners were enrolled in Algebra I compared to 19% enrollment of all students in the 2020–2021 academic year, the chances of pursuing a STEM college career are slim for many emergent bilinguals (U.S Department of Education, 2020–2021). As the Washington, D.C., Superior Court noted in a major test case on the viability of curriculum tracking as an educational practice (*Hobson v. Hansen*, 1967), sixth-grade students who are taught a grade 3 curriculum are likely to end the year with a third-grade education (Gándara et al., 2003).

Dual-language bilingual programs, which emphasize high academic achievement and "enrichment" rather than remediation, and where students' home language practices can be more deliberately affirmed and used for instruction and assessment, can potentially help reduce the risks of the deficit connotation that is attached to students designated as English learners. Pimentel (2011), for example, describes how a child who had mastered most of the pre-K curriculum was considered "at risk" when enrolled in a remedial transitional bilingual program, simply for being a Spanish speaker, but when moved to a dual-language bilingual program, he was reclassified as "gifted." Pimentel recognizes that it is the language ideologies guiding the program implementation that lead to such deficit ideas. However, as we have said, dual-language bilingual programs are not shielded from raciolinguistic (Rosa & Flores, 2017) and monoglossic ideologies that guide literacy and content assessments, English learner classification processes, and power relations in social interactions among students and educators. Research shows that even in dual-language bilingual programs, there is a danger of continuing to view minoritized emergent bilinguals as deficient, leading to persisting inequalities (Cervantes-Soon et al., 2017). García-Mateus's (2023) study of a second-grade dual-language bilingual class in a gentrifying neighborhood, for example, reveals that racialized emergent bilinguals from low-income families (who often serve as language brokers for their families) tend to be perceived as not having enough expertise in any language and as struggling learners. These perceptions have material consequences in their learning opportunities, for it leads to educators positioning emergent bilinguals as inferior to their English-speaking peers and often results in grade-level retention.

In sum, deficit thinking is an underlying ideology that affects almost all aspects of schooling, and it results in low expectations and the placement of students into a perpetual remedial track.

Little attention to content other than language. The curriculum for emergent bilinguals focuses on language and literacy, and then mathematics, subjects that are heavily tested. Thus, their understandings of the world, of science, of social studies, and of history are severely limited. Many scholars have pointed out the little attention that these subjects receive in emergent bilinguals' education. When these subjects are taught, the emphasis is again the development of vocabulary and what is seen as disciplinary literacy without taking into account the richness in knowledge production that these understandings would bring. Among the exceptions has been a group of science/engineering scholars who have challenged the limited approach to science education for emergent bilingual students (González Howard et al., 2023, 2024; Pérez, 2021; Pérez et al., in press; Suárez, 2022). We will discuss their alternative approaches later in this chapter.

High-stakes accountability. High-stakes accountability refers to assessments, typically standardized tests, that have significant consequences or implications for individuals, schools, or districts based on the results. High-stakes testing rose to prominence in the late 20th and early 21st centuries, spurred by education reform movements and reports such as *A Nation at Risk* (National Commission on Excellence in Education, 1983), which advocated for increased accountability measures like standardized testing to address perceived flaws in the U.S. education system. As we saw in Chapter 3, the passage of the No Child Left Behind Act in 2001 was pivotal, mandating standardized testing in reading and math for grades 3–8 and tying federal funding and penalties to schools' test results, heightening the significance of standardized testing in education policy. This focus on accountability drove the expansion of the standardized testing industry, with companies developing various assessments, including state exams and college entrance tests, and solidifying standardized testing's role in education. States aligned academic standards with these tests, using them to gauge student proficiency and hold schools responsible, while market-driven education reforms reinforced the importance of high-stakes testing in evaluating school performance and promoting accountability.

In practice, high-stakes accountability typically involves tying school funding, teacher salaries, or school accreditation to student performance on standardized tests. For students, the consequences may include decisions about grade retention or promotion, remedial education, and graduation eligibility. For example, under policies like the No Child Left Behind Act and its successor, the Every Student Succeeds Act, schools may face penalties or interventions if their students consistently perform poorly on standardized tests. Similarly, teachers' job evaluations and compensation may be influenced by their students' test scores.

High-stakes accountability policies are supposed to help improve educational outcomes by incentivizing schools and educators to focus on raising student achievement. However, researchers have argued that these policies can lead to teaching to the test, narrowing of the curriculum, undue stress on students and educators, the exacerbation of inequalities (Au, 2022; Darling-Hammond, 2018; McNeil, 2009; Valenzuela, 2005), and an overall culture of fear among students and educators (Counsell & Wright, 2018; DeJaynes et al., 2020). Additionally, there are concerns about the fairness and validity of using standardized test scores as the primary measure of educational quality and teacher effectiveness.

High-stakes testing poses significant challenges for emergent bilinguals due to several factors. These students, still acquiring English proficiency, may struggle to understand and demonstrate content knowledge in standardized tests (Blaise, 2018). Cultural references and assumptions in these tests can be unfamiliar to emergent bilinguals from diverse backgrounds, hindering their ability to engage with the material as intended. Moreover, the standardized format of assessments may not accommodate the linguistic diversity of emergent bilinguals, including their use of translanguaging practices, which are not recognized in most standardized testing environments. The pressure associated with high-stakes testing, such as grade promotion and graduation implications, can exacerbate test anxiety among emergent bilinguals, leading to underperformance or disengagement and other negative consequences on students' well-being (Li et al., 2018). Moreover, limited accommodations tailored to their linguistic needs further disadvantage these students and may impact the validity of test results.

High-stakes tests often prioritize certain academic skills, neglecting the cultural and linguistic assets, social-emotional development, and critical thinking skills of emergent bilinguals. It is then not surprising that this kind of testing often perpetuates deficit thinking about emergent bilinguals' academic abilities, stigmatization, and low expectations from educators and peers (Bertrand & Marsh, 2021). The pressure to increase test scores often leads low-performing schools to adopt and enforce the teaching of prescriptive curricula, thus denying opportunities for culturally sustaining pedagogies, meaningful curricula, and agentic teaching and learning (Acosta et al., 2021; Back, 2020). It has also resulted in educational policies with reduced attention to supporting students' home languages, as well as in the altering of bilingual programs to prioritize English instruction in order to help students pass the test (Menken & Solorza, 2014). It is thus essential for educators and policymakers to adopt inclusive and culturally responsive and socially just assessment practices to better support the diverse needs of emergent bilingual students in ways that value their whole selves. We will discuss assessment practices with emergent bilinguals, including more appropriate and holistic alternatives in Chapter 8.

Special needs and disability. Both over- and under-identification of emergent bilinguals with disabilities present significant concerns (Golloher et al., 2017). Over-identification leads to ineffective interventions and a label that exacerbates deficit perceptions with detrimental consequences (Cioè-Peña, 2021). On the other hand, under-identification, which is especially acute in early childhood education, means that there are students who are struggling, not being seen, and not receiving the supports that they need (Takanishi & LeMenestrel, 2017).

Since the 1960s, emergent bilinguals have tended to be overrepresented in some categories of special education (Ortiz, Fránquiz, & Lara, 2020), particularly in specific learning and intellectual disabilities and language and speech impairment classes, and most especially at the secondary level (Artiles et al., 2002; Umansky et al., 2017). The overrepresentation of emergent bilinguals in the learning disability and speech/language categories suggests that many educators may have difficulty distinguishing students with disabilities from those who are still learning English (Zehler et al., 2003). While overrepresentation of emergent bilingual learners may be less prevalent in the primary years, Samson and Lesaux's (2009) study revealed that they became more prominent by third grade, implying that educators tend to delay special education referrals until students attain English proficiency. Gándara et al. (2003) have shown that emergent bilinguals who have low proficiency scores in both English and their home language are even more vulnerable. They are 1.5 times more likely at the elementary level, and twice as likely at the secondary level, to be diagnosed as speech impaired and learning disabled. Emergent bilinguals who are in bilingual programs are less likely to be in special education than those students who are in English-only programs (Artiles et al., 2002).

According to Zehler et al. (2003), approximately 9% of the total population of emergent bilinguals in public schools had been placed in special education classes in 2001–2002. Of these, 61% were male, indicating an overrepresentation of male emergent bilinguals with disabilities, since only 51% of all emergent bilinguals were male (Zehler et al., 2003). Most emergent bilinguals in special education programs were at the elementary level (50.5%), followed by middle school (22.8%), and then high school (18.6%) (Hopstock & Stephenson, 2003).

In Zehler and colleagues' 2003 study, Latine students represented 80% of the total special education emergent bilingual population, indicating that they are slightly overrepresented in special education programs compared to English learners overall. This could relate to cultural biases against Latine students. However, it may also have to do with the abundance of assessment instruments in Spanish compared to other languages, which makes it possible to diagnose these students. There are also more Spanish–English bilingual special education teachers and school psychologists, meaning that more programs for Spanish speakers may be available.

On the other hand, even when students are correctly identified as having special needs, emergent bilingual learners with disabilities tend to experience limited access to bilingual special education services. In some cases, this has had to do with the scarcity of teachers with both bilingual and special education expertise (Wang & Woolf, 2015). Students in self-contained special education classrooms are less likely to receive instruction in their home language or English-language development supports (Hulse, 2021). Simultaneously, emergent bilinguals with disabilities may be excluded from bilingual education programs (Hulse, 2021). Under the fallacy that English-only instruction will prevent linguistic confusion and academic difficulties, educators often discourage parents of emergent bilinguals with disabilities from enrolling them in bilingual programs (Cioè-Peña, 2020; Guiberson, 2013). Bilingualism is viewed as a commodity (Cervantes-Soon, 2014), and thus it is seen as a privilege rather than a right (Cioè-Peña, 2020), and emergent bilinguals with disabilities are framed as falling short of what it takes to develop it.

Exclusion from gifted programs and Advanced Placement. The other side of the coin when it comes to accessing the most challenging educational programs is the emergent bilinguals' underrepresentation in gifted and talented programs and Advanced Placement courses.

In 2016, fewer than 3% of students who were designated gifted and talented in 2013–2014 were emergent bilinguals (U.S. Department of Education and Office for Civil Rights, 2016). Mun and colleagues' (2016) comprehensive review of the literature on gifted emergent bilinguals noted identification procedures and policies as the central issue. However, a quantitative assessment of data by the National Center for Research on Gifted Education (NCRGE, 2016) from three states with mandated gifted identification policies affirmed that emergent bilinguals were typically underrepresented in gifted and talented programs, even in states with such mandates. The NCRGE thus conducted a systematic qualitative study to address the issue and found that the primary obstacle was a widespread reluctance among teachers, parents/guardians, and other stakeholders to refer emergent bilinguals for evaluation (Gubbins et al., 2018). This reluctance has the potential to delay or completely hinder the identification of ELs as gifted and talented and manifests across all grade levels. There are also very few bilingual gifted and talented programs, assuming that giftedness is only the purview of monolingual students.

In addition, according to data from the U.S. Department of Education and the Office for Civil Rights, the proportion of emergent bilinguals in advanced math and science classes and enrolled in one Advanced Placement (AP) class was less than 5% in 2016, as shown in Table 6.1. The data suggest that because of emergent bilinguals' performance on invalid standardized tests, they are too often judged unfit for mainstream college-preparatory classes (Koelsch, n.d.).

The "English learner" label that many emergent bilinguals carry often plays a major role in this exclusionary tracking, as it prioritizes remedial English language development/ESL courses. Thus, when emergent bilingual students encounter schedule conflicts between their ESL courses and crucial core academic subjects like English language arts (ELA), math, science, or social studies, they frequently end up taking remedial courses. This separation from their English-dominant peers can hinder their progress along the paths toward college and career readiness (Callahan & Humphries, 2016; Callahan & Shifrer, 2016; Umansky, 2016).

Dual-language bilingual education programs have the potential to increase emergent bilinguals' likelihood to be placed into more advanced courses during their later secondary school years, in contrast to their peers enrolled in ESL programs (Morita-Mullaney et al., 2020). Nevertheless, dual-language bilingual

Table 6.1. Emergent Bilinguals and Advanced Math and Science and AP

Subject	% of students in schools that offer course	% of students enrolled in course
Algebra II	5%	4%
Calculus	5%	1%
Physics	5%	4%
AP (one course)	5%	2%

Source: U.S. Department of Education and Office for Civil Rights, 2016

programs operate within established institutional frameworks, including a master schedule that reflects longstanding practices and associated beliefs among guidance counselors, subject area leaders, and administrators who decide how factors such as academic performance (testing and grades), student characteristics (such as being an English learner), and specific programs (such as ESL, DLBE, or gifted and talented programs) influence course placements. These institutional "equity traps" create a distinct form of exclusionary tracking for even high-achieving emergent bilinguals from dual-language bilingual programs, which deprive them of access to advanced-level mathematics, science, engineering, and elective courses in high school (Morita-Mullaney et al., 2020).

Inequitable Resources

As has become quite evident throughout this book, emergent bilingual students have not received their due in terms of equitable resources for academic achievement in U.S. classrooms. Here, we cast further light on the lack of curricular materials and technology, poor school facilities, limited educational funding, and inequitable access to well-prepared teachers.

Instructional materials. Oakes and Saunders (2002) have argued that there is a clear link between appropriate materials and curriculum and student academic outcome. Emergent bilinguals need developmentally and culturally appropriate materials to develop and use English, but they also need appropriate rich content materials in their home languages. However, more often than not, emergent bilinguals do not have appropriate instructional resources. Only 25% of teachers surveyed in an American Institutes for Research (AIR) study reported that they used a textbook for emergent bilinguals that was different from that used for their English proficient students, and only 46% reported using any supplementary materials for them (Parrish et al., 2002). More than one-quarter of the teachers in California reported not having appropriate reading material for emergent bilinguals, and almost two-thirds of those with high percentages of emergent bilinguals in their classes had few instructional materials in Spanish or other languages (Gándara et al., 2003). Teachers with high percentages of emergent bilinguals also reported more frequently that their textbooks and instructional materials were meager, and that they and their students had less access to technology (Gándara et al., 2003; see also Chapter 9).

Bilingual teachers are often left to their own devices to translate material produced in English, taking time and energy from their attention to students and families. Even when translations are adequate (which many times they are not, for teachers are not translators), this translated material is not always culturally or experientially appropriate, failing to engage emergent bilingual students with meaningful histories, concepts, stories, and dreams.

Although federal regulations require states to have English language proficiency standards that are aligned with the state academic content standards, the alignment of instruction for emergent bilinguals with state standards is much poorer than for English proficient students (Gutiérrez et al., 2002; Hopstock & Stephenson, 2003b). There are also few instructional materials to support this alignment (Hopstock & Stephenson, 2003b).

School facilities. Emergent bilinguals attend the most impoverished and under-resourced schools, which is clearly related to their growing isolation and segregation within the public educational system (Orfield, 2001). Research has shown that classrooms for emergent bilinguals are often located on the periphery of, in the basement of, or outside of the school building (Olsen, 1997). Emergent bilinguals also go to schools in buildings that are often not clean or safe. For example, in a survey of 1,017 California teachers conducted in 2002 by the Lou Harris polling group, close to half of the teachers in schools with high numbers of emergent bilinguals reported that their schools had unclean bathrooms and that they had seen evidence of mice, compared to 26% of teachers in schools with few, if any, English learners (Gándara et al., 2003).

In 2006, a report concluded that new school buildings were needed across the country and that minoritized students, in particular, were attending schools with decrepit facilities (BEST, 2006). Despite unprecedented spending and growth in school construction since then, resources for school construction have not been equally available in all school districts. For example, between 1995 and 2004, school districts with high levels of minority student enrollment invested only $5,172 per student in school construction, while school districts with predominantly white student enrollment spent the most ($7,102 per student) (BEST, 2006). In addition, high-minority school districts used the money to fund basic repairs, such as new roofs and asbestos removal, whereas schools in wealthier districts funded science labs and performing arts studios.

Inequitable funding. One of the most important equity issues surrounding the education of emergent bilinguals has to do with the ways in which programs are funded. Today, funding for education programs for emergent bilinguals comes mostly from local and state sources.[1] In fact, the federal education funding on average represents about 11% of what local school districts spend overall (Sánchez, 2017).

Until 2002, Title VII of the Elementary and Secondary Education Act provided funding for projects and services for emergent bilingual students at the state, district, and school levels on a competitive basis—that is, they were *discretionary grants* that states and districts applied for and used to fund schools and programs serving emergent bilinguals.

In contrast, under Title III of No Child Left Behind, and continuing under ESSA, there are *formula grants that the federal government awards directly to the states.* Under No Child Left Behind, these federal grants to the states are determined by two factors that are weighted differently in the formula:

1. The number of English language learners (80% of the formula), and
2. The population of recently immigrated children and youth (relative to national counts of these populations) (20% of the formula).

The expectation under ESSA was that Title III funding would be increased. But actual funding depends on appropriation from Congress, and this promise has not been fulfilled. Since 2002 the total appropriation has remained mostly unchanged, despite the growth of this population (Vazquez Baur, 2023; Najarro, 2024).

Because Title III grants are deemed insufficient to provide adequate funding for emergent bilinguals, states provide additional funding to school districts. But even across these states, emergent bilinguals are not funded equitably or in the same way.

A report by the Education Trust authored by Morgan (2022) discovered that districts with the highest numbers of emergent bilinguals receive about 14% less state and local funding compared to districts with lower emergent bilingual enrollment even after providing extra funds for emergent bilingual education in addition to basic per-pupil allocations (Villegas, 2023). Furthermore, per-pupil funding figures assume that schools target funds to those emergent bilinguals who need services and distribute funding somewhat evenly among them. In reality, however, the money allocated for each school is given directly to the principal in one lump sum, and the principal decides what to do with it. Little information exists on how these funds are allocated at the school level.

Striving for transparency is a central part of seeking equitable funding. Since 1991, when the press for higher standards and more accountability became more intense, courts, state legislatures, and education advocacy organizations have requested "costing out" studies in order to obtain more information on how to fund students, including emergent bilingual students, equitably. Such research helps inform the legal movement to seek adequate funding for groups deemed in need of additional resources, including emergent bilinguals (AIR, 2004; Rebell, 2007, 2009).

Most studies have shown that it costs more to educate emergent bilinguals than it does to educate English speakers (Baker et al., 2004; Parrish, 1994), although a few studies have argued otherwise (AIR, 2004). Still, estimates of these additional costs per emergent bilingual student vary greatly and range from 5% more to 200% more than the cost of educating mainstream students (Baker et al., 2004; J. Crawford, personal communication, March 17, 2007). In other words, there is great variation in this literature on the cost of a meaningful education for these students. Jiménez-Castellanos and Topper (2012) conclude that there is overall agreement that current funding levels are insufficient. Despite the differences, some consensus on the cost of providing high-quality education to emergent bilinguals is beginning to emerge.

Determining the exact cost per pupil to educate English learners (ELs) is complex and varies significantly across different contexts due to a variety of factors, including the instructional model used, geographic location, the size of the emergent bilingual population within a school or district, and the level of linguistic diversity. It is also influenced by the specific needs of emergent bilingual students, which can vary depending on their English proficiency level, grade, how recently they arrived in the country, and whether they have experienced interrupted schooling. Moreover, the emergent bilingual population in the United States is becoming increasingly diverse, and funding mechanisms have struggled to keep up with these changes (Villegas, 2023).

The cost of programs for emergent bilinguals is also significantly influenced by the role of specialized teachers and class sizes (Sugarman, 2016). Self-contained grade-level emergent bilingual classes often do not require additional staff since the primary teacher handles both language and subject instruction, though costs can rise with smaller class sizes. Conversely, pull-out or push-in strategies, or co-teaching models involving both general and specialist teachers incur higher costs due to the need for extra staff. It is anticipated that, as more general education teachers gain certification to support emergent bilinguals, some expenses may be reduced. Overall, it has been established that emergent bilinguals require additional personnel at rates of approximately 20 students with one full-time teacher and one or more instructional aide per teacher (Baker et al., 2004).

Programs for emergent bilinguals also bear costs for additional learning opportunities, staff for language assessment and academic counseling, efforts to attract and retain qualified staff, materials in students' languages, and professional development. In addition to linguistic and academic assistance, school systems frequently offer various socioemotional supports to newcomer students, which may include mental health services, mentoring, and connections to additional social services. Assisting immigrant parents in understanding and engaging with their children's education may also entail additional expenses, particularly if parents are unfamiliar with the American school system or need translation or interpretation services to communicate with educators (Sugarman, 2016).

Clearly, there is a need for additional funding to provide emergent bilinguals with the educational services they require and deserve. However, before anyone can establish precisely how much more is needed for their education, it is necessary to carefully examine the local context in which these emergent bilinguals are being educated and the goals for their education.

Inequitable access to high-quality educators. Teacher and principal quality are two of the most important factors in determining school effectiveness and, ultimately, student achievement (Blase & Blase, 2001; Clewell & Campbell, 2004). But few school leaders and not enough teachers are well versed in issues surrounding bilingualism. Additionally, there is high turnover among both administrators and teachers of language-minoritized students. It is even more difficult to find high-quality teachers and school leaders for emergent bilingual students than it is for students in general. In 2016, 32 states reported having shortages of teachers who could work with emergent bilinguals (Sánchez, 2017). The issue has become more prevalent in recent years. The Office of English Language Acquisition (2023) found that while the emergent bilingual population increased 2.6% in the 2019–2020 year, the number of certified or licensed teachers in emergent bilingual education decreased 10.4%. Thus, ESL and bilingual education jobs were among the top three teaching positions with the highest vacancy rate.

Although principals and teachers at schools with large numbers of English learners are more likely to be Latine or Asian, these principals and teachers also tend to be less experienced and have fewer credentials than those at schools with few or no emergent bilingual students (De Cohen et al., 2005). Forty percent of Asian teachers and 45% of Latine teachers nationwide teach in schools with high levels of emergent bilinguals (De Cohen et al., 2005). These Latine and Asian teachers are more likely to be bilingual and knowledgeable of the students' cultures, thus enabling the support of the students' languages and identities. And yet, teachers in schools with high numbers of emergent bilinguals have fewer credentials on average than teachers at schools with few or no emergent bilinguals (De Cohen et al., 2005). Although only slightly more than 50% of teachers in schools with high levels of emergent bilinguals have full certification, almost 80% of teachers in other schools do.

States have much difficulty in finding qualified personnel to teach emergent bilinguals, with California, Texas, Florida, and Illinois having the greatest need (OLEA, 2023). Nonetheless, other states not perceived as traditional immigrant destinations, such as Alaska, Delaware, and West Virginia, have had large shares of recently arrived children (Sugarman, 2023). Schools in these and other states like Wisconsin, for example, which have seen their emergent bilingual population triple in recent decades, must adapt to accommodate new and diverse groups of students, often lacking the necessary expertise or resources that are available in states with more established immigrant communities (Lowenhaupt & Reeves, 2017).

The lack of credentialed teachers to work with emergent bilinguals is quite dire. While about 65% of all teachers in the year 2017–2018 had at least one emergent bilingual in their class, only about 5% of all teachers had a major, minor, or certificate in ESL education (OLEA, 2023).

Beyond teacher certification in specialized areas, most teachers in the United States have not had any preparation on how to teach emergent bilinguals. In 2009, the U.S. Government Accountability Office reported that nationwide, less than 20% of teacher education programs required at least one course focused on English learners and bilingualism, and less than a third exposed their students to any fieldwork experience with emergent bilinguals.

The inadequate preparation of teachers on issues affecting language-minoritized students negatively impacts their ability to teach these students. It has been found that teachers who are certified in ESL or bilingual academic development, as well as those who are bilingual, have more positive attitudes toward the bilingualism of the students and their own teaching (Lee & Oxelson, 2006). However, according to U.S. Census data, teachers are disproportionately monolingual. Nationally, only 13% of teachers are bilingual, compared with at least 21% of children. A report from the Century Foundation shows that in California, one of the states with the largest emergent bilingual populations, only 14% of teachers are bilingual compared to 40% of the K–12 student populations (Williams, 2023). Bilingual programs often struggle to recruit qualified teachers. This is particularly true in the growing dual-language bilingual programs located in new immigrant gateway states, which have to source teachers from other countries. These teachers, while fluent in the language used in the program, are often not familiar with bilingual issues or living bilingual lives. These teachers are undergoing a difficult process of acculturation and understanding of the U.S. school system themselves, and they often lack the necessary sociocultural knowledge about the U.S. racialized emergent bilinguals as well as the preparation necessary to teach them in culturally sustaining ways and to develop a sense of agency to advocate for them (Cervantes-Soon, 2014; Babino & Stewart, 2018). Moreover, due to dominant beliefs in their home countries; differences in race, language practices, and social class; and insufficient preparation, they may also internalize the hegemony of English and adopt conventional monolingual, raciolinguistic, and deficit-thinking ideologies, contributing to persistent inequalities (Dorner et al., 2021; Martínez, Hikida, & Durán, 2018).

According to Gándara, Maxwell-Jolly, and Driscoll (2005), there is a shortage not only of qualified teachers but also of school professionals to assist emergent bilinguals. Bilingual speech pathologists are sorely needed, and guidance counselors with bilingual skills are also in short supply. In California, less than 8% of the school psychologists are bilingual and capable of conducting an assessment in the home language of an emergent bilingual.

From the foregoing discussion, it is evident that emergent bilinguals have to contend with much more than language inequities. And yet, issues in their education are often reduced to purely linguistic ones. In this regard, and focusing on Latine students, Gándara and Contreras (2009) have said:

> Although Latinos have suffered many of the same inequities as blacks and other minority groups in schooling—inadequate and overcrowded facilities, underprepared teachers, inappropriate curriculum and textbooks, and segregated schools—the civil rights focus in education for Latinos has been primarily the issue of language. (p. 121)

The fact that 80% of emergent bilinguals are Latine students means that more attention has been paid to the inequities of language use instead of the inadequacies of the educational opportunity they have been given. And yet, to offer equitable curricular opportunities to emergent bilinguals would require a fundamental change in the ways in which we view the students' ways of using languages other than English, as well as their dynamic bilingualism.

ALTERNATIVE CURRICULAR PRACTICES AND PREPARING CARING EDUCATORS

A Challenging Inclusive Curriculum That Starts Early

Emergent bilinguals are fully capable of developing ways of using English for academic purposes if given the same socioeducational opportunities as wealthy white children. "The same," however, does not always mean integrated educational programs in which emergent bilinguals could be overlooked, or worse, discriminated against. An equitable curriculum and pedagogy for emergent bilinguals must adapt to their needs. A challenging inclusive curriculum for emergent bilinguals must be ecologically adaptive, as students' bilingualism and biliteracy emerge.

In *early childhood*, emergent bilinguals must be given the opportunity to engage with caring adults who not only speak their home languages and understand their linguistic and cultural practices but also can guide their bilingual development by providing opportunities for them to practice listening to and speaking English, as well as their home language repertoire. The beginnings of communication around print must include children's home language practices, the ways in which they use language to make meaning from print. Chumak-Horbatsch (2012) provides a plethora of recommendations for linguistically appropriate practice with young immigrant children.

Although it may be necessary to provide a separate instructional space away from English-only students to develop an emergent bilingual's literacy, care must be taken to also provide integrated spaces where emergent bilinguals can interact with other children whose repertoire at home includes English. This can happen during the time for snack or lunch, play, nap, music, art, dance, or any of the range of activities in which very young children are involved. These integrated spaces must function as catalysts not only of English language acquisition for emergent bilinguals but also of acquisition of other linguistic and cultural practices for young English-speaking monolingual children.

It is of primary importance that culturally and linguistically relevant early childhood programs with bilingual instruction be developed for very young emergent bilinguals (E. García & Jensen, 2009; Tazi, 2014). And it is crucial that this preschool education be state funded and provided free of charge to all 3- and 4-year-olds. An investment in bilingual preschools for all emergent bilinguals would correspond strongly with improved language development by the time the children reach elementary school.

In Chapter 5, we discussed alternative practices that foster the development of English academic literacy through complex language use. Much has been said about the ways in which a *challenging academic curriculum* can be delivered to emergent bilinguals while also developing their spoken language use in academic contexts, as well as their academic literacies (Celic, 2009; Chamot & O'Malley, 1994; Echevarría, Vogt, & Short, 2004; Freeman & Freeman, 2008; Gibbons, 2002, 2009). But in order to provide inclusive educational spaces and curricular opportunities for emergent bilinguals throughout schooling, home language practices cannot be considered suspect. An inclusive and equitable society would provide the means by which emergent bilinguals are assessed for gifted-and-talented programs with the language practices they use and know best. In turn, these gifted-and-talented programs would then include these different ways of using language and make the development of bilingualism and biliteracy a goal for all the children. As we have seen, bilingualism and biliteracy are important for improved cognitive functioning, creative performance, and critical awareness. Thus, gifted-and-talented programs would include emergent bilinguals and at the same time would make spaces where bilingualism and biliteracy would be a goal for all.

The limited teaching of *science and engineering* to emergent bilinguals is increasingly being challenged. By taking up the concept of translanguaging, some science educators are showing how curriculum can move from being based on what is called "the language of science" to a *"language for science"* (Gonzalez Howard et al., 2023). Even after the Next Generation Science Standards (NGSS) demanded that students follow the practices of scientists and engineers in making sense of real-world phenomena and designing solutions, educators focused on teaching the language of science—the technical vocabulary and terms, use of the passive voice, and impersonal use instead of first-person accounts. But by emphasizing the language for science, emergent bilinguals are free to draw upon all their language resources and practices to explore scientific phenomena and engage in scientific sensemaking (Andersen, Méndez Pérez, & González-Howard, 2022; Pérez, 2021; Pérez, González-Howard, & Suárez, 2022, in press). For example, Enrique Suárez's work has explicitly addressed how young bi-/multilingual students' translanguaging enhances their explanations of how electricity flows through circuits (Suárez, 2020, 2022), how sounds are produced (Suárez & Otero, 2024), and how to engineer objects that float (Suárez & Sousa, 2023).

If all students' language practices were given their rightful place in the U.S. curriculum as important tools for sociocognitive and academic development, more *advanced classes and Advanced Placement classes* would be taught through languages other than English. New York State policy mandates translation of some math, science, and social studies graduation exams into five languages—Spanish, Chinese, Korean, Russian, and Haitian Creole. The policy has resulted in a more challenging high school curriculum for emergent bilinguals because students who were previously relegated to ESL, music, art, and physical education classes are now included in content classes taught in these languages. Today, many high schools are also teaching AP classes in languages other than English. In one high school we know, for example, AP Biology is taught in Spanish for Latine emergent bilinguals. Although the students read the advanced biology text in English, they discuss and do experiments and scientific work in Spanish. In another high school, the teacher makes the advanced biology text available in both English and Spanish; students work collaboratively in small groups and are encouraged to use all their meaning-making resources to make sense of the text. In this classroom, the bilingual students' translanguaging is leveraged so that all can participate in accelerated classes, even those taught in English. Students are given responsibility to use all their communicative resources to research and learn advanced content.

Finally, with deeper understandings of bilingualism, educators may take a more nuanced approach when considering recommending *special education placement* for those students who have not yet developed English practices deemed as academic. Educators would know that the development of bilingualism and biliteracy takes practice over a lifetime and that using English for academic purposes to perform school tasks comes with time and practice. Moreover, it is important to understand that home language instruction is an essential support for students with disabilities and that bilingualism is a crucial aspect of their daily lives and identities and not simply a form of "enrichment" or commodified resource. This would then mean that educators may be better advocates for ensuring that emergent bilinguals with disabilities have access to a bilingual special education program that supports their linguistic, neurodiverse, academic, and cultural development.

Preparing Caring, Creative, and Qualified Educators

Perhaps no other area is so crucial to the improvement of education of emergent bilinguals as the preparation of educators for these students—school leaders, teachers, and professionals such as school psychologists, guidance counselors, therapists, and paraprofessionals. In fact, all school leaders today need to become experts on bilingualism and the education of emergent bilinguals (Reyes, 2006). Not just specialized bilingual and ESL teachers but also "mainstream" teachers have to understand issues of bilingualism in education and how to include emergent bilinguals in a high-quality and challenging education (Lucas & Grinberg, 2008). A study by López, Scanlan, and Gundrum (2013) found that states that mandate specialist certification along with requiring all teachers to possess some level of knowledge to effectively work with emergent bilinguals experienced the most successful outcomes in terms of emergent bilingual academic achievement. Moreover, López and Santibañez's (2018) analysis of teacher preparation in Arizona, California, and Texas found that over time, more rigorous training also results in improved teacher self-efficacy, which is an important factor for job satisfaction, commitment to the profession, more positive interactions with students, and confidence to teach emergent bilinguals. In general, more preparation is better for both teachers and emergent bilingual students.

With the intensified migrations of peoples and convergences of languages and cultures in today's globalized world, there cannot be language teachers on the one hand and content teachers on the other (Téllez & Waxman, 2006). All language teachers must have some expertise in the content area, just as all content teachers must have some expertise in language. To achieve this, teacher education programs would have to change significantly, making a commitment to include courses on bilingualism and language development in all curricula, and ensuring that their prospective teachers have clinical experiences with emergent bilinguals (Grant & Wong, 2003).

Teacher apprenticeship models have sprung up where prospective teachers team up with experienced teachers for a year of teaching, while pursuing university courses in partnership with the school district. One such model is that being pursued by the Internationals Network for Public Schools in New York City (see Chapter 3). Prospective teachers have a yearlong teaching apprenticeship in high-performing international high schools. The program is designed around the tenet that, like students, teachers learn best when they apply the theories and content of teaching in an authentic learning context and develop teaching abilities by practicing alongside an experienced teacher.

Teachers who provide emergent bilinguals with a challenging and creative curriculum are those who are committed to the development of language-minoritized communities, both socially and academically. A way to capitalize on this commitment would be to attract prospective teachers from the language communities themselves (Clewell & Villegas, 2001; Valenzuela, 2016). Valenzuela (2016) offers a vision for how to implement their Grow Your Own initiative, which builds bilingual teacher capacity by tapping the very communities where these teachers are needed and nurturing critical consciousness from the bottom up.

The engagement of the community is crucial to ensure that there is a supply of committed and qualified caring and creative teachers.

EDUCATING EMERGENT BILINGUALS: EMBRACING CHALLENGE AND CARE

It is evident that providing an equitable education to emergent bilinguals is not only an issue of language. And yet, unless the students' home language practices are accepted in schools and not considered suspect, there will continue to be ways of excluding emergent bilinguals from the equal educational opportunities that they deserve. Given the ways in which schools are structured, only a language rights orientation based on principles of social justice will ensure that emergent bilinguals are given equitable curricular opportunities and are included in advanced courses and gifted-and-talented programs. But language rights have to be balanced with socioeducational rights, which insist that emergent bilinguals have equitable resources, equitable funding, and equitable access to high-quality teachers. Social justice for emergent bilinguals includes providing them with a challenging inclusive and linguistically and culturally relevant curriculum that empowers them to counteract the linguistic and social oppression in which they often live.

STUDY QUESTIONS

1. What is social justice? How is social justice related to language rights? What do you think about language rights?
2. What are the characteristics of a challenging and creative curriculum for emergent bilinguals? Describe inequities in curricula that emergent bilingual students face.
3. How would you define a transformative pedagogy? What are the differences in conceptualization between culturally relevant pedagogy and culturally sustaining pedagogy? In what ways are culturally relevant and sustaining pedagogies transformative?
4. How can critical consciousness help reduce inequities and deficit thinking? How can it be fostered in the classroom through the curriculum, student interactions, and instructional practices? How can it be cultivated among educators and other adults in the school community?
5. How do deficit-oriented beliefs, such as the notion of the "word gap" or "language gap," hinder agentic opportunities for students? What are the consequences? What classroom practices would offer students opportunities for increased agency?
6. Why are emergent bilinguals often classified as special education students? Why are they often excluded from advanced courses and gifted-and-talented programs? How could this exclusion be remedied?

7. Discuss how instructional resources are often inadequate for emergent bilinguals. What would be necessary to alleviate this situation?
8. What is the situation regarding funding of high-quality educational programs for emergent bilinguals? What do "costing out" studies say?
9. Why are many educators inadequately prepared to serve emergent bilinguals? What would be a way of attracting and preparing caring, creative, and qualified teachers of emergent bilinguals?
10. Discuss what would be the characteristic of an inclusive and just curriculum for emergent bilinguals.

CHAPTER 7

Family and Community Engagement

This chapter addresses the roles of families and communities in the education of emergent bilinguals. The chapter focuses on:

- Theoretical constructs and empirical evidence for family and community engagement:
  - » Research on parental and family engagement,
  - » Building equitable collaborations, and
  - » The funds of knowledge construct.
- Inequitable practices:
  - » Stigmatization of language-minoritized families and communities,
  - » Exclusion of home language practices, and
  - » One-size-fits-all parental and family education programs.
- Alternative approaches:
  - » Parent and family engagement as a shared responsibility,
  - » Broadening the view of parental and family engagement, and
  - » Community organizing.

Both popular belief and research over the years have supported the value of parental and family[1] engagement in their children's schooling, maintaining that several caring adults (school personnel and family members), working together, can accelerate students' learning. It is "the mantra of every educational reform program" (Gonzalez, 2005, p. 42), including NCLB (2001) and the ESSA (2015) legislation, which, as we noted in Chapter 3, promotes "language instruction educational programs for the parents, families, and communities of English learners" (Section 3102, 129 STAT. 1954). In this chapter, we examine what the research tells us regarding the benefits of parental and family engagement overall and discuss specific benefits for families with emergent bilingual children. We take a critical look at what actually happens to many of these families and children when they reach the schoolhouse door—the discrimination and marginalization they experience. We argue for the implementation of alternative approaches—more promising ways in which families, schools, and communities can come together on a more equal footing to support an equitable education for emergent bilinguals.

RESEARCH AND THEORIES ON PARENTAL AND COMMUNITY INVOLVEMENT

Involvement, Engagement, or Equitable Collaboration?

Historically, the role of parents and communities in relationship to schools has been characterized in the research literature as one of "involvement" (Jeynes, 2011). Joyce Epstein, the originator of a widely cited model of parental involvement (e.g., Epstein, 1987; Epstein & Dauber, 1991), later suggested that rather than the term *parental involvement*, the phrase "school, family, and community partnerships" is more appropriate because it describes the shared responsibility that the concerned parties should have for students' education (Epstein & Sheldon, 2006). Other researchers and educators also have moved away from the concept of involvement, which they say implies a partial, subservient role that parents and families have in their own children's education in general and in the workings of the school in particular.

Thus, in the past two decades, *engagement* is the term being used to conceptualize the relationship among parents, families, communities, and schools. This preference for the term *engagement* was advanced by Shirley (1997) in the context of a community's role in organizing school reform. In introducing the term, Shirley makes a distinction between "*accommodationist* forms of parental *involvement* and *transformational* forms of parental *engagement*" (1997, p. 73; emphasis in original). Goodall and Montgomery (2014), who focus on the family's relationship to the school, outline a continuum between parents' involvement with their children's schools and parents' engagement with their learning. The latter, they say, implies parents' commitment and their exercise of agency in choice and action. In the remainder of this chapter, we use the designation *engagement* except when the studies discussed specifically describe their work in terms of involvement. We show how, when engagement becomes more than a word and translates into action, parents, communities, and schools can work as partners to educate emergent bilinguals.

More recently, based on her study of strategies from three organizational initiatives aiming to enhance family engagement, Ishimaru (2019a, 2019b) has argued that we should move from notions of family engagement, which still prioritize school-centric ideas of individual student achievement, to equitable collaborations that bring together families and communities with schools and other educational agencies to prioritize systemic and institutional educational transformation. Ishimaru (2014) argues that although family engagement "best practices" call for a "shared vision," according to the U.S. Department of Education, family engagement initiatives are required to align with the achievement goals of schools and districts and connect families with the teaching and learning objectives for students. This implies that families need to abide by the goals and vision already established by educators for their children, perpetuating imbalanced power relations. In addition, scholars have long pointed out that this is particularly problematic for the families of racialized and emergent bilingual students, as school goals predominantly reflect white and middle-class values and expectations (Auerbach, 2009; Baquedano-López, Alexander, & Hernandez, 2013). Thus, Ishimaru's (2019a) research notes that when strategies for family engagement are implemented, such as parent capacity-building, relationship-building, and systemic capacity-building, these still tend to focus on changing parents without influencing teacher learning or instruction, on relationship-building that reinforces school priorities and power dynamics, and on systemic change initiatives that lack integration for transformative outcomes.

Ishimaru's (2019a, 2019b) notion of *equitable collaboration* implies that federal family engagement frameworks should evolve from solely prioritizing individual student academic achievement to creating a comprehensive plan that places families and communities at the forefront of systemic and institutional educational reform for all students. This revised framework would explicitly tackle issues related to race, class, language, sexual orientation, citizenship status, and other power imbalances that significantly impact the involvement of families and communities as knowledgeable participants and leaders in education. Moreover, standards and evaluations for teacher and leadership preparation would need to adapt to reflect these changes. Similarly, state and local family engagement policies could transition away from implicit assumptions that focus solely on families conforming to school norms and agendas. Instead, these policies could emphasize efforts and measures aimed at fostering collective capacity and relationships among families, educators across various systems, and community partners to drive transformative change in educational systems. Furthermore, policies regarding place-based collaborative initiatives could emulate and deliberately align with equity-focused family engagement policies. This alignment would explicitly recognize the importance of involving nondominant parents and families as influential decision-makers at various levels of these initiatives.

Studies

There is general agreement that parental involvement in their children's education positively impacts children's academic success (Henderson & Mapp, 2002; Park & Holloway, 2017).

In particular, studies show that children from minoritized and low-income families gain the most from parent engagement (Epstein, 1990; Henderson, 1987; Henderson & Berla, 1994; Henderson & Mapp, 2002; Hidalgo, Siu, & Epstein, 2004; Jordan, Orozco, & Averett, 2001). However, nondominant populations, especially immigrant families, encounter language and cultural barriers, racism, poverty, and other challenges when navigating schools (Baquedano-López et al., 2013).

Psychology researchers have also found what they describe as three overarching "determinants" of parental involvement. The first is parents' beliefs regarding the support roles they have in their children's education; the second is the extent to which they believe that they possess the knowledge and tools they need as educators of their children; the third relates to their perceptions regarding the schools' (or their children's) willingness to have them participate (see Hoover-Dempsey & Sandler, 1997).

Researchers who focus on social theory examine sociocultural and socioeconomic factors of parent involvement. These scholars point out that parents who possess certain kinds of social and cultural capital—social connections, relationships, and shared understandings that provide support and access to institutional resources (Bourdieu, 1985; Portes, 1998) are successful in helping their children do well academically.[2] Becoming involved in their children's schooling requires that parents understand how the school system functions, what curricular choices are available for their children, and whether they are aware of counseling and advice for accelerated learning and other college-preparatory options. Studies show that many language-minoritized parents do not have access to these understandings (Gándara & Contreras, 2009), yet they do have uniformly high aspirations for their children (Delgado-Gaitán, 1990, 1992; Steinberg, 1996). Parents often embrace the "opportunity narrative," a belief that with their sacrifices and hard work, their children can get ahead because school represents an opportunity for success (Bartlett, 2007).

Let us examine one such study on families' educative practices at home. Concha Delgado-Gaitán (1992) showed in an early study still cited today that school *does* matter to Mexican American parents. In her close ethnographic observation and interviews of six families, Delgado-Gaitán examined family social interaction in the home, where parents, within the broader context of their local community institutions, transmit their beliefs, values, and experiences to their children. She describes three categories of parental support for their children's education. The first she calls *the physical environment*, which addresses the economic and social resources in the home and surrounding community, such as arranging study spaces and materials in close-knit quarters at home and consulting people they know in the church and workplace about their children's schooling. The second category includes *emotional and motivational climates within the home*, such as encouraging their children to study so that they improve the weekly evaluations they bring home from school and ultimately grow up to be well educated. The third category includes the *interpersonal interactions among family members around literacy* in the home. Delgado-Gaitán found that these interactions, particularly families' approaches to homework activities, varied across the families and illustrated their incomplete knowledge about school literacy practices and expectations. She summarizes parents' dedication to their children's school success this way:

> Parents share a great deal with their children in the areas of aspirations, motivations, physical resources, and face-to-face interactions, which organize the total learning environment. (Delgado-Gaitán, 1992, p. 512)

Mexican American parents' aspirations for their children are a critical factor in their academic achievement. But more is needed on the part of the school. Delgado-Gaitán (1992) concludes that schools need to "open lines of communication with families and whole communities in a systematic way in order to facilitate the families' access to necessary academic and social resources" (p. 513).

It is well documented that, while many parents of emergent bilinguals actively support their children's education at home, schools frequently fail to acknowledge their abilities or contributions (Poza, Brooks, & Valdés, 2014). This issue became particularly clear during and in the aftermath of the Covid-19 pandemic. As Ishimaru and Bang (2022) note, "discourses about 'learning loss' accompany calls for increased testing driven by deficit assumptions about the familial and communal life of children of color and the failures to imagine what is being learned" (p. 383). They also contend that these responses of educational systems not only reveal but worsen inequalities, showing the limitations of small-scale efforts for change and individual professional expertise in addressing systemic racism and its related issues, producing significant schooling challenges that create additional concerns for nondominant families compared to white parents. Ishimaru and Bang emphasize that despite obstacles, these families draw on their histories of resilience to promote culturally relevant learning. As a result, the experiences of nondominant youth and families raise broader equity questions about what counts as learning and valuable knowledge, the purpose of education, and family roles in schooling, which schools and scholars have yet to address.

It is important to move away from dominant notions of family engagement by first recognizing and building on the ways in which emergent bilingual families are already generating valuable knowledge and skills that enable their children and future generations to learn, survive, and thrive despite challenging, inequitable, and unjust conditions. Second, it also behooves educators to identify the ways in which schooling systems create burdens, reproduce deficit thinking, and exacerbate inequities through their relationships with families. And third, educators must think creatively and expand our imagination to envision, design, and carry out equitable collaborations with the potential not only to support emergent bilinguals' linguistic and academic needs as defined by conventional notions of valuable knowledge but also to create empowering learning contexts where bilingual students can be knowledge creators and agents of change.

The Funds of Knowledge Construct

Delgado-Gaitán's (1992) research laid the foundation for the concept of *funds of knowledge*. A group of anthropologists from the University of Arizona developed a program of research, spanning nearly three decades, in Mexican American communities in the United States, and observed that households possessed valuable cultural and practical knowledge that was often overlooked by schools (e.g., Esteban-Guitart & Moll, 2014; González, Moll, & Amanti, 2005; Greenberg, 1989, 1990; Moll et al., 1992; Moll & Greenberg, 1990). Funds of knowledge are a construct that refers to the rich and diverse knowledge resources that individuals and families possess based on their cultural backgrounds, histories, experiences, and everyday practices, including linguistic practices. The idea was to recognize that students' home lives are sites of valuable knowledge construction and to leverage these funds of knowledge by bringing them into the classroom.

This research has focused on teachers' visits to the homes of families of language minoritized students to learn about a variety of abilities that the families possess, such as carpentry, mechanics, music, knowledge about health and nutrition, household and ranch management, and extensive language and literacy practices. López (2001) describes parents' efforts at teaching their children the value of hard work, a value that is transferable into academic life. Other researchers have documented children's first exposures to print, known as local literacies: Bible reading, reading and writing family letters, record-keeping, and following recipes (Delgado-Gaitán & Trueba, 1991; Mercado, 2005b).

Mercado (2005a) describes funds of knowledge in two New York Puerto Rican homes as drawing from three resources: intellectual, social, and emotional. The families draw on both Spanish and English literacy to address their needs in health, nutrition, and legal matters and for spiritual development. As Mercado (2005a) says, the funds of knowledge approach "is an approach that begins with the study of households rather than the study of pedagogy . . . and transforms relationships between and among families, students, and teachers" (p. 251). Browning-Aiken (2005) and Tenery (2005) both describe how social networks are formed with extended family, friends, and the wider community. In short, parents of emergent bilinguals have a great deal to teach educators about knowledge and skills that originate in their households that can, and should, be translated into academic success in schools. By exploring their students' family and community practices, teachers can become learners when they reach out to families and communities to understand students' existing knowledge repertoires (McIntyre et al., 2001).

Research has demonstrated variation in funds of knowledge among families from different backgrounds (Llopart & Esteban-Guitart, 2016; Rodriguez, 2013). To illustrate the significance and trajectory of the application of funds of knowledge in educational research and its potential to inform equitable family/community collaborations, we will discuss some relevant studies.

Whose Funds of Knowledge?

Philips's (1983) early work on the Warm Springs Reservation in Oregon showed that children learn participation structures at home that are different from the participation structures in the school, resulting in white teachers' misinterpreting the children's turn-taking behaviors and other ways of speaking. Heath (1983) demonstrated how practices in the home sometimes clash with school practices, in her research describing the home–school relationship of three communities in the Piedmont Carolinas: Maintown (representative of the middle class) and Trackton and Roadville, representing working-class Black and white mill communities, respectively. Literacy activities in the working-class communities differ from the literacy taught in schools, which represent middle-class "ways with words." Heath argues that literacy is practiced in all three communities in situations with rich mixtures of orality and literacy, but that teachers often fail to recognize and build upon the literacy practices of some communities, particularly those most marginalized in the larger society.

Other studies have shown how teachers can learn about communication patterns in the home, which can be adapted for improved learning opportunities in the classroom. For example, Rosebery, Warren, and Conant (1992) found that speakers of Haitian Creole use certain discursive practices that are culturally congruent with the discourse of argumentation in science, thus demonstrating how the home language can be a resource rather than an impediment for learning, as is often assumed. Case studies of other work on home language and culture in science classrooms have shown similar findings (e.g., Hudicourt-Barnes, 2003; Rosebery & Warren, 2008). In a similar vein, Au (1993) described efforts to meet the needs of native Hawaiian children, with particular attention to children's reading development, demonstrating that these students' reading improves when the participation structure of reading lessons maintains a close fit with the discourse of talk-story, part of the Hawaiian storytelling practice (see also Au, 2005).

Funds of Knowledge for Teaching and Learning

Marshall and Toohey's (2010) research in Canada on Punjabi Sikh fourth- and fifth-grade children's multimedia project on intergenerational stories shows how funds of knowledge can be leveraged in classrooms. The project empowered the Punjabi students to raise questions regarding the absence of their home languages from the school. Taking the initiative to incorporate their home languages into their illustrated storybooks led them to question why, in their French–English dual-language bilingual school, Punjabi was not also included even though 73% of the children in the school were Punjabi speakers.

The authors point out that the stories the children heard and retold included more "difficult" funds of knowledge such as grandparents' traumatic memories of life in India—encounters with snakes, lightning strikes, beatings, and war. These depictions of struggle became a source of concern; the teacher was ambivalent about what would be appropriate to include in storybooks being created for the school. In the end, stories were published with the *difficult family funds of knowledge* intact. The authors conclude their research by emphasizing the need to recognize and support families' and students' agency in applying their funds of knowledge in the classroom. Marshall and Toohey (2010) state, "We speculate that such knowledge might become the impetus . . . for productive dialogues among community members, children, and teachers about how these matters might become resources for children and teachers and community" (p. 237). Pitt and Britzman (2003) also question how "difficult" knowledge might be used as a resource rather than a prohibition in schools, from a psychoanalytic perspective. They claim that such knowledge can be a source of dialogue and critical examination of what students' life experiences might bring to their learning experience in the classroom.

In a similar vein, Zipin's (2009) research draws attention to difficult knowledge by discussing what he calls the "darker" aspects of students' life worlds—crime, alcohol, drugs, bullying. In a challenge to the earlier scholarly work on funds of knowledge that circumvented difficult topics such as these, he argues that dark funds of knowledge are too often avoided in schools and should be included in the curriculum. He describes the process by which one teacher helped her students address problems of bullying and harassment through clay animation stories. This required a great deal of effort on the part of both teacher and students to take on activities that interrupt "usual institutional denial mechanisms that sustain boundaries between dark knowledge and school curriculum" (Zipin, 2009, p. 321).

Zipin, Sellar, and Hattam (2012) also call attention to the difficulty of defining funds of knowledge in today's world of migration and border crossings. These movements give rise to localities that are culturally and linguistically diverse, fluid, often poor, and without funds of knowledge in common. The researchers argue that in diverse environments like these, local schools need to rethink their curriculum. The focus should be on working with families and students to reimagine "new possibilities for *becoming community*" (2012, p. 185; emphasis in the original). This new thinking compels schools to recognize the agency of learners, who can imagine recontextualizing work beyond existing funds of knowledge toward a more just future.

Transnational and Politicized Funds of Knowledge

Despite the challenges described by Zipin and colleagues (2012), more recent research has built on the concept of funds of knowledge by relating it to immigrant and racialized emergent bilingual students' lives, particularly by recognizing transnational and languaging experiences as sites of knowledge production (i.e., Alvarez, 2018; Cuero & Valdez, 2012; Dabach & Fones, 2016; Kwon et al., 2019; Lam & Warriner, 2012). Transnational funds of knowledge acknowledge the expertise gained by immigrant students over time and space, often passed down through generations as they navigate international borders as well as the multiple borders that many continue to experience living in between worlds (Esteban-Guitart, 2021; Gallo & Link, 2015; Hedges, 2015; Nuñez, 2023).

Some scholars have also explored youths' *politicized funds of knowledge*, which Gallo and Link (2015) define as "the real-world experiences, knowledges, and skills that young people deploy and develop across contexts of learning that are often positioned as taboo or unsafe to incorporate into classroom" (p. 361). Studies have examined the ways in which immigrant families used politicized funds of knowledge to navigate borders and citizenship status within a multiplicity of dangers (Bellino & Gluckman, 2024; Mangual Figueroa, 2011; Nuñez & Urrieta, 2021), challenge educational injustice (Campano et al., 2013; Rusoja, 2024), elicit the grim realities depicted in narcocorridos regarding drug violence along the border (De la Piedra & Araujo, 2012; de Los Ríos, 2018), or transgress sanctioned language practices through humor, profanity, and play (Martínez & Morales, 2014) and through translanguaging (Nuñez, 2021).

For instance, Gallo and Link's (2015) five-year ethnographic study with Mexican immigrant students in an elementary school investigates the complexities of learning amid heightened deportations in a Pennsylvania town. They focus on the experiences of a student named Ben from kindergarten to fifth grade, delving into the impact of his father's detention and potential deportation on his education across various settings like home, school, and alternative learning environments. Gallo and Link recognize Ben's and his peers' politicized funds of knowledge acquired from their experiences crossing the border, understanding the significance of having legal documentation, or acting as liaisons between law enforcement and their families. Gallo and Link note that while children actively sought opportunities to discuss and write about these significant experiences with supportive adults, teachers were often unaware of deportation-based practices or, even if they intended to help students, felt unsure about discussing topics concerning documentation status. Instead of avoiding discussions on differences such as immigration, Gallo and Link advocate for educational approaches and policies that equip educators to acknowledge and engage with students' politicized funds of knowledge.

This body of work urges educators to treat racialized transnational and emergent bilingual students as authorities on their experiences, incorporating their knowledge to challenge curricular biases. It also emphasizes these youth's sociopolitical awareness, advocating for the acknowledgment of their critical literacy skills. Nonetheless, these forms of funds of knowledge among immigrant youth tend to be silenced in schools due to restrictive educational policies, top-down curricula, and other teaching practices that overlook their perspectives (Lima Baker & Oliveira, 2023). Recognizing and utilizing the funds of knowledge of transnational/immigrant, racialized, and emergent bilingual students offers pedagogical benefits, such as activating prior knowledge and fostering culturally sustaining learning. Integrating students' politicized funds of knowledge into classrooms could, for example, stimulate insightful discussions on topics like home countries' political systems, perceptions of U.S. affairs, and critical analyses of language and literacy practices that can help counter assimilationist discourses (Dabach & Fones, 2016).

Recent scholarship focusing on students' politicized funds of knowledge emphasizes that an important aspect of funds of knowledge is that they originate not only from immediate members of nuclear families but also from larger intergenerational and nonbiological kinships and community networks across borders, effectively redefining the meaning of family for emergent bilinguals (Rusoja, 2024). Moreover, Dorner and Kim (2024), for example, highlight the politicized funds of knowledge that emergent bilingual youth begin to develop when they serve as language brokers for their families, helping them navigate relationships and unfamiliar institutional systems. These initial experiences can later develop as *critical transliteracy practices* that youth enact to engage their own agency not as translators for their families but as advocates for their communities. Rusoja (2022, 2024) also demonstrates how the politicized funds of knowledge of students and their families are the foundation for community organizing and mobilization for human rights. In this way, politicized funds of knowledge involve not only information but also transformative action.

As will be clear now, the robust literature on the funds of knowledge approach shows its durability and value as a resource for strengthening and transforming school–community relationships by transgressing normative ideas of what families and communities look like; the role that they, including their children, should play; and the purposes of collaborations. Integrating students' politicized funds of knowledge into family/community engagement initiatives has the potential to decenter normative school-centric, deficit-oriented, and paternalistic ideas and expectations to cultivate equitable collaborations in which emergent bilingual students, families, and communities enact their own agency and build on their transgenerational, historicized, contextualized, border-crossing, and communal knowledge.

INEQUITIES IN SCHOOL AND FAMILY/COMMUNITY RELATIONS

The Stigmatization of Language-Minoritized Families and Communities

As we have said, despite the promise of family, community, and school collaboration indicated in research findings, the "involvement" view still tends to dominate family–school relations. This view is defined in terms of parental presence at school or parents' assistance with students' academic work, for example. In general, it is the school that decides how parents can become involved with their children's education, which, according to Seeley (1993), is a "delegation" model.

In this approach, the parents of emergent bilinguals, who in many cases have limited formal schooling themselves and may not communicate well in English, continue to be disadvantaged, as they are stigmatized and considered incapable educational partners (Chappell & Faltis, 2013; Ramirez, 2003). In this way, rather than being viewed as meaningful contributors and experts in the lives of their own children, low-income minoritized parents tend to be framed in deficit ways and at fault for their children's poor academic performance because "(a) students enter school without the normative cultural knowledge and skills; and (b) parents neither value nor support their child's education" (Yosso, 2005, p. 75). Parents of emergent bilinguals are thought to have substandard language skills, lack of education, "inferior" family organizational structures and values, and "lack of interest" in their children's education. Families' home language practices are devalued, and family members' "accented" English may become a marker of difference and exclusion (Lippi-Green, 1997), especially if families are newcomers to the United States (Wiley & Lukes, 1996). Thus, not only do parents feel marginalized (Chaparro, 2020; Warriner, 2009), but their children also often experience a sense of failure during school and may feel unwelcome or even excluded from extracurricular activities (Gándara, O'Hara, & Gutiérrez, 2004).

By and large, perceptions of parental involvement and even parental suitability are based on normative Western values that ignore the important knowledge and expertise that families already possess. For example, U.S. educators tend to hold negative views toward transnational Mexican and Central American families, particularly due to children's school absenteeism when families make return trips to their home countries (Urrieta & Martínez, 2011). However, Urrieta's (2016) ethnographic study of U.S.–Mexican Indigenous children's transnational experiences found that these trips were not only an essential way for U.S.-born children to sustain significant cultural, intellectual, and spiritual practices that carry ancestral knowledge in their lives but also that through these trips, the children learned and applied important border-crossing literacies that were essential for their survival and can only be acquired through lived experience. Urrieta also noted that U.S. educators often miss the importance of these trips because they judge their value based solely on what the children "might miss out on" during their absence— formalized Western knowledge—without considering the value that families place on sustaining their cultural heritage and local knowledge (2016, p.1).

Another predominant assumption is that parents should, at the very least, support their children's language, literacy, and academic development by helping them with daily homework and by engaging in bedtime book reading, which are practices typically displayed by dominant white families. Although research on homework help dispels the myth that it is essential for higher achievement and shows that in many cases it actually reproduces inequalities and contributes to high levels of stress and conflict at home, it continues to be ingrained in most American schooling (Calarco, 2020; Kohn, 2006).

Delegating school responsibilities to parents places additional burdens on families who may already be facing significant challenges (Torres & Hurtado-Vivas, 2011). Homework demands impose a greater burden on parents and children from lower socio-economic and immigrant backgrounds, as these parents often lack the necessary time, previous school experiences, English language proficiency, resources, and suitable space to complete assignments, unlike their counterparts from higher socioeconomic classes and English-dominant families (Hurtado-Vivas, 2011). The homework and book reading burdens tend to fall disproportionately on mothers, exacerbating gender inequalities and expectations of "intensive mothering" in which mothers not only bear greater responsibilities for their families but also face heightened scrutiny in doing so (Elliott & Bowen, 2018; Goodall, 2021). Because Western patriarchal and colonial ideologies have historically pathologized both mothers and racialized people, homework often becomes a colonizing tool that dehumanizes and deagenticizes immigrant parents, particularly mothers, as schools intrude into the home to tell them how to structure their family time.

Moreover, homework demands also reproduce inequities because, even when they are aware of structural inequalities faced by their students, teachers tend to perceive those who are not able to complete it to their standards as irresponsible and may tend to penalize them more harshly (Calarco, Horn, & Chen, 2022). Overall, these impositions devalue minoritized family practices by, for example, deeming storytelling inferior to bedtime book reading (Souto-Manning & Rabadi-Raol, 2018), or prioritizing school work and goals over household chores, religious/spiritual practices, family leisure, community friendships, and other strong cultural practices that have been in fact essential to the survival (Torres & Hurtado-Vivas, 2011) and sustenance of the family's ancestral knowledge (Urrieta, 2016).

Given the linguistic marginalization and the imposition of school-centric ideas of parental involvement at home, not only do parents feel marginalized (Warriner, 2009; Chaparro, 2020), but their children also often experience a sense of failure during school and may feel unwelcome or even excluded from extracurricular activities (Gándara, O'Hara, & Gutiérrez, 2004). Yet the research demonstrates that, in fact, it is the schools that are deficient—schools with the least funding and limited resources as well as teachers who have not been prepared to work with families for whom English is not part of their home language practices (Gibson, Gándara, & Koyama, 2004). As Valenzuela (1999) noted, schooling is too often a subtractive process, which ignores students' ways of knowing and speaking. As family's unique literacies and ancestral knowledge systems are dismissed and pathologized in favor of school-centric practices, opportunities for building on these resources are lost

(Torres & Hurtado-Vivas, 2011; Urrieta, 2016), and schooling eventually becomes complicit in producing failure (see also Varenne & McDermott, 1998).

Exclusion of the Most Significant Resource: Home Language Practices

Many educators still consider family practices to be barriers to student achievement. The practice that most often comes under attack is the use of the home language. There is a kind of "exceptionalist" belief (DeGraff, 2005), a deficit view of home language practices as an inadequate vehicle for education. DeGraff (2009) presents a critical examination of this deficit view of the home language using the example of school and community attitudes toward his own Haitian Creole; he shows the fallacy of this belief and its social cost for Haitian American children's education. In his article, DeGraff shares a comment that readers once sent to *The Miami Herald* about the Haitian Creole language: "Creole is not even a language. It is slave lingo. . . . Why on earth are we spending public funds to teach kids in school the language of peasants?" (cited in DeGraff, 2009, p. 124). Such comments are not only demeaning but also racist and classist. Contrary to these false beliefs, DeGraff demonstrates through detailed comparative analysis of Creole, English, and French language structures that Haitian Creole is a powerful linguistic resource.

A great deal of research shows the value of home language practices as an educative tool. Research also shows that the erosion of the language other than English among the children of immigrants has negative repercussions for family life and for the well-being of children, particularly as they move into adolescence. The absence of a shared language creates communication challenges, resulting in heightened conflict between parents and children, diminished parental effectiveness, exacerbation of preexisting issues in parent–child relationships, and heightened susceptibility of adolescents to negative influences from peers (Cox et al., 2021).

Unfortunately, immigrant parents are often exhorted to "speak English at home" in the mistaken belief that this will improve their children's performance at school (Spolsky, 2012). This advice, though well intentioned, encourages inconsistent and often weak "linguistic input" from parents who themselves may speak little or no English and, above all, devalues home language practices (Gándara & Contreras, 2009). However, even without explicit discouragement from teachers, English-only schooling policies and practices indirectly also dissuade families from sustaining their home language practices (Kaveh & Sandoval, 2020; Kaveh, 2022). As Kaveh's (2022) research revealed, teachers' appreciation and "feel-good" expressions of "bilingualism as a resource" do not translate into actual pedagogical change or the decentering of English in the curriculum, instruction, and classroom management choices. Thus, the lack of access to bilingual education clearly plays a significant role in home language erosion (Cox et al., 2021).

As we have argued in earlier chapters, the erasure of the home language through English-only school practices reinforces the deficit view that families and their children need to be linguistically "fixed" or "repaired" before they can succeed academically in the United States. Nonetheless, bilingual education programs do not always eliminate deficit thinking or result in equitable collaborative relationships with families from historically marginalized communities. As we have seen, this has been evident in the rise of dual-language bilingual programs' popularity among white, English-speaking middle/upper class families, and the lack of equitable access by minoritized families when these programs are established in affluent or gentrified neighborhoods (Dorner et al., 2021). Also, while these programs may be characterized by higher degrees of parental involvement, including that of racialized low-income families, it is intersectionally privileged families who display normative expectations of parental involvement who tend to dominate PTA participation and whose voices receive most attention (Cervantes-Soon, 2014; Cervantes-Soon et al., 2017, 2021; Freire & Alemán, 2021; Palmer & García-Mateus, 2023).

Given this research, addressing issues of language, race, class, and immigration status in parent involvement is crucial for equity, requiring engagement at both local and broader societal levels.

Teachers themselves admit that their weakest skills are in the area of making effective connections with parents from diverse ethnolinguistic backgrounds (Gándara, Maxwell-Jolly, & Driscoll, 2005). Gándara and her colleagues (2005) tell us that teachers they interviewed reported "their district's failure to devote resources to the training of teachers, aides, and other personnel to communicate with parents and/or to provide teachers the time to make useful contact with families" (p. 7). Gándara and Contreras (2009) give reasons why hiring qualified teachers from the students' own communities would be important to bridge the distance from minoritized families and communities:

> Such teachers not only better understand the challenges that students face and the resources that exist in those communities; they are also more likely to speak the language of the students and be able to communicate with them and their parents. Moreover, teachers who come from the same community in which they work are more likely to stay in the job over time, developing valuable experience and expertise that has been shown to enhance the achievement of their students. (p. 148)

Work is still needed to encourage teacher positive engagement with parents (Maxwell-Jolly & Gándara, 2012). We argue that the schools have to revise their valuation of these parents' educative role and abundant family literacy practices within minoritized families by fostering an environment of parental involvement that necessitates reshaping the entire system in order to help pave the way for family–school equitable collaborations.

One-Size-Fits-All Parent Education Programs

Historically, U.S. education policies have regulated parent–school relationships based on national interests and in attempts to remedy "problem" minoritized populations. Baquedano-López and colleagues (2013) examine various tropes used in approaches to parental involvement. First, they highlight the portrayal of "Parents as Problems," which stems from government policies aimed at safeguarding students and empowering teachers with greater control over education. Conversely, the concept of "Parents as First Teachers" acknowledges parental influence but often introduces pedagogical strategies that downplay parental roles. Additionally, the discourse of "Parents as Learners," which is particularly prevalent in discussions involving immigrant parents, undermines parental knowledge.

Under these tropes, one mainstream approach has been to develop "parent education" or "family literacy" programs to show parents how they can become involved in their children's education. The programs offer services such as providing information about the U.S. educational system; demonstrating ways to interact with teachers, school administrators, and other staff; and offering ways to help children at home—for example, by reading to them, talking with them, and encouraging them in their studies (Chrispeels & Gonz, 2004; Chrispeels & Rivero, 2001).

Although parent education programs are valuable, some focus almost exclusively on what parents do not know. Many of these programs have taken the "let us fix them" approach, assuming that parents lack the requisite motivations and skills to support their children's education. We have already shown the fallacies in any deficit model that claims there is one best way for parents to be involved in their children's education, and other scholars have concurred with this criticism (Auerbach, 1995; Taylor, 1997).

Amid educational reforms in the late 1990s, the notion of parents as partners gained traction, bolstered by Title I amendments that mandate schools to inform parents about school programs, academic standards, and assessments to foster knowledgeable partnerships (Baquedano-López et al., 2013). School–family compacts, mandated by Title I, outline shared responsibilities for academic improvement among families, school staff, and students. However, this practice still perceives a lack of parent involvement as a problem that schools must address to align parents with their agenda, especially regarding reform efforts. The partnership concept does not always clearly define meaningful interactions and shared responsibilities with families. Furthermore, a federal report revealed low compliance with school–family compacts and other Title I parent involvement components in most states. The law's language tends to limit parent responsibility to monitoring attendance, homework completion, and TV watching, reducing their role to that of a compliance officer rather than a partner in education. School compacts resemble parent–school contracts in charter schools, which often serve more as compliance mechanisms than tools for genuine inclusion and partnership.

Furthermore, Baquedano-López, Alexander, and Hernández (2013) highlight the trope of "Parents as Choosers and Consumers," which is linked to efforts promoting school choice. "School choice" encompasses policies allowing parents to select their children's educational institutions from options and to stimulate competition among schools in the hopes of enhancing educational quality. The idea of "parent choice" has become mainstream in educational reforms, including NCLB's "opt out" option, which allows parents to transfer children from low-performing schools.

School choice discourse emphasizes parents' ability to make market-based decisions, such as choosing between public and private schools, school locations, and various public school options. Parents also make choices regarding course placements, special education services, language use, and engagement activities. The parent-as-chooser discourse limits involvement to individual market-based selections. Parent-choice ideologies can be neoconservative or neoliberal, focusing on parent or market control, respectively. Progressive choice programs aim to reduce school inequality but are often undermined by colorblind discourses, which overlook systemic inequities. Such discourses neglect power dynamics and constrain parent involvement. Despite potential changes in parent involvement policies, schools, teachers, and elite families maintain privileged knowledge.

Despite the implementation of policies aimed at integrating nondominant students and their families into our public school system through diverse mechanisms, significant inequities persist, as evidenced by educational achievement data among nondominant students. Johnson (2009) provides a critique of any unitary "best practices" approach in parent education programs that do not account for diversity in families' ways of educating their children. In the section that follows, we provide alternative routes to family engagement in children's education.

ALTERNATIVE APPROACHES TO PARENT AND COMMUNITY ENGAGEMENT

Counteracting Stigmatization Through Broader Views of Parent and Community Engagement

Ways of approaching parent and community engagement have evolved in attempts to create a more equal partnership between families/communities and schools. In recommending alternative approaches, we discuss efforts to ameliorate the chasm between parents of emergent bilinguals, their communities, and school personnel. We begin by signaling more culturally sensitive programs to support parents as educators and then discuss how families and communities, often in concert, have asserted more agency in calling for educational policies and practices that take into account their children's linguistic and cultural resources for learning.

Scholars in the Global Family Research Project (formerly the Harvard Family Research Project from 1983 to 2017) have sponsored a number of initiatives and have provided tips, research reports, and policy briefs on family engagement in children's education. Their overarching approach is to demonstrate that family engagement is a shared responsibility among parents, the school, and the community.

The Family, School, and Community National Working Group (Weiss & Lopez, 2009) has developed an expanded definition of family engagement that entails three principles, which we cite here:

- First, family engagement is a shared responsibility in which schools and other community agencies and organizations are committed to reaching out to engage families in meaningful ways and in which families are committed to actively supporting their children's learning and development.
- Second, family engagement is continuous across a child's life and entails enduring commitment but changing parent roles as children mature into young adulthood.

- Third, effective family engagement cuts across and reinforces learning in the multiple settings where children learn—at home, in prekindergarten programs, in school, in after school programs, in faith-based institutions, and in the community. (Weiss & Lopez, 2009, para. 6)

These more sensitive approaches to parent education programs also acknowledge that schools must move beyond a unidirectional undertaking: Schools must learn from families, too, and come to understand how student learning occurs at home and in the community. A more useful way to benefit emergent bilinguals' success is to develop bidirectional school-community education programs.

As Rosenberg, Lopez, and Westmoreland (2009) argue, family engagement is a responsibility that must be shared by schools, parents, and communities. The first step that educators can take in taking responsibility is to counter pervasive deficit discourses about minoritized parents (Goodall, 2021) and to broaden definitions of what counts as parental involvement. That is why the funds of knowledge program of research we introduced earlier is so important (e.g., Browning-Aiken, 2005; González, Moll, & Amanti, 2005; López, 2001; Mercado, 2005a, 2005b; Moll et al., 1992; Tenery, 2005).

Broadening the View of Family and Community Engagement

A broader definition of parental engagement, which takes into account family and community practices, is that provided by Pérez Carreón, Drake, and Calabrese Barton (2005), who developed the concept of *ecologies of parental engagement* to refer to the participation of parents in a child's schooling in a manner that goes beyond the physical space of the school and is rooted in the understanding of a family's cultural practices. This approach takes into account the different styles of action taken by parents of diverse ethnolinguistic backgrounds.

Two seminal studies of families' styles of action, published in the 1990s and still read today, are good examples of parental actions that dispel deficit-oriented myths about lack of parental involvement among minoritized families. Ana Celia Zentella's (1997, 2005) research in New York and Guadalupe Valdés's (1996) research in California provide evidence that parents of various Spanish-speaking backgrounds are involved in their children's education in a variety of ways, including rich linguistic exposure to storytelling and print in the home language. Zentella (1997) explores the lives and rich language practices of working-class Puerto Rican families with a focus on five girls, whom she follows from childhood until they become young adults. Her observations of family language practices lead her to emphasize the importance of teachers building on students' home language practices for learning to support students' self-worth and identity and to help children see connections with the standard Spanish taught in school and the one used at home. For Zentella (2005), becoming bilingual gives students a chance at economic advancement. She states that parental goals for their children also include becoming *bien educado* (well educated), a term that encompasses moral values and respect along with having book knowledge.

Valdés (1996) describes first-generation Mexican parents' beliefs about their role in their children's schooling. For these parents, teachers were to be entrusted with the children's academic skills. Mothers and fathers, who did not feel that they had the academic preparation to help with these skills, focused instead on giving advice, instilling respect, and fostering moral values (see also Suárez-Orozco & Suárez-Orozco, 2001). Valdés makes a strong argument in this research that school officials' and teachers' response to these parental beliefs has been that the parents are disinterested in the children's education. As we have seen in the research reported throughout this chapter, this notion is far from the truth; parents want to learn how to help their children at home (Epstein, 1990), yet they have felt disregarded and left powerless in their attempts to be engaged with the school (Pérez Carreón, Drake, & Calabrese Barton, 2005).

Community Organizing

Research shows that rather than being naive and needy clients, parents of emergent bilinguals often question the existing power relations in the home–school relationship and strive to enact more agentic participation in schools guided by their own critical consciousness (Baez & Hurie, 2023; Dyrness, 2011; Sun, 2023). Researchers have documented agentic forms of parental actions on behalf of their children, including those of immigrant parents, such as searching out a dialogic approach with school personnel (Olivos, 2006; Olivos, Jiménez-Castellanos, & Ochoa, 2011) or approaching outside groups "such as employers, church authorities, or staff of nonprofit organizations about their rights as parents" (Poza, Brooks, & Valdés, 2014, p. 132).

Some parents form grassroots organizations to address their schools about concerns they have regarding their children's education. According to a survey of 66 community-organizing groups by Mediratta, Fruchter, and Lewis (2002), most of these groups have been in existence since 1994. Though research on these groups' impact has been limited, we know about some of their efforts. Gold, Simon, and Brown (2002) interviewed 19 community-organizing groups and conducted a case study of five of them. The authors learned that members of the community make an impact on the quality of schools by, among other things, insisting on school–community connections and developing parents' leadership skills.

Other examples include Delgado-Gaitán's (2001) study of the Comité de Padres Latinos/Committee of Latinx Parents (COPLA), where parents learned to make sense of the school system, build leadership, and become their children's advocates. Delgado-Gaitán (2001) explained: "Shaped by the lesson of their own pain, [the] parents placed their children's needs center stage, giving rise to and sustaining their activism in the community" (p. 8). Dyrness's (2011) participatory action research in Oakland, California, also documented the efforts of immigrant mothers, who united to voice their concerns and ideas in efforts to secure equitable education for their children as the district transitioned into a new small-schools model. Yet Dyrness reveals how educators, amid conflict, used their credentials to silence community voices and position themselves as experts in decision-making.

In some cities, bilingual families and communities are spearheading what Jaumont (2017) has called "a bilingual revolution," demanding that bilingual programs be accessible for their children. These efforts are examples of the type of parental engagement that involves mobilizing to change or create new education structures that truly tap into the linguistic assets of communities. However, it is important to keep in mind that not all bilingual families have been given the same degree of consideration. While this movement has been recently received more favorably, it is often because many of those seeking these programs already possess a degree of intersectional privilege, such as English proficiency, high socioeconomic status, or characteristics of elite cosmopolitanism. Moreover, the current context of school choice has also facilitated more positive responses toward these parents' demands for dual-language bilingual programs because they are used as amenities to attract more "desirable" families (Cervantes-Soon et al., 2021; Chaparro, 2021; Dorner et al., 2021).

The reality is that racialized, low-income families' struggle for bilingual education has been historically faced with dismissal, repression, and the imposition of restrictive language policies. For example, Soto's (1996) ethnographic study in "Steel Town," Pennsylvania, documented emergent bilingual families' community organizing and advocacy to reinstate the community's nationally recognized bilingual education program after the local school board and superintendent decided to eliminate it. However, during the ensuing political struggle, decision-makers disregarded the voices of bilingual community leaders, educators, and children, perpetuating asymmetrical power relations.

Community-based organizations (CBOs) with strong connections to marginalized families and communities can add leverage to families' pursuit of more active roles in engaging with schools (Shirley, 1997). For example, a case study approach was used to examine three CBOs in Chicago, Illinois; Los Angeles, California; and Newark, New Jersey, which were working to engage parents more fully in schools (Warren et al., 2009). The three core elements that they found across these diverse urban settings included a focus on building relationships among parents as well as between parents and the school, the development of parent leaders who collaborate with schools in setting agendas, and a mutual exchange of relational power. The authors concluded by stating that not only parents but also schools can benefit from the expertise of CBOs to develop partnerships with parents in the education of children and youth.

An example of a successful partnership with community-based organizations is the Padres Comprometidos program that was developed originally by the National Council of La Raza (UnidosUS since 2017). The program continues to be implemented in many sites and states. The home language and cultural practices of Latine parents are seen as assets in the curriculum designed by Padres Comprometidos. In addition to working with families, the program also works with school personnel so that relationships between families and school personnel are built and strengthened, with all equal partners.

Decolonizing Parental Engagement

Baquedano-López, Alexander, and Hernandez (2013) adopt a decolonial stance in the dynamics between school administrators, teachers, and families. A decolonial approach challenges the Eurocentric foundations underpinning notions of progress and development, which often undermine the autonomy and sovereignty of nondominant communities. It is evident that educational practices remain entrenched in dominant, white, Eurocentric paradigms, rooted in a historical legacy that glorifies colonial practices and perpetuates notions of success based on Western ideals of individual merit and supposed equality of opportunity. Moreover, our educational system reflects neoliberal principles, attributing the "crisis of education" disproportionately to communities of color. This perpetuates a narrative of education serving a "civilizing function," dictating what is deemed best for nondominant students and their families while marginalizing alternative forms of knowledge and eroding their decision-making autonomy.

Therefore, a decolonial approach seeks to redefine these power dynamics by addressing imbalances and exclusions experienced by students and parents from nondominant backgrounds. It acknowledges the imperative of restructuring economic systems to enable meaningful parental participation and decision-making for their children's education. Furthermore, decolonization efforts must confront and dismantle all forms of violence, whether epistemic, psychological, or physical, including silencing, linguistic domination, segregation, and tracking, which perpetuate the dehumanization and academic marginalization of racialized emergent bilinguals.

This transformative work requires that educators understand the complex intersections of race, class, language, immigration status, and other social structures that shape the educational experiences of nondominant students. It also necessitates deep-seated social change processes, creativity, and the fostering of families' agency. Yet education policies aimed at enhancing parent/family–school relationships have proven to be limiting. Thus, rather than relying on school contexts and educational policies to allow communities to advance decolonizing goals, some grassroots efforts have taken place within liminal spaces where families, educators, and other community members can come together to cultivate the critical consciousness, sovereignty, and knowledge systems that are disregarded in schools.

As an example of this approach, Milk-Bonilla and Valenzuela (2023) describe Academia Cuauhtli, a community-based extracurricular program offering ethnic studies to economically disadvantaged third, fourth, and fifth graders. It also offers transformative professional development for bilingual teachers, focusing on culturally enriching curriculum development, student-centered teaching methods, and fostering asset-based partnerships between homes and schools. Academia Cuauhtli's approach aims to enhance teacher awareness by challenging deficit orientations toward low-income Latine communities by prioritizing the cultivation of trusting, collaborative relationships among teachers, families, community members, and students and fostering a social framework of genuine care. This approach, known as *relational pedagogies*, integrates various forms of care for students, with a particular focus on their well-being. Milk Bonilla and Valenzuela illustrate this approach through a lesson on curanderismo, the traditional holistic healing system in Latin America. They emphasize two relational strategies—pláticas and convivios, that is, conversations and living together—as examples of how a caring-based social framework harnesses collective knowledge to support a comprehensive approach to student education. These relational approaches, built on critical consciousness and genuine and mutual care, can open new possibilities for family–school relations despite the limits imposed by sanctioned school spaces and policies.

EDUCATING EMERGENT BILINGUALS: RE-CREATING THE SCHOOL–FAMILY–COMMUNITY CONNECTIONS

We can learn a great deal from research about more empowering school–family–community linkages. In addition, we have to recognize that parents are invested in their emergent bilingual children's learning and want them to excel. Further, we should recognize that the education of emergent bilingual students is a partnership with parents and the community. By acknowledging and leveraging the knowledge and power that parents possess in their interactions with school staff, teachers can work toward redefining the dynamics between parents and schools and realizing equitable educational opportunities.

Schools can investigate the funds of knowledge that their students' families and communities hold and then build on them. The most important resource that families possess is their home language and cultural practices, which should be celebrated as a source of knowledge. Teachers also need support: They must be provided with the tools they need to communicate better with these families. Assistance should be given to families to understand the workings of the school system, to build social networks, to seek out school and community services that support their educational efforts, and to proactively initiate alternative agendas for school change. In short, the literature we report here suggests that there needs to be a balance of power with school personnel, parents, and community working to achieve closer mutual engagement for the education of emergent bilinguals. Crucially, decolonization supports a humanizing project, fostering critical reflection on practices that contribute to ongoing stigma, deficit thinking, and colonization, challenging the imposition of dominant knowledge not only in curricula and pedagogical practices but also in relationships with families.

STUDY QUESTIONS

1. Distinguish between the concepts of family/community involvement, engagement, and equitable collaboration. Why does this matter?
2. Describe what research tells us regarding the benefits of family and community engagement for emergent bilingual children's success in school.
3. What are funds of knowledge? Give some examples of these from the research; describe how the research has broadened to include difficult or dark funds of knowledge in the curriculum.
4. In what ways are families of emergent bilinguals sometimes stigmatized?
5. What are the problems and promises of parent education programs?
6. In what ways are parents showing leadership on behalf of their children's education?
7. Describe what would be a promising program to develop partnerships between families of emergent bilinguals and schools.

CHAPTER 8

Assessments

In this chapter, we will:

- Review theoretical constructs that are important for the fair assessment of emergent bilinguals, specifically:
  - » The power of assessments,
  - » The difference between language proficiency and content proficiency,
  - » The discrepancy between general language performances and language-specific performance,
  - » The validity and reliability of tests for emergent bilinguals,
  - » The fit of the assessment to the population, and
  - » The match of the language of the test to the language practices of the students.
- Identify inequities in assessment practices that arise from:
  - » Assessing prematurely and intensely,
  - » Establishing arbitrary proficiencies, or
  - » Ignoring those who need the most help.
- Consider some alternative practices, including:
  - » Observing closely,
  - » Assessing authentically and dynamically,
  - » Enabling testing accommodations,
  - » Disentangling language and content,
  - » Assessing in students' home languages, using translations and transadaptations,
  - » Assessing bilingually, and
  - » Translanguaging in assessment.

One of the key equity issues surrounding the education of emergent bilinguals concerns the ways in which these students are assessed according to national mandates and state accountability systems. Our central question in this chapter is: *Given what we know theoretically and research-wise about assessment of emergent bilinguals, are these students being assessed according to accepted theories and research evidence about language and bilingualism?* The answer to this question, as we will demonstrate here, is an emphatic *no.* As we have previously noted, it has been widely demonstrated that as a result of inadequate high-stakes tests, emergent bilinguals experience more remedial instruction, greater probability of assignment to lower curriculum tracks, higher dropout rates, poorer graduation rates, and disproportionate referrals to special education classes (Artiles, 1998; Artiles & Ortiz, 2002; Bach, 2020; Bertrand & Marsh, 2021; Cummins, 1984). In fact, given the negative repercussions on graduation eligibility and resource provisions to schools, Menken (2010) argues that no group has been punished more by high-stakes assessments than emergent bilinguals designated as English learners.

Because the English learner subgroup by definition cannot possibly meet the proficiency targets in these high-stakes tests, *all* programs serving emergent bilinguals are often questioned, including those that are conducted exclusively in English. Mandating high-stakes tests in English for all has acted as language policy, accelerating students' immersion in English without the advantage of home language support. Valenzuela (2005) maintains that high-stakes testing in Texas has been the most detrimental policy for Latines and emergent bilinguals and recommends that there be local control over assessment.

We agree with the assertion that all students have to be *included* in every assessment. But there are equity concerns regarding how assessments are currently being conducted and how the data they generate are being used. These equity issues have to do with misunderstandings of theoretical constructs for assessment that disproportionately impact emergent bilinguals. These include (1) the power of assessments, (2) the difference between language proficiency and content proficiency, (3) the discrepancy between general language performance and language-specific performance, (4) the validity and reliability of the tests for emergent bilinguals, (5) the fit of the assessment to the population, and (6) the match of the language of the test to the language practices of the students. This chapter first considers these theoretical constructs and then identifies the shortcomings of some ill-considered practices that surround assessment of emergent bilinguals. As in other chapters, we note that there is a gap between accepted theories regarding assessment for these students and the testing that takes place. We end the chapter by proposing alternative assessment policies and practices that are more effective for these students based on theory and research evidence.

THEORETICAL CONSTRUCTS IN ASSESSMENT

The Power of Assessments

As Foucault (1979) has indicated, assessment can be a way to exercise power and control (see also Shohamy, 2001). Foucault (1979) explains:

> The examination combines the technique of an observing hierarchy and those of normalizing judgement. It is a normalizing gaze, a surveillance that makes it possible to qualify, to classify and to punish. It establishes over individuals a visibility through which one differentiates them and judges them. (p. 184)

Since Alfred Binet developed his intelligence testing methods in the early 20th century, tests have been used to label and classify students, often with grave consequences. For example, the Stanford-Binet test developed by Lewis Terman was used to "prove" that "[Indians, Mexicans, and Blacks] should be segregated in special classes . . ." (Terman, cited in Oakes, 1985, p. 36). The history of assessment has been entangled from the very beginning with racism and linguistic discrimination (Wiley, 1996). Testing is used more often as a vehicle for allocating or denying educational and employment benefits rather than as a means for informing teaching and developing learning.

Bertrand and Marsh (2015) examined the use of testing data over the course of a year in six schools with large populations of African American and Latine students. Their study found that educators and administrators frequently employed data in manners that reinforced deficit perceptions of students' abilities by attributing students' performance to some aspect of the students' identity, such as being categorized as English learners, assigned to special education, or being generally and permanently a "low" student. These deficit-oriented ideas absolve educators from their responsibility, suggesting that if students are predetermined to perform poorly, then the effectiveness of the instruction they receive is irrelevant. While assessment data are supposed to inform and help improve teaching, Kim's (2017) research with secondary-level emergent bilinguals noted that assessment data sets were actually used in ways that disadvantaged these students throughout their educational journey. These students were continuously placed in remedial education and denied opportunities for high-quality curriculum, rendering them as perpetually low-achieving, struggling, and long-term English learners despite their eagerness to succeed in school. Thus, educators have to be extremely mindful of the power of tests and how they can be dangerous and discriminatory if used inappropriately.

Language Proficiency and Content Proficiency

Every assessment is an assessment of language (AERA, APA, & NCME, 2014). Thus, assessment for emergent bilinguals, who are still learning the language in which the test is administered, is not valid unless language is disentangled from content. As we have noted, English used for interpersonal communication is not the same as the more complex use required for academic tasks in English. Gottlieb (2006, 2016) describes how *academic language proficiency* is usually assessed by evaluating the comprehension and use of specialized vocabulary and language patterns in the spoken and written modes, the linguistic complexity of these modes, and the appropriate use of the sound system (phonology), grammatical structure (syntax), and meaning (semantics) of the language. *Content proficiency* refers to whether the student has actually acquired knowledge of the subject matter. When assessments use only English to test emergent bilinguals' content knowledge, both language and content proficiency are entangled.

The Discrepancy Between General Linguistic Performance and Language-Specific Performance

It is also important to keep in mind two dimensions of language performances that we call *general linguistic performance* and *language-specific performance* (García,

Johnson, & Seltzer, 2017). General linguistic performance has to do with the ability of students to deploy any of the features in their language repertoire to accomplish language and content-specific tasks. Language-specific performance refers to the ability to deploy only the features considered standard and that correspond to the specific named language demanded of the task (García et al., 2017).

All speakers use features of their language system that go beyond those sanctioned in schools to perform academic tasks. In part, schools teach students to use language for tasks that are different from those they perform outside of school. In schools, for example, students are given practice in making sense of complex texts they have read or listened to; using language to make convincing arguments, especially in writing; discussing a math problem or theorem; and so on. As we have seen, emergent bilinguals come into schools with very different schooling experiences. Some newcomers arrive in U.S. schools with strong prior education. They know how to use language to perform school tasks, although perhaps they may not have the features of English demanded in a U.S. school. Let us illustrate with two hypothetical cases. Jeehyae, newly arrived from Korea, can use Korean to do all the things that the language arts standards require. In reading, and in Korean, Jeehyae can provide text evidence of key ideas, make inferences and identify main ideas and relationships in complex texts, recognize the text's craft and structure (its chronology, comparison and contrast, identify cause and effect), and associate knowledge and ideas from multiple sources and texts. In writing, and in Korean, Jeehyae can produce text types for various purposes, such as opinion, informative, explanatory, and narrative pieces. But, of course, if in an assessment Jeehyae were asked to perform these tasks using English features exclusively, she would do very poorly.

Jeehyae's linguistic performance is different from that of Moussa, a student recently arrived from Guinea in Africa whose home language practices he identifies as Fulani, but who has been schooled in French in a poor rural school. Moussa's school did not provide him with the opportunities to use Fulani or French to perform the linguistically complex academic tasks valued in U.S. schools. His school focused on developing Moussa's standard French through mechanical drills and tasks aimed to "erase" his Fulani. When Moussa entered his U.S. school, he was assessed in English only. As a result, his lack of experience using language for academic purposes was masked by his poor English-only performance.

By not differentiating between general linguistic performance and language-specific performance, assessments run the risk of obviating the important difference between Jeehyae, a student able to use language to perform academic tasks (even if that language is Korean), and Moussa, whose poor language performance is not simply a matter of English language acquisition but of learning how to use language for school tasks. Both students' language-specific performances in English language assessments are poor. However, Jeehyae can leverage her experience with ways of using Korean in school to perform academic tasks, whereas Moussa cannot perform these tasks in French, nor can he do so in Fulani. Assessments that do not differentiate between general linguistic performance and language-specific performance mask an important difference among emergent bilinguals that has important consequences for their education. These entanglements then have important significance for test validity.

Validity and Reliability for Emergent Bilinguals

In order for test results to be equitable, emergent bilinguals must be included in the design and piloting of the instrument so that the *norming* of the test is not biased—that is, the test must have both validity and reliability for bilingual students (Abedi, 2004; Abedi & Lord, 2001).

Reliability refers to the capacity of the test or of individual test items to measure a construct consistently over time. Research by Abedi (2004); Abedi, Hofstetter, and Lord (2004); and Martiniello (2008) demonstrates that large-scale exams have differential reliability for students whose English language abilities do not match the population on whom the test was normed. Martiniello (2008) shows that emergent bilingual students and monolingual students with the same math ability perform differently on particular math test items because of unfamiliar vocabulary and complex syntactic structures.

Chatterji (2003) defines *validity* as having to do with "the *meaningfulness* of an assessment's results given the particular constructs being tapped, purposes for which the assessment is used and the populations for whom the assessment is intended" (p. 56). Given the fact that language and content are confounded in tests, there are concerns over the validity of standardized assessments for emergent bilinguals because a test may not measure what it intends. Furthermore, tests may have little *content validity* for these students because the performance of emergent bilinguals does not reveal much about their learning (Lachat, 1999). Worse still is the *consequential validity* of these tests for emergent bilinguals—the after-effects and social consequences. Emergent bilinguals often pay a price with regard to how they are taught as a result of these tests, ending up misdirected into remedial educational programs and special education (Cronbach, 1989; Kim, 2017; Messick, 1989).

Because tests are constructed for white, middle-class, monolingual populations, they always contain a built-in content bias. Tests do not always include activities or concepts from the worlds of minoritized students (Mercer, 1989). Nor do they take into account the multilingual abilities of bilingual children (Ascenzi-Moreno & Seltzer, 2021; Shohamy, 2011). These tests designed for monolingual students reflect neither the cultural practices nor the language practices with which emergent bilingual students are familiar.

Fit of Tests to Population

Criterion-referenced assessments, in which each exam is compared to a specific body of knowledge, are distinct from *norm-referenced assessments*, in which each exam is measured against the scores of other students. But criterion-referenced assessments are still not appropriate for testing emergent bilinguals. In criterion-referenced assessments, students are graded according to whether they have met a defined criterion or standard, which determines what students should know and be able to do in various subject areas. But emergent bilinguals, by definition, generally cannot meet the standard of English language proficiency; thus, they are often judged not to be competent with regard to subject knowledge.

Furthermore, because language and subject content are entangled, studies have found that there is a discrepancy between test scores and student performance in the classroom. Katz et al. (2004) studied Spanish-speaking and Chinese-speaking emergent bilinguals in San Francisco and concluded: "Test data suggested that ELL students underperformed academically compared to EO (English-only) students, but ELL students turned out to be high achievers in the classroom context" (p. 56).

It has been shown that *performance-based assessments*, tests that ask students to produce a product such as a portfolio or perform an action, are better for bilingual students because they provide a wider range of opportunities to show what they know and are able to do in both language and content areas (Abedi, 2010; Estrin & Nelson-Barber, 1995; Gottlieb, 2016, 2017; Navarrete & Gustke, 1996). Genishi and Borrego Brainard (1995) say that performance-based assessment "can be oral, written, 'performative,' as in dance, or visual/artistic" (p. 54). Goh (2004) recommends any alternative technique that can determine what a given student really knows or can do—performances, hands-on activities, and portfolios of student work—arguing that assessment must include multiple modalities. Because student problem-solving skills may be documented in different ways, performance-based multimodal assessments are less language dependent than are traditional tests, enabling teachers to better distinguish between language proficiency and content proficiency. So, although performance-based assessments tax teachers' time, they are more appropriate precisely because they require teachers' attention to the details in students' performance.

However, it is important to recognize that although performance-based assessments are a more appropriate and valid way to identify student learning, they are not necessarily neutral or objective instruments because ultimately they rely on teachers' interpretations of the results they yield. Teachers' perceptions of students and underlying ideologies play a significant role in shaping their interpretations of student performance in these assessments. For example, Ascenzi-Moreno and Seltzer's (2021) research on formative reading assessments in two different dual-language bilingual programs found that teachers tended to interpret low reading scores among Latine students differently from those of more affluent white students. While teachers analyzed low scores among white students in nuanced ways and used them to identify skills they wanted to teach, teachers of Latine students viewed their low scores as an indication of lack of literacy in their homes and discussed them as a natural result of being overall struggling learners. Thus, Ascenzi-Moreno and Seltzer argue that educators do not use assessments just to gauge students' knowledge; they may also rely on them to reinforce their preconceived beliefs.

Let us reiterate the major caveat about performance assessments: Because their interpretation relies on the judgment of those scoring the tests (Lachat, 1999), it is crucial that individuals knowledgeable about the linguistic and cultural practices of emergent bilinguals participate in the development of rubrics for scoring student work. In this way, scorers may be able to disentangle academic performance on the assessment from language proficiency. In addition, it is important to recognize the fallacy of color-blind neutrality and engage in deep reflexivity through the interpretation process.

Matching the Language of the Test to Language Practices

The language practices of both emergent and proficient bilingual students are very different from those of monolingual students. Thus, a test constructed for monolinguals cannot match the language use of bilingual individuals who draw from a language repertoire with many more linguistic features. Bachman (2001) refers to the distinction between the language of the test and actual language practices:

> That there must be a relationship between the language used on tests and that used in "real life" cannot be denied, since if there is no such relationship, our language tests become mere shadows, sterile procedures that may tell us nothing about the very ability we wish to measure. (p. 356)

Valdés and Figueroa (1994) point to the difficulties of testing emergent bilingual students with instruments that have been normed for monolinguals:

> When a bilingual individual confronts a monolingual test, developed by monolingual individuals, and standardized and normed on a monolingual population, both the test taker and the test are asked to do something that they cannot. The bilingual test taker cannot perform like a monolingual. The monolingual test cannot "measure" in the other language. (p. 87)

Clearly, monolingually constructed and administered tests cannot validly measure the complex language practices of bilingual students.

INEQUITABLE ASSESSMENT PRACTICES

The inadequate and inequitable assessment practices for emergent bilinguals are often the product of the deficit thinking and raciolinguistic ideologies that we have identified in this book. Emergent bilinguals continue to be assessed prematurely with high-stakes instruments that confound academic language and content and that do not align with their language practices. In fact, much educational time is taken up testing with invalid instruments. And despite the fact that theory and research support the use of performance-based assessments as more valid for these students, they are rarely used as high-stakes tests.

Assessing Prematurely and Intensely

Researchers contend that the high-stakes testing of the American school population mandated by NCLB (2001) and continued by ESSA (2015) has had a negative effect on all students (Nichols & Berliner, 2007). Much time and energy is being spent testing, even though there is no evidence that the testing is improving the education of emergent bilinguals. Although teachers are assessing students with more performance-based assessments, they often deem the scores on high-stakes standardized tests to be more important because schools and teachers are held accountable for the performance of students on such tests (Amrein & Berliner, 2002).

The intensity of testing means that less time is being spent in challenging and creative teaching or teaching subject matter that is not tested. The phenomenon known as *washback*, the process by which testing and formal assessments drive the curriculum, has been well documented, especially in the literature on language teaching (Bach, 2020; Cheng, Watanabe, & Curtis, 2004; Shohamy, Donitsa-Schmidt, & Ferman, 1996). A study by the Center on Education Policy (CEP) found that since 2002, 62% of districts reported they had increased the time for reading and required schools to spend a specific amount of time teaching reading, while 53% of districts had also done so for math (Center on Education Policy, 2005). In contrast, less time is being spent teaching science, social studies, and the arts. Crucially, the reading and math curricula narrowly follow the exigencies of the tests.

The Center on Education Policy (2016) surveyed teachers on a number of issues, assessment being one of them. Eighty-one percent of teachers responding believed that students spend too much time taking state-mandated tests. In high-poverty schools, one-third of teachers said they spend more than one month per school year preparing students for mandated exams. However, an overwhelming majority of teachers (86%) believed in formative teacher-made assessments. For state-mandated tests, less than a third of teachers surveyed wanted to eliminate them, but more than half (60%) wanted to reduce their frequency or length.

In 2015, the Council of the Great City Schools estimated that the average student in large city school systems will take approximately 112 mandatory standardized tests between prekindergarten and high school. Each year, students spend an average of 20 to 25 hours taking these tests.

In the aftermath of the Covid-19 pandemic with its attendant ongoing deficit discourses about "learning loss," test-related pressures have been exacerbated. A 2023 survey by the EdWeek Research Center, involving 870 teachers, principals, and district leaders, showed that nearly half feel heightened pressure after Covid-19 to ensure students perform well on these tests (Stanford, 2023). In addition, 41% of participants reported an increase in the time spent by teachers in their districts on preparing students for standardized tests since the 2018–2019 school year, which was the last full school year before the pandemic.

Concerns about excessive testing are not new. A 2015 national PDK/Gallup poll (PDK International, 2015) reported that two-thirds of public-school parents agree that there is too much emphasis on standardized testing. This has fueled the parental movement to opt out of mandated standardized testing. Although ESSA (2015) has continued to require testing, it has also made funds available to states to audit their testing systems and eliminate unnecessary assessments (U.S. Department of Education, 2016). During a speech to educators in January 2023, U.S. Secretary of Education Miguel Cardona noted that "too many generations of students, particularly Black and [B]rown students, missed out on STEM, hands-on learning, experiential learning, or project-based learning because teaching was reduced to test prep. Enough is enough!" (Long, 2023). He advocated for standardized tests to serve as "a flashlight" illuminating effective educational practices rather than "a hammer" dictating outcomes. However, transforming the culture of accountability that ultimately punishes the most vulnerable students will continue to be a challenge given over 20 years of federal policy mandating annual testing and imposing penalties on underperforming schools.

Establishing Arbitrary Proficiencies

Assessment of emergent bilinguals is done particularly to determine whether or not they are proficient in English. But different states measure English proficiency differently, using tests that have diverging views of what the construct of proficiency entails. Thus, as we have said, emergent bilinguals may be deemed to be proficient in one state and not in another.

Establishing these arbitrary language proficiencies also stems from a misunderstanding of language development and bilingualism. Proficiency assessments pay attention only to the stage in which English is being learned, as if that process could be completed, thus ignoring that all speakers are constantly adding new features to our linguistic/semiotic repertoire. The point at which the student is declared to be "proficient in English" is established arbitrarily and abstractly. Gándara and Contreras (2009) note that it is a false dichotomy to say that "One is either proficient or not; one is either an English learner or a fluent English speaker" (p. 124), and they argue that this false dichotomy is imposed because of external funding and other pressures to sort students. These assessments consider proficiency only from a monolingual English language point of view, and the emergent bilingual student is considered nothing more than an English learner.

In contrast, as we have said, speakers "do language"; they language actively; they use diverse language features, practices, and additional meaning-making modes. We have argued that the bilingual continuum is not a straight linear process but rather is one that flows unevenly as students' language practices adapt to the changing social and academic contexts and interlocutors that they encounter, as well as their bodily-emotional experiences with language. The dynamic relationship among the linguistic features that they draw on means that, although students can be placed along a bilingual continuum in terms of development of both what is considered the home language and English, there is no end point by which students leave one category and enter into another because they are always translanguaging. Bilingual proficiency is dynamic. Like a river current, what García, Johnson, and Seltzer (2017) have called the translanguaging corriente, it is always flowing and always adapting to the communicative terrain in which it is being performed and the students' own emotional sense of belonging. Emergent bilinguals are somewhere along the starting point of the bilingual continuum, and developmental progress along that continuum is contingent on their opportunities for doing language and their "feel" in doing so. However, because bilinguals are constantly selecting features from their language repertoire for very different tasks and diverse interlocutors, we cannot say that they have ever finished "having" one language or the other.

The federal requirement of ESSA that students meet AYP standards in state exams drives the construction of categories of proficiency that have little to do with students' real learning and development. Assessments are then used to categorize students arbitrarily instead of to develop deep understandings and teacher knowledge about students and their learning.

Ignoring Those Who Need the Most Help

Federal educational policy's ongoing emphasis on ensuring that all students are proficient in English and pass standardized tests means that it has become common for schools to spend enormous time and energy with those who are close to moving up a proficiency level, those whom many call "the bubble kids" (Booher-Jennings, 2006). Neal and Schanzenbach's (2010) research shows that although NCLB accountability data reveal decreased disparities in achievement between white and minoritized students, when the data are disaggregated by subgroup, Black and Latine students are still likely to be left behind because schools tend to prioritize bubble kids. Unfortunately, even new strategies intended to prevent manipulation of the system are susceptible to manipulation themselves. Lauen and Gaddis (2012) found that minoritized students who were near the proficiency threshold benefited more than those significantly below or above it, indicating, again, that teachers may have focused more attention and resources on these students. In this way, while subgroup accountability measures may reduce disparities between different groups, they may also exacerbate disparities within those groups. In sum, students at the bottom were getting very little help and students at the top were also not being challenged academically and intellectually, because their positive scores would not make a difference to the schools' AYP measures.

ALTERNATIVE ASSESSMENT PRACTICES

Observing Closely

The best way to assess emergent bilinguals is for teachers to observe and listen to their students and record these observations systematically over long periods of time. Of course, to "re-view" emergent bilinguals in the close ways described by Carini (2000a, p. 56), the observer must be familiar with the linguistic and cultural practices of the student. Carini (2000b) differentiates between assessing what students learned, made, or did, and "paying close attention to *how a child goes about learning or making something*" (p. 9). Carini (2000b) continues: "[I]t is when a teacher can see this process, *the child in motion*, the child engaged in activities meaningful to her, that it is possible for the teacher to gain the insights needed to adjust her or his own approaches to the child accordingly" (p. 9). Thus, for Carini, observing closely refers to understanding the *process of learning*, not just assessing a product. These ongoing descriptive reviews of children (Carini, 2000a, 2000b; Traugh, 2000) can develop a multidimensional portrait of bilingual learners. Rather than labeling emergent bilinguals as "limited," "at risk," or "deficient," these kinds of assessments provide avenues for understanding the capacities and strengths of emergent bilinguals. Observing closely allows the teacher/assessor to obtain valid, reliable information about the dynamics of the process of learning that then informs the teaching in a cyclical relationship.

Assessing Dynamically and Authentically With Performance Assessments

Dynamic assessment rests on the work of Vygotsky on the interactive nature of cognitive development. Its goal is to "determine the 'size' of the ZPD [zone of proximal development]" (Gutiérrez-Clellen & Peña, 2001, p. 212) and to transform students' abilities through dialogic collaboration between learners and the assessor-teacher (Poehner, 2007). Dynamic assessment and instruction mutually elaborate each other. Dynamic assessment is thus mostly formative; it simultaneously supports emergent bilinguals in the learning of language and content (Alvarez et al., 2014; Bailey & Heritage, 2014; Heritage, Walqui, & Linquanti, 2015).

Georgia García and P. David Pearson (1994), in a review of formal and alternative assessment, support the notion that emergent bilinguals be given performance-based assessments that are dynamic, in the sense that they should reveal what the student can do with or without the help of the teacher or of peers. In this way, teachers are able to evaluate the kind of support that students require in order to comprehend and complete tasks. For García and Pearson, these dynamic assessments can be conducted in English, the home language, or using practices from both languages. Through dynamic assessments that are administered bilingually, teachers may assess their students' interpretations of material and vocabulary from diverse cultural and linguistic perspectives and then use that knowledge to create further opportunities for students to learn what is appropriate. For example, through bilingual dynamic assessments, bilingual students can demonstrate their literacy understandings using their home and school language practices, and teachers can then assist them in developing academic literacy in the additional language (see also García, Johnson, & Seltzer, 2017; García, 2009, Chapter 15).

Gottlieb (2017) provides a succinct guide to assessing multilingual learners using performance assessments. She gives the following characteristics of an effective performance assessment:

- Represents students' identities, languages, and cultures,
- Consists of authentic tasks with real-life application that ideally take on social action,
- Requires hands-on student engagement, preferably in collaboration with peers,
- Exemplifies original student work that includes multiple modalities,
- Is built from features of universal design for learning,

- Connects to students' lives, interests, and experiences, and
- Offers evidence for learning based on standards-referenced criteria for success.

Portfolio assessment is an important part of these performance assessments. In portfolios, emergent bilinguals can collect artifacts of their learning and reflect on what they have learned collaboratively with one another, their teacher, and their families.

Gottlieb (2017) points to other tools that can be used in performance assessments: anecdotal notes taken by the teacher, student self-assessment, peer assessment, reading response logs, read-alouds, using translanguaging together with other meaning-making modes and the resources offered through technology (see Chapter 9). All of these are valid gauges of emergent bilingual students' academic progress, taking into account the difference between language and content proficiencies, and between general linguistic performances and language-specific performances.

Enabling Testing Accommodations

One way to improve the validity of monolingual standardized assessments is to provide students with test accommodations. Many educational authorities provide accommodations for emergent bilingual students being tested in English. As a result of the accountability-system changes associated with NCLB and continued under ESSA, emergent bilinguals must be provided with appropriate accommodations. ESSA (2015) states that such accommodations should include, "to the extent practicable, assessments in the language and form most likely to yield accurate information on what those students know and can do" (p. 129, Stat. 1826).

State accommodation policies vary substantially (Rivera & Collum, 2006). Rivera and Stansfield (2001) organize the different accommodations into five categories:

1. *Presentation:* Permits repetition, explanation, simplification, test translations into students' native languages, or test administration by a bilingual specialist
2. *Response:* Allows a student to dictate their answers, and to respond in their native language or display knowledge using alternative forms of representation
3. *Setting:* Includes individual or small-group administration of the test, or administration in a separate location or multiple testing sessions
4. *Timing/scheduling:* Allows for additional time to complete the test or extra breaks during administration
5. *Reinforcement:* Allows for the use of dictionaries and glossaries

Abedi and Lord (2001) show how *linguistic modification*, the paraphrasing of test items so that they are less complex, has resulted in significant differences in math performance among emergent bilinguals in the United States. In fact, additional research has shown that *the only accommodation that narrows the gap between emergent bilinguals and other students is linguistic modification of questions that have excessive language demands* (Abedi & Lord, 2001; Abedi et al., 2004). Test accommodations other than linguistic modifications seem to make little difference in the scores of emergent bilinguals. However, linguistic accommodations tailored to meet the language needs of emergent bilinguals, such as glossaries/dictionaries and linguistic modifications, tend to be less commonly integrated into assessments conducted in mainstream classrooms (Yang, 2020). Because teacher beliefs and knowledge play a significant role in their assessment accommodation practices, it is important to design professional development that deliberately supports teachers in this area (Ascenzi-Moreno & Seltzer, 2021; Cho, 2019; Yang, 2020).

Disentangling Language and Content

Content and language are distinct areas of learning, but they are also interconnected, suggesting that language proficiency is necessary to convey content knowledge. Notwithstanding, Mahoney (2017) stresses the importance for educators of emergent bilinguals to consistently clarify the purpose of their assessments in order to differentiate the relevant construct. Although this disentanglement is difficult, some alternatives have been proposed. Shepard (1996) has argued that a fair assessment framework for emergent bilinguals should integrate the two dimensions— *language proficiency* and *content proficiency*. Academic performance of bilinguals should be seen as a continuum that is related to a continuum of English acquisition; in this view, the language in the tests of subject-matter content is adapted according to the place along the continuum in which the student might be situated.

Duverger (2005) has suggested that another way of disentangling the effects of language proficiency on content proficiency is to have a double scale of criteria: criteria relating to the *content* being delivered and criteria relating to the *language* being used. When content learning takes place through a student's weaker language, which is English in the case of emergent bilinguals in the United States who are the major focus in this book, subject-matter knowledge should have a higher coefficient, and language should not mask satisfactory handling of the content.

Assessing Students in Their Home Language

A much more equitable practice would be to assess students in their home languages. In this section, we address why this does not happen and the ideological and technical obstacles that stand in the way. The current debate over assessment of emergent bilinguals in the United States largely results from the lack of clarity over the goal of their education, which is whether educating emergent bilinguals should focus only on English language development or more broadly on their intellectual, academic, and social development. The education of English language learners—as the naming indicates and as we have been signaling—often focuses narrowly on the acquisition of *English language skills* and not on the acquisition of content knowledge. Houser (1995) explains that if content-area knowledge were the primary goal, students would be assessed in their home language. However, assessing students in their home language is generally considered inappropriate because educational policy attends narrowly to fluency in English. Furthermore, developing translations and transadaptations of assessments in the home language is complicated, as we will see in the next two sections.

Test translations. Effective translation of tests requires collaboration among various stakeholders, including translators, ESL/bilingual teachers, content teachers, test developers, and sociolinguists (Solano-Flores, 2012; Turkan & Oliveri, 2014). Given how challenging this is, test translation is not always feasible or appropriate. Because the testing industry is a market-driven operation, it might be possible to develop translations into Spanish, since the numbers of Spanish-speaking emergent bilinguals would merit it, but developing them into less commonly used languages could be difficult and expensive. Furthermore, assessments conducted in different languages may not be psychometrically equivalent (Anderson et al., 1996). Maintaining construct equivalence is difficult when the test is either translated directly from one language to another or when tests in two languages are constructed. The nonequivalence of vocabulary difficulty between languages makes comparisons for content proficiency between tests given in different languages inappropriate (August & Hakuta, 1998). The Standards for Educational and Psychological Testing put forth conjointly by the American Educational Research Association, the American Psychological Association, and the National Council on Measurement in Education (1985) state:

> Psychometric properties cannot be assumed to be comparable across languages or dialects. Many words have different frequency rates or difficulty levels in different languages or dialects. Therefore, words in two languages that appear to be close in meaning may differ radically in other ways important for the test use intended. Additionally, test content may be inappropriate in a translated version. (p. 73)

Sometimes, emergent bilinguals are allowed to use both the home language version and the English language version of the test. But developing and validating equivalent versions of a test (two monolingual versions side by side) is difficult and costly (Anderson, Jenkins, & Miller, 1996). Furthermore, research on this issue has repeatedly shown substantial psychometric discrepancies in students' performance on the same test items across languages (August & Hakuta, 1997). This means that test items are not measuring the same underlying knowledge.

In addition, translations are only viable when emergent bilinguals have been effectively educated in their home languages. And even then, translations may privilege the standard variety of the language, which often is different from language use in bilingual contexts (Solano-Flores, 2008). If students have limited literacy in the standard variety, a translated assessment that tests content proficiency is also invalid.

An additional concern is that even appropriate translation of tests would not obviate the cultural uniqueness and register of high-stakes tests, which might not be familiar to immigrant students—the format, layout, bubbling in multiple-choice answers, and discursive styles that are specific to tests (Solano-Flores, 2008), as well as computer-based assessments.

Furthermore, translations are only appropriate if the students have been taught through the language of the test. If the language is not used for instruction, then assessment for content proficiency in the students' home language also may be counterproductive. For instance, Shanmugam and Lan (2013) discovered that Malay-speaking students expressed dissatisfaction with Malay translation assistance because English was their primary language in school. They felt they understood mathematical concepts better in English than in Malay. In short, the language of the assessment must match students' primary language of instruction (Abedi & Lord, 2001; Abedi, Lord, & Plummer, 1997; Yang, 2020).

Transadaption of tests. Transadaptation is a strategy with promise. Transadapted tests adapt test items to fit the cultural or linguistic requirement of the students who are being tested. For example, an English test item may ask about "mountain climbing," but the Spanish test may adapt this to say *"excursión,"* a more relevant cultural experience. Transadapted test items are not simple translations. They are written from the linguistic and cultural perspective of the group being tested. Transadapted tests work to eliminate cultural biases, which are prevalent in many assessments because they refer to cultural experiences or historical/social backgrounds to which many emergent bilinguals have not been exposed (Johnston, 1997). As a result, they have more validity than tests that are simply translated. They also are better able to capture content knowledge by minimizing the negative effects of language, particularly when using other accommodations such as combining transadaptation and oral delivery in math assessments (Badham & Furlong, 2022). Transadapted testing is being used in some states—for example, Texas, which uses transadapted Spanish versions of the state's test, called STAAR. However, even transadapted tests, because they are monolingual, do not take into account the full range of linguistic practices of emergent bilingual students, whose full capabilities are enmeshed with their bilingualism.

Assessing Bilingually

A valid way to assess the content proficiency of emergent bilinguals (not solely their English proficiency) is to develop large-scale assessments that build on their bilingual abilities. One example of a bilingual mode instrument designed to assess the verbal-cognitive skills of bilingual students is the Bilingual Verbal Ability Test. All subtests of the assessment are first administered in English. Any item failed is then readministered in the student's home language and the score added in order to measure the test-taker's knowledge and reasoning ability using both languages (Muñoz-Sandoval et al., 1998).

Students also could be assessed via a *bilingual mode,* a way of rendering learners' bilingual abilities and knowledge visible. For example, spoken questions can be given in one language and responses requested in another. Or written tests can have the question in English, and the responses may be produced in the home language, or vice versa. Alternatively, the written text could be supplied in English and the oral presentation in the home language, or vice versa, thereby providing the teacher with a measure of students' productive skills across two modes and for all languages, while at the same time giving emergent bilinguals the opportunity to use all their languages. Thus, this bilingual mode of assessment would not only give educators a more accurate picture of what students really know without having language as an intervening variable, but it also would offer a clearer picture of students' language capacities.

In cases where school authorities are interested exclusively in students' progress in learning English, students might also be assessed via a *bilingual tap* mode, a way of tapping into or drawing on their home language in order to produce English (García, 2009). This type of assessment would, for example, give instructions and questions in the students' home languages and ask students to respond solely in English. In this way, the home language would be used to activate knowledge for assessment in much the same way that bilingual children use their home language and culture to make sense of what they know. This bilingual tap assessment builds on work on bilingual language processing by Dufour and Kroll (1995), Jessner (2006), and Kecskes and Martínez Cuenca (2005).

A more holistic way to assess emergent bilinguals is to integrate not only the use of bilingual approaches but also various language modalities, such as reading, writing, listening, and speaking in literacy assessment. For instance, Butvilofsky and colleagues (2021) advocate for a comprehensive biliterate assessment approach that employs writing to more accurately gauge emergent bilingual learners' literacy proficiency, such as in reading fluency and phonological awareness. In their study, they selected students whose scores on the Dynamic Indicators of Basic Early Literacy Skills (DIBELS) English assessment identified them as reading below or well below benchmark and in need of intensive interventions. Yet the authors also administered the Indicadores Dinámicos del Éxito en la Lectura (IDEL), a similar test in Spanish and collected three pairs of Spanish and English writing samples. In addition to the IDEL results, the qualitative analysis of the students' writing samples revealed biliteracy strengths across Spanish and English as well as their capacity to exhibit progress throughout their second-grade academic year that DIBELS was unable to capture. This research underscores the importance of biliterate writing assessment in comprehensively evaluating emerging bilingual learners' literacy development, offering a broader and more suitable means of assessing their literacy skills along their linguistic repertoire.

Translanguaging in Assessment

Leveraging translanguaging in assessment is the only way to level the playing field between bilingual and monolingual students, giving bilingual students the opportunity that monolingual children have—to be able to show what they know and can do using *all their linguistic resources*. Teachers who leverage translanguaging in instruction can design formative and summative assessments in which students are given the opportunity to show what they know by using their full language and communicative repertoire (Ascenzi-Moreno & Seltzer, 2021; García, Johnson, & Seltzer, 2017; Gottlieb, 2017; Mahoney, 2017).

A translanguaging design for assessments ensures that students can perform using all the features of their language repertoire; at the same time, the design tracks whether students are performing independently or with moderate assistance from other people or other resources. For just these purposes, García, Johnson, and Seltzer (2017) have developed a *Teacher's Assessment Tool for Translanguaging Classrooms*. Teachers who are bilingual can apply such a tool readily. The challenge for monolingual teachers, however, is greater, because they have to rely on other individuals (peers, parents, or other colleagues) and other resources for help in interpreting students' test responses. Even so, technology is making this easier, and electronic translations are an indispensable resource for teachers today.

Translanguaging in standardized assessments is still rare, although technology is enabling more possibilities: Alexis López and his associates at ETS have been developing middle school math and science translanguaging assessments for Latine bilingual students. Students are first asked to select a bilingual avatar who is a bilingual friend or assistant and who provides a model of how to translanguage in assessments. Next, on this computer-based platform, students have the opportunity to see or hear items in two languages, English and Spanish. This way, they can say or write responses using all their linguistic resources, either oral or in writing (López, Turkan, & Guzmán-Orth, 2017). The intent is to ensure that language and content, as well as general language and language-specific capacities, are disentangled (López, 2023b; López, Guzmán-Orth, & Turkan, 2014). Additionally, these test innovations are exploring how to enable multilingual practices in content and English language proficiency assessments (López, 2023a).

EDUCATING EMERGENT BILINGUALS: ACCOUNTING FOR FAIR ASSESSMENT

The data-driven frenzy of accountability that was first spurred by NCLB (2001) puts assessments rather than teaching at the center of education today. The issue of assessment is particularly important for emergent bilinguals, for whom some of these high-stakes tests are invalid. There are, however, ways of improving the construction of valid assessments for this population, and this chapter has considered some of these alternative practices.

In sum, we see that misunderstandings about bilingualism in the United States create obstacles to developing assessment mechanisms that are fair and valid for all students. Monolingual high-stakes tests administered to emergent bilinguals have negative consequences not only for the individual students but also for the teachers who teach them, the leaders of the schools in which they are educated, the communities in which they live, and the states in which they reside. Scores on assessments are not only driving the kinds of instruction and programmatic opportunities that emergent bilinguals can access but also the salaries that their teachers receive, the funding that their schools and the states in which they reside obtain, and the real-estate value of the communities in which they live. This creates a cycle in which the victims will surely be the emergent bilinguals, as these testing practices will result in students dropping out of the school system, excluding them from all opportunities to learn. Developing fair and valid assessments for emergent bilinguals emerges as the most critical issue in education during this era of increased accountability. Continuing down the path we are on has the potential not only to exclude children from educational opportunities but also to undermine the entire public school system on which our U.S. democracy rests.

STUDY QUESTIONS

1. Why are assessments so powerful?
2. Why are assessments not always valid and reliable for emergent bilinguals?
3. How do the different kinds of tests compare in the way they assess emergent bilinguals' language and content proficiencies?
4. What are some of the complications of establishing categories of proficiencies?
5. What is the difference between observing closely and assessing students? Discuss advantages and disadvantages.
6. Describe some of the test accommodations that can be used with emergent bilinguals. Identify issues to consider and practices that work best.
7. What are the issues that surround translations and transadaptions of tests?
8. Discuss ways of assessing bilingually. In your view, what are the difficulties with implementation of such assessments?
9. What does accounting for translanguaging in assessment entail? What are the benefits and the challenges of translanguaging in assessment?

CHAPTER 9

Affordances of Technology

In this chapter, we will:

- Provide the theoretical underpinnings of multiliteracies and the "digital turn" in multimodality,
- Highlight the consequences of inequitable access to computers and the internet,
- Consider some guidelines for judicious use of artificial intelligence in the classroom, and
- Lay out the research evidence for the efficacy of such access for emergent bilinguals.

In earlier chapters, we discussed the importance of building on the linguistic resources that emergent bilingual students bring to school and of choosing appropriate pedagogical and curricular approaches to support their academic growth. Throughout, we have signaled examples of applying digital technologies to classroom instruction for these purposes. In this chapter, we bring these technologies to the fore, as our world is increasingly networked and communication is increasingly digital in our working, playing, and learning lives (Castells, 2007; Cummins, Brown, & Sayers, 2007; Kleifgen & Kinzer, 2009; Leu et al., 2013). We draw together threads of increased human mobility across national borders, new digital technologies that support collaborative learning environments for multilingual speakers, and the enhancement of multimodal resources to teach emergent bilinguals. As in the other chapters, we first provide the theoretical underpinnings for technology use, including *multiliteracies*, a term we introduced in Chapter 4, and the associated approach known as *multimodality*. Next, we point out some consequences of inequitable access to digital resources in a society permeated by new information and communication technologies (ICTs). Finally, we discuss the research evidence for the benefits of such access for emergent bilinguals.

The need to provide innovative instruction for all students, especially emergent bilinguals, has never been greater. We will show that digital technologies enhance learning and achievement and, in addition, that using these tools requires new literacy skills (Kinzer, 2010), which these students are also entitled to learn. Our argument is grounded in the theoretical and empirical underpinnings discussed next.

THEORETICAL UNDERPINNINGS

In the mid-1990s, a group of international scholars known as the New London Group (1996; see also Cope & Kalantzis, 2000) wrote a manifesto—a "pedagogy of multiliteracies"—calling on educators to recognize and respond to the intertwining of two phenomena: the increased linguistic diversity of learners populating our classrooms and the proliferation of new resources for learning owing to the rise of digital technologies. Their call rings true even today, as more of our students come to school with different language practices and bring their diverse assumptions about the world into the classroom. Our tools for learning today are providing greater access to other forms or modes of communication, such as graphics, image, sound, and video, which can be deployed conjointly with the spoken and written modes of multiple named languages during the learning process. The central argument that the New London Group made over 30 years ago still stands: All students should benefit from a pedagogy designed to provide a future of full participation in their working, civic, and private lives.

One of the authors of this manifesto, Gunther Kress, wrote extensively about the concept of *multimodality*, which seeks to explain how people communicate not only through what is perceived as "the linguistic" but also through other communicative modes (Kress, 2003, 2010). His work on multimodality is grounded in the social-semiotic theory of M. A. K. Halliday (1978, 1993). Before we discuss the link between multimodality and digital technologies, let us examine the idea behind *social semiotics* in a little more detail. Basically, semiotics is the study of signs used as elements of "making meaning," to use Halliday's phrase, in communication. Signs can take the form of words, gestures, images, sounds, and so on. Briefly, social semiotics takes the position that people draw on available signs within a particular context to make meaning. In terms of linguistic signs (spoken or written), rather than thinking of language as a "thing" made up of rule-governed forms, Halliday's approach underscores the importance of the "meaning potential" in any given communicative context because people draw on socially situated options—what he terms *semiotic resources* or *modes*—for communicating. (Notice how his approach resonates with our own shift away from focusing on *language* as a noun to *language practices*, or *languaging* as a verb, an action.) Studies on multimodality by Kress and others expand Halliday's historical focus on the spoken and written modes by identifying and examining more closely the nonlinguistic modes that people draw on in different communicative contexts. These scholars contributed detailed analyses of the functions of these other modes; examples include Kress and van Leeuwen's (1996) focus on images and van Leeuwen's (1999, 2011) work on film, music/sound, and color. These deep-dive studies of individual modes then shifted to the exploration of how the different modes are *combined* to make meaning, bringing forward a multimodal approach to analysis (e.g., Jewitt, 2009; Kress, 2010; Kress & van Leeuwen, 2001; O'Halloran, 2008).

Researchers have written extensively about the importance of multimodality in education (e.g., Bezemer & Kress, 2015; Jewitt, 2002; Jewitt & Kress, 2003; Kleifgen, 2006; Kress et al., 2001; Lemke, 1998). In some ways, this is not a new idea:

Classrooms themselves are multimodal spaces filled with textbooks, worksheets, talk, body posture, and gestures; classroom walls are adorned with posters, diagrams, images, texts, and illustrations that serve to guide student learning or to display student work; teachers design and use these resources in different ways, which can in turn affect student learning differentially, as is richly illustrated in a study of high school English classrooms in the United Kingdom (Kress et al., 2005). Learning in the disciplines such as science, mathematics, and history entails the use of linguistic modes surrounded by many nonlinguistic modes such as diagrams, maps, and photographs. Often, the educational potential of nonlinguistic modes for emergent bilinguals goes unmentioned in research: In a review of 40 studies of students studying science through an additional language, Williams and Tang (2020) reexamined the function of nonlinguistic modes, which were not prominently featured in the original findings. The authors found that integrating the nonlinguistic modes in science learning improved the language learners' science discourse in these studies. Moreover, this improvement occurred especially in contexts of translanguaging, which enhanced the use of learners' linguistic modes along with nonverbal modes in the science learning environment.

Unfortunately, however, racialized emergent bilinguals from low-income communities tend to be relegated to a limited set of modalities, namely practicing discrete reading and writing skills, which often even exclude authentic and agentic opportunities for student talk and body movement in the classroom (Adair & Colegrove, 2021). A multimodal social-semiotic theory of communication helps educators think about the interrelationships among all the modes—including the linguistic modes *together* with the other modes (Kleifgen, 2019)—that may be brought to bear during any given learning situation, and which, if integrated in the classroom, can expand the learning opportunities for emergent bilinguals.

In terms of technology, which is our focus in this chapter, students who are using computers and the internet are making meaning with vast and growing numbers of semiotic resources that reach beyond the boundaries of the classroom: still and moving images, sounds and music, colors, and spoken and written language(s). Students who are engaging with one another and exploring the multimodal resources available on the computer screens before them are participating in complex forms of communication to learn. In Kress's (2003) words, they are learning with "ensembles" of modes that may differ and change depending on the context of the learning activity (p. 70). Each mode within a given ensemble contributes to the whole of meaning-making or, shall we say, to the learning of something new. As we will see, this complexity is further heightened and enhanced when the spoken and written modes that are part of these ensembles entail the use of more than one language; emergent bilinguals can exploit this complexity by using their home language practices online to scaffold their learning.

Central to this theoretical approach is human agency. People who are interacting and learning together bring diverse languages, cultures, and understandings into this complex digital environment. Kress (2010) states:

> In a social-semiotic account of meaning, individuals, with their social histories, socially shaped, located in social environments, using socially made, culturally available

resources, are *agentive* and generative in sign-making and communication. (p. 54; emphasis added)

Using a multimodal social-semiotic approach to learning, educators can facilitate optimal ways to use the wide-ranging modes, including multiple language modes, that are available on the internet and other ICTs to build new knowledge (Bezemer & Kress, 2015; Jewitt & Kress, 2003). Two of the 10 authors who formed part of the New London Group (1996), William Cope and Mary Kalantzis, have recognized the concept of *translanguaging* as a major contribution to the spirit of the multiliteracies concept published in 1996. As we noted in Chapter 4, they now offer a different term, *transposition*, that takes into account the fluidity of translanguaging integrated with other meaning-making modes (Cope, Kalantzis, & Tzirides, 2024). Cope and his colleagues focus particularly on the educational context in the new media age. They illustrate how taking a multimodal view, where different modes mutually elaborate each other in the process of meaning-making, spotlights the fact that the linguistic modes of speech and text are radically different, where speech is closely aligned with sound and text aligned with image, for example. The affordances of these modes are different, and they become even more so in digitized form. Thus, the authors underscore the need to rethink theoretical discussions and pedagogical practices in the digital age: They advocate for a more expansive approach to understanding and teaching meaning-making that surpasses traditional language analysis, and they also argue that these pedagogical tools must be made available to all language teachers in support of all students.

But what happens when emergent bilinguals have little or no access to ICTs in their schools or homes? We outline some consequences next.

INEQUITABLE ACCESS TO DIGITAL TECHNOLOGIES

There is little doubt that to function in contemporary society, one must have digital competence, the ability to use and evaluate digital technologies for communication, learning, employment, and everyday life (Llomaki et al., 2016). The Organisation for Economic Co-Operation and Development (OECD, 2005) identified skilled technology use inside and outside the workplace as one of the key competencies that graduating students need to participate fully in society. Fortunately, the good news is that, in recent years, physical access to the internet, a prerequisite for gaining digital competence, has increased for many households. According to the Pew Research Center (2024), 95% of adults report using the internet. Nevertheless, lower income groups tend not to have broadband at home. Overcoming barriers to connectivity—physical access to the internet—is only a first step to digital competence according to van Dijk and colleagues (van Dijk, 2017; van Deursen & van Dijk, 2018). Other levels of access beyond *connectivity* include access to *devices* (computers, smartphones, tablets, etc.) and, crucially, access to *digital skills*, that is, receiving instruction on how to retrieve and evaluate information, conduct research, communicate, and create content on these devices.

Among the indicators of educational access (such as school funding, books, and highly qualified teachers and curricula) is computer use. Yet, according to a study conducted by the National Center for Education Statistics (NCES, 2018), poor and minoritized youth between the ages of 5 and 17 have less access to computer technologies than do white affluent youth. Similarly, a Pew report on digital technology use (Poushter, 2016) found that people around the world, including the United States, who have lower incomes and less education are less likely to gain access to the internet or to own smartphones than those with higher incomes and more education. In the United States, state education departments, recognizing the need to incorporate digital technologies into curricula for all students, including emergent bilinguals, are revising standards to foster the effective use of these tools. According to the State Educational Technology Directors Association (SETDA), 32 of the 50 states have developed state-wide digital education plans to date (Gifford, 2023).

Despite some gains in access to connectivity, devices, and instruction in the use of ICTs for learning, Linda Darling Hammond (2024) presents a bleak summary of what she calls an "anatomy of inequality" still present in the education system, which begins with poverty in a community, leading to inadequate allocation of school resources, fewer qualified teachers, unequal access to a high-quality curriculum, and a dysfunctional school. To address these issues, Darling-Hammond asserts that schools must be reinvented so that they are, among other things, "culturally and linguistically connected and sustaining . . . and equitable in the opportunities provided and outcomes achieved" (p. 1). The Computer Science Education Justice Collective has argued that in recent years the teaching capacity for computer science education has increased. Yet, the needs of diverse students for relevant computer science education remain unmet (Computer Science Education Justice Collective, in press).

Differential access to ICTs can exacerbate the problem of educational inequities for underserved students, many of whom are emergent bilinguals. With proactive help from policymakers and educators, emergent bilingual students, too, can benefit from appropriate uses of technology for learning. We now turn to empirical studies showing examples of ways in which these digital tools, when used judiciously and focused on these students' needs as well as the funds of knowledge they bring into the classroom, can promote educational attainment.

HOW DIGITAL TECHNOLOGIES CAN BENEFIT EMERGENT BILINGUALS

The research is clear. New digital technologies, if made available and when used thoughtfully, can enhance student learning. The emphasis on multimodality in educating emergent bilinguals is very much attuned to our conceptualization of translanguaging (see Chapters 4 and 5), which is, as we have said, an agentive process by which students select and suppress the features of their unitary language system to communicate and learn. A verbal repertoire forms part of a broader communicative repertoire (Rymes, 2014) that includes embodied modes such as gestures, facial expressions, eye movements, posture. Sometimes, certain modes in this larger communicative repertoire become more prevalent than at other times. For example, the Deaf community employs sign language accompanied by facial expressions and body posture in order to make meaning in social interaction. Emergent bilinguals select those features from their complex spoken language repertoire that, depending on the context, are best suited for communicating with one or more interlocutors. In both cases, participants may draw on additional modal resources in the surrounding environment during their interactions. In today's classrooms, students increasingly enjoy access to an expanded multimodal system facilitated by technology to select appropriate modes—linguistic, visual, and others—to collaborate and learn. Before we describe research showing how the affordances of ICTs can support emergent bilingual learners, we pause here to discuss a digital resource that has come onto the educational scene where interaction is not between human participants but between a human and a machine that can write and generate other meaning-making modes: artificial intelligence (AI). This resource brings with it some problems along with promises, and we emphasize again the importance of appropriate, thoughtful, judicious educational use of AI and other ICTs.[1]

Generative Artificial Intelligence (Generative AI)

We use the umbrella term *generative artificial intelligence* (generative AI) to refer to a type of technology that can create novel content, including text, talk, images, audio, and code (U.S. Department of Education, Office of Education Technology (2023). We focus on text-based generative AI, in which a *chatbot*—a computer program that simulates human spoken or written conversation—receives a *prompt* (a question or instructions) from a user like a teacher or student and then draws on a *large language model (LLM)*—where vast pools of data reside—to produce a response. The quality of the output depends on (1) the prompt that a user submits to a chatbot and (2) the training data that an LLM has received. The following is an overview of the affordances and challenges that generative AI presents for emergent bilinguals and for education, broadly conceived, along with some suggestions for ameliorating negative impact.

Large language models. LLMs are a specialized type of AI that is pretrained on a massive store of data extracted from the internet as well as from books, images, and other sources; most of the training data are composed of digitized texts. LLMs can comb through more bodies of digitized texts and do so more quickly than any human can. These binary computing machines

> have "read" almost every word ever published. This because almost every published word has by now been digitized and in multiple languages—an estimated five billion words. After statistical analysis of this corpus, the AI can now predict the probability of the next word after any given word. (Cope & Kalantzis, 2023, p. 7)

However, just as the internet itself contains false along with factual material, these LLM data sets can contain "hallucinations"—erroneous or misleading information; the term also encompasses biased material, such as the dominance of content in English representing mostly Western perspectives (Zhuo et al., 2023). Thus, falsehoods and *prejudicial* (Cheuk, 2021) data stored in the LLM can show up in the text produced by the chatbot in answer to a prompt.

Chatbots and prompts. Chatbots such as ChatGPT have the capability to produce original and well-designed responses, reports, or other genres of texts in answering user prompts, and they can do so rapidly. Prompts are ways of communicating with AI by entering an instruction or question into the system in order to elicit a specific result. But chatbots cannot think; they are not capable of evaluating the source material for falsehoods or bias. Thus, designing or "engineering" more sophisticated prompts is an important skill for teachers and students to acquire. For example, the prompt should set a context and give specific instructions regarding what the chatbot may select from the LLM to generate. A key point is that these models do not understand language; rather, the texts that are generated by chatbots are based purely on statistical analysis of patterns in characters (Cope & Kalantzis, 2023).

Student cheating with AI. Many educators have concerns that their students might use ChatGPT or other chatbots to cheat by submitting the output as their own original writing. Teachers may find it difficult to distinguish AI-generated text from student writing. There is no way to prevent the possibility of cheating, aside from perhaps requiring in-class handwritten submissions. Most scholars say that cheating is not the most serious drawback to the use of these tools. Instead, they recommend that educators guide students in (1) learning about how generative AI works and (2) learning how to critically assess these tools' strengths and weaknesses. (See, for example, Roschelle et al.'s [2020] expert panel report from the U.S. Department of Education's Office of Educational Technology.)

Kalantzis and Cope (2024, pp. 26–28) call for a "cyber-social literacy learning" that includes improvements in areas such as detailed prompt engineering, computer applications that sharpen the accuracy of generative AI models with facts drawn from sources external to the chatbot, and the overarching need to attend to "education justice for all."

With this background and caveats around AI, we can now examine some specific applications of ICTs to the education of emergent bilinguals, including the educational application of chatbot-prompted LLMs with novel affordances such as digital translation, speech recognition tools, and intelligent language tutors.

Empirical research has demonstrated the positive outcomes of implementing computer-based technologies in classrooms and beyond, including studies showing the learning benefits for emergent bilinguals (Darling-Aduana & Heinrich, 2018; Vogel et al., 2020). In addition, the WIDA Consortium (2014) has issued a brief focusing on the use of technology in classrooms with emergent bilinguals.

When thoughtfully used, ICTs as learning tools offer a variety of affordances: *accessibility, retrievability, interactivity* (Kleifgen et al., 2014),[2] and *creativity*. Although these affordances are tightly intertwined, and they overlap to produce a positive effect on learning, we separate them for illustrative purposes in our discussion, with examples from research findings.

Accessibility

Students need access to information so that they can become both consumers and producers of knowledge. The internet is a potential virtual library holding a massive and growing global archive of information for students to explore without the limitations of distance or time. With the internet, learning becomes ubiquitous. As Leu and his colleagues (2013) put it, the internet "has become this generation's defining technology for literacy in our global community" (p. 1159). This virtual library provides ready-to-hand multimodal content—video and sound recordings, maps, graphs, photographs, and of course, texts. Web-based texts themselves are almost entirely embedded with other semiotic resources and/or hyperlinks that take students to additional related content.

In schools where low-income students receive one-to-one access to computers and the internet, it has been found that these students take advantage of using the technology at school because their access elsewhere is limited; their increased access has resulted in achievement gains (Darling-Hammond, Zielezinski, & Goldman, 2014). A two-year longitudinal study by Grimes and Warschauer (2008), where low-income students in three diverse schools participated in a laptop program, found that the students in laptop classrooms showed positive test scores beginning in the second year of the program, and that they used laptops at school and home to write. Results showed that they were inclined to write and revise more, using multiple modes and a wide variety of genres, including project-based reports.

Students with access to mobile devices have the added benefit of ubiquitous use. Kukulska-Hulme and Wible (2008) provide examples of users learning "in the wild" with mobile phones in a range of settings, such as the transmission of video, audio, and images by undergraduates doing geology fieldwork; the building of a learning experience with photos, text, and voice in a museum; digital collaboration among students in class with students taking a tour in the outdoors; and student creation and sharing of learning games with mobile phones.

Immigrant families who have access to smartphones are using them in various ways to adjust to their new circumstances with the support of the home language and other meaning-making modes. In an ethnographic study carried out by McCaffrey and Taha (2019), Middle Eastern refugee families settling in New Jersey were observed using tools such as Google Translate, WhatsApp, and English-to-Arabic machine translation on their smartphones to negotiate resettlement issues through translanguaging and other communicative modes such as emojis, videos, and photos. Their children also used smartphones during ESL classes at school to exchange knowledge in multiple peer languages. However, the families' concerted efforts to make use of these tools to help them adjust to life in a new country did not always ensure helpful responses, leading the authors to point to the need for educators and other service providers to recognize that refugees are accessing smartphones and machine translation apps and recommending that more be done to proactively promote intercultural/translingual contact with newcomers to the United States.

Many languages and different ways of using language live on the internet. We argue that emergent bilinguals can draw on this home language resource and use today's internet to strengthen their academic English practices along with their home language practices. For example, they can improve their understanding of a text written in English by accessing translation tools on the internet to receive a translation in their home language. The advent of machine translation (MT) such as Google Translate and similar tools has brought new opportunities for student learning. For example, in a case study of an immigrant student from China, authors Vogel, Ascenzi-Moreno, and García (2018) show that when an emergent bilingual is given access to machine translation tools in a classroom where the teacher applies translanguaging strategies, the student benefits from an ensemble of modes for learning. The student in this study participated in translanguaging interactions with his classmates for better understanding of the assigned writing task, then used resources on the internet such as images and texts in Chinese for note-taking, the Google Translate tool for rendering his Chinese notes into English, and the online writing software to complete revisions of his Chinese and English responses.

The benefit of gaining access to the home language in a multimodal context was also shown in a study by Kleifgen, Lira, and Ronan (2014), which was part of a 4-year web-based intervention project funded by a federal grant to support emergent bilingual adolescents' learning. Kleifgen and her colleagues studied a bilingual science classroom of Spanish-speaking immigrants, who were just beginning to learn English. The students used a web-based research and writing system to study complex concepts about evolution.[3] The system contained a library of historical and scientific resources related to evolution, including bilingual texts, maps, labeled diagrams, images, and videos, all curated by the projects' researchers and school partners to ensure historical and scientific accuracy. Students could select from an extensive number of documents to study the key concepts in Spanish as well as English. For example, students had online access to a description of fossils in both languages [*Los fósiles proporcionan un registro de organismos que vivieron en el pasado* . . . / Fossils provide a record of organisms that lived in the past . . .].

Videos included in the digital library were used by participating teachers to introduce new instructional units. If the videos were recorded in English, Spanish subtitles were provided, as seen in Figure 9.1, a screenshot from an animated music video of Darwin's voyage to the Galápagos Islands (Borlase & Haines, n.d.). The system's collection of digital images and diagrams was gathered from the internet, scanned from science texts, or designed by the teachers. These were often accompanied by captions in Spanish to provide a mutually elaborating ensemble of information for understanding.

Over the course of six instructional sessions, students used the system's pop-up function to open a notepad and one or more resources on the screen to examine them and take notes. They used the accumulated notes to develop an essay in response to a writing prompt. Records of their notes and essay drafts showed

Figure 9.1. Mr. Darwin's Music Video With Subtitles in Spanish

that they drew on ensembles of modes for learning—images, videos, and texts in both Spanish and English—as they gained content knowledge about evolution and put their ideas into writing. Students were able to construct an argument supported by evidence and examples, thus developing foundations for academic literacy.

When a classroom teacher opens the door to translanguaging strategies and provides *access* to online tools for exploring resources in the home language, students have access to new forms of knowledge. In this way, students are able to read about topics in subjects like science, history, or language arts, which can aid their understanding of what is being studied in class. Teachers, too, can use the internet to provide home language versions of subject-matter content to support student learning. As noted throughout this book, research shows that learning subject-matter content using home language practices while adding English practices to the repertoire facilitates academic achievement. In short, by combining *access* to home language practices with other modes available online, students can go through this content-learning process efficiently and at the same time develop their bilingual language use.

Retrievability

Closely related to the accessibility of content on the internet is the notion of *retrievability* of that same content. Using the internet, emergent bilingual students can easily return to materials multiple times to examine them for deeper understanding. In the study described previously, Kleifgen et al. (2014) also analyzed log files, which captured students' digital behaviors in the web-based system, including which items in the library they chose to open and how often they returned to any given item. The authors found that the students returned often to the multimodal curricular resources and that some resources were viewed repeatedly, a signal that students deemed them important enough to review in order to gain information for note-taking and writing.

Similarly, Ronan (2014, 2017) studied student behaviors using the same web-based system in a different school. She describes how four students in a social studies class accessed a variety of multimodal resources, many of them more than once, to learn about and take notes on the civil rights movement. The digital library held 31 resources associated with this instructional unit. In her analysis of students' choices about which kinds of resources they selected from among these digitized materials—texts, video and audio recordings, photographs, maps—Ronan considered the overall counts recorded in the log files indicating how often they clicked on the resources for a pop-up view on the computer screen. In addition, she analyzed the corresponding transcripts of students' talk, writing, gestures, and their interactions with the online space to determine precisely how the students incorporated a given multimodal resource from the internet into their talk and notes. Each of the four emergent bilinguals, who represented different English language proficiency levels, took distinct paths to initial examination and subsequent retrieval of the online materials based on their interests and language choices. Ronan's (2017) work, showing students' agency as they varied in online selection and *retrieval* of bilingual materials along with other semiotic resources, provides a strong argument that "unlike traditional textbooks that impose a sequential structure upon a reader, open-ended digital spaces . . . allow students to direct their own learning" (p. 102).

Other integrated online environments that focus on language learners' writing allow students to review their developing essays as well as their teachers' feedback. For example, David Wible and his colleagues (Wible et al., 2001, 2003) describe the *retrievability* of archived essays and comments in a writing platform called IWiLL (Intelligent Web-based interactive Language Learning). Students using this system, who were Chinese speakers learning to write in English, were able to retrieve and review their collection of compositions, conduct pinpoint searches of their persistent writing difficulties, and search for their teachers' comments to find patterns of difficulty; teachers also could search and retrieve students' writing and provide targeted instruction in frequent problem areas, such as word choice, sentence fragments, subject–verb agreement, and so on.

In sum, with digital technologies, students can construct, retrieve, and review texts in one or more languages as a way to comparatively analyze the material, thus attaining a clearer understanding of concepts and improving their written language production.

Interactivity

We approach the examination of the affordance of *interactivity* by focusing on two aspects: student interactions with digital tools and interactions among students while using the tools.

Interacting with digital tools. Studies have shown that underserved students benefit academically from highly interactive activities on computer-based tools. This was one of the key findings in a literature review conducted by Zielezinski and Darling-Hammond (2016); their review of more than 50 studies confirms that when students are given the opportunity to collect and analyze data online or to engage with multiple resources such as simulations and video instruction modules to gain understanding of concepts, their learning is enhanced. One of the studies cited in their review (Bos, 2007) shows that an experimental group of 96 low-achieving high school students' mathematical achievement improved significantly when they studied quadratic equations using the Texas Instruments InterActive software lessons to manipulate interactive graphs and tables; this software was assessed as high in cognitive and mathematical fidelity (Bos, 2009). The struggling students' achievement scores were greater than those of the student control group who studied the same material in conventional classes consisting of lecture, notes, and drill and practice.

In terms of highly interactive AI applications in pedagogy, chatbots are popular for skill building, particularly when used as a conversational partner for students learning an additional language. Huang, Hew, and Fryer (2022) reviewed 25 such studies that showed a number of advantages to interacting with an AI agent on a chatbot in the target language: the nonhuman conversational partner is available around the clock for continuous practice and is adaptable to the learners' interest and learning level. Further, language learners can easily access the chatbot using their computer, tablet, or mobile phone. Besides conversational practice on specific scenarios like asking for directions or making reservations, users engage in simulations and pose grammatical, vocabulary, or other language-related questions. More advanced learners may ask academic questions such as procedures for developing a research question or a literature review. Applications for younger children are also in development, as in the integration of multiple AI models to design an embodied AI partner for shared storytelling that offers the potential of promoting early narrative skills (Li & Xu, 2023). However, it is important to note the need to develop regulatory mechanisms that take into account young children's learning and privacy needs before making available AI-supported software.

Cope and Kalantzis (2013) describe a robust web-based learning and writing platform, Scholar, developed at the University of Illinois and designed for fourth-grade level and above. They show how this digital space affords learning transformations or "openings" such as ubiquitous access to the system from any device in or out of school, student knowledge production using multiple modes, and interactive collaboration with and feedback from teachers and peers. They also stress that the system occasions another pedagogical opening: "differentiated" learning, which is based on individual students' developing understandings and requirements. This feature is particularly important for low-income students, including many minoritized emergent bilinguals, who may not have had equitable educational opportunities in school or internet connectivity at home; with the Scholar learning environment in their classrooms, they can work at their own pace, receive individualized teacher support, and find their own writing voices. More recently, to supplement the collaborative feedback given by teachers and peers on students' multimodal compositions, the authors and their research colleagues developed an app called CGMap to be used within the Scholar platform, which moderates the responses given by OpenAI's GPT through, for example, prompt engineering and the provision of additional text-based resources that have been vetted for trustworthiness. Students can now revise and resubmit their work based on *interactions* with both human and AI-based reviews (Cope & Kalantzis, 2024; Tzirides et al., 2023).

The work of MIT's Michel DeGraff (2013) and his colleagues demonstrates that putting into students' hands powerful *interactive* software translated into Haitian Creole (Kreyòl) for engaging in scientific experiments has the potential to positively impact learning in the entire country of Haiti. The MIT–Haiti Initiative began working in 2010, first to translate and design digital tools alongside nondigital materials for active learning in mathematics, physics, biology, chemistry, and biochemistry in the home language, and, second to conduct workshops and publish guides for teachers of high school and university students on ways to use these tools and materials effectively in their classrooms (DeGraff & Stump, 2018; Miller, 2016). Examples of the highly interactive science software include StarGenetics, which simulates genetics experiments with yeast, fruit flies, and Mendel's peas; PhET, which simulates physics experiments in density, electromagnets, and gas properties; and Mathlets, for learning about differential equations and complex arithmetic (MIT–Haiti Initiative, n.d.). Supporting teachers in their adoption of a discovery approach to learning and their comfort with digital tools in the classroom was crucial to the success of this work. Because the country is suffering extreme impoverishment and strife due to recent political turmoil and gang violence, the MIT–Haiti Initiative has been forced to move all of its efforts online. Fortunately, the digital platform now provides a library of instructional materials in Kreyòl for teachers of all disciplines and grade levels, including a series of active-learning guides for physics, chemistry, and biology.

While currently the Haitian people are experiencing political instability and insecurity, historically, they also have suffered impoverishment and injustice due to the postcolonial exclusion of the home language from the nation's classrooms, thus depriving Kreyòl-speaking learners of an equitable education (DeGraff, 2020). The MIT–Haiti Initiative is built on a framework that accounts for the learner's language and the school's capacity to deliver high-quality instruction using digital tools for learning.

The continued success of this support depends not only on an amelioration of political instability but also on respecting a 1982 language-education policy (the

Bernard Reform) that designated Kreyòl rather than the colonial language, French, as the language of instruction. The Bernard Reform was meant to benefit students as well as teachers, most of whom do not speak French. Yet, over time, the Ministry of Education began to promote "early transition" from Kreyòl back to French as the language of instruction, thus negatively affecting the majority of students whose home language is Kreyòl. Fortunately, the current Minister of Education is making efforts to return Kreyòl to its place as the main language of instruction at all grade levels (DeGraff, Frager, & Miller, 2022). It will take such decolonizing work to reintegrate the *home language practices* of Haitians with *technology* and *a proven instructional approach* to achieve positive attitudinal changes in pedagogy for participating teachers and students in Haiti. (For more examples of decolonial efforts to challenge linguistic domination in education both in Haiti and beyond, see DeGraff, in preparation.)

It is essential to underscore the fact that not all software claiming to be interactive is associated with positive academic outcomes. Studies have shown that when "programmed instruction" tools such as drill and practice activities for rote learning are the only digital options offered to students from low socioeconomic status backgrounds, their test scores are negatively affected (Warschauer & Matuchniak, 2010; Wenglinsky, 2005). Well-designed interactive programs for complex learning must also be available to "allow students to see and explore concepts from different angles using a variety of representations" (Darling-Hammond, Zielezinski, & Goldman, 2014, p. 7).

Interactions among learners with and through technology. Interactivity includes not only an individual's interaction with engaging software but also students' conjoint meaning-making and design. More research is demonstrating the educational value of students' collaborative interactions while using technology. For example, Ronan's (2014) study of students in a social studies class documents the collaboration among learners as they participated in a classroom activity while engaging with web-based multimodal materials to accomplish an online writing task. Multimodal transcripts were constructed and analyzed to illustrate student-pair interactions as they shared a common space on the computer screen. During this activity, the students conjointly examined online visual and textual resources, used gesture along with talk in two languages, and along the way applied these resources to construct a written note. The analysis uncovered the process of transformation of a student's writing while engaging with different modalities for examination, discussion, and note-taking. Ronan's findings help us "(understand) writing as a multimodal/multilingual, *socially interactive* practice" (2014, p. 247; emphasis added).

Besides collaboration among users as they are working in pairs or small groups on web-based activities, another setting in which technology enhances interactivity is through users' collaborations that occur almost entirely online. For example, online collaborative inquiry that leads to culminating projects can take place between classrooms located in different regions of the world. Project-based learning (PBL), said to originate in the work of John Dewey (1938), was first adopted at the turn of the century by classroom teachers to engage students in collaborative investigations around authentic problems and develop projects or presentations to address them (Thomas, 2000). Research has shown that when the PBL approach is integrated into digital environments that are thoughtfully designed and with teachers who receive professional development and support for using these alternative spaces for learning, emergent bilinguals can thrive academically (Condliffe et al., 2016).

Teachers have reported that using collaborative online PBL enhances their instructional strategies for English learners. In a collective case study, Foulger and Jimenez-Silva (2007) describe how 14 classroom teachers received technology training and sustained support from a professional developer to implement project-based activities that involved writing. One of the teachers joined a global learning group called the International Education and Resource Network (iEARN)[4] so that her class could participate in an online exchange with students in a school outside the United States. In selecting iEARN, the teacher had the benefit of a robust digital learning space with a long history of teacher-led interchanges. iEARN began in 1988 with a telecommunications project between teachers and students in New York State and Moscow and soon expanded in 1990 to nine countries. Since then, more than 140 countries have been involved in more than 150 international collaborative projects online in English and in 29 other languages. Its online platform allows teachers to connect with other teachers and their students around the world to *interact* with one another and to collaborate on meaningful projects and make contributions to local and/or global communities.

In another iEARN online project, which involved U.S. and Middle East and North African (MENA) classrooms, analyses were carried out of the online social interactions among teachers in iEARN's development workshops as well as the follow-up interactions between their students, who were collaborating on projects across languages and cultures. The findings indicated that participants—many of whom were emergent bilingual English learners from Yemen—through their online *interactions* gained ground in intercultural understanding, learned about different life worlds, and developed their communicative and technology skills in the online spaces (Kleifgen, 2017a, 2017b).

Creativity

To examine the notion of creativity as an affordance, we turn again to the work of Gunther Kress, who first introduced the concept of *design* for education in the early 1990s. For Kress, design implies that both teachers and learners exercise agency and freedom to become *creative* in their academic work. Arguing for a pedagogy of creativity, agency, and change in the curriculum, he states: "Curriculum is a design for the future" because such a curriculum has the potential to shape individuals' positive participation in society (Kress, 2000b, p. 161; see also Kress, 2000a). Design is also a way to demonstrate individual learners' agency, interests, and freedom to become creative in their academic pursuits "through the design of messages with the resources available to them in specific situations" (Kress, 2010, p. 23; see also Kress, 2003). In using the term *messages*, Kress is referring to "making" or "producing" new forms of content in today's digital age by assembling the meaning-making resources available to students in many modes. More than ever, learning is about drawing on multimodal resources to design something new.

Figure 9.2. Image of a Park Sign in the Segregationist South, Barring People of Color From Entry

Creativity occasioned by the support of technology is a process of design in environments that can range from the design of the smallest fragment of text to the construction of more extended multimodal discourse. We learn how a short note begins to be created in Ronan's (2015) work. She carried out a fine-grained analysis of two emergent bilinguals examining a multimodal resource in the digital library of a web-based system in order to take notes on the system's digital notepads. During a class lesson on the history of segregation in the United States, the two students collaboratively discuss and come to an interpretation of a historical photograph from the segregationist South showing a park sign barring people of color from entry (Figure 9.2).

Both students begin to take their own notes describing the photograph. At one point during their discussion and note-taking, one student asks her classmate in Spanish what she should write next. He suggests a reason for the discriminatory order posted on the sign: "*Porque ¿ellos son differentes razas?*" [Because they are different races?]. She transforms the message written in English on the image along with her classmate's suggestion in spoken Spanish into a new written note in her developing English:

> white people only (negros and Mexican) out. i think the white people not like that peoples of Mexican and negrous because they different countrys and different color of skin.

The student, in this unfolding creative process of interaction with a peer and drawing on and reinterpreting multiple modes—including a multimodal image and spoken and written language in Spanish and English—has transformed those resources and begun her design of a new text in written English.

Another study (Pierson, Clark, & Brady, 2021) illustrates the student creation of complex multimodal scientific artifacts. Groups of students in a sixth-grade STEM class were invited to leverage their translanguaging practices—linguistic modes—while designing different types of scientific models to represent ecosystems by combining a broad range of additional modes for learning (diagrams, physical structures, images, gestures). In varying ways, the linguistic modes conjoined with other modes provided opportunities for communicative interaction and design. For example, students discussed the advantages of the more complex and dynamic computational model over the flat, diagrammatic model. Throughout the unit, students demonstrated their *creative* design of different types of multimodal scientific models—computational, diagrammatic, and physical.

Studies give evidence that, when struggling students are challenged to engage in their own content creation using new media, they are more likely to do well on competency tests. In one such study, so-called at-risk students who were designing projects in technology-rich classrooms, compared with students who were on level but not using these tools, outperformed their peers in state-mandated exams (Maninger, 2006). Maninger's research on ninth-grade English classrooms provides illustrations of teachers guiding students as they produced blogs about the literature they were studying, used online software to compose assigned papers, and created multimodal webpages for their projects.

Other studies show the benefits when underserved minoritized students are presented with the opportunity to engage in *creative* digital storytelling. Hull and Nelson (2005) examine one young man's multimodal composition, an ensemble of modes—language, image, and music—to tell an autobiographical story called "Lyfe-N-Rhyme." The author developed his digital story at a community technology center in an urban setting where many youths have little or no access to digital tools at school or at home. The researchers' detailed analysis of a digital artifact focuses on how the *semiotic relationships across the modes* progressively elaborate one another and eventually create a new form of meaning where the whole is greater than the sum of its parts. Nevertheless, as Iedema (2003) points out, studies of "finished" designs like these demonstrate "the complexity of texts or representations as they are, and less frequently how it is that such constructs [are elaborated]" (p. 30; see also Kleifgen, 2013).

Whereas Hull and Nelson's (2005) "Lyfe-N-Rhyme" analysis is a case study of a finished product, the work by Angay-Crowder, Choi, and Yi (2013) offers a play-by-play description of how teachers can open up opportunities for their emergent bilinguals' *creative storytelling*. They provide a blueprint of lessons grounded in the New London Group's theory of pedagogy and lay out in detail the process by which 12 middle school students, all children of immigrants, were instructed in the basics of digital storytelling and in strategies for constructing a story. Ten of the students came from Spanish-speaking homes, one spoke limited Bengali, and one spoke Tagalog. They were encouraged to consult with one another and with adults in their communities to verify their narratives as well as to explore their multiple languages and literacies in the process of applying both linguistic and other semiotic modes to their stories. The students were also taught how to use the storytelling software, and they were guided in how to assess and select the different modes in order for their stories to have greater effect. The study demonstrates the importance of providing specific guidance and encouragement to emergent bilinguals to unleash their creativity throughout the process.

In Marshall and Toohey's (2010) study, Punjabi Sikh fourth- and fifth-grade students in Canada participated in a multimedia intergenerational stories project. The students took home MP3 players and recorded interviews with their grandparents in Punjabi, Malay, and Hindi about what it was like growing up in India. The students translated these spoken interviews into written English and produced the text on computers, leaving space for their illustrations. They then decided to translate their written work into the grandparents' home language (with the help of the grandparents or other adults who were literate in the language) so that they would have bilingual texts. Finally, they recorded their readings of the stories in English and Punjabi; the recordings were put on compact discs to accompany the books. In short, the students used multiple modes over time, both online and off, to complete their *creative work*.

Increasingly, learning is about drawing on multimodal resources to design something new, as these studies illustrating the affordances of creativity have shown. Although most of the examples we have given describe digital storytelling, other spaces on the internet are being used by young people for creative work. In a Pew internet survey, over half of the adolescents surveyed report that they have created web content (Lenhart & Madden, 2005). Further, emergent bilinguals can create as they learn computer science skills, as reported in a study of one sixth-grade classroom where students used translanguaging as they integrated computer code into their language arts projects (Ascenzi-Moreno, Güílamo, & Vogel, 2020). (For more, see the PiLa-CS project described later on in this chapter.) Young people today are also exploring wikis, video production, games, virtual worlds, and especially social media with YouTube, TikTok, Instagram, and Snapchat surpassing Facebook in daily use as reported by Pew Research Center (Vogels, Gelles-Watnick, & Massarat, 2022). And they are self-publishing zines with original or copied texts and images used in new ways. All of these digital spaces make use of multimodal resources, including multiple spoken and written languages.[5]

Taken together, the affordances for learning that new digital technologies can provide—*accessibility*, *retrievability*, *interactivity*, and *creativity*—demonstrate the potential that these new learning environments have for the equitable education of emergent bilinguals.

RESOURCING EMERGENT BILINGUALS' CLASSROOMS

We have argued that emergent bilinguals can benefit academically from high-quality digital tools and from teachers who have preparation, commitment, and experience in using these tools in their schools and classrooms. We know theoretically and empirically that new media technologies are good for emergent bilinguals. So, what can we do to make this happen? Here, we refer again to the four affordances described in this chapter to address this question.

First, students need *access* to digital tools in their schools. Schools require the necessary infrastructure—servers, storage, and bandwidth—for fast and reliable connectivity and to avoid the frustration of breakdowns. We know that one-to-one *access*, one device per student, is beneficial for emergent bilinguals. This is especially the case if they do not have *access* to computers or other devices at home; they need more opportunities at school to *retrieve* online materials for study, note-taking, review, and the production of new knowledge artifacts.

Second, web-based and other software materials that are well-designed and *interactive* must be made available to students. Software designed for rote learning should not be the menu of options for emergent bilinguals; technologies designed for complex and collaborative learning-in-*interaction* must be part of the digital curriculum.

Third, teachers are students' best advocates in obtaining sustained and efficacious *access* to digital technologies. Students will learn appropriate and *creative* uses of new media with the guidance of teachers who are well prepared to integrate technology into their teaching. This means that teachers must be given the opportunity to explore the scholarship on multimodality, to consider the affordances and limitations of ICTs, including AI technology, and to experiment with implementation of multimodal learning using digital resources so that they can support students' *creative* designs.

In short, ICTs for learning must be intelligently designed and tested, schools must be supplied with adequate technical infrastructure, and educators must be given the professional preparation and ongoing support to be students' guides in these alternative learning spaces. One project that takes into account these requirements illustrates what can be done to support emergent bilinguals' literacy and educational attainment: The project, Participating in Literacies and Computer Science (PiLa-CS; https://www.pila-cs.org/our-approach) has been working with teachers specifically to support emergent bilinguals and all multilingual students in computing education. The PiLa-CS approach builds and sustains the language practices, identities, and communities of multilingual learners by rejecting deficit-based framings of these students (Vogel et al., 2020).

In terms of multimodal resources, the embodied modes and those in the environment (visual, audio, etc.) are not separate scaffolds for developing the spoken and written modes; instead, they are an essential part of all the meaning-making resources at emergent bilingual students' disposal (Grapin, 2019; Kleifgen & Kinzer, 2009). Foregrounding multimodality can transform educators' conceptions of how to leverage the students' meaning-making potential beyond accessing spoken and written linguistic modes alone. Students can draw on an ecology of modes, including linguistic—spoken and written—in the home language and the emergent language, embodied modes such as gesture and facial expressions, and modes in the physical environment and through ICT. But to draw on them creatively and naturally, educators must provide an accessible and enabling environment for learning.

EDUCATING EMERGENT BILINGUALS:
THE IMPORTANT ROLE OF TECHNOLOGY

In this chapter, we have addressed the important role that digital technology has in the education of emergent bilinguals. Many studies like those reported in this chapter, which are based on multiliteracies pedagogy and the more recent thinking in social semiotics about multimodality, offer ideas for classroom instruction with technology—including the potential of AI-supported tools—that is engaging and meaningful for emergent bilingual students. The four affordances we discussed can serve as guidelines as teachers and other adults in students' lives provide motivating and educative digital materials and activities for students. Other excellent resources that suggest sensible technology implementation are available: Teachers can benefit from ideas in Cecilia Magadán's (2015, 2021) volumes (written in Spanish), which offer theoretically based, empirically demonstrated, and pedagogically effective ways of integrating technology into the classroom. Bruce, Bishop, and Budhathoki's (2014) work describes examples from a wide variety of settings that show how students use new media to support other people in their communities. A most important teacher resource to advance educational equity in computer science is the open-source textbook published by the Computer Science Education Justice Collective (in press). Written in clear language, this guide is important for any teacher who wants to implement equitable and relevant computer science instruction for diverse students taking into account issues of race, language, and ability. We conclude this chapter by calling upon leaders and school administrators to properly resource schools, classrooms, and communities with technologies for optimal learning in our increasingly diverse, digitized, and globalized world. But we also call upon educators to consider multiple modes of communication as part of students' meaning-making capacity and not as a simple scaffold. In particular, we call for a transformation of the *incomplete ways* in which schools often view emergent bilinguals' semiotic repertoire. Too often, "schooling takes place in a linguistic and digital straitjacket" (Kleifgen, 2022, p. 65). Schools many times consider only what emergent bilinguals are *missing*—English—instead of all the language features and practices that make up their existing language repertoire. When they leverage them, they often do so only as scaffolds. Likewise, when schools consider other modes, they sometimes think of them as a way to support the "language" that students do not have—again, what they are *missing*. For example, students are allowed to draw only when they can't write, or act only when they can't speak, or use technology only to contextualize tasks with images. But if we take a translanguaging view, we see *all of it—all linguistic features together with all other modes—as essential* affordances making up the students' meaning-making repertoire, transforming their capacity to learn and to be themselves.

Educators of emergent bilinguals need to remain "wide awake," as Maxine Greene (1995) tells us, as to why some students are given the opportunity to use all their meaning-making resources and others are not. And educators must remain vigilant about the reasons why emergent bilinguals often are not given equitable curricular opportunities and resources, as we have been suggesting throughout this book.

STUDY QUESTIONS

1. Discuss the concepts of multiliteracies, initiated by the New London Group; multimodality, as defined and elaborated by Gunther Kress; and social semiotics, the foundational theory proposed by M. A. K. Halliday.
2. What are some of the inequities that low-income and minoritized students face with regard to where and when they can use digital technologies?
3. What are some ways that generative AI might support emergent bilinguals? What do educators need to know about the opportunities and challenges that this tool presents?
4. Describe the four affordances offered by ICTs and give examples from the research of how they support emergent bilinguals' learning.
5. Select one or two of the practices described in the research and discuss how they illustrate more than one affordance for learning. For example, how might one technology implementation demonstrate both accessibility and retrievability? Interactivity and creativity? Other combinations?

CHAPTER 10

Signposts

Conclusion and Recommendations

In this concluding chapter, we will:

- Summarize what we have learned about:
  - » Who emergent bilinguals are and what educational programs exist for them,
  - » Language theory and research,
  - » Bilingual programs and practices,
  - » Curriculum and other practices,
  - » Family and community engagement,
  - » Assessment, and
  - » Affordances of technology.
- Offer signposts: a set of detailed recommendations for advocates, policymakers, educators, and researchers to provide a more equitable education for emergent bilinguals.

Throughout this book, we have presented the case for reconceptualizing English language learners in American schools as *emergent bilinguals*. This concept recognizes the value of the students' home language practices as resources for learning and as markers of their identity as individuals who have creative ways of knowing, being, and communicating. The term *emergent* emphasizes the "loopiness" of bilingual development and the internal connectedness of the linguistic/multimodal, the cognitive, the social, the emotional, and the lived bodily experience as students do language in meaningful interactions. The term *bilingual* challenges the current silencing of bilingualism in education; it also links the present battle against deficit thinking and raciolinguistic ideologies to the historical antiracist struggles of language-minoritized communities during the civil rights era of the 1960s. In repositioning these students from English learners to emergent bilinguals, we have been able to expose the dissonance between research findings on the best ways to educate them and the current educational policies and practices that have disregarded them.

WHAT HAVE WE LEARNED?

In Chapter 2, we began to address how emergent bilinguals have been identified and demonstrated the discrepancies in the way they have been counted and classified in federal, state, and even school district agencies. We identified problems with counting and sorting; for example, some agencies exclude from the count any bilingual students who have not been classified as English learners. What is clear is that the language-minoritized population is growing more rapidly than the monolingual English-speaking population; the number of bilingual students has increased dramatically. What the data also show is that most emergent bilinguals attend schools in high-poverty urban school districts where classrooms are often crowded, enrichment programs and material resources are lacking, and teachers are underqualified. Students in these schools have high incidences of health problems and absenteeism. Further, it cannot be assumed that because these students are speakers of languages other than English, they are all foreign born; three in four are native-born U.S. citizens. Finally, although we know that the majority of emergent bilinguals in the United States are speakers of Spanish, the census does not account for the fact that some of those categorized as such are actually speakers of the many Indigenous languages of the Americas.

In Chapter 3, we charted the types of educational programs that have been available in the United States for emergent bilinguals. These range from programs that require the exclusive use of English in the classroom to those that provide instruction and support in the home language along with English. But over the 55+ year history of language education policies, beginning with the Bilingual Education Act of 1968, inspired by the civil rights struggles of the 1960s, and continuing through ESSA (2015), we have seen a shift away from the bilingual end of the continuum to a largely English-only language policy for racialized minoritized students in U.S. schools. An exception to this trend has been the dual-language bilingual education (DLBE) program model, which has gained popularity in recent decades. This rise is largely due to its inclusion of English speakers and its status as a choice program. While these programs create new bilingual education opportunities for emergent bilinguals, they also introduce a unique set of challenges and tensions.

Against this backdrop, in subsequent chapters, we explored theories and research that support ways in which emergent bilinguals can learn both English and subject-matter content optimally and be assessed equitably. We considered the gaps between the research evidence and language education policies and practices for emergent bilinguals. Most importantly, we advocated for alternative policies and practices that have the potential to educate these students more equitably.

Language Theory and Research

In Chapter 4, we discussed key theoretical frameworks for understanding the relationship between bilingualism and learning. These interrelated frameworks have shown the cognitive, academic, and sociopolitical benefits of drawing on *all* home language practices, including those named English, as well as Haitian Creole,

Korean, Mandarin Chinese, Russian, Spanish, and so on. Translanguaging scholarship (e.g., García & Li Wei, 2014; Otheguy, García, & Reid, 2015) has argued that the distinction between named languages is social, not linguistic or cognitive: Bilingual speakers do language with their own complex language system or repertoire from which they select features guided by their *social* lives and experiences, and understandings of which features and practices might help them construct their message most successfully, given the nature of the interaction and the participants.

Scholars from an array of academic disciplines—including anthropology, education, linguistics, and psychology—have shown that language use varies in different contexts and have provided descriptive analyses of a wide range of language and literacy varieties. The research makes it clear that, in educational contexts, carrying on a simple conversation about everyday topics is not the same as discussing, reading, and writing about cognitively demanding ideas. We know from extensive research in schools in the United States and around the world that attaining competence in literacies for academic purposes requires sustained discussion, reflection, and practice. We also know that these literacies are bound up in relations of power and identity and that literacies entailing two or more named languages intensify questions of power and negotiations of identity. Skilled teachers can provide space in the classroom that empowers students to affirm their linguistic and cultural funds of knowledge even as they add to their repertoire of disciplinary knowledge and communicative practices. It is through these linguistic and literacy processes that students engage in identity work: They develop a sense of self through multiple language practices in different social situations (Norton, 2013). This is precisely what the notion of pluriliteracies addresses. As we discussed in Chapter 4, the term *pluriliteracies* describes the complex language practices that take place in multilingual communities (see García, Bartlett, & Kleifgen, 2007). It helps us understand young peoples' diverse literacy practices and values in and out of school; it also takes into account the intermingling of multiple languages and scripts as well as rapidly changing new technologies that further shape their use.

Added to this understanding is the recognition that the path to bilingualism is a dynamic process and not a linear one, as had been previously claimed. Emergent bilinguals expand their own repertoire, adding new features as they communicate and learn. Guided by social cues in an interaction, they select features and practices from their unitary repertoire to communicate. At times, they creatively use linguistic features that are socially categorized as belonging to one or another language to make meaning. By understanding what makes up a bilingual's repertoire and bringing this flexible and subtle understanding of language practices into the classroom, teachers open new spaces for optimal meaning-making, identity formation, and eventual academic achievement.

Large-scale evaluations and meta-analyses of studies on bilingual programs beginning in the 1970s and continuing into the present (Baker & Wright, 2021) have borne out these theoretical frameworks, showing that judicious use of different language practices in the classroom results in high achievement levels in both subject-matter content and English and other languages, sometimes exceeding national norms, provided that teachers and students are given adequate time to develop students' ways of "doing" language. Bilingual education has been maligned in the United States despite the fact that the most carefully designed reviews of programs have shown positive educational outcomes. The political climate has overshadowed these empirical findings, and language has been treated as a problem rather than a resource. The problem does not reside in students or their languages but rather in classroom practices that have been shaped by misguided educational policies.

Language and Classroom Practice

We have seen that emergent bilinguals generally have not been in classrooms that apply theory and research findings on the benefits of using home language practices to support learning. Further, in classrooms where both languages are used, the home language and English generally are kept strictly separated (what we called compartmentalization in Chapter 5). This ignores the potential of dynamic bilingualism and translanguaging for *scaffolding*, when students require assistance to understand concepts while at the same time developing their bilingualism; *assessment*, so teachers can distinguish between students' content knowledge and language skills; and *transformation*, in order to promote students' raciolinguistic consciousness and self-identity. Unfortunately, the number of bilingual education programs has decreased dramatically, and most emergent bilinguals today are in English-only programs. Even ESL support is being curtailed in some states.

Our response to this sad state of affairs is to put forth a strong argument for all students—majority- and minoritized-language speakers—to be given the opportunity to reap the benefits of bilingualism in their education.

Curriculum and Other Practices

If we cast a light of social justice and linguistic human rights on typical curricular and pedagogical designs for emergent bilinguals, we see the inequities, because the elements of richness and creativity are missing. We described these inequities and considered alternative practices in Chapters 5 and 6.

Both Courtney Cazden in 1986 and Linda Darling-Hammond again in 2024 pointed to the fact that two kinds of curricula exist in U.S. schools: one that has well-designed, challenging content and engages students in creative and collaborative work, and another that only pays attention to basic skills. The latter is often the kind of curriculum that emergent bilinguals are taught. They are subject to deficit models of instruction—"remediation," tracking, mistaken placement into special education, exclusion from gifted programs, and reduced curricular choice because of a narrow focus on English language skills. Moreover, inequities begin early. Emergent bilinguals seldom get a favorable start through early childhood programs, despite the fact that these programs can contribute to later educational achievement.

Challenging and creative curricula can give emergent bilinguals access to rich classroom discourse and literacy experiences across subject-matter areas. It is sustained social interactions that affirm students' identities while helping them learn.

Teacher preparation is crucial to a high-quality education for emergent bilinguals. We know that effective teachers of these students have a thorough understanding of how language works. These teachers have studied child language development and bilingualism and have acquired the knowledge that is necessary to teach the students explicitly about how language is used in different content areas (Wong-Fillmore & Snow, 2000). Well-prepared teachers understand the importance of preschool for emergent bilingual children, emergent bilinguals' rights to be assessed for bilingual gifted-and-talented programs, and the need for those with disabilities to receive bilingual special education. They use culturally sustaining pedagogies and equitable resources to enhance students' translanguaging in classroom social interaction and literacy events—all with the goal of fostering learning with critical consciousness (Freire, 1970; Palmer et al., 2019). In addition, effective teachers have received preparation to reach out to parents of emergent bilinguals to form a partnership in students' education.

Family and Community Engagement

Effective teachers know that they cannot go it alone. As we discussed in Chapter 7, research tells us that parents are emergent bilinguals' primary advocates for an equitable education. Thus, their equitable collaboration as influential decision-makers in the transformation of schools provides the potential not only to support students' linguistic and academic needs but also to foster learning environments for them to collaboratively construct new knowledge and become change agents. Parents and community members possess distinctive funds of knowledge—ways of knowing that their children learn at home (González, Moll, & Amanti, 2005; Moll et al., 1992). These too often go unrecognized in the school; worse, these endogenous competencies—home language and literacy practices, practical skills, and values—are considered by some to be inferior and inconsequential to schooling. This deficit view of home language practices requires intervention—in teacher education as well as ongoing professional development—for critical reassessment based on research demonstrating that students' home language practices are a powerful resource for learning. These home language practices are not the same as simply talking about one home language.

Even in cases where schools recognize the value of students' funds of knowledge, including linguistic knowledge, they may avoid applying some of the more "difficult" or uncomfortable funds of knowledge, which are perceived either to be too sensitive or to clash with the curriculum, such as transnational students' experiential knowledge garnered through crossing borders, learning about documentation, or fearing that a parent might be detained or deported. In fact, such experiences can be a source of dialogue and writing, with the support of a teacher, as well as an educative tool for critical thinking and problem solving.

Often, parental education programs are designed to teach parents how to educate their children; some of these programs operate in a deficit model, implicitly suggesting that parents lack adequate parenting skills (Goodall, 2021). Alternative models view family engagement as a responsibility shared among the school, the community, and the family (Rosenberg et al., 2009). Bilingual communities, including immigrants, are looking for more genuine dialogue with school personnel (Olivos, Jiménez-Castellanos, & Ochoa, 2011) and demanding access to bilingual programs for their children (Jaumont, 2017), while at the same time they are up against the pressure for "school choice" such as dual-language programs that may favor elite families. Parents of emergent bilinguals are also working within the community to demand that outside groups support their parental rights and are establishing their own grassroots organizations with an aim to reform school programs for their children. In sum, a decolonial approach regarding parental engagement is needed to challenge dominant Eurocentric paradigms and to reestablish parents' autonomy with respect to their children's education.

Assessment

Testing is the gatekeeping device that often prevents emergent bilingual students from gaining access to further education and eventually an excellent quality of life. All students, including emergent bilinguals, are over-tested under current government mandates, and some educators have applied testing data in ways that reinforce deficit perceptions of African American and Latine students' abilities (Bertrand & Marsh, 2021). For emergent bilinguals, testing is especially burdensome because they are essentially being tested for their language proficiency rather than for their knowledge of subject-matter content. Moreover, not only are the tests given in English, but they also have been normed on monolingual student populations; they do not take into account English learners' developing bilingualism or bilingual use. Finally, although performance-based assessments are an improvement over traditional tests, they still rely on teachers' interpretations of the results, which can reflect biased perceptions of minoritized emergent bilinguals (Ascenzi-Moreno & Seltzer, 2021).

In Chapter 8, we suggested several alternatives to the way emergent bilinguals are currently tested. They involve changing the ways that students take the tests or how others score them, or developing different assessments altogether, such as tests in the home language or tests that use the students' translanguaging practices as a way to tap into and assess what students know (Ascenzi-Moreno, García, & López, 2024; García, 2009a; Gottlieb, 2017). The most promising alternatives continue to be close observations of student learning in the classroom, dynamic bilingual assessments, and performance-based as well as biliterate assessments. But for testing to be effective and fair, it requires professional development around teacher beliefs and judgments in interpreting the scores of minoritized test-takers.

Affordances of Technology

Over the past several years, there has been a conceptual shift in understanding literacy not as a static, standardized, and monomodal (written) *product* but as a plural, creative, and multimodal *practice*. Multimodality entails many semiotic resources: both spoken and written communication in multiple languages, along with other modes on which people draw to make meaning. This expanded notion of literacy practices has its impact in classrooms where students can use multiple modes to study and learn.

As we have seen in Chapter 9, digital competence is essential for learning, working, and living in today's world. Yet poor and minoritized students still have less access to computers and the internet than their more privileged counterparts. Despite advances in the availability of multimodal resources as a result of the expansion of new media technologies, some emergent bilingual students still do not have access to these tools to support their learning (Darling-Hammond, 2010; Poushter, 2016). This is truly unfortunate and inequitable, especially for emergent bilingual students, since many of the nonlinguistic modes or resources for learning can act as scaffolds for the development of the spoken and written linguistic modes. And, as we have argued throughout this volume, multiple linguistic modes also can be mutually elaborative for learning, particularly for emergent bilingual students.

In Chapter 9, we also noted that the era of generative artificial intelligence has brought with it responsibilities on the part of educators and students alike to understand its promises and pitfalls for education. A chatbot, simulating human communication, can rapidly produce well-designed texts in response to user instructions or prompts. But because chatbots cannot think or distinguish between true and false information, teachers need to guide students in designing sophisticated prompts and in critically assessing the strengths and weaknesses of these tools (Kalantzis & Cope, 2024). When used judiciously, AI can support emergent bilingual learners with additional applications such as digital translation, speech recognition tools, and intelligent language tutors.

Information and communication technology (ICT) offers accessibility to a growing archive of information with the following affordances: no limitations of space or time; retrievability of materials for further study and deeper understanding; interactivity with powerful ICT applications and among learners for collaborative work in the classroom or around the world; and creativity by assembling meaning-making resources to design something new, that is, to learn. These affordances promote the educational achievement of emergent bilinguals. Leadership on the part of school administrators is needed to resource all schools with ICTs. We also need well-prepared classroom teachers who understand bilingual students' translanguaging, as they offer careful guidance in opening up translanguaging learning spaces on the internet.

Our analysis of a wide variety of issues in the education of emergent bilinguals shows an ever-growing dissonance between the research and inappropriate educational programs and instruction, limited curricular resources and funding, exclusion of parents and the community, faulty assessment procedures, and inequitable access to digital technologies. We now conclude this book by offering a series of hopeful signposts—a set of recommendations for a more equitable education for emergent bilinguals.

SIGNPOSTS: POLICY RECOMMENDATIONS

The following recommendations for transforming the education of emergent bilinguals take on greater urgency today given the increase in the number of students—citizens and noncitizens alike—coming into classrooms who speak a language other than English. Some of these recommendations can be carried out by advocacy groups and grassroots organizations; some need the leadership of government at the federal, state, and local levels, and school officials to move forward; others can be enacted by educators in their schools and classrooms; yet others belong to the realm of researchers.

For Advocates

Many people from outside the field of education—citizens, parents, other professionals, and grassroots organizations—are important advocates for emergent bilinguals and can take steps such as the following to transform education.

- Educate the U.S. public through the media, including social media, about the nature of bilingualism.

There are folk theories in the United States that "other" languages and speakers of "other" languages are somehow abnormal and in need of repair. The media and the internet could play an important role in disseminating essential knowledge about language and bilingualism to the general public. Advocates could post online articles, start blogs/vlogs, videos, and/or use other social media to offer discussions about ways in which bilingualism facilitates learning in school and creates work and social opportunities in life, especially for racialized language minoritized populations. In this way, people would come to an understanding that in acquiring English, language-minoritized students become bilingual, and thus, English language teaching helps foster bilingualism. In addition, language-majority parents would understand the advantages of bilingualism in their own lives and those of their children.

Furthermore, through the portrayal of bilingual Americans in movies and television shows, and the representation of bilingual minorities as loyal and hardworking Americans, the public would come to recognize bilingualism as a normal feature of U.S. society. The mainstream media can play an important role in bringing the sounds of languages other than English and bilingualism to all Americans.

- Educate the American public through the media about the benefits of bilingualism as an individual and national resource.

With the help of a wide range of media, the public can come to an understanding about the cognitive and creative value of bilingualism for *all* Americans. Peoples' use of the internet is ubiquitous, and they can easily be persuaded about the advantages of multilingual communication for work and education in today's globalized world, where the movement of people, goods, information, and services is no longer bound by national borders.

- Publicize the efforts of good schools and programs for emergent bilinguals, including the role of school leaders, educators, and the community in this work.

Advocates can promote exposés on schools where emergent bilinguals are learning and where school leaders and educators are making a difference. An example is the book by Kleyn and her colleagues (2024) about a school called *Dos Puentes*. The media can be convinced that portraits of school success can pique the public's interest, perhaps more than stories of failure and conflict. These and similar media presentations can help dispel negative stereotypes about bilingualism and linguistic diversity.

- Urge federal funding for high-quality schools, educational programs and resources, and teacher education programs for emergent bilinguals.

Advocates can emphasize that fair funding needs to be given to educate emergent bilinguals. They can also urge that funding not be tied entirely to test results and that other factors be taken into account so that schools, programs, and teachers who serve language-minoritized communities can be adequately supported. High-quality schools are not always those that have the best test results, but high-quality schools are safe, clean, and have adequate instructional material and resources. They enjoy teams of teachers generously committed to teaching emergent bilinguals and prepared with knowledge about how students learn and develop proficiency in English for academic purposes. Equal educational opportunity for emergent bilinguals should be the focus of the advocacy.

- Keep the federal government and state and local educational authorities accountable for the education of emergent bilinguals.

Although there has been a major focus on accountability for school leaders and teachers, there are weak accountability measures for federal and state government and educational authorities. Questions can be raised about the irrationality of the federal government imposing unfunded mandates on state governments. Questions can also be raised about the ways in which state governments and local educational authorities report their services to emergent bilinguals, as well as how they assess them and report the test scores.

- Urge federal funding for the development of valid and reliable assessment instruments for emergent bilinguals—assessment that takes into account the difference between testing academic knowledge and testing linguistic knowledge, while recognizing the value of multiple indicators of students' achievement.

Advocates can insist that the testing industry be made accountable by exposing how testing scores are being used to exclude emergent bilinguals. Advocates can urge that assessment be put back into the hands of educators. To that end, they should call for funding tied to assessment development that is user-centered. If test-makers were to spend time in classrooms, they would learn from educators what it is that emergent bilinguals can do and how they learn. Thus, test-makers would be able to work with teachers to develop tests that can adequately evaluate emergent bilinguals and help teachers understand the students' strengths and weaknesses.

Advocates could urge federal funding for the development and testing of new assessment initiatives that rely on students' bilingualism. New assessment tools should differentiate between testing students' general linguistic performance for academic purposes and testing their understanding and application of specific linguistic features. Funding might also support projects that enable schools and teachers to design their own assessments, as well as research on how teachers are using the assessment data to develop understandings about their own teaching, and about emergent bilinguals' lives and learning potential.

For Policymakers

- Develop a definition of an English learner that is stable across federal and state lines. The federal government should require stable and accurate data reporting and classification.

It is imperative that agreement be reached as to what constitutes a learner of English. Policymakers could call on scholars of bilingualism to explore how to measure and assess the English practices needed for success in schools. To be accurate, the measure should include students' home languages and their bilingual abilities. Policymakers could demand that this measure not define a category from which students exit and move to a "proficient" category, but designate points on a continuum of emergent bilingualism that require different kinds of educational programs and different levels of academic intervention.

- Design educational policy based on current theory and research regarding the benefits of an equitable education for emergent bilinguals.

The research evidence supporting the use of emergent bilinguals' home language practices in their education is incontrovertible. Policymakers could become well versed in this research and empirical evidence so that this takes center stage in developing policy.

- Support and expand educational programs that have demonstrated success in providing a challenging, high-quality education, and that build on the strengths children and youth bring to school, particularly their home linguistic and cultural practices.

Policymakers could discontinue portraying categories of educational programs as if they were in opposition to each other—ESL or bilingual, for example. Instead, informed policymakers could support the students' translanguaging and leverage it in educating emergent bilinguals in all programs. They could support and encourage educational programs that follow research findings to the extent that the community situation permits.

- Support and expand student access to high-quality materials, including new technologies, especially in high-poverty schools, to facilitate access to the changing communication mediascape and give students a better chance to reach academic attainment.

Policymakers need to provide schools with multimodal, including multilingual, resources—books as well as digital audio and video materials. Access to technology infrastructure for fast connectivity to the internet, one-to-one access to computers, and high-quality interactive tools including carefully curated generative AI with intelligent language tutors, digital translation, and speech recognition capabilities are especially important for emergent bilinguals. Policymakers should ensure that these resources are readily available in all classrooms so that students can read, write, and carry out research and creative design using all the languages and other meaning-making modes at their disposal.

- Start bilingual educational support early through meaningful bilingual early childhood programs.

Policymakers should ensure that multilingual early childhood programs are available and that early assessment and intervention, when appropriate, are done following children's home language practices. Language-majority children could also benefit from these multilingual early childhood programs, participating and becoming familiar with different linguistic and cultural practices early in life.

- Pay particular attention to the middle school years.

Emergent bilinguals who are supported in elementary schools—through either ESL or bilingual programs—often receive fewer services when they reach middle school. Policymakers must pay particular attention to the middle school years, because students who continue to be categorized as English learners after having received five to six years of education may face serious educational barriers. These students cannot be educated in the same ways as emergent bilinguals who are newcomers; educational programs have to be designed to meet the needs of these middle school emergent bilinguals.

- Support strong programs for emergent bilinguals at the secondary level.

Emergent bilinguals need challenging educational programs at all levels, but especially at the secondary level. Policymakers should require that schools provide these adolescents with the challenging academic content they need and with guidance to take Advanced Placement courses. A rigorous academic program that can also develop advanced English literacy is essential to make these adolescents college-ready.

- Support bilingual families and communities in the development of more flexible structures for bilingual education programs.

Bilingual families often prefer a bilingual education program for their children. Bilingual education programs hold much promise in developing the bilingualism not just of those classified as English learners but also of English-speaking children growing up in bilingual homes or of those who identify with ancestors who spoke languages other than English, and even of those who do not. However, because of the ways in which many dual-language bilingual education programs in the United States have been constructed with a strict definition of what is considered "two-way," many children are left out of a bilingual education experience. Flexibility is needed in the implementation of bilingual education programs. Policymakers need to support all families in the development of bilingual education programs for all children in U.S. schools, especially for those who have been racialized and minoritized.

- Require all school leaders, teachers, and other school personnel to be well versed in issues of bilingualism and to understand the importance of the home language and culture for children.

Policymakers could make understanding bilingualism and translanguaging a requirement for teacher certification and employment. Beyond teachers who specialize in ESL and bilingual programs, all teachers should be required by policymakers to demonstrate an ability to work with emergent bilinguals and their families.

- Promote strong preservice/in-service education and professional development that prepares teachers to work with emergent bilinguals.

Given the growing numbers of emergent bilingual children in American schools, policymakers could require that all teacher education programs include coursework on bilingualism and the education of emergent bilinguals. Policymakers could also require that all teachers receive professional development that specifically targets emergent bilinguals as part of their professional commitment.

- Provide incentives for the preparation and hiring of additional bilingual staff—from school leaders and teachers to paraprofessionals, school psychologists, school counselors, therapists, and the like.

Because it is more difficult to recruit, prepare, and retain bilingual school staff, policymakers should provide financial incentives to those institutions of higher education that prepare bilingual staff and to schools that hire them. Financial incentives should be targeted to members of language-minoritized groups who are particularly needed in the teaching profession. Incentives for community members to become paraprofessionals are especially important, as are programs in which these paraprofessionals could then extend their preparation and eventually become teachers. The inclusion of family and community members who can contribute their endogenous local knowledge to the life of the school would be a value-added policy measure.

- Provide incentives for bilinguals to join specialized professional organizations such as Teaching English to Speakers of Other Languages (TESOL) or the National Association of Bilingual Education (NABE) or attend conferences like La Cosecha or the New Mexico Translanguaging Institute.

Bilingual individuals who can become ESL and bilingual teachers need to be offered incentives to become acquainted with the profession and join professional organizations. Different states and regions may offer incentives to encourage attendance at their conferences and meetings.

- Require all teachers to develop some learning experience as emergent bilinguals themselves.

Academic study of an additional language is a worthy aim. However, a richer experience could be considered. Teacher education programs could arrange for prospective teachers to experience a period of time abroad or in an ethnolinguistic community in the United States other than the teacher's own.

- Promote the integration of ESL/bilingual education programs so that all ESL teachers would know about bilingualism and translanguaging, and all bilingual teachers would be experts in developing the English literacy and the biliteracy of their students.

Policymakers could require that, with the exception of the coursework required of bilingual teachers in teaching content in the home language, the preparation of ESL and bilingual teachers be the same. Being in classes together would ameliorate the divisions between programs that often exist. All teachers should know how to teach content in English to emergent bilinguals, as well as support the development of their academic English practices. Additionally, all should understand how to leverage the students' translanguaging in educating them.

- Require schools to recognize the funds of knowledge that exist in emergent bilingual students' families and communities, be accountable to them, and achieve closer mutual engagement for a higher-quality education.

Policymakers could also require that all teachers have coursework on how to work with families of emergent bilinguals. This coursework might also include information on how community-based organizations can serve as catalysts in building school–family–community partnerships. The coursework ideally would require that all teachers learn an additional language to maximize the bilingualism of the U.S. teaching force in the 21st century. In addition, the coursework would make teachers aware of what they could learn from the funds of knowledge of the community and parents by developing the prospective teachers' skills in ethnographic observations and interviews. This specialized coursework would help teachers design assignments that build on the families' funds of knowledge in ways that do not place additional burdens on their parents.

For Educators

- Consider the whole child.

To be effective, teachers would not focus narrowly on the language of the student but instead "cast [their] inner eye on a particular child," as Carini (2000a, p. 57) would say. Teachers can follow Carini's advice about paying attention to students' physical presence and gesture, their disposition and temperament, their connection to other people, their strong interests and preferences, and their modes of thinking and learning.

- Consider students in the context of their communities.

Effective teachers become familiar with the community in which the children live and with the histories of the cultural practices and knowledge systems in which the children and youth are immersed at home and in the community. If the community has a large immigrant population, educators should understand their histories of (im)migration, their cultural practices, their religion, their language practices, and their knowledge systems. They could also become familiar with community-based organizations that support language-minoritized groups and with after-school and weekend community bilingual programs that the students might attend.

- Observe and listen to language practices closely.

Effective teachers are listeners and observers of their students. Teachers should listen to the students on the playground, in the gym, and in the cafeteria. They might also listen to the parents as they pick up their children or to the youth as they make their way home when the school day is over. What languages are they speaking? What are they saying? Teachers could pay attention to the signage in the community and around the school. Are signs written in other languages? Other scripts? They might also inquire about TV programs, computer games, social media, and other digital media that children and youth engage with, sometimes in languages other than English.

- Learn something about the home languages and linguistic practices of students.

Teachers could ask parents to teach them how to say simple phrases such as "Good morning," "Good afternoon," "Thank you," "Please," and "Good-bye." They might experience what it means to write in a nonalphabetic script. Elementary school teachers can try to learn a short song (or obtain a recording) in an additional language to teach the children in the class to sing. Families can be asked to bring in multilingual materials and devise classroom signage in different languages so that the classroom can become a multilingual setting.

- Speak, speak, speak. Read, read, read. Write, write, write.

Language is learned through practice in different contexts. Teachers can give students opportunities to use the English language richly—by listening to different discourses on various media, by reading broadly across both fiction and nonfiction, and by writing different genres frequently. Teachers should give students opportunities to leverage their home language practices by taking up translanguaging pedagogy. A school's access to the internet can facilitate these practices; teachers can use computers and whiteboards in the classroom to promote digital literacy, collaborative online research, and projects using multiple language and other modal resources. Finally, teachers should encourage generative dialogue and opportunities to engage in lively, thoughtful, high-quality interactions.

- Engage in ongoing reflection, individually and collectively.

Given the pervasiveness of raciolinguistic ideologies and deficit thinking, it is imperative that teachers remain reflexive about their own beliefs and practices and about the ways in which dominant discourses about racialized emergent bilinguals—including students with disabilities and students from low-income backgrounds—are constructed.

Reflexivity helps teachers recognize and challenge biases within their schools and their own classrooms that can lead to unequal treatment and lower expectations for racialized emergent bilinguals. It can also help identify ways in which certain policies, materials, assessments, discourse structures, and other practices can lead to unequal power relations among students and families on the basis of language, race, gender, ability, and other categories. Reflexivity requires humility and observation; it fosters ideological clarity and can help educators grow as advocates and agents of change.

- Encourage students to think critically about language practices and the power of language.

Emergent bilinguals need to become language architects (Flores, 2020)—comfortable analyzing language practices, developing metalinguistic skills, comparing named languages, thinking aloud about languages, and critiquing the way languages are used in print and digital media, as well as in public life. They also should have sustained practice learning content and selecting the features from their repertoire that are most appropriate in different contexts. In addition, emergent bilinguals need to become aware of the different powers of named languages in society and in their schools. Teachers can support this development by ensuring that their pedagogy is collaborative and culturally and linguistically relevant. A critical multilingual awareness curriculum would help students develop the ability to analyze social and political issues of language that are relevant to their lives.

- Use bilingual instructional practices and translanguaging pedagogy as a sense-making mechanism.

Instead of compartmentalizing English and excluding home language practices from instruction, all educators should engage in bilingual instructional practices—to render one assignment in the other language, to authorize students to conduct research in that language, to use what they have learned in one language in the service of the other, and/or to discuss and think in any language as they read and write in another. This is important for ESL teachers and bilingual teachers. Furthermore, educators should understand the implications of the concept of translanguaging for the instruction of bilingual students. Teachers need to view bilingual students' language system as unitary, helping students add new linguistic features and appropriate them, and helping them select those that are most appropriate to successfully participate in the task at hand. Teachers should empower emergent bilingual students to use their translanguaging as sense-making in the service of deeper understandings and more advanced development of English and other languages.

- Provide a challenging and creative curriculum with challenging and relevant material.

Teachers should elaborate the instructional sessions for emergent bilinguals by providing different scaffolds. This does not mean teachers should simplify; they should search for instructional material that is challenging. Whenever possible, they should provide opportunities to read and write in the students' home languages, enabling the development of complex ideas that can be expressed better in a language one knows while the other language is still being developed. Teachers should encourage the use of technology and the internet because these can be important resources for students to find challenging material written in their home languages, material that is relevant to students' lives, and because this encourages positive identity development and engages them with complex ideas. Educators can leverage ICTs to empower their students to create digital content that showcases the strengths of emergent bilinguals and engages with bilingual communities on topics of interest and advocacy. This approach allows students to become agents of change, all while engaging their creative and bilingual skills through writing, drawing, acting, game creation, and audiovisual design. Additionally, it promotes media literacy and connects students with real bilingual audiences globally in culturally sustaining ways. At the same time, educators should inculcate in their students a critical and judicious use of AI, especially by evaluating the strengths and weaknesses of the material generated by AI.

- Provide differentiated instruction for emergent bilingual students with different educational profiles.

Some emergent bilinguals are new to the school language; they have come to school from homes in which English is not spoken or is spoken in ways that are different from the language practices in school. They also may come from schools in other countries where instruction was in a language other than English. Some of the newcomer students have well-developed literacy practices in their home language, but others do not. Many have had their education interrupted by war, poverty, and other social conditions. Still other emergent bilinguals have been in U.S. classrooms for a long time and yet have failed to develop academic literacy in English. And there are also bilingual students who have been labeled as disabled. Educators need to be aware of these differences and provide students with appropriate lessons and pedagogy. They should also advocate for computer use in their classrooms to enable online access for differential learning and to unleash students' diverse interests and creativity.

- Become an advocate of emergent bilinguals and their instruction.

Individuals and groups outside the school system are not the only ones who can become advocates. Besides parents, effective teachers know what the best academic path is for emergent bilinguals. Teachers should use the data generated from standardized assessments but supplement it with their own close observations, performance assessments, and professional judgments. They should resist educational decisions made for emergent bilinguals that are based on one score on a standardized test. They should be advocates for what these students need when communicating with other school professionals, other teachers, the school leadership team, and the community.

- Develop a strong relationship with students' families.

Teachers should learn as much as they can about and from families of emergent bilinguals and the community's funds of knowledge. When it comes to newcomers to the United States, teachers need information regarding whether the family or other relatives were separated because of immigration, with whom the children/ youth immigrated, and who was left behind. They can encourage parents and other community members to participate in classroom activities, inviting them to give presentations about their cultural and linguistic histories and practices. Above all, they can promote greater family and community engagement by inviting parents to learn more about the school's structures and processes and by listening to parents' and the community's demands for alternative educational practices.

- Inculcate in emergent bilingual students a hunger for inquisitiveness, and model dreams of inclusion, equity, and social justice.

Teachers should be particularly focused on high expectations for emergent bilingual students, as well as ways of releasing their imagination. At the same time, teachers should convey their convictions about the need for acceptance and social justice to build a more inclusive and just world.

For Researchers

- Study the cognitive and creative advantages of bilingualism.

Neurolinguistic research that focuses on the cognitive and creative consequences of bilingualism has just begun to emerge. This research needs to be advanced.

- Develop assessments that differentiate between language and content knowledge and that distinguish between general linguistic performances and language-specific performances. Take translanguaging into account in the design of assessments.

Assessment is the most serious gap in research on emergent bilinguals' education. Researchers—in particular, neurolinguists, psycholinguists, and sociolinguists—need to join with psychometricians and educators in developing assessments for bilingual children that reflect their complex language practices rather than simply reflecting monolingual practices.

- Develop measures of dynamic bilingual proficiency.

As researchers recognize the fallacy of a linear conception of bilingualism, it becomes necessary to develop ways of assessing the complex dynamic nature of language practices and bilingualism. Research in this area needs to be strengthened.

- Conduct research on the effects of translanguaging for the teaching and learning of emergent bilinguals.

Past conceptions of bilingualism were constructed based on monolingual notions of language practices. As a result, English compartmentalization has been a preferred instructional approach in the United States. But, as studies of bilingualism begin to rest on heteroglossic (Bakhtin, 1981) notions of language use, translanguaging has become a more accepted concept. More research is needed in this area.

- Strengthen research on bilingual acquisition and evaluation of education for emergent bilinguals by conducting, for example, more multidisciplinary and mixed-method studies that will help educators and school officials in making informed decisions about the fit between children and programs and practices.

Research on the education of emergent bilinguals, focused on the students themselves and the teachers' pedagogies and practices (rather than on whether bilingual or ESL programs are more adequate), needs to be encouraged.

- Interrogate the assumptions present in traditional research methodology and design research that takes into account different epistemologies and translanguaging.

Felix Ndhlovu (2018) reminds us that the world cannot be fully understood "through the use of methods that arose out of a colonial metropolitan reading of the world" (p. 10) and that *decolonizing research approaches* are necessary when working with people who have been oppressed by colonial legacies and whose knowledges have been silenced. Instead of asking what language is spoken, by whom, to whom, and when, translanguaging researchers are asking: "How are these speakers deploying their linguistic repertoires to make meaning for themselves and others?"

EDUCATING EMERGENT BILINGUALS: ALTERNATIVE PATHS

As we have tried to demonstrate in this book, current policies and practices for the education of emergent bilinguals remain largely misguided. They contradict what theory and research have concluded and what scholars and educators have maintained. They also diverge from the realities of engagement in a globalized world with its growing multilingualism. However, despite restrictive educational policies, we see, on the ground, reflective educators who continue to use a commonsense approach in teaching the growing number of these students by building on the strengths of their home language and cultural practices. Educators, however, should not be left alone—or even worse, forced to hide what they are doing—when implementing practices that make sense for the students and the communities they are educating. For emergent bilinguals to move forward and not be left behind, educators need to be supported by policy and resources that bolster their expertise and advance their teaching. Educators need to be given time and space at school to observe students closely and document their work and learning *with* and *through* language, instead of being required to focus only on their performance through poorly designed tests and assessments. They need the opportunity to teach individual students instead of seeing teaching as a master plan of scores. With better preparation on the nature of bilingualism and translanguaging, teachers can find ways to work with the good aspects of governmental policy at the federal, state, and local levels.

Educators, and all who are concerned about this growing student population, should advocate for changes in aspects of the policy that make no sense for emergent bilinguals. For changes to be effective, the different levels of policy must work in tandem with educators and language-minority communities. Only then will we begin to close the gap between levels of abstract policies and local realities through which most disadvantaged students, such as emergent bilinguals, fall. We must start closing the gap of inequity for emergent bilinguals by naming the inequities, as we have done in this book, and then taking action to support their meaningful education.

Afterword

When the first edition of *Educating Emergent Bilinguals* was published in 2010, I'm pretty sure I was among the very first people to purchase a copy. As a teacher educator, early career researcher, and former bilingual teacher, I was hungry for a compelling, critical, and authoritative resource that could inform my own research and teaching and that I could share with the many teachers with whom I worked on a daily basis. There was an urgent need at that time not only for new terminology but also for a new perspective on teaching students classified as English learners. In many ways, that need persists. The deficit perspectives that predominated in 2010 continue to circulate widely in schools and society, and schooling for emergent bilingual students continues to be structured in ways that perpetuate those perspectives and contribute to unequal educational opportunities and outcomes. In this sense, the third edition of *Educating Emergent Bilinguals* comes not a moment too soon.

In their most recent edition of this groundbreaking book, Ofelia García, Jo Anne Kleifgen, and Claudia Cervantes-Soon essentially double down on what made the first two editions so pivotal and impactful while also incorporating new research and critical perspectives from younger scholars in ways that speak directly to the current historical moment. In addition to reiterating the continued need for a shift in perspective and terminology, this new addition zooms out to situate the history of U.S. language policy within longer colonial histories while also zooming back in to make concrete connections to contemporary issues and contexts. Above all else, this new edition continues to remind us that emergent bilingual students bring multiple strengths and tremendous potential that can be practically leveraged to promote their academic success. By providing practical, principled, and theoretically informed guidance for how to support emergent bilinguals, this new edition serves as a timely and essential resource for the task at hand in today's schools.

As we look ahead toward more just and equitable futures for emergent bilingual students, will a fourth or fifth edition of this book be necessary? In my view, almost certainly. What remains to be seen, however, is exactly how much schools will have changed for the better for emergent bilingual students between now and then. I continue to be hopeful in this regard, and I look for positive signs wherever I can find them. Perhaps the most positive development that I've noticed in schools since the first edition of this book was published is a dramatic shift in how we refer to students classified as English learners. Rather than continue to call these students "English learners" or "English language learners" or "limited English proficient," educators in schools around the country have increasingly embraced more affirming and appreciative language, and I attribute this shift, in large part, to the influence of this book and the teaching and research it has inspired. It matters that we care about how we refer to emergent bilingual students and that we're making a deliberate and collective effort to have our terminology reflect our values and commitments.

This shift in terminology is a huge step in the right direction, but we still have much further to go. As a community of educators, researchers, and policymakers, we must continue to insist on reframing emergent bilinguals as brilliant learners who are replete with potential. We must continue to reject the perverse logic that would frame their bilingualism as a deficit. We must continue to explore and build on their many linguistic strengths. And we must redouble our efforts to both highlight the tremendous diversity and heterogeneity of this group of learners and normalize what they are doing in schools—speaking and learning additional languages.

In my own research on multilingualism in schools, I've had the pleasure and privilege of spending many years with an amazing group of children who were initially classified as English learners. They were all children of immigrants who shared the same "English learner" label, but they were a tremendously diverse group. Some of these students truly were learning English as an additional language for the very first time in school, and reframing them as emergent bilinguals made it easier for teachers to see their potential and then identify and build on their strengths. Some of these students, however, already spoke quite a bit of English when I met them, and I believe that some of them had been initially *misclassified* as English learners. As I spent year after year watching these children grow up, one of my biggest takeaways was that, for some of these students, there was nothing emergent at all about their bilingualism. On the contrary, some of them were already very fully and brilliantly bilingual in kindergarten. And some of them even spoke three or more languages at that very young age, adding even more languages to their expansive linguistic repertoires by the time they had finished high school. While *emergent bilingual* is a label that moves us in the right direction by helping us reframe some students, it truly did not do justice to many of the amazingly multilingual children I knew. As a label, it wasn't generous or expansive enough to capture their tremendous linguistic complexity and ingenuity.

As I marveled at these amazing students, it struck me that they were actually part of a bigger group of *multilingual* children. All of them—from the students who started out truly learning English as an additional language to those who already spoke three or more languages when they entered school—were part of a larger population of children who speak and/or are learning multiple languages. And, of course, this population of multilingual children actually constitutes the majority of children worldwide. Most children on Earth speak two or more languages simultaneously from early childhood on, and most children on Earth go on to learn additional languages in schools and society. In other words, there is nothing abnormal or atypical about this. It is simply the reality for the majority of the children on our planet.

As a thought experiment, what would happen if we deliberately restructured schools in response to this multilingual reality? What if we deliberately reframed emergent bilingual students as part of the majority population of multilingual children on this planet? How might this help us perceive and treat these students differently? How might it help us normalize these children and what they're doing in schools? How might it encourage us to be more attentive to their strengths and to their potential? At my most hopeful, I like to imagine such scenarios. I like to imagine schools that are aligned with and supportive of students' multilingual realities. Indeed, I hope for the kind of schools that would make a book like *Educating Emergent Bilinguals* unnecessary—schools in which we normalize speaking and learning multiple languages; schools in which we wouldn't dream of framing multilingualism as a deficit; schools in which our default starting point is to presume brilliance and potential. As I continue to hope and work for such a future, *Educating Emergent Bilinguals* will continue to be an indispensable resource for me and for all teachers who seek to make schools more joyful, supportive, and equitable spaces for the amazing multilingual students with whom we are privileged to work.

—Ramón Antonio Martínez
Stanford University

Notes

Preface

1. We choose not to capitalize white in this book to avoid recentering whiteness (Crenshaw, 1991) and to distinguish it from the white supremacist practice of capitalizing it.

Chapter 1

1. We use the term *emergent bilingual* in this book for students who are speakers of *one or more languages* other than English and who are developing English literacy in school. Some might say that students who are already bilingual and who are learning in English in school might be better called *emergent multilinguals*. But we use the term *bilingual* because of its ties to sociopolitical struggles that surrounded the civil rights era in the United States. Although in this book we use *emergent bilingual* to call attention to those learning English who are minoritized in U.S. society, in fact, the term can be also used to designate those who are acquiring languages other than English—for example, English speakers in two-way dual-language bilingual programs.

2. Throughout this book, we prefer the term *home language practices* to *mother tongue*, *native language*, or *first language*. *Mother tongue* is extensively used, especially to refer to the language of minoritized communities, although it has been called inaccurate (Baker & Prys Jones, 1998; Kaplan & Baldauf, 1997; Skutnabb-Kangas, 1981). Skutnabb-Kangas (1981) reminds us that one can identify a mother tongue based on different criteria—the language one learned first, the language one knows best, the language one uses most, the language one identifies with, and the language with which others identify one. The term *native language* has also been discredited because of its ties to exclusivity, privilege, and whiteness (see, for example, Bonfiglio, 2010). Our preference for the use of *language practices*, rather than simply *language*, has to do with the epistemological understandings of language that are clarified throughout the book.

3. Sometimes, building on home language practices is accomplished through bilingual education, about which we say more in subsequent chapters. At other times, this can be accomplished in programs where only English is formally used as a medium of instruction, but where teachers acknowledge and build on the language practices that the students bring to the classroom.

Chapter 2

1. As in all cases where we use U.S. Census figures, we calculate emergent bilinguals by adding up all those who claim to speak English less than "very well."

2. *Indo-European* is not synonymous with European languages. In this survey, the category Indo-European includes all languages of this linguistic family except for English

and Spanish. French, German, Hindi, and Persian are all classified as Indo-European. Hungarian, a European language that belongs to the Uralic language family, is included in the "other language" category.

3. Asian/Pacific languages include languages indigenous to Asia and Pacific Island areas that are not also Indo-European languages. Chinese, Japanese, Telugu, and Hawaiian are all in this category.

4. Scholars point out that categories of race and ethnicity are confounded in the U.S. Census as well as in educational policy, where the terms *linguistic minority*, *race*, and *ethnicity* are often ambiguously used (Macías, 1994; Wiley, 1996).

5. *Temporary sojourners* are usually businesspersons who are on a short-term visit.

6. The term *migrant workers* usually refers to persons who work at seasonal jobs and move around; in the United States, it usually describes low-wage laborers in the field of agriculture.

Chapter 3

1. Some of the history in this section is taken from O. García (2009a). A valuable source for this information is Crawford (2004). See also Baker and Wright (2021).

2. Otheguy and Otto (1980) argue that a simple maintenance bilingual education is not possible because language always has to be developed. Thus, we prefer to call these programs *developmental bilingual education programs*.

3. The original model for International High Schools in New York mixed newcomers of different language backgrounds. However, in scaling up the model, they were confronted with the reality that some neighborhoods were almost exclusively Spanish speaking. Two schools in New York that are exclusively for Spanish-speaking newcomers were then established, following the same pedagogical principles of collaborative grouping and use of home languages to support English language development. At the time of this writing, the Internationals Network for Public Schools consisted of 31 schools and academies in New York City, California, New Jersey, and the D.C. Metro area.

4. The subgroups of students were racial and ethnic groups (Asian/Pacific Islander, Black, Hispanic, American Indian, white), economically disadvantaged (those receiving free/reduced-price lunch), students with disabilities, and limited English proficient.

5. Title I, Improving the Academic Achievement of the Disadvantaged, provides financial assistance to schools with high numbers or high percentages of poor children to help ensure that all children meet challenging state academic standards.

Chapter 4

1. In this book, language is viewed not as a fixed or bound system tied to a specific nation or community but as a dynamic, fluid set of semiotic resources that speakers draw upon to communicate and make meaning, emphasizing how multilingual individuals use their entire linguistic repertoire in flexible and creative ways, depending on context, purpose, and audience. However, in much of the language acquisition research, language practices are operationalized and defined in traditional ways as static codes that belong to separate named languages. Therefore, we use the terms *two languages* or *home, first*, and *second* languages as applicable in various parts of this book when referring to specific studies using these constructs and to avoid distraction and redundancy in unpacking the terms.

2. Notice that we are not using the term *academic language* or *academic English*, but instead *language/English for academic purposes* in this volume. The term *academic English* is problematic because it implies a set of static autonomous features that describe

it and that students can "have" (see, for example, Flores, 2020; García & Solorza, 2020; Valdés, 2017). Further, as we explain later in this chapter, the term *academic language* can also suggest a raciolinguistic ideology. Our use of *English for academic purposes* makes it clear that these features change depending on what students are doing with language.

3. The term *decontextualized* has been considered controversial because no language, however abstract, can truly be considered separated from a context (see, for example, Gee, 2014).

4. It is important to understand that the Canadian immersion bilingual education programs resulted from an initiative of Anglophone-majority parents to support their children's acquisition of French in Francophone Québec—that is, to make their children bilingual. Thus, the use of *immersion*, or more precisely, *submersion* for English-only programs in the United States has little to do with Canadian immersion programs. Furthermore, today Canada has to respond to much more than the two "official languages" of Canada, as per the 1972 Official Languages Act. The great number of speakers of languages of Canadian First Nations, as well as the high influx of immigrants in Canada, have also disrupted the orthodoxy of Canadian immersion programs in using only French to teach Anglophone children (see, for example, Cummins, 2008).

5. It is well known that immigrants to the United States have traditionally shifted to English by the third generation (see, for example, Fishman, 1966).

Chapter 5

1. In 2008, a dual-language immersion initiative in Utah created enormous interest. By 2020 there were 106 immersion programs in elementary programs and 16 two-way dual-language programs in elementary schools (J. Freire, personal communication, 5/1/2020). The 2008 DLI (dual-language immersion) initiative was then followed by Senate Bill 117 (2018) and House Bill 161 (2023), which provide ongoing funding for programs the state calls Dual Language Education, both immersion and two-way. However, the DLI Utah state policy only supports one-way immersion for language majority children and two-way programs, while it excludes one-way DLBE programs or developmental bilingual education for language minoritized students. Utah's discourse in the media about dual language has shifted from one of equity and heritage to one focused on global human capital (Cervantes-Soon et al., 2021; Valdez, Freire, & Delavan, 2016). Currently Delaware and Georgia have replicated the so-called DL Utah model and have excluded one-way DLBE programs for language-minoritized students from their state programs (Freire et al., 2021).

2. For more on the structure of CUNY-NYSIEB, see García and Kleyn (2016), García and Menken (2015), and García and Sánchez (2015); see also CUNY-NYSIEB (2021). The project has created teaching guides in different areas: general strategies (Celic & Seltzer, 2012), curriculum (Seltzer, Hesson, & Woodley, 2014), writing (Espinosa, Ascenzi-Moreno, & Vogel, 2016), and Latino literature (Pérez Rosario, 2014). These guides and other resources and videos can be downloaded from the website.

Chapter 6

1. Typically, state and local tax revenues provide most of the money in the United States for public education, 92% of the total on average, but this has not always been so for English learners and not for all states where the funding often comes from federal initiatives, as do other categorical programs to serve "disadvantaged" students.

Chapter 7

1. We use the terms *parent* and *family* interchangeably in this chapter, with a view toward a broader definition of what constitutes a parent or a family in today's diverse society. Our use of these terms encompasses other adults such as stepparents, grandparents, guardians, and caretakers, and varied family structures such as families with single or same-sex parents. See also Yosso (2005) on community cultural capital.

2. Shifting the focus away from the school to local communities, Compton-Lilly (2007) describes the tension between the "official reading capital" and local communities' reading capital, which schools ignore.

Chapter 9

1. For more detailed insights and research into AI and education, see Cope and Kalantzis (2024); Cope, Kalantzis and Searsmith (2020); and Kalantzis and Cope (2024).

2. We wish to acknowledge and thank Clifford Hill of Teachers College, Columbia University, who first proposed to colleagues and students these affordances for learning with ITCs.

3. For a description of the web-based system design and instructional approach developed for this intervention, along with a detailed example of its use in the classroom, see Kleifgen et al. (2014).

4. Although most iEARN learning group exchanges are in English, many teacher-initiated projects are in other languages such as Arabic, Chinese, French, Japanese, and Spanish (https://iearn.org).

5. More examples of research exploring children's and adolescents' use of these internet spaces include Hung (2011), Kleifgen (2022), Kleifgen and Kinzer (2009), Knobel and Lankshear (2009), and Lam and Christiansen, (2022).

References

Abedi, J. (2004). The No Child Left Behind Act and English language learners: Assessment and accountability issues. *Educational Researcher*, *33*(1), 4–14.

Abedi, J. (2010). *Performance assessments for English language learners*. Stanford University, Stanford Center for Opportunity Policy in Education.

Abedi, J., Hofstetter, C. H., & Lord, C. (2004). Assessment accommodations for English language learners: Implications for policy-based empirical research. *Review of Educational Research*, *74*(1), 1–28.

Abedi, J., & Lord, C. (2001). The language factor in mathematics tests. *Applied Measurement in Education*, *14*(3), 219–234.

Abedi, J., Lord, C., & Plummer, J. R. (1997). *Final report of language background as a variable in NAEP mathematics performance* (CSE Tech. Rep. No. 429). University of California at Los Angeles, National Center for Research on Evaluation, Standards, and Student Testing.

Abutalebi, J., Della Rosa, P. A., Green, D. W., Hernández, M., Scifo, P., Keim, R., Cappa, S. F., & Costa, A. (2012). Bilingualism tunes the anterior cingulate cortex for conflict monitoring. *Cerebral Cortex*, *22*(9), 2076–2086. https://doi.org/10.1093/cercor/bhr287

Ackerman, D. J., & Tazi, Z. (2015). *Enhancing young Hispanic dual language learners' achievement: Exploring strategies and addressing challenges* (Policy Information Report, ETS Research Report No. RR-15-01). Educational Testing Service. https://doi.org/10.1002/ets2.12045

Acosta, S. T., Chen, X., Goltz, H., Goodson, P., & Padrón, Y. (2021). A case study of novice bilingual education teachers conducting action research and diffusing teaching innovations. *Urban Education*, *56*(9), 1576–1607. http://dx.doi.org/10.1177/004208591 8805148

Adair, J. K., & Colegrove, K. S. S. (2021). *Segregation by experience: Agency, racism, and learning in the early grades*. University of Chicago Press.

Adair, J. K., Colegrove, K. S. S., & McManus, M. E. (2017). How the word gap argument negatively impacts young children of Latinx immigrants' conceptualizations of learning. *Harvard Educational Review*, *87*(3), 309–334.

Adams, D. W. (1995). *Education for extinction: American Indians and the boarding school experience, 1875–1928*. University Press of Kansas.

Ajayi, L. (2015). Critical multimodal literacy: How Nigerian female students critique texts and reconstruct unequal social structures. *Journal of Literacy Research*, *47*(2), 216–244. https://doi.org/10.1177/1086296X15618478

Alim, S., Rickford, R., & Ball, A. (Eds.). (2016). *Raciolinguistics: How language shapes our ideas about race*. Oxford University Press.

Alvarez, A. (2018). Drawn and written funds of knowledge: A window into emerging bilingual children's experiences and social interpretations through their written narratives and drawings. *Journal of Early Childhood Literacy, 18*(1), 97–128. https://doi.org/10.1177/14687984177406

Alvarez, L., Ananda, S., Walqui, A., Sato, E., & Rabinowitz, S. (2014). *Focusing formative assessment on the needs of English language learners.* WestEd.

American Councils for International Education. (2017). *The national K–12 foreign language enrollment survey report.* Defense Language and National Security Education Office. https://www.americancouncils.org/sites/default/files/FLE-report-June17.pdf

American Educational Research Association, American Psychological Association, & National Council on Measurement in Education (AERA, APA, & NCME). (1985). *Standards for educational and psychological testing.* American Psychological Association.

American Educational Research Association, American Psychological Association, & National Council on Measurement in Education (AERA, APA, & NCME). (2014). *The standards for educational and psychological testing.* American Psychological Association.

American Immigration Council. (2021, June 24). *U.S. citizen children impacted by immigration enforcement.* https://www.americanimmigrationcouncil.org/research/us-citizen-children-impacted-immigration-enforcement

American Institutes for Research (AIR). (2004). *Determining the cost of providing all children in New York an adequate education.* https://www.air.org/resource/determining-cost-providing-all-children-new-york-adequate-education

Amrein, A. L., & Berliner, D. C. (2002, March 28). High-stakes testing, uncertainty, and student learning. *Education Policy Analysis Archives, 10*(18). http://epaa.asu.edu/epaa/v10n18/

Andersen, S., Méndez Pérez, K., & González-Howard, M. (2022). Reimagining science lessons through translanguaging: Supporting multilingual students' scientific sense-making in the context of science and engineering practices. *Science Scope, 46*(2), 25–31.

Anderson, N. E., Jenkins, F. F., & Miller, K. E. (1996). *NAEP inclusion criteria and testing accommodations: Findings from the NAEP 1995 fieldtest in mathematics.* National Center for Education Statistics.

Angay-Crowder, T., Choi, J., & Yi, Y. (2013). Multimodal literacies and technology: Digital storytelling for multilingual adolescents in a summer program. *TESL Canada Journal, 30*(2), 36–45.

Ansari, A., & Crosnoe, R. (2018). The transition into kindergarten for English language learners. In A. Mashburn, J. LoCasale-Crouch, & K. Pears (Eds.), *Kindergarten transition and readiness: Promoting cognitive, social-emotional, and self-regulatory development* (pp. 185–204). Springer.

Anstrom, K. (1997). *Academic achievement for secondary language minority students: Standards, measures, and promising practices.* National Clearinghouse for Bilingual Education.

Anzaldúa, G. (1987). *Borderlands/La frontera: The new mestiza.* Aunt Lute Books.

Anzaldúa, G., & Keating, A. L. (Eds.). (2002). *This bridge we call home: Radical visions for transformation.* Routledge.

Arizona Proposition 203. (2000). Arizona Revised Statues 15-751-755.

Arnoux, E. de N. (2014). Glotopolítica: Delimitación del campo y discusiones actuales con particular referencia a Sudamérica. In por Lenka Zajícová y Radim Zámec (Ed.),

Lengua y política en América Latina: Perspectivas actuales (pp. 19–43). Univerzita Palackého v Olomouci (Olomouc, Czech Republic).

Arthur, J., & Martin, P. (2006). Accomplishing lessons in postcolonial classrooms: Comparative perspectives from Botswana and Brunei Darussalam. *Comparative Education, 42*(2), 177–202. https://doi.org/10.1080/03050060600628009

Artiles, A. J. (1998). The dilemma of difference: Enriching the disproportionality discourse with theory and context. *The Journal of Special Education, 32*(1), 32–36.

Artiles, A. J., & Ortiz, A. A. (Eds.). (2002). *English language learners with special education needs: Identification, assessment, and instruction.* Center for Applied Linguistics and Delta System.

Artiles, A. J., Rueda, R., Salazar, J., & Higareda, I. (2002). English-language learner representation in special education in California urban school districts. In D. Losen & G. Orfield (Eds.), *Racial inequity in special education* (pp. 117–136). Harvard Education Press.

Ascenzi-Moreno, L. (2018). Translanguaging and responsive assessment adaptations: Emergent bilingual readers through the lens of possibility. *Language Arts, 95*(6), 355–369.

Ascenzi-Moreno, L., Espinosa, C., & Lehner-Quam, A. (2022). Move, play, language: A translanguaged, multimodal approach to literacies with young emergent bilinguals. In S. Brown & L. Hao (Eds.), *Multimodal literacies with young emergent bilinguals: Beyond print-centric practices* (pp. 117–130). Multilingual Matters.

Ascenzi-Moreno, L., García, O., & López, A. A. (2024). Latinx bilingual students' translanguaging and assessment: A unitary approach. In S. Melo-Pfeifer & C. Ollivier (Eds.), *Assessment of plurilingual competence and plurilingual learners in educational settings* (pp. 48–61). Routledge.

Ascenzi-Moreno, L., Güílamo, A., & Vogel, S. (2020). Integrating coding and language arts: A view into sixth graders' multimodal and multilingual learning. *Voices from the Middle, 27*(4), 47–52.

Ascenzi-Moreno, L., & Seltzer, K. (2021). Always at the bottom: Ideologies in assessment of emergent bilinguals. *Journal of Literacy Research, 53*(4), 468–490. https://doi.org /10.1177/1086296X211052255

Asson, S., Frankenberg, E., Darriet, C., Santibañez, L., Cervantes-Soon, C., & López, F. (2023). Racial, linguistic, and economic diversity across schools with two-way dual language immersion programs: Evidence from Los Angeles Unified School District. EdWorkingPaper No. 23–822. Annenberg Institute for School Reform at Brown University.

Au, K. H. (1993). *Literacy instruction in multicultural settings.* Harcourt Brace.

Au, K. H. (2005). *Multicultural issues and literacy achievement.* Lawrence Erlbaum.

Au, W. (2022). *Unequal by design: High-stakes testing and the standardization of inequality.* Routledge.

Auer, P. (2005). A postscript: Code-switching and social identity. *Journal of Pragmatics, 37*(3), 403–410.

Auerbach, E. A. (1995). Deconstructing the discourse of strengths in family literacy. *Journal of Reading Behavior, 27*(4), 643–661.

Auerbach, S. (2009). Walking the walk: Portraits in leadership for family engagement in urban schools. *School Community Journal, 19*(1), 9–31. http://www.adi.org/journal/ ss09/AuerbachSpring2009.pdf

August, D., & Hakuta, K. (1997). *Improving schooling for language-minority children: A research agenda.* National Academies Press.

August, D., & Hakuta, K. (Eds.). (1998). *Educating language-minority children.* Committee on Developing a Research Agenda on the Education of Limited-English-Proficient and Bilingual Students, National Research Council, Institute of Medicine, and National Academies Press.

August, D., & Shanahan, T. (Eds.). (2006). *Developing literacy in second-language learners: Report of the National Literacy Panel on language-minority children and youth.* Lawrence Erlbaum.

Babino, A., & Stewart, M. A. (2018). Remodeling dual language programs: Teachers enact agency as critically conscious language policy makers. *Bilingual Research Journal, 41*(3), 272–297. https://doi.org/10.1080/15235882.2018.1489313

Baca, G., & Gándara, P. (2008). *NCLB and California's English language learners: The perfect storm.* Springer Science Business and Media B.V.

Bach, A. J. (2020). High-stakes, standardized testing and emergent bilingual students in Texas: An overview of study findings and a call for action. *Texas Journal of Literacy Education, 8*(1), 18-37.

Bachman, L. F. (2001). *Fundamental considerations in language testing* (5th ed.). Oxford University Press.

Bachman, L. F. (2002). Alternative interpretations of alternative assessments: Some validity issues in educational performance assessments. *Educational Measurement: Issues and Practice, 21*(3), 5–18.

Back, A. J. (2020). High-stakes, standardized testing and emergent bilingual students in Texas: An overview of study findings and a call for action. *Texas Journal of Literacy Education, 8*(1), 18–37.

Badham, L., & Furlong, A. (2022). Summative assessments in a multilingual context: What comparative judgment reveals about comparability across different languages in Literature. *International Journal of Testing, 23*(2), 111–134. https://doi.org/10.1080/15305058.2022.2149536

Baetens Beardsmore, H. (2018). Plurilingualisme et créativité. In J. Erfurt, E. Carporal, & A. Weirich (Eds.), *L'éducation bi-/plurilingue pour tous. Enjeux politiques, sociaux et éducatifs.* Peter Lang.

Báez, L. "Tony," & Hurie, A. H. (2023). Contextualizing parent activism in one of Milwaukee's bilingual public schools. In L. Dorner, D. Palmer, C. Cervantes-Soon, & D. Heiman (Eds.), *Critical consciousness in dual language bilingual education: Case studies on policy and practice* (pp. 158–167). Routledge. https://doi.org/10.4324/9781003240594-20

Bailey, A. L., & Heritage, M. (2014). The role of language learning progressions in improved instruction and assessment of English language learners. *TESOL Quarterly, 48*(3), 480–506.

Bailey, A. L., & Kelly, K. R. (2013). Home language survey practices in the initial identification of English learners in the United States. *Educational Policy, 27*(5), 770–804.

Baker, B. D., Green, P. C., & Markham, P. (2004). Legal and empirical analysis of state financing of programs for children with English language communication barriers. Paper presented at the annual meeting of the National Association for Bilingual Education, Albuquerque, NM. http://www.ku.edu/%7Ebdbaker/papers/nabe04.pdf

Baker, C. (2001). *Foundations of bilingual education and bilingualism* (3rd ed.). Multilingual Matters.

Baker, C. (2011). *Foundations of bilingual education and bilingualism* (5th ed.). Multilingual Matters.

Baker, C., & Prys Jones, S. (1998). *Encyclopedia of bilingualism and bilingual education.* Multilingual Matters.

Baker, C., & Wright, W. (2021). *Foundations of bilingual education and bilingualism* (7th ed.). Multilingual Matters.

Bakhtin, M. (1981). *The dialogic imagination. Four essays.* The University of Texas Press.

Ballenger, C. (1997). Social identities, moral narratives, scientific argumentation: Science talk in a bilingual classroom. *Language and Education, 11*(1), 1–14.

Baltodano, M. P. (2004). Latino immigrant parents and the hegemony of Proposition 227. *Latino Studies, 2*(2), 246–253.

Baquedano-López, P., Alexander, R. A., & Hernandez, S. J. (2013). Equity issues in parental and community involvement in schools: What teacher educators need to know. *Review of Research in Education, 37*(1), 149–182. http://dx.doi.org/10.3102/00917 32X12459718

Barac, R., & Bialystok, E. (2012). Bilingual effects on cognitive and linguistic development: Role of language, cultural background, and education. *Child Development, 83*(2), 413–422.

Barnett, W. S., & Masse, L. N. (2007). Comparative benefit–cost analysis of the Abecedarian program and its policy implications. *Economics of Education Review, 26*(1), 113–125.

Barter-Storm, B., & Wik, T. (2020). Using social justice graphic novels in the ELL classroom. *TESOL Journal, 11*(4), e551. https://doi.org/10.1002/tesj.551

Bartlett, L. (2007). Bilingual literacies, social identification, and educational trajectories. *Linguistics and Education, 18*(3–4), 214–231. https://doi.org/10.1016/j.linged.2007 .07.005

Bartlett, L., & García, O. (2011). *Additive schooling in subtractive times. Bilingual education and Dominican immigrant youth in the Heights.* Vanderbilt University Press.

Batalova, J., Fix, M., & Murray, J. (2007). *Measures of change: The demography and literacy of adolescent English learners—A report to Carnegie Corporation of New York.* Migration Policy Institute.

Bauer, E. B., Colomer, S. E., & Wiemelt, J. (2020). Biliteracy of African American and Latinx kindergarten students in a dual-language program: Understanding students' translanguaging practices across informal assessments. *Urban Education, 55*(3), 331–361.

Beeman, K., & Urrow, C. (2013). *Teaching for biliteracy: Strengthening bridges between languages.* Caslon.

Bellino, M. J., & Gluckman, M. (2024). Learning in transit: Crossing borders, waiting, and waiting to cross. *Social Sciences, 13*(2), 121. https://doi.org/10.3390/socsci1302 0121

Ben-Zeev, S. (1977). The effect of bilingualism in children from Spanish-English low-income neighborhoods on cognitive development and cognitive strategy. *Working Papers on Bilingualism, 14.* Ontario Institute for Studies in Education, Bilingual Education Project.

Bernstein, K. A., Katznelson, N., Amezcua, A., Mohamed, S., & Alvarado, S. L. (2020). Equity/social justice, instrumentalism/neoliberalism: Dueling discourses of dual language in principals' talk about their programs. *TESOL Quarterly, 54*(3), 652–684. https://doi.org/10.1002/tesq.582

Bertrand, M., & Marsh, J. (2021). How data-driven reform can drive deficit thinking. *Phi Delta Kappan, 102*(8), 35–39. https://doi.org/10.1177/003172172110139

Building Educational Success Together (BEST). (2006). *Growth and disparity: A decade of U.S. public school construction.* BEST.

Bezemer, J., & Kress, G. (2015). *Multimodality, learning and communication: A social semiotic frame.* Routledge.

Bialik, K., Scheller, A., & Walker, K. (2018, October 2). Six facts about English language learners in U.S. public schools. *Pew Research Center.* https://www.pewresearch.org /short-reads/2018/10/25/6-facts-about-english-language-learners-in-u-s-public-schools/

Bialystok, E. (2004). Language and literacy development. In T. K. Bhatia & W. C. Ritchie (Eds.), *The handbook of bilingualism* (pp. 577–601). Blackwell.

Bialystok, E. (2007). Cognitive effects of bilingualism: How linguistic experience leads to cognitive change. *International Journal of Bilingual Education and Bilingualism, 10*(3), 210–223.

Bialystok, E. (2011). Reshaping the mind: The benefits of bilingualism. *Canadian Journal of Experimental Psychology, 65*(4), 229–235.

Bialystok, E. (2015). Bilingualism and the development of executive function: The role of attention. *Child Development Perspectives, 9*(2), 117–121.

Bialystok, E. (2016). Bilingual education for young children: Review of the effects and consequences. *International Journal of Bilingual Education and Bilingualism, 21*(6), 666–679. https://doi.org/10.1080/13670050.2016.1203859

Bialystok, E., Craik, F. I., & Luk, G. (2012). Bilingualism: Consequences for mind and brain. *Trends in Cognitive Sciences, 16*(4), 240–250.

Bilingual Education Act. (1968). Title VII, Bilingual Education, Language Enhancement, and Language Acquisition Programs of Elementary and Secondary Education Act. P. L. 90–247.

Bilingual Education Act. (1974). Title VII of Elementary and Secondary Education Act, 1974 reauthorization, P. L. 93–380.

Bilingual Education Act. (1978). Title VII of Elementary and Secondary Education Act, 1978 reauthorization, P. L. 95–561.

Bilingual Education Act. (1984). Title VII of Elementary and Secondary Education Act, 1984 reauthorization, P. L. 98–511.

Bilingual Education Act. (1988). Title VII of Elementary and Secondary Education Act, 1988 reauthorization, P. L. 100–297.

Bilingual Education Act. (1994). Title VII of Improving America's Schools Act of 1994. P. L. 103–382.

Birch, B. M. (2002). *English L2 reading: Getting to the bottom.* Lawrence Erlbaum.

Blackledge, A., & Creese, A. (2010). *Multilingualism: A critical perspective.* Continuum Press.

Blaise, J. G. (2018). The effects of high-stakes accountability measures on students with limited English proficiency. *Urban Education, 53*(9), 1154–1181. http://dx.doi.org/10 .1177/0042085915613549

Blanc, M., & Hamers, J. (Eds.). (1985). *Theoretical and methodological issues in the study of languages/dialects in contact at macro- and micro-logical levels of analysis.* Proceedings of the International Conference DALE (University of London)/ICRB (Laval University, Quebec).

Blase, J., & Blase, J. (2001). *Empowering teachers: What successful principals do* (2nd ed.). Corwin Press.

Block, D. (2014). Moving beyond "lingualism": Multilingual embodiment and multimodality in SLA. In S. May (Ed.), *The multilingual turn: Implications for SLA, TESOL and Bilingual Education* (pp. 54–77). Routledge.

Blommaert, J. (2010). *The sociolinguistics of globalization.* Cambridge University Press.

Blommaert, J., & Rampton, B. (2011). Language and superdiversity. *Diversities, 13*(2), 1–22.

Bonfiglio, T. H. (2010). *Mother tongues and nations. The invention of the native speaker.* Mouton de Gruyter.

Booher-Jennings, J. (2006). Rationing education in an era of accountability. *Phi Delta Kappan, 87*(10), 756–761.

Borlase, K., & Haines, D. (n.d.). Mr. Darwin music video. https://www.youtube.com/watch?v=SSFL1Z1rMoE

Bos, B. (2007). The effect of the Texas Instrument interactive instructional environment on the mathematical achievement of eleventh grade low achieving students. *Journal of Educational Computing Research, 37*(4), 351–368.

Bos, B. (2009). Technology with cognitive and mathematical fidelity: What it means for the math classroom. *Computers in the Schools, 26,* 107–114. https://doi.org/10.1080/07380560902906088

Bourdieu, P. (1985). The forms of capital. In J. G. Richardson (Ed.), *Handbook of theory and research for the sociology of education* (pp. 241–258). Greenwood.

Brown v. Board of Education, 347 U.S. 483 (1954).

Browning-Aiken, A. (2005). Border crossing: Funds of knowledge within an immigrant household. In N. González, L. C. Moll, & C. Amanti (Eds.), *Funds of knowledge: Theorizing practices in households, communities, and classrooms* (pp.167–181). Lawrence Erlbaum.

Bruce, B. C., Bishop, A. P., & Budhathoki, N. R. (Eds.). (2014). *Youth community inquiry: New media for community and personal growth.* Peter Lang.

Burton, J. (2023). Supporting multilingual English language learners through spoken word poetry and multimodal identity-text activities. *Concordia Working Papers in Applied Linguistics, 7.* https://doe.concordia.ca/copal/documents/7_Burton.pdf

Busch, B. (2012). The linguistic repertoire revisited. *Applied Linguistics, 33*(5), 503–523, https://doi.org/10.1093/applin/ams056

Butvilofsky, S. A., Escamilla, K., Gumina, D., & Silva Diaz, E. (2021). Beyond monolingual reading assessments for emerging bilingual learners: Expanding the understanding of biliteracy assessment through writing. *Reading Research Quarterly, 56*(1), 53–70. https://doi.org/10.1002/rrq.292

Calarco, J. M. (2020). Avoiding us versus them: How schools' dependence on privileged "helicopter" parents influences enforcement of rules. *American Sociological Review, 85*(2), 223–246. https://doi.org/10.1177/0003122420905793

Calarco, J. M., Horn, I. S., & Chen, G. A. (2022). "You need to be more responsible": The myth of meritocracy and teachers' accounts of homework inequalities. *Educational Researcher, 51*(8), 515–523. https://doi.org/10.3102/0013189X221111337

California Department of Education. (2006a). Number of English learner students enrolled in specific instructional settings. http://dq.cde.ca.gov/dataquest/ElP2_State.asp?RptYear=2005-

California Department of Education. (2006b). English learners, instructional settings and services. www.dq.cde.ca.gov/dataquest/ELP2_State.asp?RptYear=200405&RPTType =ELPart2_1a

California Proposition 227. (1998). California Education Code, Sections 300–311.

Calkins, L. (1994). *The art of teaching writing* (2nd ed.). Heinemann.

Callahan, R. (2003). *Tracking and English language proficiency: Variable effects on academic achievement of high school ELs.* [Unpublished doctoral dissertation, University of California, Davis].

Callahan, R. (2005). Tracking and high school English learners: Limiting opportunities to learn. *American Educational Research Journal, 42*(2), 305–328.

Callahan, R., & Gándara, P. (2014). *The bilingual advantage: Language, literacy and the US labor market.* Multilingual Matters.

Callahan, R., & Humphries, M. (2016). Undermatched? School-based linguistic status, college going, and the immigrant advantage. *American Educational Research Journal, 53*(2), 263–295. https://doi.org/10.3102/0002831215627857

Callahan, R., & Shifrer, D. (2016). Equitable access for secondary English learner students: Course taking as evidence of EL program effectiveness. *Educational Administration Quarterly, 52*(3), 463–496. https://doi.org/10.1177/ 0013161X16648190

Cammarota, J., & Fine, M. (2008). *Revolutionizing education: Youth participatory action research in motion.* Routledge.

Cammarota, S., Griffith, B., & Zeigler, K. (2017). *Mapping the impact of immigration on public schools.* Center for Immigration Studies. https://cis.org/Report/Mapping-Impact -Immigration-Public-Schools

Campano, G., Ghiso, M. P., Yee, M., & Pantoja, A. (2013). Toward community research and coalitional literacy practice for educational justice. *Language Arts, 90*(5), 314–326. https://www.jstor.org/stable/24574990

Campbell, L., & Bright, W.O. (2016). North American Indian languages. *Encyclopedia Britannica.* https://www.britannica.com/topic/North-American-Indian-languages

Canagarajah, S. (1999). *Resisting linguistic imperialism in English teaching.* Oxford University Press.

Canagarajah, S. (2011). Translanguaging in the classroom: Emerging issues for research and pedagogy. *Applied Linguistics Review, 2* (2011), 1–28. https://doi.org/10.1515 /9783110239331.1

Canagarajah, S. (2013). *Translingual practice: Global Englishes and cosmopolitan relations.* Routledge.

Canale, M., & Swain, M. (1980). Theoretical bases of communicative approaches to second language teaching and testing. *Journal of Applied Linguistics, 1*(1), 1–47.

Capps, R., Fix, M., Murray, J., Ost, J., Passel, J. S., & Herwantoro, S. (2005). *The new demography of America's schools: Immigration and the No Child Left Behind Act.* Urban Institute.

Carini, P. (2000a). A letter to parents and teachers on some ways of looking at and reflecting on children. In M. Himley & P. Carini (Eds.), *From another angle: Children's strengths and school standards. The Prospect Center's descriptive review of the child* (pp. 56–64). Teachers College Press.

Carini, P. (2000b). Prospect's descriptive processes. In M. Himley & P. Carini (Eds.), *From another angle: Children's strengths and school standards. The Prospect Center's descriptive review of the child* (pp. 8–20). Teachers College Press.

Carlo, M. S., August, D., McLaughlin, B., Snow, C. E., Dressler, C., & Lippman, D. N. (2004). Closing the gap: Addressing the vocabulary needs of English-language learners in bilingual and mainstream classrooms. *Reading Research Quarterly, 39*(2), 188–215.

Carlson, D. (2023). *Charter schools and English learners in the Lone Star State*. Thomas B. Fordham Institute. https://fordhaminstitute.org/national/research/charter-schools-and-english-learners-lone-star-state

Carrasquillo, A., & Rodriguez, V. (2002). *Language minority students in the mainstream classroom* (2nd ed.). Multilingual Matters.

Castañeda v. Pickard. (1981). 648 F.2d 989 (5th Cir., 1981).

Castells, M. (2007). Communication, power and counter-power in the network society. *International Journal of Communication, 1*(1), 238–266.

Cazden, C. (1986). ESL teachers as advocates for children. In P. Rigg & D. S. Engirgh (Eds.), *Children and ESL: Integrating perspectives* (pp. 7–21). TESOL.

Celic, C. (2009). *English language learners day by day K–6*. Heinemann.

Celic, C., & Seltzer, K. (2012). Translanguaging: A CUNY-NYSIEB guide for educators. CUNY-NYSIEB, The Graduate Center, CUNY. http://www.cuny-nysieb.org

Cenoz, J., & Gorter, D. (Eds.). (2015), *Multilingual education: Between language learning and translanguaging*. Cambridge University Press.

Cenoz, J., & Gorter, D. (2022). *Pedagogical translanguaging*. Cambridge University Press.

Center on Education Policy. (2016, May). *Listen to us: Teachers' views and voices*. George Washington University. http://files.eric.ed.gov/fulltext/ED568172.pdf

Cerat, M. L. (2017). *Haitian linguistic and cultural practices* [Doctoral dissertation, The Graduate Center, City University of New York].

Cervantes-Soon C. G. (2014). A critical look at dual language immersion in the new Latin@ diaspora. *Bilingual Research Journal, 37*(4), 64–82. http://doi.org/10.1080/1523 5882.2014.893267

Cervantes-Soon, C., Gambrell, J., Kasun, G. S., Sun, W., Freire, J. A., & Dorner, L. M. (2021). "Everybody wants a choice" in dual language education of El Nuevo Sur: Whiteness as the gloss for everybody in media discourses of multilingual education. *Journal of Language, Identity & Education, 20*(6), 394–410.

Cervantes-Soon, C. G., & Carrillo, J. F. (2016). Toward a pedagogy of border thinking: Building on Latin@ students' subaltern knowledge. *The High School Journal, 99*(4), 282–301.

Cervantes-Soon, C. G., Degollado, E. D., & Nuñez, I. (2020). The Black and Brown search for agency: African American and Latinx children's plight to bilingualism in a two-way dual language program. In N. Flores, A. Tseng, & N. Subtirelu (Eds.), *Bilingualism for all? Raciolinguistic perspectives on dual language education in the United States* (pp. 199–219). Multilingual Matters.

Cervantes-Soon, C., Dorner, L. M., Palmer, D., Heiman, D., Schwerdtfeger, R., & Choi, J. (2017). Combating inequalities in two-way language immersion programs: Toward critical consciousness in bilingual education spaces. *Review of Research in Education, 41*(1), 403–427. https://doi.org/10.3102/0091732X17690120

Cervantes-Soon, C., & García, O. (2023). Literacy in multilingual classrooms. In *The encyclopedia of applied linguistics* (2nd ed.). John Wiley & Sons. https://doi.org/10 .1002/9781405198431.wbeal20251

Cervantes-Soon, C., Gambrell, J., Kasun, G. S., Sun, W., Freire, J. A., & Dorner, L. M. (2021). "Everybody wants a choice" in dual language education of el Nuevo Sur: Whiteness as the gloss for everybody in media discourses of multilingual education.

Journal of Language, Identity & Education, 20(6), 394–419. https://doi.org/10.1080/15348458.2020.1753201

Chamot, A. U., & O'Malley, J. M. (1994). *The CALLA handbook: Implementing the cognitive academic language learning approach.* Addison-Wesley.

Chang-Bacon, C. K. (2021). Generation interrupted: Rethinking "students with interrupted formal education" (SIFE) in the wake of a pandemic. *Educational Researcher, 50*(3), 187–196. https://journals.sagepub.com/doi/full/10.3102/0013189X21992368

Chang-Bacon, C. K., Khote, N., Schell, R., & Crookes, G. V. (2022). Critical literacy in English language teaching, bi/multilingualism, and translanguaging. In J. Pandya, R. A. Mora, J. H. Alford, N. A. Golden, & R. Santiago de Roock (Eds.), *The handbook of critical literacies* (pp. 40–49). Routledge.

Chaparro, S. (2020). Pero aquí se habla Inglés: Latina immigrant mothers' experiences of discrimination, resistance, and pride through antropoesía. *TESOL Quarterly, 54*(3), 599–628. https://doi.org/10.1002/tesq.593

Chaparro, S. E. (2021). Creating fertile grounds for two-way immersion: Gentrification, immigration, & neoliberal school reforms. *Language Policy, 20*(3), 435–461.

Chappell, S. V., & Faltis, C. J. (2013). *The arts and emergent bilingual youth: Building culturally responsive, critical and creative education in school and community contexts.* Routledge.

Chatterji, M. (2003). *Designing and using tools for educational assessment.* Allyn & Bacon/Pearson.

Chávez-Moreno, L. C. (2020). Researching Latinxs, racism, and white supremacy in bilingual education: A literature review. *Critical Inquiry in Language Studies, 17*(2), 101–120.

Chávez-Moreno, L. C. (2023). A raciolinguistic and racial realist critique of dual language's racial integration. *Journal of Latinos and Education, 22*(5), 2085–2101.

Chávez-Moreno, L. C. (2024). *How schools make race: Teaching Latinx racialization in America.* Harvard Education Press.

Cheng, L., Watanabe, Y., & Curtis, A. (Eds.). (2004). *Washback in language testing: Research contexts and methods.* Lawrence Erlbaum.

Cheuk, T. (2021). Can AI be racist? Color-evasiveness in the application of machine learning to science assessments. *Science Education, 105*(5), 825–836. https://doi.org/10.1002/sce.21671

Cho, S. (2019). Secondary content-area teachers' perceptions of English language learners in classroom assessments. *NYS TESOL Journal, 1*(6), 42–52.

Chrispeels, J. H., & Gonz, M. (2004). Do educational programs increase parents' practices at home?: Factors influencing Latino parent involvement. Harvard Family Research Project. http://www.hfrp.org/family-involvement/publications-resources/do-educational-programs-increase-parents-practices-at-home-factors-influencing-latino-parent-involvement#_ftnref1

Chrispeels, J. H., & Rivero, E. (2001). Engaging Latino families for student success: How parent education can reshape parents' sense of place in the education of their children. *Peabody Journal of Education, 76*(2), 119–169.

Chumak-Horbatsch, R. (2012). *Linguistically appropriate practice. A guide for working with young immigrant children.* University of Toronto Press.

Chun, C. W. (2009). Critical literacies and graphic novels for English-language learners: Teaching Maus. *Journal of Adolescent & Adult Literacy, 53*(2), 144–153.

Cimasko, T., & Dong-shin, S. (2017). Multimodal resemiotization and authorial agency in an L2 writing classroom. *Written Communication, 34*(4), 387–413. https://doi.org/10.1177/0741088317727246

Cioè-Peña, M. (2020). Bilingualism for students with disabilities, deficit or advantage?: Perspectives of Latinx mothers. *Bilingual Research Journal, 43*(3), 253–266. http://dx.doi.org/10.1080/15235882.2020.1799884

Cioè-Peña, M. (2021). Raciolinguistics and the education of emergent bilinguals labeled as disabled. *Urban Review, 53*(3), 443–469. https://doi.org/10.1007/s11256-020-00581-z

Civil Rights Act, Title VI, Section 601. (1964).

Clewell, B. C., & Campbell, P. (2004). *Highly effective US schools: An outlier study.* The Urban Institute/Campbell-Kibler Associates, Inc.

Clewell, B. C., & Villegas, A. M. (2001). *Absence unexcused: Ending teacher shortages in high-need areas.* The Urban Institute.

Cloud, N., Genesee, F., & Hamayan, E. (2000). *Dual language instruction. A handbook for enriched education.* Heinle and Heinle.

Collier, V. P., & Thomas, W. (2017). Validating the power of bilingual schooling: Thirty-two years of large-scale, longitudinal research. *Annual Review of Applied Linguistics, 37*, 203–217. https://doi.org/10.1017/S0267190517000034

Collins, B., & Cioè-Peña, M. (2016). Declaring freedom: Translanguaging in the social studies classroom to understand complex texts. In O. García & T. Kleyn (Eds.), *Translanguaging with multilingual students. Learning from classroom moments* (pp. 118–139). Routledge.

Common Core State Standards. (2010). http://www.corestandards.org/

Compton-Lilly, C. (2007). The complexities of reading capital in two Puerto Rican families. *Reading Research Quarterly, 42*(1), 72–98.

Computer Science Educational Justice Collective. (in press). *Advancing educational equity in computer science.* SUNY Press.

Condliffe, B., Visher, M. G., Banger, M. R., Drohojowska, S., & Saco, L. (2016). *Project-based learning: A literature review.* MDRC.

Conteh, J., & Meier, G. (Eds.). (2014). *The multilingual turn in languages education: Opportunities and challenges for individuals and societies.* Multilingual Matters.

Cook, V. (2002). Background to the L2 user. In V. Cook (Ed.), *Portraits of the L2 user* (pp. 1–28). Multilingual Matters.

Cook, V. (2008). *Second language learning and language teaching* (4th ed.). Hodder.

Cooper, B. R., & Lanza, S. T. (2014). Who benefits most from Head Start? Using latent class moderation to examine differential treatment effects. *Child development, 85*(6), 2317-2338. https://doi.org/10.1111/cdev.12278.

Cope, B., & Kalantzis, M. (2013). Towards a new learning: The scholar social knowledge workspace, in theory and practice. *E-Learning and Digital Media, 10*(4), 332–356.

Cope, B., & Kalantzis, M. (Eds.). (2000). *Multiliteracies: Literacy learning and the design of social futures.* Routledge.

Cope, B., & Kalantzis, M. (2024). A multimodal grammar of artificial intelligence: Measuring the gains and losses in generative AI. *Multimodality & Society, 4*(2), 123–152. https://doi.org/10.1177/26349795231221699.

Cope, B., Kalantzis, M., & Searsmith, D. (2020). Artificial intelligence for education: Knowledge and its assessment in AI-enabled learning ecologies. *Educational Philosophy and Theory, 52*(16), 1–17. http://doi.org/10.1080/00131857.2020.1728732.

Cope, B., Kalantzis, M., & Tzirides, A. O. O. (2024). Meaning without borders. In K. K. Grohmann (Ed.), *Multifaceted multilingualism*, (pp. 327–368). John Benjamins.

Corey, M. (2016, December 7). Majority of English learner students are born in the United States, analysis finds. *Education Week*. https://www.edweek.org/teaching-learning /majority-of-english-learner-students-are-born-in-the-united-states-analysis-finds /2016/12

Council of Chief State School Officers (CCSSO). (2016, February). Major provisions of Every Student Succeeds Act (ESSA) related to the education of English learners. http:// www.ccsso.org/Documents/2016/ESSA/CCSSOResourceonESSAELLs02.23.2016.pdf

Council of Europe. (2000). *Common European framework of reference for languages: Learning, teaching, assessment*. Language Policy Division. www.coe.int/t/dg4/linguisic /CADRE_EN.asp

Council of the Great City Schools. (2015). *Student testing in America's Great City Schools: An inventory and preliminary analysis*. http://www.cgcs.org/cms/lib/DC00001581/ Centricity/ Domain/87/Testing%20Report.pdf

Counsell, S. L., & Wright, B. L. (2018). High-stakes accountability systems: Creating cultures of fear. *Global Education Review*, 5(2), 189–202.

Cox, R. B., Jr., deSouza, D. K., Bao, J., Lin, H., Sahbaz, S., Greder, K. A., Larzelere, R., Washburn, I., Leon-Cartagena, M., & Arredondo-Lopez, A. (2021). Shared language erosion: Rethinking immigrant family communication and impacts on youth development. *Children*, 8(4), 256. https://doi.org/10.3390/children8040256

Crawford, J. (2003). A few things Ron Unz would prefer you didn't know about English learners in California. http://ourworld.compuserve.com/homepages/ JWCRAWFORD /castats.htm

Crawford, J. (2004). *Educating English learners: Language diversity in the classroom* (5th ed.). Bilingual Educational Services.

Crawford, J. (2007). The decline of bilingual education in the USA: How to reverse a troubling trend? *International Multilingual Research Journal*, 1(1), 33–37.

Creese, A., & Blackledge, A. (2010). Translanguaging in the bilingual classroom: A pedagogy for learning and teaching? *Modern Language Journal*, 94(1), 103–115.

Crenshaw, K. (1991). Mapping the margins: Intersectionality, identity politics, and violence against women of color. *Stanford Law Review*, 43(6), 1241–1299. https://doi .org/10.2307/1229039

Cronbach, L. J. (1989). Construct validation after thirty years. In R. L. Linn (Ed.), *Intelligence: Measurement theory and public policy* (pp. 147–171). University of Illinois Press.

Crump, A. (2014). Introducing LangCrit: Critical language and race theory. *Critical Inquiry in Language Studies*, 11(3), 207–224.

Cuero, K. K., & Valdez, V. E. (2012). "Good" students and "involved" mothers: Latin@ responses to normalization pressures in schools. *International Journal of Qualitative Studies in Education*, 25(3), 317–338. http://dx.doi.org/10.1080/09518398.2010.529845

Cummins, J. (1979). Cognitive/academic language proficiency, linguistic interdependence, the optimum age question, and some other matters. *Working Papers on Bilingualism*, 19, 121–129.

Cummins, J. (1979). Linguistic interdependence and the educational development of bilingual children. *Review of Educational Research*, 49(2), 222–251.

Cummins, J. (1981). *Bilingualism and minority language children*. Ontario Institute for Studies in Education.

Cummins, J. (1984). *Bilingualism and special education: Issues in assessment and pedagogy*. Multilingual Matters.

Cummins, J. (2000). *Language, power, & pedagogy: Bilingual children caught in the crossfire*. Multilingual Matters.

Cummins, J. (2003). *Biliteracy, empowerment and transformative pedagogy*. http://www.iteachilearn.com/cummins/biliteratempowerment.html

Cummins, J. (2006). Identity texts: The imaginative construction of self through multiliteracies pedagogy. In O. García, T. Skutnabb-Kangas, & M. Torres-Guzmán (Eds.), *Imagining multilingual schools: Languages in education and glocalization* (pp. 51–68). Multilingual Matters.

Cummins, J. (2007). Rethinking monolingual instructional strategies in multilingual classrooms. *The Canadian Journal of Applied Linguistics*, 10(2), 221–240.

Cummins, J. (2008). Teaching for transfer: Challenging the two solitudes assumption in bilingual education. In N. H. Hornberger (Ed.), *Encyclopedia of language and education*, 65–75.

Cummins, J. (2009). Foreword. In D. Fu (Ed.), *Writing between languages: How English language learners make the transition to fluency, grades 4–12* (pp. ix–xii). Heinemann.

Cummins, J. (2017). Teaching minoritized students: Are additive approaches legitimate? *Harvard Educational Review*, 87(3), 404–425.

Cummins, J., Brown, K., & Sayers, D. (2007). *Literacy, technology and diversity: Teaching for success in changing times*. Allyn & Bacon.

City University of New York-New York State Initiative on Emergent Bilinguals (CUNY-NYSIEB) (Eds.). (2021). *Translanguaging and transformative teaching for emergent bilingual students. Lessons from the CUNY-NYSIEB Project*. Routledge.

Custodio, B., & O'Loughlin, J. B. (2020). Students with interrupted formal education: Understanding who they are. American Federation of Teachers. https://www.aft.org/ae/spring2020/custodio_oloughlin

Dabach, D. B., & Fones, A. (2016). Beyond the "English learner" frame: Transnational funds of knowledge in social studies. *International Journal of Multicultural Education*, 18(1), 7–27. https://doi.org/10.18251/ijme.v18i1.1092

Darder, A. (2012). *Culture and power in the classroom: Educational foundations for the schooling of bicultural students*. Routledge.

Darling-Aduana, J., & Heinrich, C. J. (2018). The role of teacher capacity and instructional practice in the integration of educational technology for emergent bilingual students. *Computers & Education*, 126, 417–432. https://doi.org/10.1016/j.compedu.2018.08.002

Darling-Hammond, L. (2010). *The flat world and education: How America's commitment to equity will determine our future*. Teachers College Press.

Darling-Hammond, L. (2018). From "separate but equal" to "No Child Left Behind": The collision of new standards and old inequalities. In D. Meier & G. Wood (Eds.), *Thinking about schools* (pp. 419–437). Routledge.

Darling-Hammond, L. (2024). Reinventing systems for equity. *ECNU Review of Education*, 7(2), 214–229. https://doi.org/10.1177/20965311241237238

Darling-Hammond, L., Zielezinski, M. B., & Goldman, S. (2014). *Using technology to support at-risk students' learning*. Stanford Center for Opportunity Policy in Education (SCOPE) and Alliance for Excellent Education.

Darriet C., Santibañez L. (2024). Examining two-way dual language program dispersion in the context of neighborhood change, charter school expansion, and enrollment decline. *American Journal of Education*, 131(1), 55–91. https://doi.org/10.1086/732395

De Cohen, C. C., Deterding, N., & Chu Clewell, B. (2005). *Who's left behind? Immigrant children in high and low LEP schools*. Program for Evaluation and Equity Research. Urban Institute. http://www.urban.org/UploadedPDF/411231_whos_left_behind.pdf

de Jong, E. J., & Bearse, C. (2011). The same outcomes for all? High school students reflect on their two-way immersion program experiences. In D. J. Tedick, D. Christian, & T. W. Fortune (Eds.), *Immersion education: Practices, policies, possibilities* (pp. 104–122). Multilingual Matters.

De la Luz Reyes, M. (2012). Spontaneous biliteracy: Examining Latino students' untapped potential. *Theory into Practice*, 51(4), 248–255.

De la Piedra, M., & Araujo, B. (2012). Transfronterizo literacies and content in a dual language classroom. *International Journal of Bilingual Education and Bilingualism*, 15(6), 705–721. https://doi.org/10.1080/13670050.2012.699949

de los Ríos, C., & Seltzer, K. (2017). Translanguaging, coloniality and English classrooms: An exploration of two bicoastal urban classrooms. *Research in the Teaching of English*, 52(1), 55–76.

de los Ríos, C. V. (2018). Toward a corridista consciousness: Learning from one transnational youth's critical reading, writing, and performance of Mexican corridos. *Reading Research Quarterly*, 53(4), 455–471. https://doi.org/10.1002/rrq.210

De Souza, L. M. T. M. (2007) Entering a culture quietly: Writing and cultural survival in Indigenous education in Brazil. In S. Makoni & A. Pennycook (Eds.), *Disinventing and reconstituting languages* (pp. 135–169). Multilingual Matters.

Degollado, E. D., Nuñez, I., & Romero, M. A. (2021). Border literacies: A critical literacy framework from nepantla. In J.Z. Panda, R.A. Mora. J.H. Alford, N.H. Golden and R.S. de Roock (Eds.), *The handbook of critical literacies* (pp. 456–464). Routledge.

DeGraff, M. (2005). Linguists' most dangerous myth: The fallacy of Creole exceptionalism. *Language in Society*, 34(4), 533–591.

DeGraff, M. (2009). Creole exceptionalism and the (mis)-education of the Creole speaker. In J. Kleifgen & G. C. Bond (Eds.), *The languages of Africa and the diaspora: Educating for language awareness* (pp. 124–144). Multilingual Matters.

DeGraff, M. (2013). MIT-Haiti initiative uses Haitian Creole to make learning truly active, constructive, and interactive. *Educational Technology Debate: Exploring ICT and learning in developing countries*. https://edutechdebate.org/cultural-heritage-and-role-of-education/mit-haiti-initiative-uses-haitian-creole-to-make-learning-truly-active-constructive-and-interactive/

DeGraff, M. (2020). The politics of education in post-colonies: Kreyòl in Haiti as a case study of language as technology for power and liberation. *Journal of Postcolonial Linguistics*, 3, 89–125.

DeGraff, M. (in preparation). *Our own language. Linguistics and education for decolonization, liberation, and nation-building in Haiti and beyond*. MIT Press.

DeGraff, M., Frager, W. S., & Miller, H. (2022). Language policy in Haitian education. *Journal of Haitian Studies*, 28(2), 33–95.

DeGraff, M., & Stump, G. S. (2018). Kreyòl, pedagogy, and technology for opening up quality education in Haiti: Changes in teachers' metalinguistic attitudes as first steps in a paradigm shift. *Language*, 94(2), e127–e157.

DeJaynes, T., Cortes, T., & Hoque, I. (2020). Participatory action research in schools: Unpacking the lived inequities of high stakes testing. *English Teaching: Practice & Critique, 19*(3), 287–301. http://dx.doi.org/10.1108/ETPC-10-2019-0136

Del Valle, J. (2017). La perspectiva glotopolítica y la normatividad. *Anuario de Glotopolítica, 1*, 17–40.

Delavan, M. G., Freire, J. A., & Menken, K. (2021). Editorial introduction: A historical overview of the expanding critique (s) of the gentrification of dual language bilingual education. *Language Policy, 20*(3), 299–321.

Delavan, M. G., Freire, J. A., & Menken, K. (Eds.). (2024). *Overcoming the gentrification of dual language, bilingual and immersion education: Solution-oriented research and stakeholder resources for real integration.* Multilingual Matters.

Delgado-Gaitán, C. (1990). *Literacy for empowerment: The role of parents in children's education.* Falmer Press.

Delgado-Gaitán, C. (1992). School matters in the Mexican-American home: Socializing children to education. *American Educational Research Journal, 29*(3), 495–513.

Delgado-Gaitán, C. (2001). *The power of community: Mobilizing for family and schooling.* Rowman & Littlefield.

Delgado-Gaitán, C., & Trueba, H. (1991). *Crossing cultural borders: Education for immigrant families in America.* Falmer Press.

Dewey, J. (1938). *Experience and education.* Macmillan.

Díaz, R., & Klinger, C. (1991). Towards an explanatory model of the interaction between bilingualism and cognitive development. In E. Bialystok (Ed.), *Language processing in bilingual children* (pp. 167–192). Cambridge University Press.

Doerr, N. M. (Ed.). (2009). *The native speaker concept: Ethnographic investigations of native speaker effect.* De Gruyter/Mouton.

Dorner, L. M., Cervantes-Soon, C. G., Heiman, D., & Palmer, D. (2021). "Now it's all upper-class parents who are checking out schools": Gentrification as coloniality in the enactment of two-way bilingual education policies. *Language Policy, 20*(3), 1–27. https://doi.org/10.1007/s10993-021-09580-6

Dorner, L. M., & Kim, S. (2024). Language brokering over time: A study of citizenship becoming through a transliteracies framework. *Journal of Language, Identity & Education, 23*(3), 1–15.

Dorner, L. M., Moon, J. M., Freire, J., Gambrell, J., Kasun, G. S., & Cervantes-Soon, C. (2023). Dual language bilingual education as a pathway to racial integration? A place-based analysis of policy enactment. *Peabody Journal of Education, 98*(2), 185–204.

Dorner, L. M., Palmer, D., Cervantes-Soon, C. G., Heiman, D., & Crawford, E. R. (Eds.). (2022). *Critical consciousness in dual language bilingual education: Case studies on policy and practice.* Multilingual Matters.

Dual Language Schools. (2020). https://duallanguageschools.org/

Duarte, B. J. (2022). The effects of school choice competition on an underserved neighborhood public school. *Educational Policy, 37*(7), 1950–1988. https://doi.org/10.1177/089590482211345

Dufour, R., & Kroll, J. F. (1995). Matching words to concepts in two languages: A test of the concept mediation model of bilingual representation. *Memory & Cognition, 23*(2), 166–180.

Duncan, J. (2013, February 7). No Child Left Behind: Early lessons from state flexibility waivers. Testimony of Secretary of Education Arne Duncan to the U.S. Senate

Committee on Health, Education, Labor and Pensions. http://www.ed.gov/news/speeches/no-child-left-behind-early-lessons-state-flexibility-waivers

Durán, L. (2017). Audience and young bilingual writers: Building on strengths. *Journal of Literacy Research, 49*(1), 92–114.

Dussias, A. M. (1999). Waging war with words: Native Americans' continuing struggle against the suppression of their languages. *Ohio State Law Journal, 60*(3), 901–993.

Duverger, J. (2005). *L'Enseignment en classe bilingue* [Teaching in a bilingual class]. Hachette.

Dworin, J. E. (2003). Insights into biliteracy development: Toward a bidirectional theory of bilingual pedagogy. *Journal of Hispanic Higher Education, 2*(2), 171–186.

Dyrness, A. (2011). *Mothers united: An immigrant struggle for socially just education.* University of Minnesota Press.

Ebe, A. E. (2016). Student voices shining through: Exploring translanguaging as a literary device. In O. García & T. Kleyn (Eds.), *Translanguaging with multilingual students. Learning from classroom moments* (pp. 57–82). Routledge.

Echevarría, J., Vogt, M. E., & Short, D. J. (2004). *Making content comprehensible for English learners. The SIOP model* (2nd ed.). Allyn & Bacon.

Eisner, E. W. (2001). What does it mean to say a school is doing well? *The Phi Delta Kappan, 82*(5), 367–372.

Elliott, S., & Bowen, S. (2018). Defending motherhood: Morality, responsibility, and double binds in feeding children. *Journal of Marriage and Family, 80*(2), 499–520. https://doi.org/10.1111/jomf.12465

English Language Learners Sub-Committee of the Massachusetts Board of Elementary and Secondary Education's Committee on the Proficiency Gap. (2009). *Halting the race to the bottom: Urgent interventions for the improvement of English language learners in Massachusetts and selected districts.* Gastón Institute Publications.

Epstein, J. L. (1987). What principals should know about parent involvement. *Principal, 66*(3), 6–9.

Epstein, J. L. (1990). School and family connections: Theory, research, and implications for integrating sociologies of education and family. In D. G. Unger & M. B. Sussman (Eds.), *Families in community settings: Interdisciplinary perspectives* (pp. 99–126). Haworth Press.

Epstein, J. L., & Dauber, S. L. (1991). School programs and teacher practices of parent involvement in inner-city elementary and middle schools. *The Elementary School Journal, 91*(3), 289–305.

Epstein, J. L., & Sheldon, S. B. (2006). Moving forward: Ideas for research on school, family, and community partnerships. In C. F. Conrad & R. Serlin (Eds.), *SAGE handbook for research in education: Engaging ideas and enriching inquiry* (pp. 117–137). Sage Publications.

Escamilla, K., Hopewell, S., Butvilofsky, S., Sparrow, W., Soltero-González, L., Ruiz-Figueroa, O., & Escamilla, M. (2014). *Biliteracy from the start: Literacy squared in action.* Caslon Publishing.

España, C., & Herrera, L.Y. (2020). *En Comunidad. Lesson for centering the voices and experiences of bilingual Latinx students.* Heinemann.

Espinosa, C., & Ascenzi-Moreno, L. (2021). *Rooted in strength. Using translanguaging to grow multilingual readers and writers.* Scholastic.

Espinosa, C., Ascenzi-Moreno, L., & Vogel, S. (2016). *A translanguaging pedagogy for writing. A CUNY-NYSIEB guide for educators.* CUNY-NYSIEB, The Graduate

Center, CUNY. http://www.cuny-nysieb.org/wp-content/uploads/2016/05/TLG-Peda gogy-Writing-04-15-16.pdf

Espinosa, C., & Herrera, L. (2016). Reclaiming bilingualism: Translanguaging in a science class. In O. García & T. Kleyn (Eds.), *Translanguaging with multilingual students. Learning from classroom moments* (pp. 160–178). Routledge.

Espinosa, L. (2013a). *Early education for dual language learners: Promoting school readiness and early school success.* Migration Policy Institute.

Espinosa, L. (2013b). *PreK-3rd: Challenging common myths about dual language learners. An update to the seminal 2008 report.* No. 10. Foundation for Child Development.

Esteban-Guitart, M. (2021). Advancing the funds of identity theory: A critical and unfinished dialogue. *Mind, Culture, and Activity, 28*(2), 169–179. https://doi.org/10.1080 /10749039.2021.1913751

Esteban-Guitart, M., & Moll, L. C. (2014). Funds of identity: A new concept based on the funds of knowledge approach. *Culture & Psychology, 20*(1), 31–48.

Estrin, E. T., & Nelson-Barber, S. (1995). Bringing Native American perspectives to mathematics and science teaching. *Theory into Practice, 34*(3), 174–185.

Every Student Succeeds Act of 2015 (ESSA). (2015). Pub.L.No. 114–95 § 114 Stat.1177 (2015–2016).

Fabina, J., Hernandez, E., & Meirath, K. (2023, June). *School enrollment in the United States: 2021.* American Community Survey Reports. ACS-55.

Fairclough, N. (1999). Global capitalism and critical awareness of language. *Language Awareness, 8*(2), 71–83.

Fairclough, N. (Ed.). (1992). *Critical language awareness.* Longman.

Ferguson, G. (2006). *Language planning and education.* Edinburgh Press.

Figueras-Daniel, A., & Li, Z. (2021). Evidence of support for dual language learners in a study of bilingual staffing patterns using the Classroom Assessment of Supports for Emergent Bilingual Acquisition (CASEBA). *Early Childhood Research Quarterly, 54,* 271–285. https://doi.org/10.1016/j.ecresq.2020.09.011

Fishman, J. A. (1965). Language maintenance and language shift: The American immigrant case within a general theoretical perspective. *Sociologus, 16*(1), 19–39.

Fishman, J. A. (1966). *Language loyalty in the United States. The maintenance and perpetuation of non-English mother tongues by American ethnic and religious groups.* Mouton.

Fitts, S. (2006). Reconstructing the status quo: Linguistic interaction in a dual-language school. *Bilingual Research Journal, 30*(2), 337–365.

Fleischman, H. F., & Hopstock, P. J. (1993). *Descriptive study of services to limited English proficient students: Volume I. Summary of findings and conclusions.* Report submitted to the U.S. Department of Education. Development Associates, Inc.

Flores, B. (2005). The intellectual presence of the deficit view of Spanish-speaking children in the educational literature during the 20th century. In *Latino education: An agenda for community action research,* 75–98.

Flores, N. (2013). The unexamined relationship between neoliberalism and plurilingualism: A cautionary tale. *TESOL Quarterly, 47*(3), 500–521.

Flores, N. (2016). A tale of two visions: Hegemonic whiteness and bilingual education. *Educational Policy, 30*(1), 13–38. http://doi.org/10.1177/0895904815616482

Flores, N. (2019). Translanguaging into raciolinguistic ideologies: A personal reflection on the legacy of Ofelia García. *Journal of Multilingual Education Research, 9*(1), 45–60. https://research.library.fordham.edu/jmer/vol9/iss1/5/

Flores, N. (2020). From academic language to language architecture: Challenging raciolinguistic ideologies in research and practice. *Theory Into Practice*, *59*(1), 22–31.

Flores, N. (2024). *Becoming the system. A raciolinguistic genealogy of bilingual education in the post-civil rights era*. Oxford.

Flores, N., & Lewis, M. (2022). False positives, re-entry programs and long term English learners: Undoing dichotomous frames in US language education policy. *Equity & Excellence in Education*, *55*(3), 257–269.

Flores, N., & Rosa, J. (2015). Undoing appropriateness: Raciolinguistic ideologies and language diversity in education. *Harvard Educational Review*, *85*(2), 149–171.

Flores, N., Tseng, A., & Subtirelu, N. (Eds.). (2020). *Bilingualism for all? Raciolinguistic perspectives on dual language education in the United States*. Multilingual Matters.

Foucault, M. (1979). *Discipline and punish: The birth of the prison*. Vintage Books.

Foulger, T. S., & Jimenez-Silva, M. (2007). Enhancing the writing development of English learners: Teacher perceptions of common technology in project-based learning. *Journal of Research on Childhood Education*, *22*(2), 109–124.

Frankenberg, E., Ee, J., Ayscue, J. B., & Orfield, G. (2019). Harming our common future: America's segregated schools 65 years after Brown. *The Civil Rights Project*. https://escholarship.org/content/qt23j1b9nv/qt23j1b9nv.pdf

Free, J. L., & Križ, K. (2022). The not-so-hidden curriculum: How a public school system in the United States minoritizes migrant students. *Equity & Excellence in Education*, *55*(1–2), 50–72.

Freeman, Y., & Freeman, D. (2008). *Academic language for English language learners and struggling readers*. Heinemann.

Freire, J. A., & Alemán, E., Jr. (2021). "Two schools within a school": Elitism, divisiveness, and intra-racial gentrification in a dual language strand. *Bilingual Research Journal*, *44*(2), 249–269. https://doi.org/10.1080/15235882.2021.1942325

Freire, J. A., Alfaro, C., & de Jong, E. (Eds.). (2024). *The handbook of dual language bilingual education*. Routledge.

Freire, J. A., & Delavan, M. G. (2021). The fiftyfication of dual language education: One-size-fits-all language allocation's "equality" and "practicality" eclipsing a history of equity. *Language Policy*, *20*(3), 351–381. https://doi.org/10.1007/s10993-021-09579-z

Freire, J. A., Gambrell, J., Kasun, G. S., Dorner, L. M., & Cervantes-Soon, C. (2021). The expropriation of dual language bilingual education: deconstructing neoliberalism, whitestreaming, and English-hegemony. *International Multilingual Research Journal*, *16*(1), 27–46. https://doi.org/10.1080/19313152.2021.1929762

Freire, P. (1970). *Pedagogy of the oppressed*. Herder and Herder.

Freire, P., & Macedo, D. (1987). *Literacy: Reading the word and the world*. Routledge.

Fry, R., & López, M. H. (2012). *Hispanic student enrollments reach new highs in 2011*. http://www.pewhispanic.org/2012/08/20/hispanic-student-enrollments-reach-new-highs-in-2011/

Fu, D. (2003). *An island of English: Teaching ESL in Chinatown*. Heinemann.

Fu, D. (2009). *Writing between languages: How English language learners make the transition to fluency*. Heinemann.

Fu, D., Hadjioannou, X., & Zhou, X. (2019). *Translanguaging for emergent bilinguals*. Teachers College Press.

Funk, C., & Lopez, M. H. (2022, June 14). *A brief statistical portrait of U.S. Hispanics*. Pew Research Center. https://www.pewresearch.org/science/2022/06/14/a-brief-statistical-portrait-of-u-s-hispanics/

Gallo, S., & Link, H. (2015). "Diles la verdad": Deportation policies, politicized funds of knowledge, and schooling in middle childhood. *Harvard Educational Review, 85*(3), 357–382. https://doi.org/10.17763/0017-8055.85.3.357

Gándara, P. (1999). *Review of research on the instruction of Limited English Proficient Students: A report to the California legislature.* Linguistic Minority Research Institute.

Gándara, P., & Aldana, U. S. (2014). Who's segregated now? Latinos, language, and the future of integrated schools. *Educational Administration Quarterly, 50*(5), 735–748.

Gándara, P., & Contreras. F. (2009). *The Latino education crisis. The consequences of failed social policies.* Harvard University Press.

Gándara, P., & Hopkins, M. (Eds.). (2010). *Forbidden language: English learners and restrictive language policies.* Teachers College Press.

Gándara, P., Maxwell-Jolly, J., & Driscoll, A. (2005). *Listening to teachers of English language learners.* Center for the Future of Teaching and Learning.

Gándara, P., & Orfield, G. (2010). A return to the "Mexican room." The segregation of America's English learners. The Civil Rights Project. https://files.eric.ed.gov/fulltext/ED511322.pdf

Gándara, P., & Orfield, G. (2012). Segregating Arizona's English learners: A return to the "Mexican room"? *Teachers College Record, 114*(9), 1–27.

Gándara, P., O'Hara, S., & Gutiérrez, D. (2004). The changing shape of aspirations: Peer influence on achievement behavior. In G. Gibson, P. Gándara, & J. Koyama (Eds.), *School connections: U.S. Mexican youth, peers, and achievement* (pp. 39–62). Teachers College Press.

Gándara, P., Rumberger, R., Maxwell-Jolly, J., & Callahan, R. (2003). English learners in California schools: Unequal resources, unequal outcomes. *Education Policy Analysis Archives.* http://epaa.asu.edu/epaa/v11n36/

García, E. (2005). *Teaching and learning in two languages: Bilingualism and schooling in the United States.* Teachers College Press.

García, E., & Gonzalez, D. (2006, July). *Pre-K and Latinos: The foundation for America's future.* Pre-K Now Research Series.

García, E., & Jensen, B. (2009). Early educational opportunities for children of Hispanic origins. *Social Policy Report, 23*(2), 1–19.

García, G., & Pearson, P. D. (1994). Assessment and diversity. *Review of Research in Education, 20,* 337–391.

García, O. (2006, fall). Equity's elephant in the room. Multilingual children in the U.S. are being penalized by current education policies. *TC Today, 31*(1), 40.

García, O. (2009a). *Bilingual education in the 21st century: A global perspective.* Wiley-Blackwell.

García, O. (2009b). Emergent bilinguals and TESOL. What's in a name? *TESOL Quarterly, 43*(2), 322–326.

García, O. (2015). Racializing the language practices of US Latinos: Impact on their education. In J. A. Cobas, J. Duany, & R. Feagin (Eds.), *How the United States racializes Latinos* (pp. 101–115). Routledge.

García, O. (2016). The language valued at school. In G. Valdés, K. Menken, & M. Castro (Eds.), *Common core bilingual and English language learners. A resource for educators* (pp. 47–48). Caslon Publishing.

García, O. (2017). Critical multilingual awareness and teacher education. In J. Cenoz, D. Gorter, & S. May (Eds.), *Encyclopedia of language and education: Language awareness and multilingualism* (pp. 263–279). Springer International Publishing Switzerland. https://doi.org/10.1007/978-3-319-02325-0_30-11

García, O. (2023). Translanguaged TESOL in transit. *NYS TESOL Journal, 10*(1), 5–18. http://journal.nystesol.org/Vol10no1/García_V10_1.pdf

García, O., Alfaro, C., & Freire, J. (2024). Theoretical foundations of dual language-bilingual education. In J. Freire, C. Alfaro, & E. de Jong (Eds.), *The handbook of dual language bilingual education* (pp. 13–32). Routledge.

García, O., & Alvis, J. (2019). The decoloniality of language and translanguaging: Latinx knowledge-production. *Journal of Postcolonial Linguistics, 1*(1), 26–40.

García, O., Bartlett, L., & Kleifgen, J. (2007). From biliteracy to pluriliteracies. In P. Auer & Li Wei (Eds.), *Multilingualism and multilingual communication: Handbook of applied linguistics* (Vol. 5, pp. 207–228). Mouton de Gruyter.

García, O., & Cervantes-Soon, C. (2023). Best practices to support the literacy development of bilingual learners. In L. Morrow, E. Morrell, & H. Casey (Eds.), *Best practices in literacy instruction* (7th ed., pp. 335–353). Guilford Press.

García, O., Cioè-Peña, M., & Frieson, B. (2024). Bilingual education: Leaving (and not leaving) race behind. In L. Padilla & R. Vana (Eds.), *Representation, inclusion, and social justice in world language teaching: Research and pedagogy for inclusive classrooms* (pp. 102–121). Routledge.

García, O., & Flores, N. (2014). Multilingualism and Common Core State Standards in the U.S. In S. May (Ed.), *Addressing the multilingual turn: Implications for SLA, TESOL and Bilingual Education* (pp. 147–166). Routledge.

García, O., Flores, N., & Chu, H. (2011). Extending bilingualism in U.S. secondary education: New variations. *International Multilingual Research Journal, 5*(1), 1–18.

García, O., Flores, N., Seltzer, K., Li, W., Otheguy, R., & Rosa, J. (2021). Rejecting abyssal thinking in the language and education of racialized bilinguals: A manifesto. *Critical Inquiry in Language Studies, 18*(3), 203–228. https://doi.org/10.1080/15427587.2021 .1935957

García, O., Flores, N., & Spotti, M. (Eds.). (2017). *Oxford handbook of language and society.* Oxford University Press.

García, O., Flores, N., & Woodley, H. H. (2015). Constructing in-between spaces to "do" bilingualism: A tale of two high schools in one city. In J. Cenoz & D. Gorter (Eds.), *Multilingual education: Between language learning and translanguaging* (pp. 199–224). Cambridge University Press.

García, O., Johnson, S., & Seltzer, K. (2017). *The translanguaging classroom. Leveraging student bilingualism for learning.* Caslon.

García, O., & Kleifgen, J. (2019). Translanguaging and literacies. *Reading Research Quarterly, 55*(4), 553–571. https://doi.org/10.1002/rrq.286

García, O., Kleifgen, J., & Falchi, L. (2008). *Equity perspectives: From English language learners to emergent bilinguals.* Teachers College, Campaign for Educational Equity.

García, O., & Kleyn, T. (Eds.). (2016). *Translanguaging with multilingual students: Learning from classroom moments.* Routledge.

García, O., & Leiva, C. (2014). Theorizing and enacting translanguaging for social justice. In A. Blackledge & A. Creese (Eds.), *Heteroglossia as practice and pedagogy* (pp. 199–216). Springer.

García, O., & Li Wei (2014). *Translanguaging: Language, bilingualism and education.* Palgrave Macmillan Pivot.

García, O., & Menken, K. (2015). Cultivating an ecology of multilingualism in schools. In B. Spolsky, O. Inbar, & M. Tannenbaum (Eds.), *Challenges for language education and policy: Making space for people* (pp. 95–108). Routledge.

García, O., Menken, K., Velasco, P. & Vogel, S. (2018). Dual language bilingual education in NYC: A potential unfulfilled. In M. B. Arias & M. Fee (Eds.). *Profiles of dual language education in the 21st century* (pp. 38–55). Center for Applied Linguistics and Multilingual Matters.

García, O., & Nuosy, S. (2024). Actionable translanguaging love in education and research. *Critical Inquiry in Language Studies*. https://doi.org/10.1080/15427587.2024.2336449.

García, O., & Otheguy, R. (2020). Interrogating the language gap of young bilingual and bidialectal students. In E. J. Johnson (Ed.), *Critical perspectives of the language gap* (pp. 53–66). Routledge.

García, O., Phyak, P., Lee, J.W; Li, W. (in press). Navigating translanguaging: Decoloniality, fluid simultaneity and multimodalities. In Li Wei, P. Phyak, J. W. Lee, & O. García (Eds.). *Handbook of translanguaging*. Wiley.

García, O., & Sánchez, M. (2015). Transforming schools with emergent bilinguals: The CUNY-NYSIEB Project. In I. Dirim, I. Gogolin, D. Knorr, M. Krüger-Potratz, D. Lengyel, H. Reich, & W. Weiße (Eds.), *Intercultural education: Festchrift for Ulla Neumann* (pp. 80–94). Waxmann-Verlag.

García, O., Seltzer, K., & Witt, D. (2018). Disrupting linguistic inequalities in US urban classrooms: The role of translanguaging. In S. Slembrouck, K. Van Gorp, S. Sierens, K. Maryns, & P. Van Avermaet (Eds.), *The multilingual edge of education* (pp. 414–456). Palgrave Macmillan UK.

García, O., & Solorza, C. (2020). Academic language and the minoritization of U.S. bilingual Latinx students. *Language and Education*, *35*(6), 505–521. https://doi.org/10.1080/09500782.2020.1825476

García, O., & Sung, K. K-F. (2018). Critically assessing the 1968 Bilingual Education Act at 50 years: Taming tongues and Latinx communities. *The Bilingual Review Journal*, *4*(4), 318–333. https://doi.org/10.1080/15235882.2018.1529642

García, O., & Sylvan, C. (2011). Pedagogies and practices in multilingual classrooms: Singularities in pluralities. *Modern Language Journal*, *95*(3), 385–400.

García, O., & Traugh, C. (2002). Using descriptive inquiry to transform the education of linguistically diverse U.S. teachers and students. In Li Wei, J. Dewaele, & A. Housen (Eds.), *Opportunities and challenges of (societal) bilingualism* (pp. 311–328). Walter de Gruyter.

García, O., & Wong, N. (in press). Translanguaging: Uncovering networks for unspeakable significance. In Li Wei, P. Phyak, J. W. Lee, & O. García. (Eds.), *Handbook of translanguaging*. Wiley.

García, O., Zakharia, Z., & Otcu, B. (Eds.). (2013). *Bilingual community education and multilingualism: Beyond heritage languages in a global city*. Multilingual Matters.

García-Mateus, S. (2023). Bilingual student perspectives about language expertise in a gentrifying two-way immersion program. *International Journal of Bilingual Education and Bilingualism*, *26*(1), 34–49.

Gay, G. (2002). Preparing for culturally responsive teaching. *Journal of Teacher Education*, *53*(2), 106–116.

Gee, J. P. (2014). Decontextualized language: A problem, not a solution. *International Multilingual Research Journal*, *8*(1), 9–23.

Genesee, F., Lindholm-Leary, K., Saunders, W. M., & Christian, D. (Eds.). (2006). *Educating English language learners*. Cambridge University Press.

Genishi, C., & Borrego Brainard, M. (1995). Assessment of bilingual children: A dilemma seeking solutions. In E. García & B. McLaughlin (Eds.), *Meeting the challenge of linguistic and cultural diversity in early childhood education* (pp. 49–63). Teachers College Press.

Gibbons, P. (2002). *Scaffolding language, scaffolding learning. Teaching second languages in the mainstream classroom*. Heinemann.

Gibbons, P. (2009). *English learners' academic literacy and thinking. Learning in the challenge zone*. Heinemann.

Gibson, M. A., Gándara, P., & Koyama, J. P. (2004). The role of peers in the schooling of U.S. Mexican youth. In M. A. Gibson, P. Gándara, & J. P. Koyama (Eds.), *School connections: U.S. Mexican youth, peers, and school achievement* (pp. 1–17). Teachers College Press.

Gifford, A. (2023). Which states have digital learning plans? https://www.govtech.com/education/k-12/which-states-have-digital-learning-plans

Gilmore, P. (2016). *Kisisi (our language): The story of Colin and Sadiki*. Wiley-Blackwell.

Giroux, H. (1988). *Teachers as intellectuals*. Bergin and Garvey.

Givens, J. (2023). *Fugitive pedagogy*. Harvard University Press.

Goh, D. S. (2004). *Assessment accommodations for diverse learners*. Pearson.

Gold, E., Simon, E., & Brown, C. (2002). *Strong neighborhoods, strong schools: The indicators project on education organizing*. Cross City Campaign for Urban School Reform.

Goldenberg, C. (2008). Teaching English language learners. What the research does—and does not—say. *American Educator, 32*(2), 8–23, 42–44.

Goldenberg, C., & Coleman, R. (2010). *Promoting academic achievement among English learners. A guide to the research*. Corwin Press.

Golloher, A. N., Whitenack, D. A., Simpson, L. A., & Sacco, D. (2018). From the ground up: Providing support to emergent bilinguals to distinguish language difference from disability. *Insights into Learning Disabilities, 15*(2), 127–147.

González, N. (2005). Beyond culture: The hybridity of funds of knowledge. In N. González, L. C. Moll, & C. Amati (Eds.), *Funds of knowledge: Theorizing practices in households, communities, and classrooms* (pp. 29–46). Lawrence Erlbaum.

González, N., Moll, L. C., & Amanti, C. (2005). *Funds of knowledge. Theorizing practices in households, communities, and classrooms*. Lawrence Erlbaum.

González-Howard, M., Andersen, S., Méndez Pérez, K., & Suárez, E. (2023). Language views for scientific sensemaking matter: A synthesis of research on multilingual students' experiences with science practices through a translanguaging lens. *Educational Researcher, 52*(9), 570–579. https://doi.org/10.3102/0013189X231206172

González-Howard, M., Méndez Pérez, K., & Andersen, S. (2024). Learning to notice multilingual students' language use for scientific sensemaking: Integrating translanguaging theory and pedagogy in an elementary science methods course. In O. Andrews & A. Tomlin (Eds.), *When we hear them: Attuning teachers to language diverse learners* (pp. 213–226). Information Age Publishing.

Goodall, J. (2021). Parental engagement and deficit discourses: Absolving the system and solving parents. *Educational Review, 73*(1), 98–110. https://doi.org/10.1080/001319 11.2018.1559801

Goodall, J., & Montgomery, C. (2014). Parental involvement to parental engagement. A continuum. *Educational Review, 66*(4), 399–410.

Gormley, W., Jr. (2008). The effects of Oklahoma's pre-K program on Hispanic children. *Social Science Quarterly, 89*(4), 916–936.

Gort, M. (2015). Transforming literacy learning and teaching through translanguaging and other typical practices associated with "doing being bilingual." *International Multilingual Research Journal, 9*(1), 1–6.

Gort, M. (Ed.). (2018). *The complex and dynamic languaging practices of emergent bilinguals. Translanguaging across diverse educational and community contexts.* Routledge.

Gort, M., & Sembiante, S. F. (2015). Navigating hybridized language learning spaces through translanguaging pedagogy: Dual language preschool teachers' languaging practices in support of emergent bilingual children's performance of academic discourse. *International Multilingual Research Journal, 9*(1), 7–25. https://doi.org/10.1080/19313152.2014.981775

Gorter, D., Marten, H. F., & Van Mensel, L. (Eds.). (2012). *Minority languages in the linguistic landscape.* Palgrave Macmillan.

Gottlieb, M. (2006). *Assessing English language learners: Bridges from language proficiency to academic achievement.* Corwin Press.

Gottlieb, M. (2016). *Assessing English language learners: Bridges to educational equity. Connecting academic language proficiency to student achievement.* Corwin Press.

Gottlieb, M. (2017). *Assessing multilingual learners. A month-by-month guide.* ASCD.

Grant, E. A., & Wong, S. D. (2003). Barriers to literacy for language-minority learners: An argument for change in the literacy education profession. *Journal of Adolescent & Adult Literacy, 46*(5), 386–394.

Grantmakers for Education. (2013). Educating English language learners: Grantmaking strategies for closing America's other achievement gap. https://edfunders.org/sites/default/files/Educating%20English%20Language%20Learners_April%202013.pdf

Grapin, S. (2019). Multimodality in the new content standards era: Implications for English learners. *TESOL Quarterly, 53*(1), 30–55. https://doi.org/10.1002/tesq.443

Graves, M. (2006). *The vocabulary book: Learning and instruction.* Teachers College Press.

Green, D. W. (2011). Bilingual worlds. In V. Cook & B. Bassetti (Eds.), *Language and bilingual cognition* (pp. 229–240). Psychology Press.

Greenberg, J. (1989, June). Funds of knowledge: Historical constitution, social distribution, and transmission. Paper presented at the annual meeting of the Society for Applied Anthropology.

Greenberg, J. (1990). Funds of knowledge: Historical constitution, social distribution, and transmission. In W. T. Pink, D. S. Ogle, & B. F. Jones (Eds.), *Restructuring to promote learning in America's schools: Selected readings* (Vol. 2, pp. 317–326). North Central Regional Educational Laboratory.

Greene, J. (1997). A meta-analysis of the Rossell and Baker review of bilingual education research. *Bilingual Research Journal, 21*(2–3), 103–122.

Greene, M. (1995). *Releasing the imagination. Essays on education, the arts and social change.* Jossey-Bass.

Grimes, D., & Warschauer, M. (2008). Learning with laptops: A multi-method case study. *Journal of Educational Computing Research, 38*(3), 305–332.

Grosjean, F. (1985). The bilingual as a competent but specific speaker-hearer. *Journal of Multilingual and Multicultural Development, 6*(6), 467–477.

Grosjean, F. (1989). Neurolinguists, beware! The bilingual is not two monolinguals in one person. *Brain and Language, 36*(1), 3–15.

Gubbins, E. J., Siegle, D., Hamilton, R., Peters, P., Carpenter, A. Y., O'Rourke, P., . . . Estepar-García, W. (2018, June). *Exploratory study on the identification of English learners for gifted and talented programs*. National Center for Research on Gifted Education. https://ncrge.uconn.edu/wp-content/uploads/sites/982/2020/09/NCRGE -EL-Report.pdf

Guiberson, M. (2013). Bilingual myth-busters series: Language confusion in bilingual children. *Perspectives on Communication Disorders & Sciences in Culturally & Linguistically Diverse (CLD) Populations, 20*(1), 5–14. https://doi.org/10.1044/cds20.1.5

Gumperz, J. J. (1964). Linguistic and social interaction in two communities. *American Anthropologist, 66*(6–2), 137–153.

Gumperz, J. J. (1976). The sociolinguistic significance of conversational code-switching. *Working Papers of the Language Behavior Research Laboratory, 46*. University of California, Berkeley.

Gutiérrez, K. D., Asato, J., Pacheco, M., Moll, L. C., Olson, K., Horng, E., Ruiz, R., García, E., & McCarty, T. L. (2002). "Sounding American": The consequences of new reforms on English language learners. *Reading Research Quarterly, 37*(3), 328–343.

Gutiérrez, K., Baquedano-López, P., & Álvarez, H. (2001). Literacy as hybridity: Moving beyond bilingualism in urban classrooms. In M. Reyes & J. J. Halcón (Eds.), *The best for our children. Critical perspectives on literacy for Latino students* (pp. 122–141). Teachers College Press.

Gutierrez-Clellen, V., & Peña, E. (2001). Dynamic assessment of diverse children: A tutorial. *Language, Speech and Hearing Services in Schools, 32*(4), 212–224.

Hakuta, K. (1986). *Cognitive development of bilingual children*. University of California at Los Angeles, Center for Language, Education, & Research.

Hakuta, K., Goto Butler, Y., & Witt, D. (2000). *How long does it take English learners to attain proficiency?* University of California, Linguistic Minority Research Institute.

Hale, J. (2011). The student as a force for social change: The Mississippi Freedom Schools and student engagement. *Journal of African American History, 96*(3), 325–347.

Halliday, M. A. K. (1978). *Language as social semiotic: The social interpretation of language and meaning*. University Park Press.

Halliday, M. A. K. (1993). Towards a language-based theory of learning. *Linguistics and Education, 5*(2), 93–116.

Harklau, L. (1994). Tracking and linguistic minority students: Consequences of ability grouping for second language learners. *Linguistics and Education, 6*(3), 217–244.

Harmer, J. (1998). *How to teach English*. Pearson.

Hart, B., & Risley, T. R. (1995). *Meaningful differences in the everyday experience of young American children*. Paul H. Brookes Publishing.

Harvey-Torres, R., & Degollado, E. D. (2021). "And I did it with my writing": Bilingual teachers storying resilience and resistance through autohistoria. *Research in the Teaching of English, 56*(1), 60–84.

Haskins, R., & Rouse, C. (2005). Closing achievement gaps. *The Future of Children, 15*, 1–7.

Heath, S. B. (1983). *Ways with words*. Cambridge University Press.

Hedges, H. (2015). Sophia's funds of knowledge: Theoretical and pedagogical insights, possibilities and dilemmas. *International Journal of Early Years Education, 23*(1), 83–96. https://doi.org/10.1080/09669760.2014.976609

Heiman, D., Cervantes-Soon, C. G., & Hurie , A. H. (2021). "Well good para quién?": Disrupting two-way bilingual education gentrification and reclaiming space through a critical translanguaging pedagogy. In Sánchez, M.T. & García, O. (Eds.), *Transformative translanguaging espacios: Latinx students and their teachers rompiendo fronteras sin miedo* (pp. 47–70). Multilingual Matters.

Heiman, D., Cervantes-Soon, C., Palmer, D. K., & Dorner, L. M. (2023). Establishing a transformative foundation for dual language bilingual education: Critical consciousness at the core. In J. Freire, C. Alfaro, & E. J. de Jong (Eds.), *The handbook of dual language bilingual education* (pp. 51–71). Routledge.

Heiman, D., & Murakami, E. (2019). "It was like a magnet to bring people in": School administrators' responses to the gentrification of a two-way bilingual education (TWBE) program in central Texas. *Journal of School Leadership*, 29(6), 454–472.

Heller, M. (1999). *Linguistic minorities and modernity: A sociolinguistic ethnography.* Longman.

Henderson, A. T. (Ed.). (1987). *The evidence continues to grow: Parent involvement improves student achievement.* National Committee for Citizens in Education.

Henderson, A. T., & Berla, N. (1994). *A new generation of evidence: The family is critical to student achievement.* National Committee for Citizens in Education.

Henderson, A. T., & Mapp, K. L. (2002). *A new wave of evidence: The impact of school, family, and community connections on student achievement.* Southwest Educational Development Laboratory.

Herdina, P., & Jessner, U. (2002). *A dynamic model of multilingualism: Changing the psycholinguistic perspective.* Multilingual Matters.

Heritage, M., Walqui, A., & Linquanti, R. (2015). *English language learners and the new standards. Developing language, content knowledge, and analytical practices in the classroom.* Harvard Education Press.

Hernando-Lloréns, B., & Cervantes-Soon, C. (2023). Gubernamentalidad y formación de maestros: Hacia una historización de la intervención educativa en los niños bilingües. *Bilingual Review/Revista Bilingüe*, 35(2), 18–38.

Herrera, L. Y., & España, C. (2022). Se hace camino al andar: Translanguaging pedagogy for justice. *English Journal*, 111(5), 27–34.

Hidalgo, N. M., Siu, S. F., & Epstein, J. L. (2004). Research on families, schools, and communities: A multicultural perspective. In J. Banks & C. Banks (Eds.), *Handbook of research on multicultural education* (2nd ed.), pp. 631–655. Jossey-Bass.

Hobson v. Hansen. (1967). 269 F. Supp. 401, 490; DDC 1967.

Honig, B. (1996). *Teaching our children to read: The role of skills in a comprehensive reading program.* Corwin Press.

Hoover-Dempsey, K. V., & Sandler, H. M. (1997). Why do parents become involved in their children's education? *Review of Educational Research*, 67(1), 3–42.

Hopstock, P. J., & Stephenson, T. G. (2003). Descriptive study of services to LEP students and LEP students with disabilities. Special Topic Report #2: Analysis of Office for Civil Rights Data related to LEP students. U.S. Department of Education, OELA.

Hornberger, N. (1990). Creating successful learning contexts for bilingual literacy. *Teachers College Record*, 92(2), 212–229.

Hornberger, N. (2005). Opening and filling up implementational and ideological spaces in heritage language education. *Modern Language Journal*, 89(4), 605–609.

Hornberger, N. (2006). Nichols to NCLB: Local and global perspectives on U.S. language education policy. In O. García, T. Skutnabb-Kangas, & M. Torres-Guzmán (Eds.), *Imagining multilingual schools: Languages in education and glocalization* (pp. 223–237). Multilingual Matters.

Hornberger, N. (Ed.). (2003). *Continua of biliteracy. An ecological framework for educational policy, research, and practices in multilingual settings.* Multilingual Matters.

Hornberger, N., & Link, H. (2012). Translanguaging and transnational literacies in multilingual classrooms: A bilingual lens. *International Journal of Bilingual Education and Bilingualism, 15*(3), 261–278.

Hornberger, N., & Skilton-Sylvester, P. (2003). Revisiting the continua of biliteracy: International and critical perspectives. In N. Hornberger (Ed.), *Continua of biliteracy. An ecological framework for educational policy, research, and practices in multilingual settings* (pp. 35–70). Multilingual Matters.

Houser, J. (1995). Assessing students with disabilities and Limited English Proficiency. *Working Paper Series. Working Paper 95–13.* National Center for Education Statistics.

Huang, W., Hew, K. F., & Fryer, L. K. (2022). Chatbots for language learning—Are they really useful? A systematic review of chatbot-supported language learning. *Journal of Computer Assisted Learning, 38*(1), 237–257. https://doi.org/10.1111/jcal.12610

Hudicourt-Barnes, J. (2003). The use of argumentation in Haitian Creole science classrooms. *Harvard Educational Review, 73*(1), 73–93.

Hull, G., & Nelson, M. (2005). Locating the semiotic power of multimodality. *Written Communication, 22*(2), 224–261.

Hulse, E.C. (2021). Disabling Language: The Overrepresentation of Emergent Bilingual Students in Special Education in New York and Arizona, *Fordham Urban Law Journal* 48(2), 381-448. https://ir.lawnet.fordham.edu/ulj/vol48/iss2/2

Hung, A. (2011). *The work of play: Meaning making in video games.* Peter Lang.

Iedema, R. (2003). Multimodality, resemiotization: Extending the analysis of discourse as multi-semiotic practice. *Visual Communication, 2*(1), 29–57.

Institute of Education Science. National Center for Education Statistics. (2023). English learners in public schools. *Condition of Education.* U.S. Department of Education, Institute of Education Sciences. https://nces.ed.gov/programs/coe/indicator/cgf.

Ishimaru, A. (2014). Rewriting the rules of engagement: Elaborating a model of district–community collaboration. *Harvard Educational Review, 84*(2), 188–216. https://doi.org/10.17763/haer.84.2.r2007u165m8207j5

Ishimaru, A. M. (2019a). From family engagement to equitable collaboration. *Educational Policy, 33*(2), 350–385. https://doi.org/10.1177/0895904817691841

Ishimaru, A. M. (2019b). *Just schools: Building equitable collaborations with families and communities.* Teachers College Press.

Ishimaru, A. M., & Bang, M. (2022). Solidarity-driven codesign: Evolving methodologies for expanding engagement with familial and community expertise. In D. J. Peurach, J. L. Russell, L. Cohen-Vogel, and W. R. Penuel (Eds.), *The foundational handbook on improvement research in education* (pp. 383–402). Rowman & Littlefield.

Iyengar, M. M. (2014). Not mere abstractions: Language policies and language ideologies in US settler colonialism. *Decolonization: Indigeneity, Education & Society, 3*(2), 33–59.

Jacobson, R., & Faltis, C. (1990). *Language distribution issues in bilingual schooling.* Multilingual Matters.

Jacoby, J. W., & Lesaux, N. K. (2014). Support for extended discourse in teacher talk with linguistically diverse preschoolers. *Early Education and Development, 25*(8), 1162–1179. https://doi.org/10.1080/10409289.2014.907695

Jaumont, F. (2017). *The bilingual revolution: The future of education is in two languages.* TBR Books.

Jessner, U. (2006). *Linguistic awareness in multilinguals: English as a third language*. Edinburgh University Press.

Jewitt, C. (2002). The move from page to screen: The multimodal reshaping of school English. *Journal of Visual Communication, 1*(2), 171–196.

Jewitt, C. (Ed.). (2009). *The Routledge handbook for multimodal analysis*. Routledge.

Jewitt, C., & Kress, G. (Eds.). (2003). *Multimodal literacy*. Peter Lang.

Jeynes, W. H. (2011). *Parent involvement and academic success*. Routledge.

Jiménez-Castellanos, O., García, O., de Jong, E. & Morita, P. (Eds.) (2024). From access to meaningful instruction to equitsble access to high quality bilingual instruction. Lau 50th anniversary special issue, *Bilingual Research Journal* (2024). 47(4) (entire issue).

Jiménez-Castellanos, O., & Topper, A. M. (2012). The cost of providing an adequate education to English language learners. A review of the literature. *Review of Educational Research, 82*(2), 179–232. https://doi.org/10.3102/0034654312449872

Jimenez, K. (2022). Latinos will make up nearly a third of U.S. students in 2030. USA Today (Oct. 11, 2022). https://www.usatoday.com/in-depth/news/2022/10/11/latino-student-population-us-schools/10426950002/

Jin, J., & Liu, Y. (2023). Towards a critical translanguaging biliteracy pedagogy: The "aha moment" stories of two Mandarin Chinese teachers in Canada. *Literacy, 57*(2), 171–184.

Johnson, E. J., & Johnson, D. C. (2015). Language policy and bilingual education in Arizona and Washington State. *International Journal of Bilingual Education and Bilingualism, 18*(1), 92–112. https://doi.org/10.1080/13670050.2014.882288

Johnson, E. J., & Zentella, A. C. (2017). Introducing the language gap. *International Multilingual Research Journal, 11*(1), 1–4. https://doi.org/10.1080/19313152.2016.1258184

Johnson, L. R. (2009). Challenging "best practices" in family literacy and parent education programs: The development and enactment of mothering knowledge among Puerto Rican and Latina mothers in Chicago. *Anthropology & Education Quarterly, 40*(3), 257–276.

Johnston, P. (1997). *Knowing literacy: Constructive literacy assessment*. Stenhouse Publishers.

Jordan, C., Orozco, E., & Averett, A. (2001). *Emerging issues in school, family, and community connections*. Southwest Educational Development Laboratory.

Kagan, S. (1986). Cooperative learning and sociocultural factors in schooling. In California State Department of Education (Ed.), *Beyond language: Social and cultural factors in schooling language minority students* (pp. 231–298). Evaluation, Dissemination and Assessment Center, California State University at Los Angeles.

Kagan, S., & McGroarty, M. (1993). Principles of cooperative learning for language and content gains. In D. D. Holt (Ed.), *Cooperative learning: A response to linguistic and cultural diversity* (pp. 47–66). Delta Systems and Center for Applied Linguistics.

Kalantzis, M., & Cope, B. (2024, April 4). *Literacy in the time of artificial intelligence*. https://doi.org/10.35542/osf.io/es5kb

Kaplan, R., & Baldauf, R. (1997). *Language planning from practice to theory*. Multilingual Matters.

Karoly, L., & Bigelow, J. (2005). *The economics of investing in universal preschool education in California*. RAND Labor and Population Program.

Karp, F., & Uriarte, M. (2010). *Educational outcomes of English language learners in Massachusetts: A focus on Latino/a students.* Gastón Institute Publications, 159. https://scholarworks.umb.edu/gaston_pubs/159

Katz, A., Low, P., Stack, J., & Tsang, T. (2004). *A study of content area assessment for English language learners.* Prepared for the Office of English Language Acquisition and Academic Achievement for Limited English Proficient Students, U.S. Department of Education. ARC Associates.

Kaveh, Y. M. (2022). Beyond feel-good language-as-resource orientations: Getting real about hegemonic language practices in monolingual schools. *TESOL Quarterly*, 56(1), 347–362. https://doi.org/10.1002/tesq.3053

Kaveh, Y. M., Bernstein, K. A., Cervantes-Soon, C., Rodriguez-Martinez, S., & Mohamed, S. (2022). Moving away from the 4-hour block: Arizona's distinctive path to reversing its restrictive language policies. *International Multilingual Research Journal*, 16(2), 113–135.

Kaveh, Y. M., & Sandoval, J. (2020). "No! I'm going to school, I need to speak English!": Who makes family language policies? *Bilingual Research Journal*, 43(4), 362–383. https://doi.org/10.1080/15235882.2020.1825541

Kecskes, I., & Martínez Cuenca, I. (2005). Lexical choice as a reflection of conceptual fluency. *International Journal of Bilingualism*, 9(1), 49–69.

Kharkhurin, A. (2015). Bilingualism and creativity. An educational perspective. In W. Wright, S. Boun, & O. García (Eds.), *The handbook of bilingual and multilingual education* (pp. 109–126). Wiley-Blackwell.

Kibler, A., Valdés, G., & Walqui, A. (Eds.). (2021). *Reconceptualizing the role of critical dialogue in American classrooms. Promoting equity through dialogic education.* Routledge.

Kibler, A., Walqui, A., Bunch, G., & Faltis, C. (Eds.). (2024). *Equity in multilingual schools and communities: Celebrating the contributions of Guadalupe Valdés* (pp. 231–242). Multilingual Matters.

Kieffer, M. J., & Lesaux, N. K. (2007). Breaking down words to build meaning: Morphology, vocabulary, and reading comprehension in the urban classroom. *The Reading Teacher*, 61(2), 134–144.

Kim, S. (2018). "It was kind of a given that we were all multilingual": Transnational youth identity work in digital translanguaging. *Linguistics and Education*, 43, 39–52. https://doi.org/10.1016/j.linged.2017.10.008

Kim, W. G. (2017). Long-term English language learners' educational experiences in the context of high-stakes accountability. *Teachers College Record*, 119(9), 1–32. https://doi.org/10.1177/016146811711900903

Kinzer, C. K. (2010). Considering literacy and policy in the context of digital environments. *Language Arts*, 88(1), 51–61.

Kleifgen, J. (1991). Kreyòl ekri, Kreyòl li: Haitian children and computers. *Educational Horizons*, 59(3), 152–158.

Kleifgen, J. (2006). Variation in multimodal literacies: How new technologies can expand or constrain modes of communication. *WORD*, 57(3), 303–324.

Kleifgen, J. (2009). Discourses of linguistic exceptionalism and linguistic diversity in education. In J. Kleifgen & G. C. Bond (Eds.), *The languages of Africa and the diaspora: Educating for language awareness* (pp. 1–21). Multilingual Matters.

Kleifgen, J. (2013). *Communicative practices at work: Multimodality and learning in a high-tech firm.* Multilingual Matters.

Kleifgen, J. (2017a). *BRIDGE evaluation progress report: Analysis and findings for Group B teacher online training class.* iEARN.

Kleifgen, J. (2017b). *BRIDGE evaluation progress report: Analysis for Group A students "My Identity, Your Identity" project.* iEARN.

Kleifgen, J. (2019, December). The "translanguaging and multimodality" conundrum: How to avoid reification pitfalls. Paper presented at the Multilingual and Multicultural Learning: Policies and Practices Conference, Charles University, Faculty of Arts, Prague, Czech Republic.

Kleifgen, J. (2022). Emergent bilinguals and trans-semiotic practices in the new media age. In B. Otcu-Grillman & M. Borjian (Eds.), *Re-making multilingualism: A translanguaging approach* (pp. 43–65). Multilingual Matters.

Kleifgen, J., & Bond, G. C. (Eds.). (2009). *The languages of Africa and the diaspora: Educating for language awareness.* Multilingual Matters.

Kleifgen, J., & Kinzer, C. (2009). Alternative spaces for education with and through technology. In H. Varenne & E. Gordon (Eds.), *Theoretical perspectives on comprehensive education: The way forward* (pp. 139–186). Mellen Press.

Kleifgen, J., Kinzer, C. K., Hoffman, D. L., Gorski, K., Kim, J., Lira, A., & Ronan, B. (2014). An argument for a multimodal, online system to support English learners' writing development. In R. S. Anderson & C. Mims (Eds.), *Digital tools for writing instruction in K–12 settings: Student perceptions and experiences* (pp. 171–192). IGI Global.

Kleifgen, J., Lira, A., & Ronan, B. (2014, December). Developing content knowledge and science literacy in a transitional bilingual classroom. In C. Kinzer (Chair), *Collaborative design and implementation of alternative spaces for Latina/o Adolescent writers: The STEPS to Literacy intervention.* Symposium organized for the annual meeting of the Literacy Research Association, Marco Island, FL.

Kleyn, T. (2016). The grupito flexes their listening and learning muscles. In O. García & T. Kleyn (Eds.), *Translanguaging with multilingual students. Learning from classroom moments* (pp. 100–117). Routledge.

Kleyn, T., Hunt, V., Jaar, A., Madrigal, R., & Villegas, C. (2024). *Lessons from a dual language bilingual school. Celebrando una década de Dos Puentes Elementary.* Multilingual Matters.

Knobel, M., & Lankshear, C. (2009). Wikis, digital literacies, and professional growth. *Journal of Adolescent & Adult Literacy, 52*(7), 631–634.

Koelsch, N. (n.d.). *Improving literacy outcomes for English language learners in high school: Considerations for states and districts in developing a coherent policy framework.* http://www.betterhighschools.org/docs/NHSC_AdolescentS_110806.pdf

Kohn, A. (2006). *The homework myth: Why our kids get too much of a bad thing.* Da Capo Press.

Kramsch, C. (1997). The privilege of the nonnative speaker. *Modern Language Journal, 112*(3), 359–369.

Kress, G. (2000a). A curriculum for the future. *Cambridge Journal of Education, 30*(1), 133–145.

Kress, G. (2000b). Design and transformation: New theories of meaning. In B. Cope & M. Kalantzis (Eds.), *Multiliteracies: Literacy learning and the design of social futures* (pp. 153–161). Routledge.

Kress, G. (2003). *Literacy in the new media age.* Routledge.

Kress, G. (2010). *Multimodality: A social semiotic approach to contemporary communication.* Routledge.

Kress, G., & van Leeuwen, T. (1996). *Reading images: The grammar of visual design*. Routledge.

Kress, G., & van Leeuwen, T. (2001). *Multimodal discourse*. Arnold.

Kress, G., Jewitt, C., Bourne, J., Franks, A., Hardcastle, J., Jones, K., & Reid, E. (2005). *English in urban classrooms. A multimodal perspective on teaching and learning*. RoutledgeFalmer.

Kress, G., Jewitt, C., Ogborn, J., & Tsatsarelis, C. (2001). *Multimodal teaching and learning: The rhetorics of the science classroom*. Continuum.

Krizman, J., Marian, V., Shook, A., Skoe, E., & Kraus, N. (2012). Subcortical encoding of sound is enhanced in bilinguals and relates to executive function advantages. *Proceedings of the National Academy of Sciences of the United States of America, 109*(20), 7877–7881.

Kroll, J., & Bialystok, E. (2013). Understanding the consequences for bilinguals for language processing and cognition. *Journal of Cognitive Psychology, 25*(5), 497–514. http://dx.doi.org/10.1080/20445911.2013.799170

Kukulska-Hulme, A., & Wible, D. (2008). *Context at the crossroads of language learning and mobile learning*. Proceedings from ICCE 2008, October 27–31, 2008, Taiwan.

Kwon, J., Ghiso, M. P., & Martínez-Álvarez, P. (2019). Showcasing transnational and bilingual expertise: A case study of a Cantonese English emergent bilingual within an after-school program centering Latinx experiences. *Bilingual Research Journal, 42*(2), 164–177. https://doi.org/10.1080/15235882.2019.1589605

Lachat, M. (1999). *What policymakers and school administrators need to know about assessment reform for English language learners*. Brown University, Northeast and Islands Regional Education Laboratory.

Ladson-Billings, G. (1994). *The dreamkeepers: Successful teachers of African-American children*. Jossey-Bass.

Ladson-Billings, G. (1995). Toward a theory of culturally relevant pedagogy. *American Educational Research Journal, 32*(3), 465–491.

Lam, W. S. E., & Christiansen, M. S. (2022). Transnational Mexican youth negotiating languages, identities, and cultures online: A chronotopic lens. *TESOL Quarterly, 56*(3), 907–933.

Lam, W. S. E., & Warriner, D. S. (2012). Transnationalism and literacy: Investigating the mobility of people, languages, texts, and practices in contexts of migration. *Reading Research Quarterly, 47*(2), 191–215. https://doi.org/10.1002/RRQ.016.

Lambert, W. E. (1974). Culture and language as factors in learning and education. In F. E. Aboud & R. D. Meade (Eds.), *Cultural factors in learning and education* (pp. 91–122). Western Washington State College.

Lambert, W. E. (1984). *An overview of issues in immersion education*. In California State Department of Education (Ed.), *Studies on immersion education: A collection for United States educators* (pp. 8–30). California State Department of Education.

Lanauze, M., & Snow, C. (1989). The relation between first- and second-language writing skills: Evidence from Puerto Rican elementary school children in bilingual programs. *Linguistics and Education, 1*(4), 323–329.

Landry, R., & Bourhis, R. Y. (1997). Linguistic landscape and ethnolinguistic vitality. An empirical study. *Journal of Language and Social Psychology, 16*(1), 23–49. https://doi.org/10.1177/0261927X970161002

Language Instruction for Limited English Proficient and Immigrant Students. (2001). Public Law 107–110. Title III of No Child Left Behind (NCLB), Section 3001.

Larsen-Freeman, D., & Cameron, L. (2008). *Complex systems and applied linguistics.* Oxford University Press.

Lau Remedies. (1975). *Task-force findings specifying remedies available for eliminating past educational practices ruled unlawful under Lau v. Nichols.* Office for Civil Rights. http://www.stanford.edu/~kenro/LAU/LauRemedies.htm

Lau v. Nichols, 414 U.S. 563 (1974).

Lau, S. M. C., Juby-Smith, B., & Desbiens, I. (2017). Translanguaging for transgressive praxis: Promoting critical literacy in a multiage bilingual classroom. *Critical Inquiry in Language Studies, 14*(1), 99–127.

Lauen, D. L., & Gaddis, S. M. (2012). Shining a light or fumbling in the dark? The effects of NCLB's subgroup-specific accountability on student achievement. *Educational Evaluation and Policy Analysis, 34*(2), 185–208. http://dx.doi.org/10.3102/0162373711429989

Lave, J., & Wenger, E. (1991). *Situated learning: Legitimate peripheral participation.* Cambridge University Press.

Lee, J. S., & Oxelson, E. (2006). "It's not my job": K–12 teacher attitudes toward students' heritage language maintenance. *Bilingual Research Journal, 30*(2), 453–477.

Lee, J. W. (2017). *The politics of translingualism: After English.* Routledge.

Lee, J. W. (2022). *Locating translingualism.* Cambridge University Press.

Lemke, J. (1998). Multiplying meaning: Visual and verbal semiotics in scientific text. In J. R. Martin & R. Veel (Eds.), *Reading science* (pp. 87–113). Routledge.

Lenhart, A., & Madden, M. (2005). *Teen content creators and consumers.* Pew Internet and American Life Project.

Leonard, W. Y. (2017). Producing language reclamation by decolonising "language." *Language Documentation and Description, 14.* https://doi.org/10.25894/ldd146

Leu, D., Kinzer, C. K., Coiro, J., Castek, J., & Henry, L. A. (2013). New literacies: A dual level theory of the changing nature of literacy, instruction, and assessment. In D. E. Alvermann, N. J. Unrau, & R. B. Ruddell (Eds.), *Theoretical models and processes of reading* (6th ed.), pp. 1150–1181. International Reading Association.

Lewis, G., Jones, B., & Baker, C. (2012a). Translanguaging: Developing its conceptualisation and contextualisation. *Educational Research and Evaluation, 18*(7), 655–670.

Lewis, G., Jones, B., & Baker, C. (2012b). Translanguaging: Origins and development from school to street and beyond. *Educational Research and Evaluation, 18*(7), 641–654.

Li, C., Kruger, L. J., Beneville, M., Kimble, E., & Krishnan, K. (2018). The unintended consequences of high-stakes testing on English-language learners: Implications for the practice of school psychology. *School Psychology Forum, 12*(3), 79.

Li, W. (2011). Moment analysis and translanguaging space: Discursive construction of identities by multilingual Chinese youth in Britain. *Journal of Pragmatics, 43*(5), 1222–1235.

Li, W. (2014). Who's teaching whom? Co-learning in multilingual classrooms. In S. May (Ed.), *The multilingual turn: Implications for SLA, TESOL and bilingual education* (pp. 167–190). Routledge.

Li, W. (2018). Translanguaging as a practical theory of language. *Applied Linguistics, 39*(1), 9–30. https://doi.org/10.1093/applin/amx039

Li, W., & García, O. (2022). Not a first language but one repertoire: Translanguaging as a decolonizing project. *RELC Journal. A Journal of Language Teaching and Research*, *53*(2), 313–324. https://doi.org/10.1177/00336882221092841

Li, Z., & Xu, X. (2023). Designing a realistic peer-like embodied conversational agent for supporting children's storytelling. *arXiv*, 2304.09399, 2023. https://doi.org/10.48550/arXiv.2304.09399.

Lima Becker, M., & Oliveira, G. (2023). "This is a very sensitive point": Bilingual teachers' interactions with neo-nationalism in a two-way immersion program in the United States. *TESOL Quarterly*, *57*(3), 890–915. https://doi.org/10.1002/tesq.3244

Lin, A. M. Y. (2013). Classroom code-switching: Three decades of research. *Applied Linguistics Review*, *4*(1), 195–218.

Lindholm-Leary, K. (2001). *Dual language education*. Multilingual Matters.

Lindholm-Leary, K. J., & Block, N. C. (2010). Achievement in predominantly low SES/Hispanic dual language schools. *International Journal of Bilingual Education and Bilingualism*, *13*(1), 43–60. https://doi.org/10.1080/13670050902777546

Lindholm-Leary, K., & Genesee, F. (2014). Student outcomes in one-way and two-way immersion and Indigenous language education. *Journal of Immersion and Content-Based Language Education*, *2*(2), 165–180.

Linquanti, R. (2001). *The redesignation dilemma: Challenges and choices in fostering meaningful accountability for English learners*. University of California, Linguistic Minority Research Institute.

Linquanti, R., & Bailey, A. L. (2014). *Reprising the home language survey: Summary of a national working session on policies, practices, and tools for identifying potential English learners*. Council of Chief State School Officers. http://www.ccsso.org/Documents/2014/CCSSO%20Common%20EL%20Definition%20Reprising%20the%20Home%20Language%20Survey%2001242014.pdf

Linquanti, R., & Cook, H. G. (2013). *Toward a "common definition of English learner": Guidance for states and state assessment consortia in defining and addressing policy and technical issues and options*. Council of Chief State School Officers.

Lippi-Green, R. (1997). *English with an accent: Language, ideology, and discrimination in the United States*. Routledge.

Llomaki, L., Paavola, S., Lakkala, M., & Kantosalo, A. (2016). Digital competence—An emergent boundary concept for policy and educational research. *Education and Information Technologies*, *21*(3), 655–679.

Llopart, M., & Esteban-Guitart, M. (2016). Funds of knowledge in 21st century societies: inclusive educational practices for under-represented students. A literature review. *Journal of Curriculum Studies*, *50*(2), 145–161. https://doi.org/10.1080/00220272.2016.1247913

Long, C. (2023, July). Secretary of Education Miguel Cardona: "Time to end toxic disrespect." *National Education Association News*. https://www.nea.org/nea-today/all-news-articles/secretary-education-miguel-cardona-time-end-toxic-disrespect

Lopez, A. A. (2023a). Enabling multilingual practices in English language proficiency assessments for young learners. In K. Raza, D. Reynolds, & C. Coombe (Eds.), *Handbook of multilingual TESOL in practice*. Springer. https://doi.org/10.1007/978-981-19-9350-3_24

Lopez, A. (2023b). Examining how Spanish-speaking English language learners use their linguistic resources and language modes in a dual language mathematics assessment task.

Journal of Latinos and Education, 22(1), 198–210. https://doi.org/10.1080/15348431.2020.1731693

López, A. A., Guzmán-Orth, D., & Turkan, S. (2014, March). A study on the use of translanguaging to assess the content knowledge of emergent bilingual students. Paper presented at the Invited Colloquium, Negotiating the Complexities of Multilingual Assessment at the 2014 AAAL Conference. Portland, United States.

López, A. A., Turkan, S., & Guzman-Orth, D. (2017). *Conceptualizing the use of translanguaging in initial content assessments for newly arrived emergent bilingual students* (Research Report). Educational Testing Service. http://onlinelibrary.wiley.com/doi/10.1002/ets2.12140/full

López, F. (2016). When desegregation limits opportunities to Latino Youth: The strange case of the Tucson Unified School District. *Chicanx-Latinx Law Review, 34*(1), 1–34. https://www.jstor.org/stable/48648092

López, F., & Santibañez, L. (2018). Teacher preparation for emergent bilingual students: Implications of evidence for policy. *Education Policy Analysis Archives, 26*(36). https://doi.org/10.14507/epaa.26.2866

López, F., Scanlan, M., & Gundrum, B. (2013). Preparing teachers of English language learners: Empirical evidence and policy implications. *Education Policy Analysis Archives,* 2120. http://dx.doi.org/10.14507/epaa.v21n20.2013

López, G. L. (2001). The value of hard work: Lessons on parent involvement from an (im)migrant household. *Harvard Educational Review, 71*(3), 416–437.

López, M. P. (2005). Reflections on educating Latino and Latina undocumented children: Beyond Plyler v. Doe. *Seton Hall Law Review, 35,* 1373–1406.

Lovato, K. (2019). Forced separations: A qualitative examination of how Latino/a adolescents cope with parental deportation. *Children and Youth Services Review, 98,* 42–50. https://doi.org/10.1016/j.childyouth.2018.12.012

Lowenhaupt, R. & Reeves, T. (2017). Changing demographics, changing practices: Teacher learning in new immigrant destinations. *Journal of Professional Capital and Community, 2(1),* 50-71. https://doi.org/10.1108/JPCC-09-2016-0023.

Lucas, T., & Grinberg, J. (2008). Responding to the linguistic reality of mainstream classrooms: Preparing all teachers to teach English language learners. In M. Cochran-Smith, S. Feiman-Nemser, & J. McIntyre (Eds.), *Handbook of research in teacher education: Enduring issues in changing contexts* (3rd ed., pp. 606–636). Lawrence Earlbaum.

Lucas, T., & Katz, A. (1994). Reframing the debate: The roles of native languages in English-only programs for language minority students. *TESOL Quarterly, 28*(3), 537–562.

Machimana, P. N. N., & Genis, G. (2024). Centering indigenous knowledge through multimodal approaches in English first additional language learning. *Apples-Journal of Applied Language Studies, 18*(1), 1–20.

Macías, R. F. (1994). Inheriting sins while seeking absolution: Language diversity and national statistical data sets. In D. Spener (Ed.), *Adult biliteracy in the United States* (pp. 15–45). Center for Applied Linguistics and Delta Systems.

MacSwan, J. (2017). A multilingual perspective on translanguaging. *American Educational Research Journal, 54*(1), 167–201. https://doi.org/10.3102/0002831216683935

Madden, M., Lenhart, A., Duggan, M., Cortesi, S., & Gasser, U. (2013). Teens and technology. *Pew Research Center Report.* http://www.pewinternet.org/Reports/2013/03/teens-and-tech.aspx

Magadán, C. (2015). *Integración de la tecnología educativa en el aula. Enseñar lengua y literatura con las TIC*. Cenage Learning.

Magadán, C. (2021). Textos figurados: Apuntes sobre la escritura multimodal en intercambios adolescentes. *Enunciación, 26*, 102–119.

Mahoney, K. (2017). *The assessment of emergent bilinguals: Supporting English language learners*. Multilingual Matters.

Makoni, S., & Pennycook, A. (2007). *Disinventing and reconstituting languages*. Multilingual Matters.

Mangual Figueroa, A. (2011). Citizenship and education in the homework completion routine. *Anthropology & Education Quarterly, 42*(3), 263–280. https://doi.org/10.1111/j.1548-1492.2011.01131.x

Maninger, R. M. (2006). Successful technology integration: Student test scores improved in an English literature course through the use of supportive devices. *TechTrends: Linking Research and Practice to Improve Learning, 50*(5), 37–45.

Manyak, P. (2004). What did she say? Translation in a primary-grade English immersion class. *Multicultural Perspectives, 6*(1), 12–18. https://doi.org/10.1207/S15327892mcp0601_3

Marshall, F., & Toohey, K. (2010). Representing family. Community funds of knowledge, bilingualism and multimodality. *Harvard Education Review, 80*(2), 221–241.

Martínez, E. (2002). Fragmented community, fragmented schools: The implementation of educational policy for Latino immigrants. In S. Wortham, E. G. Murillo, Jr., & E. T. Hamann (Eds.), *Education in the new Latino diaspora: Policy and the politics of identity* (pp. 143–168). Ablex Publishing.

Martínez, R. A. (2017). Dual language education and the erasure of Chicanx, Latinx, and Indigenous Mexican children: A call to re-imagine (and imagine beyond) bilingualism. *Texas Education Review, 5*(1), 81–92.

Martínez, R. A., Hikida, M., & Durán, L. (2018). *Unpacking ideologies of linguistic purism: How dual language teachers make sense of everyday translanguaging*. Routledge.

Martínez, R. A., & Morales, P. (2014). ¿Puras groserías?: Rethinking the role of profanity and graphic humor in Latin@ students' bilingual wordplay. *Anthropology & Education Quarterly, 45*(4), 337–354. https://doi.org/10.1111/aeq.12074

Martiniello, M. (2008). Language and the performance of English language learners in math word problems. *Harvard Educational Review, 98*(2), 333–368.

Martin-Jones, M., & Jones, K. (Eds.). (2000). *Multilingual literacies: Comparative perspectives on research and practice*. John Benjamins.

Massachusetts Question 2. (2002). G.L. C. 71A.

Maxwell-Jolly, J., Gándara, P. (2012). Teaching all our children well. Teachers and teaching to close the academic achievement gap. In T. Timar & J. Maxwell Jolly (Eds.), *Narrowing the achievement gap: Perspectives and strategies for challenging times* (pp. 163–186). Harvard Education Press.

May, S. (2011). *Language and minority rights: Ethnicity, nationalism and the politics of language*. Routledge.

May, S. (Ed.). (2015). *Addressing the multilingual turn: Implications for SLA, TESOL and bilingual education* (2nd ed.). Routledge.

Mazak, C., & Carroll, K. (Eds.). (2017). *Translanguaging in higher education. Beyond monolingual ideologies*. Multilingual Matters.

Mazur, E. (2005). Online and writing: Teen blogs as mines of adolescent data. *Teaching of Psychology, 32*(3), 180–182.

McCaffrey, K. T., & Taha, M. C. (2019). Rethinking the digital divide: Smartphones as translanguaging tools among Middle Eastern refugees in New Jersey. *Annals of Anthropological Practice, 43*(2), 26–38. https://doi.org/10.1111/napa.12126

McIntyre, E., Rosebery, A., & González, N. (Eds.). (2001). *Classroom diversity: Connecting curriculum to students' lives.* Heinemann.

McKay, J., & Devlin, M. (2016). "Low income doesn't mean stupid and destined for failure": Challenging the deficit discourse around students from low SES backgrounds in higher education. *International Journal of Inclusive Education, 20*(4), 347–363. https://doi.org/10.1080/13603116.2015.1079273

McNeil L. (2009). Standardization, defensive teaching, and the problems of control. In A. Dader, M. P. Baltodano, & R. D. Torres (Eds.), *The critical pedagogy reader* (pp. 385–396). Routledge.

Mediratta, K., Fruchter, N., & Lewis, A. (2002). *Organizing for school reform: How communities are finding their voice and reclaiming their public schools.* New York University Institute for Education and Social Policy. http://steinhardt.nyu.edu/iesp/papers #2002

Mehan, H., Datnow, A., Bratton, E., Tellez, C., Friedlander, D., & Ngo, T. (1992). Untracking and college enrollment (Cooperative Agreement No. R117G10022). University of California, San Diego, National Center for Research on Cultural Diversity and Second Language Learning.

Melamed, J. (2011). *Represent and destroy. Rationalizing violence in the new racial capitalism.* Minnesota University Press.

Menchaca, M., & Valencia, R. R. (1990). Anglo-Saxon ideologies in the 1920s-1930s: Their impact on the segregation of Mexican students in California. *Anthropology & Education Quarterly, 21*(3), 222–249.

Menken, K. (2008). *English language learners left behind: Standardized testing as language policy.* Multilingual Matters.

Menken, K. (2010). NCLB and English language learners: Challenges and consequences. *Theory Into Practice, 49*(2), 121–128. https://www.jstor.org/stable/40650725

Menken, K. (2013). Emergent bilingual students in secondary school: Along the academic language and literacy continuum. *Language Teaching, 46*(4), 438–476.

Menken, K., & García, O. (Eds.). (2010). *Negotiating language policies in schools. Educators as policymakers.* Routledge.

Menken, K., & Kleyn, T. (2009). The difficult road for long-term English learners. *Educational Leadership, 66*(7). http://doi.org/10.1080/15348431.2011.605686 and http://www.ascd.org/publications/educational_leadership/apr09/vol66/num07/The _Difficult_Road_for_Long-Term_English_Learners.aspx.

Menken, K., & Solorza, C. (2013). Where have all the bilingual programs gone?!: Why prepared school leaders are essential for bilingual education. *Journal of Multilingual Education Research, 4*(1), 9–39.

Menken, K., & Solorza, C. (2014). No child left bilingual: Accountability and the elimination of bilingual education programs in New York City schools. *Educational Policy, 8*(1), 96–125.

Menken, K., Kleyn, T., & Chae, N. (2012). Spotlight on long-term English language learners: Characteristics and prior schooling experiences of an invisible population. *International Multilingual Research Journal, 6*(2), 121–142.

Mercado, C. (2005a). Reflections on the study of households in New York City and Long Island: A different route, a common destination. In N. González, L. C. Moll, &

C. Amanti (Eds.), *Funds of knowledge: Theorizing practices in households, communities, and classrooms* (pp. 233–255). Lawrence Erlbaum.

Mercado, C. (2005b). Seeing what's there: Language and literacy funds of knowledge in New York Puerto Rican homes. In A. C. Zentella (Ed.), *Building on strength: Language and literacy in Latino families and communities* (pp. 134–147). Teachers College Press.

Mercer, J. R. (1989). Alternative paradigms for assessment in a pluralistic society. In J. A. Banks & C. M. Banks (Eds.), *Multicultural education* (pp. 289–303). Allyn & Bacon.

Messick, S. (1989). Validity. In R. L. Linn (Ed.), *Educational measurement* (3rd ed., pp. 13–103). Macmillan.

Mignolo, W. (2000). *Local histories/global designs: Coloniality, subaltern knowledges, and border thinking.* Princeton University Press.

Mignolo, W., & Walsh, C. (2018). *On decoloniality: Concepts, analytics, praxis.* Duke University Press.

Milk-Bonilla, C., & Valenzuela, A. (2023). Relational pedagogies and the building of a social architecture of authentic cariño in the teaching of healing practices at academia cuauhtli. In L. Dorner, D. Palmer, C. Cervantes-Soon, D. Heiman, & E. Crawford (Eds.), *Critical consciousness in dual language bilingual education: Case studies on policy and practice* (pp. 168–175). Routledge. https://doi.org/10.4324/9781003240594-21

Millard, M. (2015). *State funding mechanisms for English language learners.* Education Commission of the States. http://www.ecs.org/clearinghouse/01/16/94/11694.pdf

Miller, H. (2016). The MIT-Haiti Initiative: An international engagement. *MIT Faculty Newsletter, 29*(1). http://web.mit.edu/fnl/volume/291/miller.htmlhttp://web.mit.edu/fnl/volume/291/miller.html

Mills, K. A., Davis-Warra, J., Sewell, M., & Anderson, M. (2016). Indigenous ways with literacies: Transgenerational, multimodal, placed, and collective. *Language and Education, 30*(1), 1–21. https://doi.org/10.1080/09500782.2015.1069836

Minicucci, C., & Olsen, L. (1992, Spring). *Programs for secondary limited English proficient students: A California study* (Occasional Papers in Bilingual Education, No. 5). National Clearinghouse for Bilingual Education.

MIT-Haiti Initiative. (n.d.). Resources/STEM tools. https://haiti.mit.edu/resources/

Moll, L. C., Amanti, C., Neff, D., & Gonzalez, N. (1992). Funds of knowledge for teaching: Using a qualitative approach to connect homes and classrooms. *Theory Into Practice, 31,* 132–141.

Moll, L. C., & Greenberg, J. B. (1990). Creating zones of possibilities: Combining social contexts for instruction. In L. C. Moll (Ed.), *Vygotsky and education: Instructional implications and applications of sociohistorical psychology* (pp. 319–348). Cambridge University Press.

Montero, K., Newmaster, S., & Ledger, S. (2014). Exploring early reading instructional strategies to advance the print literacy development of adolescent SLIFE. *Journal of Adolescent and Adult Literacy, 58*(1), 59–69.

Morgan, I. (2022, December). *Equal is not good enough: An analysis of school funding equity across the U.S. and within each state.* The Education Trust. https://edtrust.org/wp-content/uploads/2014/09/Equal-Is-Not-Good-Enough-December-2022.pdf

Morita-Mullaney, T., Renn, J., & Chiu, M. M. (2020). Obscuring equity in dual language bilingual education: A longitudinal study of emergent bilingual achievement, course placements, and grades. *TESOL Quarterly*, *54*(3), 685–718. http://dx.doi.org/10.1002/tesq.592

Morrell, E. (2008). *Critical literacy and urban youth: Pedagogies of access, dissent, and liberation*. Routledge.

Mun, R. U., Langley, S. D., Ware, S., Gubbins, E. J., Siegle, D., Callahan, C. McCoach, D. B., & Hamilton, R. (2016). *Effective practices for identifying and serving English learners in gifted education: A systematic review of the literature*. University of Connecticut, National Center for Research on Gifted Education.

Muñoz-Sandoval, A. F., Cummins, J., Alvarado, C. G., & Ruef, M. L. (1998). *Bilingual verbal abilities test: Comprehensive manual*. The Riverside Publishing Company.

Murnane, R. J., & Phillips, R. R. (1981). Learning by doing, vintage, and selection: Three pieces of the puzzle relating teaching experience and teaching performance. *Economics of Education Review*, *1*(4), 453–465.

Myers-Scotton, C. (2005). *Multiple voices: An introduction to bilingualism*. Wiley.

National Assessment of Education Progress (NAEP). (2022). NAEP reading assessment. https://www.nationsreportcard.gov/highlights/reading/2022/

Nagy, W., & Anderson, R. (1984). How many words are there in printed school English? *Reading Research Quarterly*, *19*, 304–330.

Najarro, I. (2024, April 26). Title III funding for English learners, explained. *Education Week*. https://www.edweek.org/teaching-learning/title-iii-funding-for-english-learners-explained/2024/04

National Center for Education Statistics (NCES). (2018). The digital divide: Differences in home internet access. https://nces.ed.gov/blogs/nces/post/the-digital-divide-differences-in-home-internet-access

National Center for Research on Gifted Education. (2016). *NCRGE gifted English learner theory of change* (Appendix B). Storrs.

National Clearinghouse for English Language Acquisition and Language Instruction Educational Programs (NCELA). (2006). Frequently asked questions. http://www.ncela.gwu.edu/faqs/http://www.ncela.gwu.edu/faqs/

National Commission on Excellence in Education. (1983). A nation at risk: The imperative for educational reform. *The Elementary School Journal*, *84*(2), 113–130.

National Research Council (NRC). (2011). *Allocating federal funds for state programs for English language learners. Panel to review alternative sources for the limited English proficiency allocation formula under Title III, Part A., Elementary and Secondary Education Act, Committee on National Statistics and Board Testing and Assessment*. National Academies Press.

National Task Force on Early Childhood Education for Hispanics. (2007). Para nuestros niños: Expanding and improving early education for Hispanics. http://www.ecehispanic.org/

National Telecommunications and Information Administration (NTIA). (2011). *Digital nation: Expanding internet usage*. US Department of Commerce.

Navarrete, C., & Gustke, C. (1996). *A guide to performance assessment for linguistically diverse students*. Evaluation Assistance Center—Western Region, New Mexico Highlands University.

NCES. (2018, October 31). The digital divide: Differences in home internet access. *NCES Blog*. https://nces.ed.gov/blogs/nces/post/the-digital-divide-differences-in-home-internet-access

Ndhlovu, F. (2018). Omphile and his soccer ball: Colonialism, methodology, translanguaging research. *Multilingual Margins: A Journal of Multilingualism from the Periphery, 5*(2), 2–19. https://doi.org/10.14426/mm.v5i2.95

Neal, D., & Schanzenbach, D. W. (2010). Left behind by design: Proficiency counts and test-based accountability. *The Review of Economics and Statistics, 92*(2), 263–283.

New London Group. (1996). A pedagogy of multiliteracies: Designing social futures. *Harvard Educational Review, 66*(1), 60–92.

New York City Public Schools. (2022–23). ELL demographics at a glance (2022–2023). https://infohub.nyced.org/docs/default-source/default-document-library/2022-23-ell-demographics-at-a-glance.pdf

Nichols, S. L., & Berliner, D. C. (2007). *Collateral damage: How high stakes testing corrupts America's schools*. Harvard University Press.

No Child Left Behind Act of 2001 (NCLB). (2001). 20 U.S.C. 6301 et seq. (2002).

Noguerón-Liu, S. (2020). Expanding the knowledge base in literacy instruction and assessment: Biliteracy and translanguaging perspectives from families, communities and classrooms. *Reading Research Quarterly, 55*(51), 5307–5318. https://doi.org/10.1002/rrq.354

Noguerón-Liu, S., Shimek, C. H., & Bahlmann Bollinger, C. (2020). "Dime de que se trató/Tell me what it was about": Exploring emergent bilinguals' linguistic resources in reading assessments with parent participation. *Journal of Early Childhood Literacy, 20*(2), 411–433.

Nores, M., Belfield, C., Barnett, W., & Schweinhart, L. (2005). Updating the economic impacts of the High/Scope Perry Preschool Program. *Educational Evaluation and Policy Analysis, 27*(3), 245–261.

Norton, B. (2013). *Identity and language learning: Extending the conversation* (2nd ed.) Multilingual Matters.

Nuñez, I. (2018). *Literacies of surveillance: Transfronterizo children translanguaging identity across borders, inspectors and surveillance*. Doctoral dissertation, University of Texas, Austin.

Nuñez, I. (2021). "Because we have to speak English at school": Transfronterizx children translanguaging identity to cross the academic border. *Research in the Teaching of English, 56*(1), 10–32. https://doi.org/10.58680/rte202131341

Nuñez, I. (2022). "Siento que el inglés está tumbando mi español": A transfronteriza child's embodied critical language awareness. *International Journal of Bilingual Education and Bilingualism, 25*(7), 2608–2620.

Nuñez, I. (2023). Toward border-crossing biliteracies: Pláticas of midwest transnational Latinx families reading and (re) writing the world. *Reading Research Quarterly, 58*(4), 475–494. https://doi.org/10.1002/rrq.512

Nuñez, I., & Urrieta, L., Jr. (2021). Transfronterizo children's literacies of surveillance and the cultural production of border crossing identities on the US–Mexico border. *Anthropology & Education Quarterly, 52*(1), 21–41. https://doi.org/10.1111/aeq.12360

Nuñez, I., Villarreal, D. A., DeJulio, S., Harvey, R., & Cardenas Curiel, L. (2021). Sustaining bilingual–biliterate identities: Latinx preservice teachers' narrative representations of bilingualism and biliteracy across time and space. *Journal of Teacher Education, 72*(4), 419–430. https://doi.org/10.1177/0022487120954360

NYC DoE, Department of English Language Learners and Student Support. (2013–2014). *School tear 2013–2014: Demographic report*. New York City Department of Education.

O'Halloran, K. L. (2008). Systemic functional-multimodal discourse analysis (SF-MDA): Constructing ideational meaning using language and visual imagery. *Visual Communication, 7*(4), 443–475. https://doi.org/10.1177/1470357208096210

Oakes, J. (1985). *Keeping track: How schools structure inequality.* Yale University Press.

Oakes, J. (1990). *Multiplying inequalities: The effects of race, social class, and tracking on opportunities to learn mathematics and science.* RAND.

Oakes, J., & Saunders, M. (2002). *Access to textbooks, instructional materials, equipment, and technology: Inadequacy and inequality in California's public schools, found in the Williams Watch Series* (wws-rr001-1002). UCLA/IDEA.

Office of English Language Acquisition (OELA). (2006). *Biennial evaluation report to congress on the implementation of title III, Part A of the ESEA.*

Office of English Language Acquisition (OELA). (2015, October). English learner students who are Hispanic/Latino: Fast facts. https://www2.ed.gov/about/offices/list/oela/fast-facts/index.html

Office of English Language Acquisition (OELA). (2021, February). *English learners in gifted and talented programs.* Brief.

Office of English Language Acquisition (OELA). (2021, August). *English learners with disabilities.* Brief.

Office of English Language Acquisition (OELA). (2022, August). *English learners, Demographic trends.* ELA Brief.

Office of English Language Acquisition (OELA). (2023). *Educators of English learners: Availability, projected need, and teacher preparation.* U.S. Department of Education. https://ncela.ed.gov/sites/default/files/2023-06/ELsTeachers-Infographic-20230616-508.pdf

Office of English Language Acquisition (OELA). (2023, February). Languages spoken by English learners: Fast facts. https://ncela.ed.gov/sites/default/files/2023-02/OELATopLanguagesFS-508.

Office of English Language Acquisition (OELA). (2023, June). Graduation rates for English learners. https://ncela.ed.gov/sites/default/files/2023-06/ELGradRates-FS-20230602-508.pdf

Olivos, E. M. (2006). *The power of parents: A critical perspective of bicultural parent involvement in public schools.* Peter Lang.

Olivos, E. M., Jiménez-Castellanos, O., & Ochoa, A. M. (2011). *Bicultural parent engagement: Advocacy and empowerment.* Teachers College Press.

Olsen, L. (1997). *Made in America.* The Free Press.

Olsen, L. (2014). *Meeting the unique needs of long term English learners: A guide for educators.* National Education Association.

OpenAI. (2023). ChatGPT (Mar14 version) [Large Language Model]. https://chat.openai.com/chat

Orfield, G. (2001). *Schools more separate: Consequences of a decade of resegregation.* The Civil Rights Project, Harvard University.

Orfield. G., & Frankenberg, E. (May 15, 2014). *Brown at 60: Great progress, a long retreat and an uncertain future.* The Civil Rights Project. https://civilrightsproject.ucla.edu/research/k-12-education/integration-and-diversity/brown-at-60-great-progress-a-long-retreat-and-an-uncertain-future/Brown-at-60-051814.pdf

Organisation for Economic Co-operation and Development (OECD). (2005). The definition and selection of key competencies: Executive summary. *The DeSeCo Project.* http://www.oecd.org/dataoecd/47/61/35070367.pdf

Ortega, L. (2014). Ways forward for a bi/multilingual turn in SLA. In S. May (Ed.), *The multilingual turn: Implications for SLA, TESOL and bilingual education* (pp. 32–53). Routledge.

Ortiz, A. (2001). *English language learners with special needs: Effective instructional strategies*. Center for Applied Linguistics. http://www.cal.org/resources/digest/0808ortiz .htmlwww.cal.org/resources/digest/0808ortiz.html

Ortiz, A. A., Fránquiz, M. E., & Lara, G. P. (2020). The education of emergent bilinguals with disabilities: State of practice. *Bilingual Research Journal, 43*(3), 245–252. https:// doi.org/10.1080/15235882.2020.1823734

Otheguy, R., García, O., & Reid, W. (2015). Clarifying translanguaging and deconstructing named languages: A perspective from linguistics. *Applied Linguistics Review, 6*(3), 281–307. https://doi.org/10.1515/applirev-2015-0014

Otheguy, R., García, O., & Reid, W. (2019). A translanguaging view of the linguistic system of bilinguals. *Applied Linguistics Review, 10*(4), 625–651. https://doi.org/10 .1515/applirev-2018-0020.

Otheguy, R., & Otto, R. (1980). The myth of static maintenance in bilingual education. *Modern Language Journal, 64*(3), 350–357.

Ovando, C., & Collier, V. (1998). *Bilingual and ESL classrooms: Teaching in multicultural contexts* (2nd ed.). McGraw-Hill.

Pacheco, M., & Chávez-Moreno, L. (2022). Bilingual education for self-determination: Re-centering Chicana/o/x and Latina/o/x student voices. *Bilingual Research Journal, 44*(4), 522–538. https://doi.org/10.1080/15235882.2022.2052203

Padrón, Y. N., & Waxman, H. C. (1999). Classroom observations of the five standards for effective teaching in urban classrooms with ELLs. *Teaching and Change, 7*(1), 79–100.

Palmer, D. (2010). Race, power, and equity in a multiethnic urban elementary school with a dual language "strand" program. *Anthropology & Education Quarterly, 41*(1), 94–114.

Palmer, D. K., Cervantes-Soon, C., Dorner, L., & Heiman, D. (2019). Bilingualism, biliteracy, biculturalism, and critical consciousness for all: Proposing a fourth fundamental goal for two-way dual language education. *Theory into Practice, 58*(2), 121–133.

Palmer, D., Cervantes-Soon, C. & Freire, J. (2024). When You Let White Kids in the Door: Unpacking Whiteness and Integration in Dual-language Bilingual Education. In A. Kibbler, A. Walqui, G. C. Bunch and C. J. Faltis (Eds.), *Equity in multilingual schools and communities: Celebrating the contributions of Guadalupe Valdés* (pp. 231-242). Multilingual Matters.

Palmer, D. K., & García-Mateus, S. (2023). *Gentrification and bilingual education: A Texas TWBE school across seven years*. Rowman & Littlefield Publishing Group.

Palmer, D. K., & Henderson, K. I. (2016). Dual language bilingual education placement practices: Educator discourses about emergent bilingual students in two program types. *International Multilingual Research Journal, 10*(1), 17–30. http://dx.doi.org/10 .1080/19313152.2015.1118668

Palmer, D. K., & Martínez, R. A. (2016). Developing biliteracy: What do teachers really need to know about language? *Language Arts, 93*(5), 379–384.

Palmer, D. K., Martínez, R. A., Mateus, S. G., & Henderson, K. (2014). Reframing the debate on language separation: Toward a vision for translanguaging pedagogies in the dual language classroom. *The Modern Language Journal, 98*(3), 757–772. https://doi .org/10.1111/modl.12121

Paris, D., & Alim, S. (2014). What are we seeking to sustain through culturally sustaining pedagogy? *Harvard Education Review, 84*(1), 85–100.

Park, S., & Holloway, S. D. (2017). The effects of school-based parental involvement on academic achievement at the child and elementary school level: A longitudinal study. *The Journal of Educational Research, 110*(1), 1–16.

Parra, E. B., Evans, C. A., Fletcher, T., & Combs, M. C. (2014). The psychological impact of English language immersion on elementary age English language learners. *Journal of Multilingual Education Research, 5*(1), 33–65.

Parrish, T. B. (1994). A cost analysis of alternative instructional models for limited English proficient students in California. *Journal of Education Finance, 19,* 256–278.

Parrish, T. B., Linquanti, R., Merickel, A., Quick, H. E., Laird, J., & Esra, P. (2002). *Effects of the implementation of Proposition 227 on the education of English learners K–12: Year two report.* American Institutes for Research. http://lmri.ucsb.edu/resdiss /pdf files/062802yr2finalreport.pdf

Partika, A., Johnson, A. D., Phillips, D. A., Luk, G., Dericks, A., & Tulsa SEED Study Team. (2021). Dual language supports for dual language learners? Exploring preschool classroom instructional supports for DLLs' early learning outcomes. *Early Childhood Research Quarterly, 56,* 124–138. https://doi.org/10.1016/j.ecresq.2021 .03.011

Passel, J., & Cohn, D. V. (2009). A portrait of unauthorized immigrants in the United States. Pew Hispanic Center. http://www.pewhispanic.org/2009/04/14/a-portrait-of -unauthorized-immigrants-in-the-united-states/

Passel, J., & Krogstad, J. M. (2023, November 16). What we know about unauthorized immigrants living in the U.S. Pew Research Center. https://www.pewresearch.org/short -read/2023/11/16/what-we-know-about-unauthorized-immigrants-living-in-the-us/

Paulsrud, B. A., Tian, Z., & Toth, J. (Eds.). (2021). *English medium instruction and translanguaging.* Multilingual Matters.

PDK International. (2015, September). Testing doesn't measure up for Americans: 47th annual PDK/Gallup poll of the public's attitudes about the public schools. *Phi Delta Kappan.* http://pdkpoll2015.pdkintl.org

Peal, E., & Lambert, W. (1962). The relation of bilingualism to intelligence. *Psychological Monographs, 76*(546), 1–23.

Pedraza, P., & Rivera, M. (Eds.). (2005). *Latino education: An agenda for community action research.* Routledge.

Pennock-Román, M. (1994). Background characteristics and future plans of high-scoring GRE general test examinees. Research report ETS-RR9412 submitted to EXXON Education Foundation. Educational Testing Service.

Pennycook, A. (2006). *Global Englishes and transcultural flows.* Routledge.

Pennycook, A. (2007). The myth of English as an international language. In S. Makoni & A. Pennycook (Eds.), *Disinventing and reconstituting languages* (pp. 90–115). Multilingual Matters.

Pennycook, A. (2010). *Language as a local practice.* Routledge.

Pennycook, A. (2024). *Language assemblages.* Cambridge University Press.

Pérez Carreón, G., Drake, C., & Calabrese Barton, A. (2005). The importance of presence: Immigrant parents' school engagement experiences. *American Educational Research Journal, 42*(3), 465–498.

Pérez Rosario, V. (2014). *The CUNY-NYSIEB guide to translanguaging in Latino literature.* CUNY-NYSIEB, The Graduate Center, The City University of New York.

http://www.nysieb.ws.gc.cuny.edu/files/2015/02/CUNY-NYSIEB-Latino-Literature
-Guide-Final-January-2015.pdf

Pérez, G. (2021). *Beyond representation: Uncovering the role of language and cognition for multicompetent students in engineering and science.* Doctoral dissertation, Stanford University.

Pérez, G., González-Howard, M., & Suárez, E. (2022). Special issue: Examining translanguaging in science and engineering education research. *Journal of Research in Science Teaching, 59*(9), 1733–1735. https://doi.org/10.1002/tea.21825

Pérez, G., González-Howard, M., & Suárez, E. (in press). Translanguaging in science and engineering education. *Journal of Research in Science Teaching* (entire issue).

Petrovic, J. E. (2005). The conservative restoration and neoliberal defenses of bilingual education. *Language Policy, 4*(4), 395–416. http://doi.org/10.1007/s10993-005-2888-y

Pew Research Center. (2024). Internet, broadband fact sheet. https://www.pewresearch.org/internet/fact-sheet/internet-broadband/

Peyton, J. K., Ranard, D. A., & McGinnis, S. (Eds.). (2001). *Heritage languages in America: Preserving a national resource.* CAL/ERIC/Delta Systems Inc.

Philips, S. U. (1983). *The invisible culture: Communication in classroom and community on the Warm Springs Indian Reservation.* Waveland Press.

Pierson, A. E., Clark, D. B., & Brady, C. E. (2021). Scientific modeling and translanguaging: A multilingual and multimodal approach to support science learning and engagement. *Science Education, 105*(4), 776–813.

Pimentel, C. (2011). The color of language: The racialized educational trajectory of an emerging bilingual student. *Journal of Latinos and Education, 10*(4), 335–353. http://doi.org/10.1080/15348431.2011.605686

Pitt, A., & Britzman, D. (2003). Speculations on qualities of difficult knowledge in teaching and learning: An experiment in psychoanalytic research. *Qualitative Studies in Education, 16*(6), 755–776.

Poehner, M. E. (2007). Beyond the test: L2 dynamic assessment and the transcendence of mediated learning. *The Modern Language Journal, 91*(3), 323–340.

Pollard-Durodola, S. D. (2020). Vocabulary instruction among English learners. In E. Cardenas-Hagan (Ed.), *Literacy foundations for English learners.* Brookes Publishing.

Portes, A. (1998). Social capital: Its origins and applications in modern sociology. *Annual Review of Sociology, 24*, 1–24.

Poushter, J. (2016, February 22). *Smartphone ownership and internet usage continues to climb in emerging economies.* Pew Research Center. http://www.pewglobal.org/2016/02/22/smartphone-ownership-and-internet-usage-continues-to-climb-in-emerging-economies/

Poza, L., Brooks, M., & Valdés, G. (2014). Entre familia: Immigrant parents' strategies for involvement in children's schooling. *The School Community Journal, 24*(1), 119–148.

Pratt, R. (1892). Kill the Indian, save the man. In *Official report of the Nineteenth Annual Conference of Charities and Correction* (pp. 46–59).

Privette, C., & Saechao, K. (2024). Black languaging IS translanguaging: We not just talkin bout it, we bout it bout it! *Perspectives of the ASHA Special Interest Group,* 1–10. https://doi.org/10.1044/2024_PERSP-23-00297

Quintero, D., & Hansen, M. (2021). As we tackle school segregation, don't forget about English learner students. *Brookings* (January 14, 2021). https://www.brookings.edu/articles/as-we-tackle-school-segregation-dont-forget-about-english-learner-students/

Rafa, A., Erwin, B., Brixey, E., McCann, Me., & Perez, Z. (2020). *Fifty state comparison.* Education Commission of the States. https://www.ecs.org/50-state-comparison-english-learner-policies/

Ramirez, A. Y. F. (2003). Dismay and disappointment: Parental involvement of Latino immigrant parents. *The Urban Review, 35*(2), 93–110.

Ramírez, J. D. (1992). Executive summary, final report: Longitudinal study of structured English immersion strategy, early-exit and late-exit transitional bilingual education programs for language-minority children. *Bilingual Research Journal, 16*(1–2), 1–62.

Rebell, M. (2007). Professional rigor, public engagement and judicial review: A proposal for enhancing the validity of education adequacy studies. *Teachers College Record, 109*(4). https://doi.org/10.1177/016146810710900604

Rebell, M. (2009). *Courts and kids. Pursuing educational equity through the state courts.* Chicago University Press.

Restrepo-Widney, C., & Sembiante, S. F. (2023). Culturally sustaining practices in a culturally and linguistically diverse preschool classroom. In K. Raza, D. Reynolds, & C. Coombe (Eds.), *Handbook of multilingual TESOL in practice* (pp. 23–40). Springer Nature Singapore. http://doi.org/10.1007/978-981-19-9350-3_2

Reyes, A. (2006). Reculturing principals as leaders for cultural and linguistic diversity. In K. Téllez & H. C. Waxman (Eds.), *Preparing quality educators for English language learners* (pp. 145–156). Lawrence Erlbaum.

Ricciardelli, L. A. (1992). Bilingualism and cognitive development in relation to threshold theory. *Journal of Psycholinguistic Research, 21*, 301–316.

Ricento, T. (2005). Problems with the "language as resource" discourse in the promotion of heritage languages in the U.S.A. *Journal of Sociolinguistics, 9*(3), 348–368. https://doi.org/10.1111/j.1360-6441.2005.00296.x

Riches, C., & Genesee, F. (2006). Cross-linguistic and cross-modal aspects of literacy development. In F. Genesee, K. Lindholm-Leary, W. Saunders, & D. Christian (Eds.), *Educating English language learners: A synthesis of research evidence* (pp. 64–108). Cambridge University Press.

Ríos-Aguilar, C., González Canché, M. S., & Sabetghadam, S. (2012). Evaluating the impact of restrictive language policies: The Arizona 4-hour English language development block. *Language Policy, 11*(1), 47–80. http://doi.org/10.1007/s10993-011-9226-3

Rivera, C., & Collum, E. (Eds.). (2006). *A national review of state assessment policy and practice for English language learners.* Lawrence Erlbaum.

Rivera, C., & Stansfield, C. W. (2001). Leveling the playing field for English language learners: Increasing participation in state and local assessments through accommodations. In R. Brandt (Ed.), *Assessing student learning: New rules, new realities* (pp. 65–92). Educational Research Service. http://ceee.gwu.edu/standards_assessments/research LEP_accommodintro.htm

Rodriguez, G. M. (2013). Power and agency in education: Exploring the pedagogical dimensions of funds of knowledge. *Review of Research in Education, 37*(1), 87–120.

Rojas-Flores, L., Clements, M. L., Hwang Koo, J., & London, J. (2017). Trauma and psychological distress in Latino citizen children following parental detention and deportation. *Psychological Trauma: Theory, Research, Practice, and Policy, 9*(3), 352. https://psycnet.apa.org/doi/10.1037/tra0000177

Rolstad, K., Mahoney, K., & Glass, G. (2005). The big picture: A meta-analysis of program effectiveness research on English language learners. *Educational Policy Review, 19*(4), 572–594.

Ronan, B. (2014). *Moving across languages and other modes: Emergent bilinguals and their meaning making in and around an online space.* Unpublished doctoral dissertation, Teachers College, Columbia University.

Ronan, B. (2015). Intertextuality and dialogic interaction in students' online text construction. *Literacy Research: Theory, Method, and Practice, 64*(1), 379–397.

Ronan, B. (2017). Digital tools for supporting English language learners' content area writing. In M. Carrier, R. M. Damerow, & K. M. Bailey (Eds.), *Digital language learning and teaching: Research, theory and practice* (pp. 93–103). Routledge.

Rosa J., & Flores N. (2017), Unsettling race and language: Toward a raciolinguistic perspective. *Language in Society, 46*(5), 621–647. https://doi.org/10.1017/S004740451 7000562

Roschelle, J., Lester, J., & Fusco, J. (Eds.). (2020). AI and the future of learning: Expert panel report. *Digital Promise.* https://circls.org/reports/ai-report.

Rosebery, A. S., & Warren, B. (Eds.). (2008). *Teaching science to English language learners: Building on students' strengths.* NSTA Press.

Rosebery, A. S., Warren, B., & Conant, F. (1992). Appropriating scientific discourse: Findings from language minority classrooms. *Journal of the Learning Sciences, 2*(1), 61–94.

Rosenberg, H., Lopez, M. E., & Westmoreland, H. (2009). *Family engagement: A shared responsibility.* Harvard Family Research Project. http://www.hfrp.org/family-involvement/publications-resources/family-engagement-a-shared-responsibility

Ruiz de Velasco, J., Fix, M., & Chu Clewell, T. (2000). *Overlooked and underserved: Immigrant children in U.S. secondary schools.* Urban Institute Press.

Ruiz, R. (1984). Orientations in language planning. *NABE Journal, 8*(2), 15–34.

Rusoja, A. (2022). "Our community is filled with experts": The critical intergenerational literacies of Latinx immigrants that facilitate a communal pedagogy of resistance. *Research in the Teaching of English, 56*(3), 301–327. https://doi.org/10.58680/rte20 2231639

Rusoja, A. (2024). "Estás luchando . . . por toda la comunidad": The communal organizing literacies of Latine/x immigrant families. *Journal of Language, Identity & Education, 23*(3), 380–395. https://doi.org/10.1080/15348458.2024.2324271

Rymes, B. (2014). *Communicating beyond language: Everyday encounters with diversity.* Routledge.

Samson, J. F., & Lesaux, N. K. (2009). Language-minority learners in special education: Rates and predictors of identification for services. *Journal of Learning Disabilities, 42*(2), 148–162. https://doi.org/10.1177/0022219408326221

Sánchez, C. (2017, February 23). English language learners: How your state is doing. *NPREd. How Learning Happens.* http://www.npr.org/sections/ed/2017/02/23/5124 51228/5-million-english-language-learners-a-vast-pool-of-talent-at-risk

Sánchez, M. T., & García, O. (Eds.). (2022). *Transformative translanguaging Espacios: Latinx students and teachers rompiendo fronteras sin miedo.* Multilingual Matters.

Sánchez, M. T., García, O., & Solorza, C. (2017). Reframing language allocation policy in dual language bilingual education. *Bilingual Research Journal, 41*(1), 37–51. https://doi.org/10.1080/15235882.2017.1405098

Santos, B. de S. (2007). Beyond abyssal thinking: From global lines to ecologies of knowledges. *Review Fernand Braudel Center, 30*(1), 45–89.

Sayer, P. (2013). Translanguaging, TexMex, and bilingual pedagogy: Emergent bilinguals learning through the vernacular. *TESOL Quarterly, 47*(1), 63–88.

Schissel, J. L. (2020). Moving beyond deficit positioning of linguistically diverse test takers: Bi/multilingualism and the essence of validity. In S. Mirhosseini & P. I. De Costa (Eds.), *Sociopolitics of English language testing* (pp. 91–108). Bloomsbury Publishing.

Seeley, D. S. (1993). Why home–school partnership is difficult in bureaucratic schools. In F. Smit, W. van Esch, & H. J. Walberg (Eds.), *Parental involvement in education* (pp. 49–58). Institute for Applied Social Sciences.

Selinker, L. (1972). Interlanguage. *International Review of Applied Linguistics, 10,* 209–231.

Selinker, L., & Han, Z-H. (2001). Fossilization: Moving the concept into empirical longitudinal study. In C. Elder, A. Brown, E. Grove, K. Hill, N. Iwashita, T. Lumley, T. McNamara, & K. O'Loughlin (Eds.), *Studies in language testing: Experimenting with uncertainty* (pp. 276–291). Cambridge University Press.

Seltzer, K. (2019). Reconceptualizing "home" and "school" language: Taking a critical translingual approach in the English classroom. *TESOL Quarterly, 53*(4), 986–1007. https://doi.org/10.1002/tesq.530

Seltzer, K. (2022). Enacting a critical translingual approach in teacher preparation: Disrupting oppressive language ideologies and fostering the personal, political, and pedagogical stances of preservice teachers of English. *TESOL Journal, 13*(2). https://doi .org/10.1002/tesj.649

Seltzer, K., & Collins, B. (2016). Navigating turbulent waters: Translanguaging to support academic and socioemotional well-being. In O. García & T. Kleyn (Eds.), *Translanguaging with multilingual students. Learning from classroom moments* (pp. 140–159). Routledge.

Seltzer, K., Hesson, S., & Woodley, H. H. (2014). *Translanguaging in curriculum and instruction: A CUNY-NYSIEB guide for educators.* CUNY-NYSIEB, The Graduate Center, The City University of New York. http://www.nysieb.ws.gc.cuny.edu/files /2014/12/Translanguaging-Guide-Curr-Inst-Final-December-2014.pdf

Shanmugam, S., & Lan, O. S. (2013). Bilingual test as a test accommodation to determine the mathematics achievement of mainstream students with limited English proficiency. *Malaysian Journal of Learning and Instruction, 10,* 29–55.

Shepard, L. A. (1996). Research framework for investigating accommodations for language minority students. Presentation made at CRESST Assessment Conference, UCLA, 1996.

Shirley, D. (1997). *Community organizing for urban school reform.* University of Texas Press.

Shohamy, E. (2001). *The power of tests: A critical perspective on the uses of language tests.* Longman.

Shohamy, E. (2006). *Language policy: Hidden agendas and new approaches.* Routledge.

Shohamy, E. (2011). Assessing multilingual competencies: Adopting construct valid assessment policies. *The Modern Language Journal, 95,* 418–429. https://doi.org/10.1111/j .1540-4781.2011.01210.x

Shohamy, E., Donitsa-Schmidt, S., & Ferman, I. (1996). Test impact revisited: Washback effect over time. *Language Testing, 13*(3), 298–317.

Shohamy, E., & Gorter, D. (Eds.). (2009). *Linguistic landscape: Expanding the scenery.* Routledge.

Short, D., & Fitzsimmons, S. (2007). *Double the work: Challenges and solutions to acquiring language and academic literacy for adolescent English language learners—A report to Carnegie Corporation of New York.* Alliance for Excellent Education.

Skutnabb-Kangas, T. (1981). *Bilingualism or not. The education of minorities.* Multilingual Matters.

Skutnabb-Kangas, T. (2000). *Linguistic genocide in education—or worldwide diversity and human rights?* Lawrence Erlbaum.

Skutnabb-Kangas, T. (2006). Language policy and linguistic human rights. In T. Ricento (Ed.), *An introduction to language policy: Theory and method* (pp. 273–291). Blackwell.

Skutnabb-Kangas, T., & Phillipson, R. (1994). *Linguistic human rights: Overcoming linguistic discrimination.* Mouton.

Skutnabb-Kangas, T., & Phillipson, R. (2017). *Language rights.* Routledge.

Skutnabb-Kangas, T., & Toukomaa, P. (1976). Semilingualism and middle-class bias: A reply to Cora Brent-Palmer. *Working Papers on Bilingualism, 19.* Ontario Institute for Studies in Education, Bilingual Education Project.

Slama, R. (2014). Investigating whether and when English learners are reclassified into mainstream classrooms in the United States: A discrete-time survival analysis. *American Educational Research Journal, 51*(2), 220–252. https://doi.org/10.3102/0002831214528277

Slavin, R., & Cheung, A. (2005). A synthesis of research on reading instruction for English language learners. *Review of Educational Research, 75*(7), 247–284.

Smith, B. E., Amgott, N., & Malova, I. (2022). "It made me think in a different way": Bilingual students' perspectives on multimodal composing in the English language arts classroom. *TESOL Quarterly, 56*(2), 525–551.

Smith, B. E., Pacheco, M. B., & Khorosheva, M. (2021). Emergent bilingual students and digital multimodal composition: A systematic review of research in secondary classrooms. *Reading Research Quarterly, 56*(1), 33–52.

Snow, C. E. (2017). The role of vocabulary versus knowledge in children's language learning: A fifty-year perspective. *Infancia y Aprendizaje, 40*(1), 1–18. http://dx.doi.org/10.1080/02103702.2016.1263449

Solano-Flores, G. (2008). Who is given tests in what language by whom, when, and where? The need for probabilistic views of language in the testing of English language learners. *Educational Researcher, 37*(4), 189–199.

Solano-Flores, G. (2012). *Translation accommodations framework for testing English language learners in mathematics.* Smarter Balanced Assessment Consortium. https://files.eric.ed.gov/fulltext/ED536955.pdf

Solorzano, D. G., & Yosso, T. J. (2001). From racial stereotyping and deficit discourse toward a critical race theory in teacher education. *Multicultural Education, 9*(1), 2–8. https://doi.org/info:doi/

Soto, L. D. (1996). *Language, culture, and power: Bilingual families and the struggle for quality education.* State University of New York Press.

Souto-Manning, M., & Rabadi-Raol, A. (2018). (Re)centering quality in early childhood education: Toward intersectional justice for minoritized children. *Review of Research in Education, 42*(1), 203–225. https://doi.org/10.3102/0091732X1875955

Spolsky, B. (2012). Family language policy—the critical domain. *Journal of Multilingual and Multicultural Development, 33*(1), 3–11. https://doi.org/10.1080/01434632.2011.638072

Stanford, L. (2023, September 1). Educators feel growing pressure for students to perform well on standardized tests. *Education Week.* https://www.edweek.org/teaching-learn

ing/educators-feel-growing-pressure-for-students-to-perform-well-on-standardized
-tests/2023/09

Statista (2019). Children who speak another language than English at home in the U.S. in 2019, by poverty status. https://www.statista.com/statistics/476863/children-who-speak -another-language-than-english-at-home-in-the-us-by-poverty-status/

Statista. (2024). Hispanic population in the United States: Statistics and facts. https://www .statista.com/topics/3806/hispanics-in-the-united-states/#topicOverview

Steele, C., Dovchin, S., & Oliver, R. (2022). "Stop measuring Black kids with a White stick": Translanguaging for classroom assessment. *RELC Journal, 53*(2), 400–415.

Steele, J. L., Slater, R., Zamarro, G., Miller, T., Li, J., Burkhauser, S., & Bacon, M. (2017). Effects of dual-language immersion programs on student achievement. *American Educational Research Journal, 54,* 282S–306S. https://doi.org/10.3102/0002831216634463

Steinberg, L. (1996). *Beyond the classroom: Why school reform has failed and what parents need to do.* Simon & Schuster.

Stolarick, K., & Florida, R. (2006). Creativity, connections and innovation: A study of linkages in the Montréal region. *Environment and Planning, 38*(10), 1799–1817.

Street, B. V. (1985). *Literacy in theory and practice.* Cambridge University Press.

Street, B. V. (1996). Academic literacies. In D. Baker, J. Clay, & C. Fox (Eds.), *Alternative ways of knowing: Literacies, numeracies, sciences* (pp. 101–134). Falmer Press.

Street, B. V. (2003). What's "new" in new literacy studies? Critical approaches to literacy in theory and practice. *Current Issues in Comparative Education, 5*(2), 77–91.

Street, B. V. (Ed.). (2005). *Literacies across educational contexts: Mediating, learning and teaching.* Caslon Press.

Suárez, E. (2020). "Estoy explorando science": Translanguaging in an out-of-school science program for emergent bilingual students. *Science Education, 104*(5), 791–826.

Suárez, E. (2022). Communicating with objects: Supporting translanguaging practices of emergent bilingual students during scientific modeling. In A. J. Rodríguez & R. Suriel (Eds.), *Equity in STEM education research: Advocating for equitable attention* (pp. 11–32). Springer.

Suárez, E., & Otero, V. (2024). Ting, tang, tong: Emergent bilingual students reasoning mechanistically about sound production. *Journal of Research in Science Teaching, 61*(1), 137–169.

Suárez, E., & Sousa, K. (2023). "What did you learn?" Emergent bilingual students write their understandings about sinking and floating. *Language Arts, 100*(4), 323–328.

Suárez-Orozco, C., & Suárez-Orozco, M. (2001). *Children of immigration.* Harvard University Press.

Suárez-Orozco, C., Suarez-Orozco, M., & Todorova, I. (2008). *Learning a new land: Immigrant students in American society.* The Belknap Press of Harvard University Press.

Sugarman, J. (2016). *Funding an equitable education for English learners in the United States.* Migration Policy Institute. https://www.migrationpolicy.org/sites/default/files /publications/US-Funding-FINAL.pdf

Sugarman, J. (2023). *Recent immigrant children: A profile of new arrivals to U.S. schools.* Migration Policy Institute. https://www.migrationpolicy.org

Sun, W. (2023). Fostering critical consciousness with immigrant families: The story of a Chinese immigrant mother in a Mandarin–English dual language program. In L. Dorner, D. Palmer, C. Cervantes-Soon, & D. Heiman (Eds.), *Critical consciousness in dual language bilingual education: Case studies on policy and practice* (pp. 131–138). Routledge.

Swinney, R., & Velasco, P. (2011). *Connecting content and academic language for English learners and struggling students*. Corwin Press.

Sylvan, C., & Romero, M. (2002). Reversing language loss in a multilingual setting: A native language enhancement program and its impact. In T. Osborn (Ed.), *The future of foreign language education in the United States* (pp. 139–166). Greenwood Publishing Group.

Takanishi, R. (2004). Leveling the playing field: Supporting immigrant children from birth to eight. *The Future of Children, 14*(2), 61–79. http://www.futureofchildren.org/usr _doc/takanishi.pdfhttp://www.futureofchildren.org/usr_doc/takanishi.pdf

Takanishi, R., & LeMenestrel, S. (Eds.). (2017). *Promoting the educational success of children and youth learning English: Promising futures*. The National Academies Press. https://doi.org/10.17226/24677

Taylor, D. (1997). *Many families, many literacies: An international declaration of principles*. Heinemann.

Tazi, Z. (2014). Ready for la escuela: School readiness and the languages of instruction in kindergarten. *Journal of Multilingual Education Research, 5*(3), 11–31.

Téllez, K., & Waxman, H. C. (Eds.). (2006). *Preparing quality educators for English language learners. Research, policies, and practices*. Lawrence Erlbaum.

Tenery, M. F. (2005). La visita. In N. González, L. C. Moll, & C. Amanti (Eds.), *Funds of knowledge: Theorizing practices in households, communities, and classrooms* (pp. 119–130). Lawrence Erlbaum.

Tharp, R. G., Estrada, P., Dalton, S. S., & Yamauchi, L. A. (2000). *Teaching transformed: Achieving excellence, fairness, inclusion and harmony*. Westview Press.

Thomas, J. W. (2000). *A review of research on project based learning*. The Autodesk Foundation. http://www.bobpearlman.org/BestPractices/PBL_Research.pdf

Thomas, W. P., & Collier, V. (1997). *School effectiveness for language minority students*. National Clearinghouse for Bilingual Education, George Washington University, Center for the Study of Language and Education.

Thomas, W. P., & Collier, V. P. (2002). *A national study of school effectiveness for language minority students' long term academic achievement: Final report*. http://www .crede.ucsc.edu/research/llaa/1.1_final.html

Thompson, K. D. (2015). English learners' time to reclassification: An analysis. *Educational Policy, 31*(3), 330–363. https://doi.org/10.1177/0895904815598394

Tian, Z., Aghai, L., Sayer, P., & Schissel, J. (Eds.). (2020.) *Envisioning TESOL through a translanguaging lens*. Springer.

Tierney, R. J., & Pearson, P. D. (2024). *Fact-checking the Science of Reading: Opening up the conversation*. Literacy Research Commons. https://literacyresearchcommons.org /wp-content/uploads/2024/04/Fact-checking-the-SoR.pdf

Torrance, E. P., Gowan, J. C., Wu, J., & Aliotti, N. C. (1970). Creative functioning of monolingual and bilingual children in Singapore. *Journal of Educational Psychology, 61*(1), 72–75.

Torres, M. N., & Hurtado-Vivas, R. (2011). Playing fair with Latino parents as parents, not teachers: Beyond family literacy as assisting homework. *Journal of Latinos and Education, 10*(3), 223–244. https://doi.org/10.1080/15348431.2011.581108

Traugh, C. (2000). Whole-school inquiry: Values and practice. In M. Himley & P. Carini (Eds.), *From another angle: Children's strengths and school standards. The Prospect Center's descriptive review of the child* (pp. 182–198). Teachers College Press.

Turkan, S., & Oliveri, M. E. (2014). Considerations for providing test translation accommodations to English language learners on common core standards-based assessments. *ETS Research Report Series, 2014*(1), 1–13. https://doi.org/10.1002/ets2.2014.2014.issue-1

Tzirides, A. O., Zapata, G., Saini, A., Searsmith, D., Cope, B., Kalantzis, M., Castro, V., Kourkoulou, T., Jones, J., Abrantes da Silva, R., Whiting, J., & Polyxeni Kastania, N. (2023). Generative AI: Implications and applications for education. *arXiv,* 2305.07605, 2023. https://doi.org/10.48550/arXiv.2305.07605.

U.S. Census Bureau. (1979). Current population survey 1979. U.S. Government Printing Office.

U.S. Census Bureau. (1989). Current population survey 1989, November supplement. U.S. Government Printing Office.

U.S. Census Bureau. (1995). Current population survey 1995, October supplement. U.S. Government Printing Office.

U.S. Census Bureau. (2005, November). *American Community Survey (ACS), 2000–2004,* U.S. Government Printing Office.

U.S. Census Bureau. (2008). *American Community Survey (ACS), 2008.* U.S. Government Printing Office.

U.S. Census Bureau. (2014). *American Community Survey (ACS), 2014.* U.S. Government Printing Office.

U.S Census Bureau. (2021). American Community Survey (ACS), 1-year estimates, 2021.

U.S. Census Bureau. (2022a). American Community Survey (ACS) 2022 1-year. Age by language spoken at home by ability to speak English for the population 5 years and over. Table C16004.

U.S. Census Bureau. (2022b). American Community Survey (ACS). Age by language spoken at home for population 5 years and over in limited English speaking households. Table B16003. https://data.census.gov/table?q=B16003%202022

U.S. Department of Education. (2015). *National Assessment of Educational Progress (NAEP).* National Center for Education Statistics. http://www.nationsreportcard.gov/reading_math_2015/#?grade=4

U.S. Department of Education. (2016, September 23). *Non-regulatory guidance: English learners and Title III of the Elementary and Secondary Education Act (ESEA), as amended by the Every Student Succeeds Act (ESSA).* September 23, 2016.

U.S. Department of Education. (2021). *English learners in charter schools factsheet.* Office of English Language Acquisition. https://ncela.ed.gov/sites/default/files/legacy/files/fast_facts/20211109-FactSheet-ELsCharterSchools-508.pdf

U.S. Department of Education (NCELA). (2015). *English learner toolkit for state and local education agencies.* Author. http://www2.ed.gov/about/offices/list/oela/english-learner-toolkit/eltoolkit.pdf

U.S. Department of Education and Office for Civil Rights. (2016). Key data highlights on equity and opportunity gaps in our nation's public schools. http://www2.ed.gov/about/offices/list/ocr/docs/2013-14-first-look.pdf

U.S. Department of Education, National Center for Education Statistics (NCES). (2006). Author.

U.S. Department of Education, National Center for Education Statistics. (2015a). *The condition of education 2015 (NCES 2015–144). English language learners.* http://nces.ed.gov/programs/coe/indicator_cgf.asp

U.S. Department of Education, National Center for Education Statistics. (2015b). *Digest of education statistics,* Table 204.27. http://nces.ed.gov/programs/digest/d15/tables /dt15_204.27.asp and Table 204.20. https://nces.ed.gov/programs/digest/d14/tables /dt14_204.20.asp

U.S. Department of Education, National Center for Education Statistics. (2016). *The condition of education.* https://nces.ed.gov/pubsearch/pubsinfo.asp?pubid=2016144

U.S. Department of Education, National Center for Education Statistics. (2021). Common core of data: State nonfiscal public elementary/secondary education survey data (v.1a). 2020–2021; and Office of Civil Rights, Civil Rights data collection, 2020–2021. Featured 2020–2021 data. Algebra across the nation. https://civilrightsdata.ed.gov

U.S. Department of Education, Office of Educational Technology. (2023). *Artificial intelligence and the future of teaching and learning: Insights and recommendations.* Author. https://tech.ed.gov.

U.S. Department of Education. (2015, January 7). U.S. Departments of Education and Justice release joint guidance to ensure English learner students have equal access to high-quality education. http://www.ed.gov/news/press-releases/us-departments-education-and-justice-release-joint-guidance-ensure-english-learn

U.S. Department of Education. (2016). Fiscal year 2017 budget summary. http://www2.ed .gov/about/overview/budget/budget17/summary/17summary.pdf

U.S. Department of Education. (2022). Academic performance and outcomes for ELs. https://www2.ed.gov/datastory/el-outcomes/index.html

U.S. Department of Education, Institute of Education Science, National Center for Education Statistics. (2020a, Fall). *English learners in public schools.* https://nces.ed.gov /programs/coe/indicator/cgf/english-learners

U.S. Department of Education, Institute of Education Science, National Center for Education Statistics. (2020b). Table 204.27 https://nces.ed.gov/programs/digest/d22/tables /dt22_204.27.asp

U.S. Department of Education, Institute of Education Science, National Center for Education Statistics. (2023). *Status dropout rates: Condition of education.* https://nces.ed .gov/programs/coe/indicator/coj

U.S. Department of Education, Office for Civil Rights. (2024, March). *Profile of English learner students in U.S. public schools during the 2020-2021 school year.* https:// www2.ed.gov/about/offices/list/ocr/docs/crdc-el-students-snapshot.pdf

U.S. Department of Education. (2018). Our nation's English learners. What are their characteristics? https://www2.ed.gov/datastory/el-characteristics/index.html

U.S. Department of Health and Human Services. (2024a, April 1). Unaccompanied children fact sheet. https://www.hhs.gov/sites/default/files/uac-program-fact-sheet.pdf

U.S. Department of Health and Human Services, Office of Refugee Resettlement. (2024b, April 1). *Unaccompanied children released to sponsors by state.* https://www.acf.hhs .gov/orr/grant-funding/unaccompanied-children-released-sponsors-state

U.S. Government Accountability Office (GAO). (July 2009). Teacher preparation. GOA-09.573. http https://www.gao.gov/assets/300/294197.pdf

Umansky, I. (2016). Leveled and exclusionary tracking: English learners' access to core content in middle school. *American Educational Research Journal, 53*(6), 1792–1833. https://doi.org/10.3102/0002831216675404

Umansky, I. M., Thompson, K. D., & Díaz, G. (2017). Using an ever-English learner framework to examine disproportionality in special education. *Exceptional Children, 84*(1), 76–96. https://doi.org/10.1177/0014402917707470

Umansky, I., & Reardon, S. F. (2014). Reclassification patterns among Latino English learner students in bilingual, dual immersion, and English immersion classrooms. *American Educational Research Journal, 51*(5), 879–912. https://doi.org/10.3102/0002831214545110

UNESCO. (1960, December 14). *Convention against discrimination in education.* Adopted by General Conference at 11th session, Paris, France.

Urrieta, L., Jr. (2010). Whitestreaming: Why some Latinas/os fear bilingual education. *Counterpoints, 371,* 47–55.

Urrieta, L., Jr. (2016). Diasporic community smartness: Saberes (knowings) beyond schooling and borders. *Race Ethnicity and Education, 19*(6), 1186–1199. https://doi.org/10.1080/13613324.2016.1168541

Urrieta, L., Jr., & Martínez, S. (2011). Diasporic community knowledge and school absenteeism: Mexican immigrant Pueblo parents' and grandparents' postcolonial ways of educating. *Interventions, 13*(2), 256–277. https://doi.org/10.1080/1369801X.2011.573225

Uzzell, E. M., & Ayscue, J. B. (2021). Racial integration through two-way dual language immersion: A case study. *Education Policy Analysis Archives, 29*(48), 1–35. https://doi.org/10.14507/epaa.29.5949

Valdés, G. (1996). *Con respeto. Bridging the distances between culturally diverse families and schools. An ethnographic portrait.* Teachers College Press.

Valdés, G. (1997). Dual-language immersion programs: A cautionary note concerning the education of language-minority students. *Harvard Educational Review, 67*(3), 391–429.

Valdés, G. (2001). *Learning and not learning English: Latino students in American schools.* Teachers College Press.

Valdés, G. (2002). Enlarging the pie: Another look at bilingualism and schooling in the US. *International Journal of the Sociology of Language, 2002*(155–156), 187–195.

Valdés, G. (2005). Bilingualism, heritage language learners and second language acquisition research: Opportunities lost or seized? *Modern Language Journal, 89*(3), 410–416.

Valdés, G. (2017). Entry visa denied: The construction of symbolic language borders in educational settings. In O. García, N. Flores, & M. Spotti (Eds.), *Handbook of language and society* (pp. 321–348). Oxford University Press.

Valdés, G. (2018). Analyzing the curricularization of language in two-way immersion education: Restating two cautionary notes. *Bilingual Research Journal, 41*(3), 1–25.

Valdés, G., & Figueroa, R. A. (1994). *Bilingualism and testing: A special case of bias.* Ablex Publishing.

Valdez, V. E., Delavan, G., & Freire, J. A. (2014). The marketing of dual language education in Utah print media. *Educational Policy, 30*(6), 849–883. https://doi.org/10.1177/0895904814555675

Valdez, V. E., Freire, J. A., & Delavan, M. G. (2016). The gentrification of dual language education. *The Urban Review, 48,* 601-627. https://doi.org/10.1007/s11256-016-0370-0.

Valencia, R. R. (2010). *Dismantling contemporary deficit thinking: Educational thought and practice.* Routledge.

Valencia, R. R. (2012). *The evolution of deficit thinking: Educational thought and practice.* Routledge.

Valenzuela, A. (1999). *Subtractive schooling: U.S. Mexican youth and the politics of caring.* SUNY Press.

Valenzuela, A. (Ed.). (2005). *Leaving children behind: How "Texas-style" accountability fails Latino youth.* State University of New York Press.

Valenzuela, A. (Ed.). (2016). *Growing critically conscious teachers: A social justice curriculum for educators of Latino/a youth.* Teachers College Press.

van Deursen, J. A. M., & van Dijk, J. A. G. M. (2018). The first-level digital divide shifts from inequalities in physical access to inequalities in material access. *New Media & Society, 21*(2). https://doi.org/10.1177/1461444818797082

van Dijk, J. A. G. M. (2017). Digital divide: Impact of access. In P. Rössler, C. A. Hoffnery, & L. van Zoonen (Eds.), *The international encyclopedia of media effects* (pp. 1–11). Wiley-Blackwell. https://doi.org/10.1002/9781118783764.wbieme0043

van Dijk, T. (2008). *Discourse and power.* Palgrave.

van Leeuwen, T. (1999). *Speech, music, sound.* Macmillan.

van Leeuwen, T. (2011). *The language of colour: An introduction.* Routledge.

van Lier, L. (2000). From input to affordance: Social-interactive learning from an ecological perspective. In J. P. Lantolf (Ed.), *Sociocultural theory and second language learning* (pp. 245–260). Oxford University Press.

van Lier, L., & Walqui, A. (2012, January 13–14). Language and the Common Core State Standards. Paper presented at the Understanding Language Conference, Stanford University, Stanford, CA.

Varela, F. (1995). The emergent self. In Brockman, J., (Ed.). *The third culture: Beyond the scientific revolution* (pp. 209–222). Simon & Schuster.

Varenne, H., & McDermott, R. (1998). *Successful failure: The schools America builds.* Westview Press.

Varghese, M. M., & Park, C. (2010). Going global: Can dual-language programs save bilingual students. *Journal of Latinos and Education, 10*(4), 335–353.

Vázquez Baur, A. (2022, September 21). How to ensure Title III funds reach every newcomer student. Report. *Next 100.* https://thenext100.org/how-to-ensure-title-iii-funds-reach-every-newcomer-student/

Villegas, A., & Lucas, T. (2002). *Educating culturally responsive teachers.* State University of New York Press.

Villegas, L. (2023). English learner funding equity and adequacy in K–12 education. *New America.* https://www.newamerica.org/education-policy/briefs/english-learner-funding-equity-and-adequacy-in-k12-education/

Vogel, S., Ascenzi-Moreno, L., & García, O. (2018). An expanded view of translanguaging: Leveraging the dynamic interactions between a young multilingual writer and machine translation software. In J. Choi & S. Ollerhead (Eds.), *Plurilingualism in teaching and learning* (pp. 89–106). Taylor & Francis Ltd. https://doi.org/10.4324/9781315392462-6

Vogel, S., Hoadley, C., Castillo, A. R., & Ascenzi-Moreno, L. (2020). Languages, literacies and literate programming: Can we use the latest theories on how bilingual people learn to help us teach computational literacies? *Computer Science Education, 30*(4), 420–443. https://doi.org/10.1080/08993408.2020.1751525

Vogels, E. A., Gelles-Watnick, R., & Massarat, N. (2022). *Teens, social media and technology.* Pew Research Center.

Vygotsky, L. S. (1978). *Mind and society.* Harvard University Press.

Walqui, A. (2006). Scaffolding instruction for English learners. A conceptual framework. *International Journal of Bilingual Education and Bilingualism, 9*(2), 159–180.

Walqui, A., & Bunch, G. C. (Eds.). (2019). *Amplifying the curriculum: Designing quality learning opportunities for English learners.* Teachers College Press.

Walqui, A., García, O., & Hamburger, L. (2004). Quality teaching for English language learners. In *Classroom observation scoring manual*. WestEd.

Walqui, A., & van Lier, L. (2010). *Scaffolding the academic success of adolescent English language learners: A pedagogy of promise*. WestEd.

Wang, P., & Woolf, S. B. (2015). Trends and issues in bilingual special education teacher preparation: A literature review. *Journal of Multilingual Education Research, 6*(1), 4.

Ward, N., & Batalova, J. (2023, June 15). Refugees and asylees in the United States. Migration Policy Institute Spotlight. https://www.migrationpolicy.org/article/refugees-and-asylees-united-states

Ward, T. B., Smith, S. M., & Vaid, J. (1997). Conceptual structures and processes in creative thought. In T. B. Ward, S. M. Smith, & J. Vaid (Eds.), *Creative thought: An investigation of conceptual structures and processes* (pp. 1–27). American Psychological Association.

Warren, M. R., Hong, S., Leung Rubin, C., & Uy, P. S. (2009). Beyond the bake sale: A community-based relational approach to parent engagement in schools. *Teachers College Record, 111*(9), 2209–2254.

Warriner, D. (2009). Continued marginalization: The social cost of exceptionalism for African refugee learners of English. In J. Kleifgen & G. C. Bond (Eds.), *The languages of Africa and the diaspora: Educating for language awareness* (pp. 199–213). Multilingual Matters.

Warschauer, M., & Matuchniak, T. (2010). New technology and digital worlds: Analyzing evidence of equity in access, use, and outcomes. *Review of Research in Education, 34*(1), 179–225.

Weiss, H., Caspe, M., & Lopez, M. E. (2006). *Family involvement makes a difference: Family involvement in early childhood education*. Harvard Family Research Project. http://www.hfrp.org/publications-resources/browse-our-publications/family-involvement-in-early-childhood-education

Weiss, H., & Lopez, M. E. (2009). Redefining family engagement in education. *FINE Newsletter, 1*(3). Harvard Family Research Project. http://www.hfrp.org/family-involvement/publications-resources/redefining-family-engagement-in-education

Wenglinsky, H. (2005). *Using technology wisely: The keys to success in schools*. Teachers College Press.

Wenworth, L., Pellegrin, N., Thompson, K., & Hakuta, K. (2010). Proposition 227 in California: A long-term appraisal of its impact on English learner student achievement. In P. Gándara & M. Hopkins (Eds.), *Forbidden language: English learners and restrictive language policies* (pp. 37–49). Teachers College Press.

Wesley, L. (2017). Producing language reclamation by decolonizing "language." *Language Documentation and Description, 14*, 15–36. http://doi.org/10.25894/ldd146

Whitebook, M., McLean, C., Austin, L. J., & Edwards, B. (2018). *Early childhood workforce index 2018*. Center for the Study of Child Care Employment. https://cscce.berkeley.edu/wp-content/uploads/2022/04/Early-Childhood-Workforce-Index-2018.pdf

Wible, D., Kuo, C., Chien, F., Liu, A., & Tsao, N. (2001). A web-based EFL writing environment: Integrating information for teachers, learners, and researchers. *Computers & Education, 37*(3–4), 297–315.

Wible, D., Kuo, C., Tsao, N., Liu, A., & Lin, H-L. (2003). Bootstrapping in a language learning environment. *Journal of Computer-Assisted Learning, 19*(1), 90–102.

WIDA. (2014). Focus on technology in the classroom. https://wida.wisc.edu/sites/default/files/resource/FocusOn-Technology-in-the-Classroom.pdf

Wiley, T. G. (1996). *Literacy and language diversity in the United States.* Center for Applied Linguistics.

Wiley, T. G., & Lukes, M. L. (1996). English-only and standard English ideologies in the U.S. *TESOL Quarterly, 30*(3), 511–535.

Wiley, T. G., & Wright, W. (2004). Against the undertow: Language minority education policy and politics in the "Age of Accountability." *Educational Policy, 18*(1), 142–168.

Williams, C. (1994). *Arfarniad o Ddulliau Dysgu ac Addysgu yng Nghyd-destun Addysg Uwchradd Ddwyieithog [An evaluation of teaching and learning methods in the context of bilingual secondary education].* Unpublished doctoral thesis, University of Wales, Bangor.

Williams, C. (2015, January 5). New America's dual language learner national work group sets up shop. https://www.newamerica.org/education-policy/edcentral/dllworkgrouplaunch/

Williams, C. (2023). America's missing bilingual teachers. The Century Foundation. https://tcf.org/content/commentary/americas-missing-bilingual-teachers/

Williams, M., & Tang, K. S. (2020). The implications of the non-linguistic modes of meaning for language learners in science: A review. *International Journal of Science Education, 42*(7), 1041–1067. https://doi.org/10.1080/09500693.2020.1748249

Willig, A. C. (1985). A meta-analysis of selected studies on the effectiveness of bilingual education. *Review of Educational Research, 55*(3), 269–317.

Wolfe, P. (2006). Settler colonialism and the elimination of the native. *Journal of Genocide Research, 8*(4), 387–409.

Wong-Fillmore, L., & Fillmore, C. J. (n.d.). What does text complexity mean for English learners and language minority students? *Understanding Language.* Stanford University. http://ell.stanford.edu/sites/default/files/pdf/academic-papers/06-LWF%20CJF%20Text%20Complexity%20FINAL_0.pdf

Wong-Fillmore, L., & Snow, C. (2000). *What teachers need to know about language.* U.S. Department of Education, Office of Educational Research and Improvement.

Woodley, H. (2016). Balancing windows and mirrors: Translanguaging in a linguistically diverse classroom. In O. García & T. Kleyn (Eds.), *Translanguaging with multilingual students. Learning from classroom moments* (pp. 83–99). Routledge.

Wright, W. E. (2010). *Foundations for teaching English language learners: Research, theory, policy, and practice.* Caslon Publishing.

Wyman, L. T., McCarty, T. L., & Nicholas, S. E. (Eds.). (2013). *Indigenous youth and multilingualism: Language identity, ideology, and practice in dynamic cultural worlds.* Routledge.

Yang, X. (2020). Assessment accommodations for emergent bilinguals in mainstream classroom assessments: A targeted literature review. *International Multilingual Research Journal, 14*(3), 217–232. https://doi.org/10.1080/19313152.2019.1681615

Yip, J. (2016). *Educational histories of newcomer immigrant youth: From countries of origin to the United States.* Doctoral dissertation, The Graduate Center, City University of New York.

Yosso, T. (2005). Whose culture has capital? A critical race theory discussion of community cultural wealth. *Race Ethnicity and Education, 8*(1), 69–91. https://doi.org/10.1080/1361332052000341006

Zehler, A., Fleischman, H., Hopstock, P., Stephenson, T., Pendizick, M., & Sapru, S. (2003). *Descriptive study of services to LEP students and LEP students with disabilities* (Vol. 1). Development Associates. https://ncela.ed.gov/sites/default/files/legacy/files/rcd/BE021199/special_ed4.pdf

Zentella, A. C. (1997). *Growing up bilingual*. Blackwell.

Zentella, A. C. (2005). Premises, promises, and pitfalls of language socialization research in Latino families and communities. In A. C. Zentella (Ed.), *Building on strength: Language and literacy in Latino families and communities* (pp. 13–30). Teachers College Press.

Zhuo, T. Y., Huang, Y., Chen, C., & Xing, Z. (2023). Exploring AI ethics of ChatGPT: A diagnostic analysis. *ArXiv*: abs/2301.12867

Zielezinski, M. B., & Darling-Hammond, L. (2016). *Promising practices: A literature review of technology use by underserved students*. Stanford Center for Opportunity Policy in Education.

Zipin, L. (2009). Dark funds of knowledge, deep funds of pedagogy: Exploring boundaries between lifeworlds and schools. *Discourse: Studies in the Cultural Politics of Education, 30*(3), 317–331.

Zipin, L., Sellar, S., & Hattam, R. (2012). Countering and exceeding "capital": A "funds of knowledge" approach to re-imagining community. *Discourse: Studies in the Cultural Politics of Education, 33*(2), 179–192.

Zong, J., & Batalova, J. (2015a). *Frequently requested statistics on immigrants and immigration in the United States*. Migration Policy Institute. http://www.migrationpolicy .org/article/frequently-requested-statistics-immigrants-and-immigration-united-states -4#Current and Historical

Zong, J., & Batalova, J. (2015b). The limited English proficient population in the U.S. Migration Policy Institute. http://www.migrationpolicy.org/article/limited-english-profi cient-population-united-states06&RptType=ELPart2_1

Index

263

About the Authors

Ofelia García is professor emerita in the PhD programs in urban education and Latin American, Iberian, and Latino cultures at The Graduate Center, City University of New York. She has also been professor at Columbia University's Teachers College and The City College of New York, and dean of the School of Education at the Brooklyn Campus of Long Island University. García has published widely in the areas of bilingualism and bilingual education, sociolinguistics, and language education and policy. Her scholarship is grounded in her life experience living in New York City after leaving Cuba at the age of 11, teaching language minoritized students bilingually, educating bilingual and ESL teachers, and working with doctoral students researching these topics. García has received Distinguished Scholar Lifetime Awards from the American Education Research Association (AERA) (Social Contexts in Education, 2019, and Bilingual Education, 2017); from the Modern Language Association (MLA) (2022); and from The Literacy Research Association (LRA), (2024). In 2017 she received the Charles Ferguson Award in Applied Linguistics, and in 2016 she was awarded an honorary doctorate of humane letters from Bank Street Graduate School of Education. She was elected to The Academy of Arts and Sciences (2023) and to the National Academy of Education (2018). Her website is www.ofeliagarcía.org.

Jo Anne Kleifgen is professor emerita of linguistics and education at Teachers College, Columbia University's graduate school of education. She has been a member of the International Linguistic Association's Executive Committee since 1991, serving twice as president and chairing the committee that oversees ILA's journal, *WORD*. Her research has focused on discourse practices in multilingual settings and the use of technologies to strengthen learners' bilingualism and biliteracy. Among her book contributions are *Communicative Practices at Work: Multimodality and Learning in a High-Tech Firm*, which describes her multiple-year study of a multilingual workplace in Silicon Valley, and *The Languages of Africa and the Diaspora: Educating for Language Awareness*, which examines the social cost of linguistic exceptionalism. Her research is published widely in book chapters and journals of linguistics/literacy and anthropology. She has directed funded projects on using new media to support Latines' language/literacy development, supervised an international program bringing classrooms in the United States and Middle East/North Africa together for online collaborative learning, and worked as an EL specialist for the U.S. Department of State. She serves on several editorial boards and as a visiting scholar at U.S. universities. She has conducted workshops and consultations in Argentina, Cambodia, China, Dominican Republic, Hong Kong, Italy, Korea, Mexico, Morocco, Panama, Taiwan, Turkey, and Vietnam. Kleifgen has enjoyed a life-long teaching career—since 1964—with students at home and abroad ranging from preschool age to senior citizens.

Claudia Cervantes-Soon is an associate professor of bilingual education at Mary Lou Fulton College for Teaching and Learning Innovation (Arizona State University) and a former K–12 bilingual educator. She is renowned for her expertise in bilingual education and the intersections of language, identity, and power. Utilizing critical ethnographic methods, decolonial theory, critical pedagogies, and Chicana/Latina feminisms, Dr. Cervantes-Soon investigates the sociocultural, pedagogical, and policy factors affecting the educational experiences of children, youth, and families from racialized and historically marginalized communities, particularly in bilingual, bicultural, and borderlands contexts. She is the author of the award-winning book *Juárez Girls Rising: Transformative Education in Times of Dystopia* and coeditor of *Critical Consciousness in Dual Language Bilingual Education: Case Studies on Policy and Practice*. Her research has also been published in prestigious journals such as the *Harvard Educational Review*, *Review of Research in Education*, and the *Bilingual Research Journal*. Her scholarship has earned recognition through an American Association of University Women Fellowship, a Spencer/National Academy of Education Postdoctoral Fellowship, and early career awards from the American Educational Research Association's Bilingual Education Research SIG and the Council on Anthropology and Education, among others.